The Mammoth Book of
1000 GREAT LIVES

The Mammoth Book of
1000 GREAT LIVES

Edited by

JONATHAN LAW

CARROLL & GRAF PUBLISHERS, INC.

New York

Carroll & Graf Publishers, Inc.
260 Fifth Avenue
New York
NY 10001

First published in the UK by Robinson Publishing 1996

First Carroll & Graf edition 1996

ISBN 0-7867-0298-2

Printed and bound in the United Kingdom

10 9 8 7 6 5 4 3 2 1

PREFACE

This book provides brief, reliable, and illuminating biographies of some 1100 men and women whose lives have made a difference to the world around them. The people included in this survey have been drawn from all ages, cultures, and fields of endeavour; the only real qualification is that their lives should have been in some way remarkable. The resulting portrait gallery is both wide and colourful. Semilegendary figures of the distant past (*Arthur*) rub shoulders with personalities of the modern media (*Madonna, O. J. Simpson*); kings, commanders, philosophers, and scientists jostle with entertainers and sportspeople. After one has included the greatest names from politics, science, and the arts – an elite who virtually select themselves – the scope for choice is almost bewilderingly vast. While the great majority of those included here have outstanding positive achievements to their name, a few, inevitably, have gained their entrée through the enormity of their crimes or errors.

The individual entries aim to provide a maximum of useful and interesting information without unnecessary padding. Although there is no strict formula, most give a brief sketch of the subject's origins and background (where relevant), followed by an outline of the main events in his or her life; here the emphasis falls squarely on the achievements or influence that brought the subject recognition and a continuing name.

A special feature of this book is the inclusion of about 250 boxes focusing on some of the more colourful and curious aspects of the careers under discussion. These boxes contain brief anecdotes and quotations by or about the person concerned to supplement what could otherwise have been a rather bare recital of biographical fact. They are intended to shed an interesting light on some aspects of the subject's character or career and as they are often amusing we hope they add to the fun of the book.

The history of the world is but the biography of great men.

Thomas Carlyle (1795–1881)

A

Abelard, Peter (1079–1142). French philosopher, theologian, and teacher. He was a canon of the cathedral of Notre Dame in Paris and fell in love with one of his pupils, Héloïse. After the birth of a son they were secretly married, but their affair was eventually discovered. Angry at the damage to Héloïse's reputation, her relatives hired men to beat Abelard and castrate him. Although Héloïse became a nun and Abelard entered a monastery they continued to write to each other; their correspondence is famous. Both are buried at the Père Lachaise cemetery in Paris.

Adam, Robert (1728–92). Scottish architect, the second son of William Adam, a leading Edinburgh architect, who trained him and his two brothers, **John** (1721–92) and **James** (1730–94). On his Grand Tour of Europe (1754–58) Robert studied classical architecture, which influenced his later work. Back in Britain, he concentrated particularly on interior decoration, evolving the so-called 'Adam style' with his brother James. They also designed furniture and fittings. His works include the interiors of Harewood House (1759–71) and Syon House (1762–69), and the Adelphi, London (1768–72, now demolished).

Addison, Joseph (1672–1719). English essayist, who founded the periodical *The Spectator* with his schoolfriend Richard Steele in 1711. Using various names, Addison contributed nearly 300 essays during its 21 months of daily publication. He also held various offices in the Whig government of 1714–18. He is considered a master of English prose.

> ❟ Whoever wishes to attain an English style, familiar but not coarse and elegant but not ostentatious, must give his days and nights to the volumes of Addison.
>
> Samuel Johnson, *Lives of the Poets* (1779) ❟

Adenauer, Konrad (1876–1967). German statesman. He served as *Oberbürgermeister* (Lord Mayor) of Cologne from 1917 until dismissed by the Nazis in 1933. Under the Nazis he was arrested several times by the Gestapo. Having entered national German politics in 1946 as chairman of the Christian Democratic Union in the British zone, he subsequently became chancellor of the new Federal German Republic (1949–55). Under his leadership the Republic achieved a remarkable political and economic recovery.

Adler, Alfred (1870–1937). Austrian psychologist. After studying in Vienna, he became associated with Sigmund Freud but soon developed opposing theories. He claimed that aggression, not sexuality, is central to human behaviour and that man's striving for perfection is an attempt to overcome a feeling of inferiority (often misnamed an 'inferiority complex'). In 1921 he founded the first of 30 or more child-guidance clinics in Vienna.

Aeschylus (c. 525–456 BC). Athenian dramatist, considered the father of Greek tragedy. His plays, which deal with moral and political issues, were also noted for their impressive theatrical effects. Only seven of his more than 80 works survive, including *The Persians* (472 BC), about the Persian Wars in which Aeschylus himself fought, and the *Oresteia* (458 BC), a trilogy concerned with the curse on the house of Atreus.

Aeschylus and the Eagle

According to tradition, Aeschylus died when an eagle, mistaking his bald head for a stone, dropped a tortoise upon it to break the shell. He is buried at Gela in Sicily.

Aesop (6th century BC). According to tradition, the Greek author of a number of fables about animals. Aesop is said to have been a slave living on the island of Samos but may have been a legendary figure. Although his name and reputation were known in the 5th century BC, the earliest existing collection of Aesop's fables dates from about 100 AD.

Akbar, Jalal-ud-Din (1542–1605). Mogul emperor of India. Crowned king of a small north-west Indian kingdom at 14, he began his personal rule in 1560 and embarked on a campaign of conquest. By 1586 he ruled an area now covered by Pakistan, northern India, and Bangladesh. Although a Muslim, Jalal-ud-Din allied himself with the Hindus and founded his empire on stable administration and religious toleration.

Akhenaten (d. c. 1350 BC). Egyptian pharaoh. His attempt to replace traditional Egyptian religion with the cult of the sun god Aten caused violent internal disorders and the downfall of the Egyptian empire in Asia. The royal portraits at Tell el-Amarna, the capital he founded, are unlike any others in Ancient Egypt, showing Akhenaten with his wife Nefertiti and his children in informal situations.

Alcock, Sir John William (1892–1919). British aviator. *See* Sir Arthur Whitten **Brown**.

Alexander the Great (356–323 BC). King of Macedonia and conqueror of the Persian Empire. Educated by Aristotle, he succeeded his father Philip II in 336. In 334 he began his ten-year campaign against Persia. In Egypt he was hailed as the son of the god Ra and founded Alexandria, which became a centre of Greek culture. He continued through Babylon and

---

The Death of Alexander

Ironically Alexander, the greatest conqueror the world had known, was defeated by a tiny insect; he died of malarial fever from a mosquito bite. As he lay dying in his tent he was asked to whom he left his empire. "To the strongest" was his bitter reply.

Afghanistan, and married the Asian princess Roxane. In 327 he set out for India but after a fierce battle his men refused to follow him any further and he was forced to turn back. At Susa he took the daughter of Darius, king of Persia, for his second wife. A great tactician and leader, he was often led by his headstrong character into deeds of extravagant bravery. He was taken ill after a banquet and died ten days later, aged 32. As he had left no heir, his empire was divided up by his generals. However, his forceful personality ensured that his name lived on after his death and he has become a legendary hero.

Alexander Nevski (1220–63). Russian prince. He was appointed prince of Novgorod and defeated the Swedes on the River Neva (1240), from which he acquired the name Nevski. In 1242 he secured a decisive victory against the Teutonic Knights on the ice of Lake Peipus. He became grand prince of Vladimir and was canonized after his death.

Alfred (849–899 AD). King of Wessex from 871 and founder of the English nation. During his entire reign Alfred was at war with the Danes and in 878 he was forced to take refuge from invaders in the Somerset marshes. A swift counter-attack restored the situation, and thereafter Alfred's naval and land defences made the Danish raids less effective. A notable administrator, he had special concern for education and personally translated several Latin works into English. He was regarded as the greatest Western European ruler since Charlemagne.

Ali, Muhammad, former name *Cassius Clay* (1942–   ). US boxer. He won the Olympic light-heavyweight gold medal in 1960 and is the only man to have won the world heavyweight championship three times (1964, 1974, 1978). In 1967, having become a Black Muslim and changed his name, he was deprived of his title and forbidden to box for three years for refusing to serve in the US Army on religious grounds. With his slogan "I'm the greatest", he became well known for his flamboyant and colourful style. he now suffers from Parkinson's disease as a result of blows to the head.

Allen, Woody, stage name of *Allen Stewart Konigsberg* (1935–   ). US film director, writer, and actor. As a young stand-up comedian, Allen developed his familiar persona of the neurotic wisecracking Jewish intellectual. He later enjoyed success in his own Broadway plays and his first film *What's New Pussycat?* (1965). Since the late 1960s he has directed his own films, which range from light comedies to more sombre work such as *September* (1988). His best-known films

> ❛ If it turns out that there's a God…basically he's an underachiever.
> Woody Allen, *Love and Death*
> (1975)

> If only God would give me some clear sign! Like making a large deposit in my name at a Swiss bank.
> Woody Allen, *The New Yorker*
> 5 November 1973 ❜

include *Sleeper* (1973), the Oscar-winning *Annie Hall* (1977), *Hannah and Her Sisters* (1986), and *Bullets over Broadway* (1994). In the 1990s his popularity was affected by the damaging publicity surrounding his separation from Mia Farrow, his companion of a decade.

Altman, Robert (1922–   ). US film director, screenwriter, and producer. Altman worked in the film business for many years before making his name with the Korean War comedy *M*A*S*H* (1972). His subsequent films include the highly praised *Nashville* (1975), *The Player* (1992), *Short Cuts* (1994), and *Prêt-à-Porter* (1995). A prolific and unpredictable film-maker, he is considered one of Hollywood's true mavericks.

Amin, Idi (1925–   ). Ugandan army officer and politician. He was for ten years the heavyweight boxing champion of the army. In 1971 he led the military coup that seized power in President Obote's absence and became president himself. In the same year he expelled about 80,000 Asians from Uganda and began a reign of terror. He promoted himself to field marshal and awarded himself the Victoria Cross. Following an invasion of Tanzanian forces and Ugandan exiles in 1979, Amin was overthrown and fled to Libya, later settling in Saudi Arabia.

Amis, Sir Kingsley (1922–95). British novelist and writer. His first novel, the irreverent *Lucky Jim* (1954), was an immediate success. Subsequent novels include *Take a Girl Like You* (1960), the supernatural tale *The Green Man* (1969), *The Old Devils* (1986), which won the Booker Prize, and *The Biographer's Moustache* (1995). He also published poetry and a volume of *Memoirs* (1991). His second wife was the novelist Elizabeth Jane Howard. His son **Martin Amis** (1949–   ) is also a novelist, who established his reputation with *The Rachel Papers* (1974) and other black comedies. In the 1980s and 1990s such works as *Money* (1983), *London Fields* (1989), and *The Information* (1995) made Amis one of the most widely praised British writers of his generation.

Ampère, André-Marie (1775–1836). French physicist. A child prodigy, he was a proficient mathematician by the age of 12. His research into the connection between electricity and magnetism resulted in the formulation of Ampère's law, which established the basis for the study of electromagnetism. His use of a freely moving needle to measure the flow of electric current led to the development of the galvanometer. The unit of electric current, usually abbreviated to 'amp', was named after him.

Amundsen, Roald (1872–1928). Norwegian explorer. He successfully navigated the North-West Passage in 1903 with a crew of six. Forestalled by Robert Peary in the discovery of the North Pole, he became the first man to reach the South Pole (1911), ahead of Robert Scott, having completed the final stage with four men and a team of 52 dogs. In 1926 he made the first crossing from Spitzbergen to Alaska over the North Pole in an airship. He died in a rescue operation, when his plane came down in the Arctic Ocean.

Andersen, Hans Christian (1805–75). Danish writer of fairy tales, such as 'The Ugly Duckling' and 'The

Snow Queen'. The son of a cobbler, he ran away at 14 to Copenhagen, where he found a rich patron who financed his education. His first volume of fairy tales, of which he wrote more than 150, was published in 1835 and included 'The Tinderbox' and 'The Princess and the Pea'. Although Andersen also wrote novels and plays, his international fame rests on the tales, which have been translated into many languages. The statue of the Little Mermaid in Copenhagen harbour is a tribute to him.

Andersen's Death March

Shortly before his death, Hans Christian Andersen was asked about the march for his funeral by the man commissioned to write it. "Make the beat keep time with little steps", he is said to have replied, "as most of the people who walk after me will be children."

Angelico, Fra, real name *Guido di Pietro* (c. 1400–55). Italian religious artist and Dominican friar. He led a simple, quiet, and virtuous life, earning the name *Angelico* ('angelic') after his death. Some of his frescoes can be seen in the monastery of S. Marco, Florence, and in a chapel of the Vatican. His other paintings include *The Coronation of the Virgin*, which is now in the Louvre.

Anne (1665–1714). Queen of Britain. The daughter of James II, she succeeded her brother-in-law William III in 1702. Until 1710 she was greatly influenced by the Duke of Marlborough and his dominating wife Sarah, and this, combined with her lack of intelligence and energy, encouraged the growing supremacy of Parliament. She married Prince George of Denmark in 1683, but her only child (of 17) to survive infancy died before her and she was succeeded by George I, Elector of Hanover, the nearest Protestant heir.

Anouilh, Jean (1910–87). French dramatist. He studied law and worked in an advertising agency before turning to the theatre. His first success *Traveller Without Luggage* (1937), was followed by such works as the controversial *Antigone* (1944) and *Ring Round the Moon* (1947). *The Lark* (1953) is a version of the story of Joan of Arc.

Aquinas, St Thomas (1225–74). Italian Catholic philosopher and theologian. He became a Dominican

---

Not so Dumb

As a student in Paris, Aquinas failed to impress his contemporaries, who referred to him as the 'dumb ox' because of his stout girth and taciturn manner. However, his teacher, the great scholar Albertus Magnus, quickly saw beyond this unimpressive exterior. After a private tutorial with Thomas, during which the two men ranged across all areas of human knowledge, Albertus announced at his next lecture: "You call your brother Thomas a dumb ox; let me tell you that one day the whole world will listen to his bellowings."

---

friar in 1243, against the wishes of his family, who imprisoned him for two years. After escaping to Cologne, where he studied under Albertus Magnus, he taught in Cologne, Paris, and Rome. His writings, especially the complete theological system attempted in the *Summa Theologiae*, continue to exert enormous influence.

Arafat, Yasser (1929–) Palestinian leader, chairman of the Palestine Liberation Organization since 1968. An engineer by training, Arafat helped to found the militant Palestinian group al Fatah in 1956. As chairman of the PLO, he brought the cause of the Palestinians to worldwide attention in the 1970s and 1980s. Having renounced terrorism, he concluded a peace treaty with Israel (1993), under which the Palestinians were granted limited self-government in Jericho and the Gaza Strip. For this he was awarded the Nobel Prize for peace (with Israel's Yitzhak Rabin and Shimon Peres) in 1993. Since then hardline opposition to the agreement on both sides has threatened Arafat's position within the Palestinian movement.

Archimedes (287–212 BC). Greek mathematician. Amongst his inventions was a spiral pump for raising water, known as Archimedes' screw, which is still used today. Best remembered for his discovery of the principles of buoyancy, he is alleged to have leapt out of his bath, shouting "Eureka!" ("I've found it!") when he first realized that his body displaced the water in the bath. He also invented war machines for the defence of Syracuse but was killed by a Roman soldier when the city was captured.

Ariosto, Ludovico (1474–1533) Italian poet. He spent most of his adult life as a courtier in the service of the Estes, the ruling family in Ferrara. Although he also wrote plays, satires, and lyrics, his fame rests on the epic *Orlando Furioso* (1516, 1532), one of the great works of the Italian Renaissance. The poem concerns the adventures and love affairs of Charlemagne's knights.

Aristophanes (c. 448–380 BC). Greek comic dramatist. His 11 surviving plays combine satirical comment on politics and literature with lyrical poetry and comic invention. His *Clouds* (423) satirized Socrates, while *Peace* (421) and *Lysistrata* (411) urged peace with Sparta.

Aristotle (384–322 BC). Greek philosopher and scientist. After studying under Plato, he became tutor to Alexander the Great. When Alexander became king of Macedonia in 336, Aristotle founded the Lyceum in Athens as a community for research. On Alexander's death in 323 Aristotle left Athens for political reasons, dying the following year. He wrote more than 400 books, covering every branch of learning; his work in biology, logic, and political science was of particular importance.

The Living and the Dead

Aristotle was once asked by how much educated men were superior to uneducated. "As much", he replied, "as the living are to the dead."

Arkwright, Sir Richard (1732–92). British pioneer of mechanical spinning. In 1768 Arkwright designed a spinning frame, a machine capable of producing a cotton thread strong enough to be used as the warp in weaving. He built and patented a number of machines, many of which were copied by other manufacturers. Popular feeling against the machines was strong, as it was felt they would replace the handicraft of the spinners, and in 1779 Arkwright's mill at Chorley was destroyed by a mob. Nevertheless his business prospered. In 1786 he was knighted and in 1790 he introduced steam power into his Nottingham works.

Armstrong, Louis (1900–71). Black US jazz musician and singer, nicknamed *Satchmo*. He first played the cornet at the age of 14 in the Waifs' Home in New Orleans, where he was sent after firing a gun in the street on New Year's Eve. He was playing the trumpet professionally by his mid teens, and formed his own band, the Armstrong Hot Five or Hot Seven, in 1924. His style of trumpet-playing in such numbers as 'Potato Head Blues' (1927) and 'West End Blues' (1928) became very popular. In later years he turned more to singing, his most famous hit song being 'What a Wonderful World'.

Armstrong, Neil (1930–   ). US astronaut. He got his first pilot's licence at 16 and became a naval aviator in the Korean War. In 1955 he joined NASA as an aeronautical research pilot. He started astronaut training in 1962 and went on two Gemini missions. On 20 July 1969, as command pilot of Apollo XI, he became the first man to set foot on the moon. He was professor of engineering at the University of Cincinnati from 1971 until 1979.

Arnold, Matthew (1822–88). British poet and critic, son of the educationalist Dr Thomas Arnold. For most of his life he worked as an inspector of schools while publishing collections of poetry and essays. *Poems* (1853) contains most of his important early poetry, while *New Poems* (1867) includes 'Thyrsis', an elegy for the poet Arthur Hugh Clough. Arnold was professor of poetry at Oxford from 1857 to 1867. In later life he was better known for his literary and cultural criticism and for *Culture and Anarchy* (1869).

Arthur (5th–6th century AD). A semi-legendary war leader of the Britons, known as *King Arthur*. His victories against the invading Saxons temporarily halted their settlement in south-west England. Subsequently Welsh, Breton, French, and English poets and romancers surrounded his name with legends, such as those of his magic sword Excalibur, his court at Camelot (perhaps the hill-fort of South Cadbury in Somerset), and his knights of the Round Table. A tomb at Glastonbury supposed to be his was opened in 1191.

Ashcroft, Dame Peggy (1907–91). British actress. Among her many performances, two of the most outstanding have been in *Romeo and Juliet* (1935) and *Hedda Gabler* (1954). She was created DBE in 1956 for her services to the theatre and was made a director of the Royal Shakespeare Company in 1968. The Ashcroft Theatre in Croydon, where she was born, is named after her.

Ashkenazy, Vladimir (1937–   ). Russian concert pianist. He studied at the Moscow Conservatoire, and gained the second prize in the International Chopin Competition when he was only 17. In 1962 he was joint winner of the Tchaikovsky competition. He made his London debut in 1963 and settled in Iceland ten years later. Ashkenazy became widely known through his recordings, especially of Chopin and Mozart.

Ashton, Sir Frederick (1906–88). British choreographer and ballet dancer. He studied under Léonide Massine and Marie Rambert and in 1935 became resident choreographer with the Vic-Wells company. In 1963 he was knighted and succeeded Ninette de Valois as director of the Royal Ballet (until 1970). He created both traditional and abstract ballets, including *Symphonic Variations* (1946), *Cinderella* (1948), *The Dream* (1964), and *Rhapsody* (1980).

Astaire, Fred, stage name of *Frederick Austerlitz* (1899–1987). US dancer and film star. In 1911 he formed a partnership with his sister Adele and they were highly successful vaudeville dancers on Broadway until Adele retired to get married. Astaire went to Hollywood in 1932, where his debonair style and genius as a dancer ensured the success of many musical films. In some of the best of these Ginger Rogers co-starred as his partner. His films include *Top Hat* (1935), *Easter Parade* (1948), and *Funny Face* (1957).

Astor, Nancy, Lady (1879–1964). The first female MP to sit in the House of Commons. Born *Nancy Witcher Langhorne* in the US, she stood for her husband's

Plymouth constituency when he succeeded to his father's peerage (1919). She won the seat and retained it until her retirement in 1945. In Parliament she tirelessly supported women's interests and children's welfare and opposed the drink trade. As a political hostess at Cliveden, her country house, she had considerable influence on government policy.

> ❛ I married beneath me – all women do.
> Nancy, Lady Astor ❜

Atatürk, title adopted by *Mustafa Kemal* (1881–1938). Turkish soldier and statesman, the founder of modern Turkey. As a young army officer he founded a secret society to remedy the deplorable state of his country. During World War I he commanded the defence of the Dardanelles and the Caucasus. He led Turkey to victory in the Greek war (1919–23) and played an important role in the abolition of the sultanate. As first president of a secular Turkish republic (1923) he used dictatorial methods to reform and modernize the country.

Attenborough, Richard, Lord (1923–) British film director, actor, and producer. Attenborough became a star of the British cinema with his appearances in such films as *In Which We Serve* (1942) and *Brighton Rock* (1947). He later moved into film production and made his debut as a director with *Oh, What a Lovely War!* (1969). In 1982 his biopic *Gandhi*, a project that he had cherished for some 20 years, earned eight Oscars. Subsequent films have included *Cry Freedom* (1987), *Chaplin*

(1992), and *Shadowlands* (1993). Attenborough, who was knighted in 1979 and made a baron in 1993, has continued to appear in such films as *Jurassic Park* (1993) and *Miracle on 34th Street* (1994). His brother is the naturalist, broadcaster, and maker of wildlife films **Sir David Attenborough** (1926–   ).

Attila (c. 406–453 AD). King of the Huns, a nomadic central Asian tribe that settled near the Danube. Nicknamed the 'Scourge of God', Attila claimed sovereignty over all the tribes between the Baltic and the Danube. At the height of his power, Attila's kingdom extended from the Rhine to the frontiers of China. In 451 he crossed the Rhine and invaded Gaul but was defeated by the Romans and Visigoths. In 452 he raided Italy but ended his invasion at the request of Pope Leo I. He died the following year, on the night of his marriage, and his empire disintegrated.

Attlee, Clement, Earl (1883–1967). British Labour politician. The son of a solicitor, he became converted to socialism at Oxford and abandoned a legal career for social work in London. After serving in World War I, he entered Parliament and held office in the two prewar Labour governments, becoming leader of the

> Few thought him even a starter
> There were many who thought themselves smarter
> But he ended PM, CH, and OM
> An Earl and a Knight of the Garter.
>
> Clement Attlee on himself

party in 1935. He served as deputy prime minister in Churchill's wartime coalition and became prime minister after the sweeping Labour victory in 1945. During his term of office he presided over the creation of the Welfare State and the nationalization of major industries. He retired from active politics in 1955.

Auden, W(ystan) H(ugh) (1907–73). British poet, considered the leader of the young left-wing writers of the 1930s. His first volume, *Poems* (1930), was an immediate success. He served as an ambulance driver in the Spanish Civil War before emigrating to the US in 1939. He later became a committed Anglican and revised many of his earlier political poems. As well as poetry, Auden's works include criticism, translations, and a libretto for Stravinsky's opera *The Rake's Progress* (1951). In 1956 he became professor of poetry at Oxford.

Augustine of Hippo, St (354–430 AD). North African theologian and philosopher. Born in Tagaste, he studied in Carthage and subsequently taught rhetoric in Rome and Milan. Although his mother was a Christian, he became a Manichaean in his youth and was also influenced by Neoplatonism. He converted to Christianity in 386 and returned to Africa, where he lived as a monk. After being ordained he was made Bishop of Hippo in 396. His writings include *The City of God*, a monumental defence of Christian belief, and the *Confessions*, a spiritual autobiography, as well as numerous letters, sermons, and treatises. He is considered the most important of the early Christian thinkers.

Augustus (63 BC–14 AD). Roman emperor, founder of the Roman empire. Born *Gaius Octavius*, he was known as *Octavian* from 44 to 27 BC, when he was given the title *Augustus* ('venerable'). He was introduced to public life by his great-uncle Julius Caesar and was appointed as his successor (44 BC). Octavian emerged from the civil wars that followed Caesar's death as triumvir (joint ruler) of the Roman world with Mark Antony and Lepidus. Lepidus was forced to retire from the triumvirate and Antony was defeated at Actium (31 BC) and died the next year, leaving Octavian in supreme control. During his long reign, peace and stability prevailed throughout the Roman world; new public buildings were constructed and a fire brigade and police force were established in Rome.

Austen, Jane (1775–1817). British novelist. A shrewd observer of people, she only settled seriously to writing after the death of her father, a clergyman, in 1805. *Sense and Sensibility* (1811) at once brought her a large readership. All her novels, including *Pride and Prejudice* (1813) and *Emma* (1815), were written in the family

> ❛ 'Oh! it is only a novel!...'in short, only some work in which the most thorough knowledge of human nature, the happiest delineation of its varieties, the liveliest effusions of wit and humour are conveyed to the world in the best chosen language.
> Jane Austen, *Northanger Abbey* (1818) ❜

sitting-room at Chawton in Hampshire and hidden when visitors called. Her novels are witty and ironic and provide interesting information about the everyday life of middle-class families in the early 19th century.

Avogadro, Count Amedeo (1776–1856). Italian physicist. Avogadro became professor of mathematics at Turin University in 1820. In 1811 he formulated the hypothesis known as Avogadro's law. This states that equal volumes of gases contain the same number of molecules when temperature and pressure are constant. The number of molecules in one gram molecular weight of any substance is known as Avogadro's number. His work was neglected in his lifetime but was rediscovered in the 19th century.

B

Bach, Johann Sebastian (1685–1750). German composer. He came from a musical family, and at 19 went to the court at Weimar as an organist and chamber musician. After this he became musical director to Prince Leopold at Cothen, where he wrote the Brandenburg Concertos, and later held the same position in Leipzig, where he stayed until his death. His *Christmas Oratorio*, *Mass in B Minor*, *St Matthew Passion*, and *St John Passion* are among the most famous religious works in the history of music. He also wrote much keyboard music and many cantatas. Three of his 13 children, Wilhelm Friedemann, Karl Philip Emanuel, and Johann Christian, were also accomplished composers.

Bacon, Francis (1561–1626). English philosopher and politician, the son of a courtier of Elizabeth I. He deserted his patron, the Earl of Essex, during the latter's trial for treason and worked with the prosecution to ensure his conviction (1601). He rapidly rose in power under James I until 1621, when he was banished from Parliament for taking bribes. Bacon's fame now rests on his philosophy, which advocates observation and experience as the source of knowledge and truth, and can be regarded as the theoretical basis of modern science. He died from a chill caught while conducting an experiment in food preservation by stuffing a chicken with snow.

> ❝ If a man will begin with certainties, he shall end in doubts, but if he will be content to begin with doubts, he shall end in certainties.
>
> Francis Bacon, *The Advancement of Learning* (1605) ❞

Bacon, Francis (1909–92) British artist, noted for his paintings of anguished distorted figures. Born in Dublin, Bacon was self-taught as an artist and found little recognition until his *Three Studies for Figures at the Base of a Crucifixion* was exhibited in 1945. His later works, which continue to explore themes of pain and isolation, include a series of 'Screaming Popes' inspired by a portrait by Velázquez.

Baden-Powell, Robert, Lord (1857–1941). British general, founder of the Scout movement. He served in India and Africa, commanding the defence of Mafeking (1899–1900) with a small garrison during the Boer War. His training book *Aids to Scouting* (1899) began to be used for training boys, and this led to the creation of the Boy Scouts in 1908. In 1910 he left the army to lead the Scouts full-time, and with his sister **Agnes** (1858–1945) founded the Girl Guides.

Baird, John Logie (1888–1946). Scottish inventor of television. Baird began his research into the problems of televising moving objects at the age of 18. In 1926 he televised objects in outline, using a flying spot of light to scan a cathode ray tube. The German post office began using his system, which he had successfully applied to moving objects, in 1929. The BBC also adopted Baird's system in that year but abandoned it in 1937 for the rival system of the Marconi Company. Baird produced the first colour television pictures in 1941.

Baldwin, Stanley (1867–1947). British Conservative statesman. After leaving Cambridge, Baldwin joined his father's iron and steel business and did not enter Parliament until 1908. He served as chancellor of the exchequer under Bonar Law (1922–23) and was prime minister twice (1924–29; 1935–37). His calm handling of the General Strike (1926) and Edward VIII's abdication (1936) made him popular, but he was blamed for Britain's unpreparedness for war in 1939.

Balzac, Honoré de (1799–1850). French novelist, who achieved his first success with *Les Chouans* (1829). His major novels fit into an overall scheme, *The Human Comedy*, which Balzac planned to contain 143 novels about 19th-century life. The 90 novels completed analyse various aspects of human nature, such as miserliness in *Eugénie Grandet* (1833), doting parenthood in *Father Goriot* (1834–35), and jealousy in *Cousin Bette* (1846). A poor businessman, Balzac lived extravagantly and was often in debt. He married a Polish countess shortly before his death.

Balzac and the Stranger

In the first flush of his fame as a writer, Balzac received an intriguing letter from abroad signed only 'The Stranger'. After some investigation, he discovered that the writer was Evelina Hanska, the wife of a Polish count. Their correspondence led to a passionate and lasting affair. Although Evelina's husband died in 1841, she did not marry Balzac until several months before his own death. A remark attributed to the writer may suggest why: "It is easier to be a lover than a husband", he is reported to have said, "for the same reason that it is more difficult to show a ready wit all day long than to produce an occasional *bon mot.*"

Bannister, Sir Roger (1929–   ). British athlete. On 6 May 1954 he became the first man to run a mile in less than four minutes (3 minutes 59.4 seconds), and subsequently improved on that time. By 1993 the world record for the mile was 3 minutes 4.39 seconds. A neurologist by profession, he later held a number of senior academic positions. In 1995 he caused controversy by suggesting that Black athletes may have innate physical advantages.

Banting, Sir Frederick (1891–1941). Canadian medical scientist. In 1921, while working at the University of Toronto, he and Charles Best discovered insulin, a hormone produced in the pancreas that is either obtained from animals or synthesized for use in treating diabetes. Banting was a joint winner of the 1923 Nobel Prize for physiology or medicine, sharing his portion of the prize with Best.

Bardot, Brigitte, stage name of *Camille Javal* (1933–   ). French film actress. A former model, she began her film career in 1954. *And God Created Woman* (1956), directed by her then husband, Roger Vadim, made her a star. Her sex appeal was highly publicized and exploited in subsequent films, which include *The Truth* (1961), *Contempt* (1964), and *Viva Maria* (1965). Since retiring from the cinema in 1973 she has devoted her time to campaigning for animal rights.

Barenboim, Daniel (1942–   ). Israeli pianist and conductor. Barenboim was born in Argentina and studied in Salzburg, Paris, and Rome. He made his debut at the age of 13 and soon became well known, particularly for his performances of Beethoven's piano sonatas. He married the cellist Jacqueline du Pré in 1967. Barenboim was musical director of the Orchestre de Paris from 1975 until 1989, when he was sacked amid much controversy. He became conductor of the Chicago Symphony Orchestra in 1991.

Barnard, Christiaan (1922–   ). South African surgeon. After much practical research into heart surgery at the Groote Schuur Hospital in Cape Town, he performed the first human heart transplant there in 1967. Although the operation was itself a success, the patient died of pneumonia 18 days later.

Barnardo, Dr Thomas John (1845–1905). British phil-anthropist. He studied medicine in London and founded the first 'Dr Barnardo's Home' for destitute children in Stepney in 1870. Dr Barnardo's is still a thriving charity and now administers over 100 homes and other child-care establishments.

Barrie, J(ames) M(atthew) (1860–1937). Scottish drama-tist and novelist. He is best known for the children's fairy-tale play *Peter Pan* (1904), which developed from a series of stories told to the sons of a friend. His other theatrical successes include *Quality Street* (1901) and *The Admirable Crichton* (1902). Barrie was knighted in 1913.

Barrymore, John (1882–1942). US actor, a member of a distinguished Anglo-American family of actors. He made his stage debut in 1903 and was soon idolized by the public for his striking good looks and dashing per-sonality. From 1912 he acted mainly in films and on radio. His private life was notoriously unsettled and troubled by alcoholism. His films include *Dr Jekyll and Mr Hyde* (1920), *Svengali* (1931), and *Grand Hotel* (1932). His brother **Lionel** (1878–1954) was a character actor in many films, including *A Free Soul* (1931) and *Duel in the Sun* (1946). Their sister **Ethel** (1897–1959) was a success-ful actress on the New York stage from 1901. She oc-casionally appeared in films and won an Academy Award for her supporting role in *None But the Lonely Heart* (1944). The dynasty has continued to the present with John Barrymore's children Diana (1921–60) and John Jnr (1932–) and his granddaughter Drew Barrymore (1975–).

Barrymore and the Booze

By the early 1930s John Barrymore's golden career had begun to suffer from the heavy drinking and wild behaviour that would make him one of Hollywood's most notorious legends. In his later films he was often unable to remember his lines, which had to be written on concealed cue cards. Stories of his erratic behaviour are legion. On one occasion he blundered drunkenly into a ladies' lavatory to be greeted by the distressed cry "This is for women!" "And so," Barrymore retorted, "is this!" Once, while performing in the theatre, he became so enraged by the continual coughing of the audience that he left the stage and returned with a large fish, which he hurled into the auditorium. "Here you damned walruses," he cried, "busy yourselves with this while we go on with the play!"

Bartók, Béla (1881–1945). Hungarian composer and pianist. Having first appeared in public at the age of ten, he became a concert pianist as a young man. While studying music in Budapest he developed an interest in Hungarian folk music, whose rhythms and melodies he incorporated into his concertos, songs, and choral music. His six string quartets are also of particular importance.

Basie, Count, real name *William Basie* (1904–84). Black US jazz bandleader. He studied the piano as a child and joined Bennie Moten's big band in the early 1930s. When Moten died (1935) Basie took the best musicians and formed his own band. He specialized in the 12-bar blues form and developed a relaxed style of performance.

Baudelaire, Charles (1821–67). French poet. He became addicted to hashish and opium in his youth and contracted the syphilis of which he eventually died. In 1842 he came into his inheritance but his extravagant and dissolute behaviour led his guardians to obtain a judgment placing his capital in trust. His first collection of poems, *Fleurs du mal* (1857; revised 1861), led to trial and conviction for obscenity and blasphemy; some of them remained banned until 1949. In 1862 he was declared bankrupt and from 1866 he was paralysed and spent the rest of his life in hospitals.

Beardsley, Aubrey (1872–98). British illustrator. His stylized black and white drawings, which were influenced by Japanese painting, are typical of the Art Nouveau style. His use of sensuous elongated human forms aroused much controversy in his day. Amongst his best-known works are the illustrations for the periodical *The Yellow Book* (1894–95) and for Oscar Wilde's play *Salome* (1894). He became a Roman Catholic a year before his death from consumption.

> ❛ He had a sort of innocent familiarity with evil, he communed with leering dwarfs, the bloated epicene figures that peopled the depraved landscapes and grotesque interiors designed by his pen, as a child might talk to fairies.
> William Gaunt, *The Aesthetic Adventure* ❜

Beatles, The. British rock group, consisting of **George Harrison** (1943–   ), **John Lennon** (1940–80), **Paul McCartney** (1942–   ), and **Ringo Starr** (1940–   ), real name *Richard Starkey*. The Beatles were formed in 1959 and in 1962 they appeared at the Cavern Club in Liverpool. Soon afterwards they recorded 'Love Me Do' and 'She Loves You', which rose to the top of the record charts in 1963. The Beatles rapidly achieved world-wide popularity and revolutionized the pop world. They made a successful tour of the US, appeared in the films *A Hard Day's Night* and *Help!*, and in 1965 were awarded the MBE. Most of their best-selling singles were written by Lennon and McCartney. Their most original album, *Sergeant Pepper's Lonely Hearts Club Band* (1967), reflected their experience of drugs and Eastern mysticism. The Beatles continued to record together until 1969 but thereafter disbanded to pursue their separate careers, with McCartney enjoying the greatest commercial success. Any hope of a reunion was shattered in 1980, when Lennon was shot dead by a demented 'fan'. Nevertheless, 'Free as a Bird', a 'new' Beatles song featuring Lennon's voice and backing from the surviving members, was released in 1995.

Beaufort, Sir Francis (1774–1857). British admiral and hydrographer. In 1808 Beaufort drafted the scale of wind strengths that has become the standard table for measuring the forces of winds. The scale ranges from calm (0) to hurricane force (12–17). Beaufort classified the grades by the amount of sail that could be carried by a warship in each wind force.

Beauvoir, Simone de (1908–86). French novelist, writer, and existentialist thinker. In 1929 she began a lifelong association with Jean-Paul Sartre at the Sorbonne, where she later taught philosophy. Her works include the feminist landmark *The Second Sex* (1949), *The Mandarins* (1956), a novel set in the French intellectual circles of the 1940s; she also wrote an autobiography in several volumes, beginning with *Memoirs of a Dutiful Daughter* (1958) and ending with *Adieux: A Farewell to Sartre* (1981).

Becket, St Thomas à (1118–70). English churchman and martyr. A skilled administrator, he was chosen as chancellor by Henry II in 1154. In this post he invariably put the king's interests above everything and in 1162 Henry had Becket elected Archbishop of Canterbury, expecting him to continue in this style. To his annoyance Becket took his new religious duties very seriously and resigned as chancellor. Henry and Becket quarrelled and Becket was forced into exile. In 1170 a reconciliation took place and Becket returned to England, only to anger the king again by asserting the rights of the Church and papacy. He was murdered in Canterbury Cathedral by four of the king's knights; according to tradition they carried out the bloody deed

> ❛ Thomas à Becket won for himself an outstanding place in history by his genius for manoeuvring other parties into the wrong.
> John Harvey,
> *The Plantagenets* (1949) ❜

after hearing their king ask in a rage, "Who will rid me of this meddlesome priest!" Soon miracles were reported at Becket's tomb and he was canonized by the pope in 1173. The king did public penance at his shrine, which became one of the most popular places of pilgrimage in Europe. Becket's feast day is 29 December.

Beckett, Samuel (1906–89). Irish novelist and dramatist. He lived in France from 1932 onwards and wrote most of his works in French, producing his own English translations. He is best known for his plays, such as *Waiting for Godot* (1954) and *Endgame* (1957), both of which illustrate the pointlessness of life and the failure of human communication. His novels include the important trilogy *Molloy* (1951), *Malone Dies* (1951), and *The Unnamable* (1953). Latterly he concentrated on short experimental works. He received the Nobel Prize for literature in 1969.

Bede, the Venerable (673–735 AD). Monk, biblical scholar, and the first English historian. Bede devoted his life to teaching, writing, and study at the monastery of Jarrow, where he wrote the *Ecclesiastical History of the English People*. He died while working on an English translation of the Gospel of St John. Within 50 years he was revered as a saint. In the 11th century his bones were taken to Durham Cathedral, where they still remain.

Beecham, Sir Thomas (1879–1961). British conductor. The grandson of the founder of a pharmaceutical firm, he established his New Symphony Orchestra in London in 1906. He helped to popularize the music of Frederick Delius and introduced audiences in London to Russian ballet and opera. After World War II he founded the Royal Philharmonic Orchestra (1947), and made a number of world tours. Beecham was noted for his eccentric opinions and sayings. He is reputed to have opposed the introduction of female musicians into his orchestras, reasoning that the attractive ones would distract the male players and the ugly ones would distract him.

Beethoven, Ludwig van (1770–1827). German composer. The son of a musician, Beethoven published his earliest known composition when he was ten and a year later he was appointed deputy organist in the Court Opera House in Cologne. He was influenced by Mozart and Haydn, under whom he studied in Vienna (1787; 1792–94). The development of his style, which is usually divided into three periods, can be seen in his nine symphonies (1800–23); these become increasingly complex and expressive, with the ninth (the *Choral Symphony*) being regarded as the greatest. Among his other works are five piano concertos, the opera *Fidelio*, and 17 string quartets. Beethoven was supported by a number of rich patrons, despite his unattractive manners and appearance and his stormy temper. By 1802 he had begun to lose his hearing, and some of his greatest works were written when he was totally deaf.

Bell, Alexander Graham (1847–1922). Scottish inventor. A teacher of elocution and speech correction, Bell went to live in Canada in 1870. He developed a method of teaching speech to the deaf and in 1873 became

> **The First Telephone Conversation**
> On 10 March 1876, Alexander Graham Bell
> became the first person to speak over the
> telephone. His words, transmitted to an-
> other room in the same house in Boston,
> were recorded by his assistant, Thomas
> Watson: "Come here, Mr Watson, I want you."

professor of vocal physiology at Boston University. In 1876 he obtained a patent for the telephone, which he had developed during long evening sessions with the mechanic Thomas Watson. He subsequently spent much time in legal action against infringement of the patent. Bell's other inventions included the photophone, a device that transmitted sound on a beam of light, and the graphophone, which recorded sound on wax discs. He also carried out research in the field of aerodynamics, conducting experiments with giant kites and hydrofoils.

Bellini, Giovanni (c. 1430–1516). Venetian painter. He came from an artistic family, his father Jacopo and his elder brother Gentile both being accomplished painters. Giovanni painted many devotional works for churches, such as *The Agony in the Garden* and *St Jerome* (1513), which are noted for the naturalistic landscapes in which the figures are placed. He also painted portraits of the doges of Venice and semi-mythological subjects such as *Feast of the Gods* (1514).

Belloc, Hilaire (1870–1953). Catholic writer of Anglo-French parentage, who became a British citizen in 1902.

He was a great friend of G. K. Chesterton and together they founded a weekly newspaper, the *Eye-Witness*. Belloc was a Liberal MP (1906–10) but was soon disillusioned with party politics. His works include poetry, such as the collection of humorous verse for children *Cautionary Tales* (1907), historical works, biographies, and travel books.

Bellow, Saul (1915–   ). US novelist, born in Quebec, Canada. The son of poor Russian Jewish immigrants, Bellow published his first novel, *Dangling Man*, in 1944. His reputation as the leading US novelist of his generation was then established by such books as *Henderson the Rain King* (1959), the highly autobiographical *Herzog* (1964), and *Mr Sammler's Planet* (1970). Many of his novels and stories concern the plight of the modern urban intellectual in the US. Later publications include *The Dean's December* (1982) and *Something to Remember Me By* (1991). He was awarded the Nobel Prize for literature in 1976.

Benedict of Nursia, St (c. 480–550 AD). Italian monk, founder of monasticism in the West. After living as a hermit and founding several monasteries, he and a group of followers settled at Monte Cassino, between Rome and Naples. Here he wrote the Rule, later known as the Benedictine Rule, which became the accepted monastic code of Western Europe. His feast day is 11 July. In 1964 he was proclaimed patron saint of Europe.

Ben Gurion, David (1886–1973). First prime minister of Israel. Born in Poland, he emigrated to Palestine in

1906. Expelled by the Turks in 1915, he later fought against them with the Jewish Legion, which he organized in the US. In the 1920s and 1930s he led the Jewish Trade Union Movement and the Mapai (Labour) party, and from 1935 he was chairman of the Zionist movement in Palestine. Having proclaimed the State of Israel in 1948, he remained its prime minister until 1963, except for a brief interval (1953–55).

Bentham, Jeremy (1748–1832). British philosopher. His philosophical writings promote the Utilitarian doctrine, which defines good conduct as that which produces "the greatest happiness of the greatest number". Bentham was a founder of University College, London, where his skeleton serves as the framework of a commemorative waxwork figure.

> ❛ The father of English innovation, both in doctrines and in institutions, is Bentham: he is…the great *critical* thinker of his age and country.
> John Stuart Mill, *Dissertations and Discussions* (1859)

> The arch-philistine Jeremy Bentham was the insipid, pedantic, leather-tongued oracle of the bourgeois intelligence of the 19th century.
> Karl Marx, *Das Kapital* (1867–83) ❜

Bergman, Ingmar (1918–). Swedish stage and film director, writer, and producer. He became internationally known for his films, over which he had complete control. They are noted for their technical excellence and for the distinguished performances of the small group of actors who appear in most of them. They include *The Seventh Seal* (1956), *Wild Strawberries* (1957), *The Virgin Spring* (1959), *Persona* (1966), the television film *Scenes from a Marriage* (1974), and *Fanny and Alexander* (1982).

Beria, Laventi Pavlovich (1899–1953). Soviet politician, head of the secret police (1938–53). Born in Georgia, the son of peasants, Beria joined the Bolshevik Party in 1917 and participated in the October Revolution. After ten years as director of the secret police in Georgia (1921–31), he rose to national prominence as a trusted associate of Stalin. As head of the notorious NKVD, he became one of the most powerful and feared men in the country. He was actively involved in the purging of Stalin's opponents and organized the deportation of many thousands to labour camps. On Stalin's death in 1953, leading figures in the party arranged for Beria's immediate arrest, believing that their own lives might otherwise be in danger. According to some rumours, he had even had Stalin poisoned. In December 1953 official sources stated that Beria had been shot as a traitor. Further details of his cruelty and corruption emerged in the *glasnost* era.

Berkeley, George (1685–1753). Irish philosopher, a friend of Jonathan Swift. His philosophy stresses the importance of perception, denying the reality of what cannot be observed, and states that "to exist is to be perceived". Berkeley also wrote extensively on social questions. He travelled in Europe from 1713 to 1720 and was made dean of Derry in 1721. He became bishop of Cloyne (1734) after three years spent in the US fostering higher education. Having resigned his bishopric in 1752, he died in Oxford a few months later.

Berlin, Irving, real name *Israel Baline* (1888–1989). US songwriter and composer, born in Russia. Amongst his most famous songs are 'Alexander's Ragtime Band', 'White Christmas', and 'Anything You Can Do'. 'God Bless America' was awarded a special gold medal by Congress. He also wrote a number of popular musicals, including *Annie Get Your Gun* (1946).

Berlioz, Hector (1803–69). French composer. He started to study medicine in Paris, but soon gave it up in favour of music. He married the Irish actress Henrietta Smithson in 1833 but they separated seven years later and he remarried in 1854. The most notable of the French Romantic composers, he is remembered for his *Symphonie fantastique*, and the choral works *The Damnation of Faust* and *L'Enfance du Christ*. He also wrote three operas and several books on music.

Bernhardt, Sarah, stage name of *Rosine Bernard* (1844–1923). French actress. She was trained at the Paris Conservatoire and first appeared on stage in 1862 at the Comédie Française. By the 1880s she was an international celebrity, touring Europe, the Americas, and Australia. She was famous for a number of tragic roles, including the title roles in *Hamlet* and Racine's *Phèdre*,

Bernhardt's Leg

In 1915, as the result of an accident incurred during a performance of Sardou's *La Tosca*, Sarah Bernhardt had to have one of her legs removed. While she was recovering, an enterprising US showman offered her $100,000 for the right to exhibit the amputated limb. Neither this misfortune nor the coming of old age (she was now in her seventies) inhibited the actress in her choice of roles; with the aid of a wooden leg, she was widely acclaimed for her performance as the 18-year-old Joan of Arc.

and was created Chevalier of the Legion of Honour in 1914. She lost her right leg in an accident (1915) but continued to perform. Her autobiography is entitled *My Double Life* (1907).

Bernini, Gian Lorenzo (1598–1680). Italian sculptor and architect. He specialized in classical subjects such as *Apollo and Daphne* (1624), with some religious works such as *The Ecstasy of St Theresa* (1645). He designed many of the churches, tombs, and fountains in Rome and also the colonnade around St Peter's Square. The three rows of columns in the colonnade were carefully aligned so that from a certain point in the square only one row can be seen.

Bernstein, Leonard (1918–90). US conductor, composer, and pianist. He became assistant conductor of the New York Philharmonic Orchestra in 1943 and had his first success later that year when the conductor was taken ill. He went on to conduct the New York Symphony Orchestra (1945–47). He was noted for his books and concerts for young people and also lectured widely on music. His compositions include both classical and light music, his best-known Broadway score being the popular musical *West Side Story* (1957).

Bessemer, Sir Henry (1813–98). British metallurgist and engineer. His most famous invention was the Bessemer process for making steel (1856), in which air is forced through molten pig iron, oxidizing such impurities as carbon and silicon. The Bessemer process has now been largely replaced by the basic-oxygen process.

Best, Charles (1899–1978). Canadian medical scientist. *See* Sir Frederick **Banting**.

Betjeman, Sir John (1906–84). English poet. His popular volumes of poetry include *A Few Late Chrysanthemums* (1954) and a verse autobiography, *Summoned by Bells* (1960). He also wrote on the architecture, churches, and countryside of Britain. He was knighted in 1969 and was Poet Laureate from 1972 until his death.

Bevan, Aneurin (1897–1960). Welsh Labour politician. The son of a miner, Bevan worked in the pits from the age of 13. A prominent trade unionist at 19, he led the Welsh miners in the 1926 General Strike. He entered Parliament as MP for Ebbw Vale in 1929 and made a reputation as an orator. During World War II he was one of Churchill's few opponents. As minister of health in the post-war Labour government he established the National Health Service, but the widening gap between his socialist ideals and the policies of the Labour party leaders led to his resignation as minister of labour in 1951.

> ❛ No amount of cajolery, and no attempts at ethical or social seduction, can eradicate from my heart a deep burning hatred for the Tory Party...so far as I am concerned they are lower than vermin.
>
> Aneurin Bevan, speech
> 4 July 1949 ❜

Bhutto, Benazir (1953–) Pakistani stateswoman. The daughter of Zulfikar Ali Bhutto, president (1971–73) and subsequently prime minister (1973–77) of Pakistan, Benazir was educated at Harvard and Oxford. Following her father's deposition (1977; he was executed in 1979), she spent seven years under house arrest and a further period in exile. In 1988 she made a triumphant return to Pakistan and was elected the first woman leader of a Muslim country. However, following increased ethnic violence she was dismissed by the president in 1990. Charges of corruption were subsequently dropped and she was re-elected in 1993.

Bismarck, Otto von (1815–98). German statesman, nicknamed the 'Iron Chancellor'. A member of an ancient Prussian family, he served as a diplomat (1849–62) in Frankfurt, Russia, and Paris, until he was appointed prime minister of Prussia by King Wilhelm I. His successful wars with Denmark (1864), Austria (1866), and France (1870) led to the unification of Germany under Prussian leadership. He dominated German politics until his sudden dismissal in 1890 by the young emperor Wilhelm II.

Bizet, Georges (1838–75). French composer. He studied music at the Paris Conservatoire from the age of ten and won a number of prizes, including the Prix de Rome in 1857. His first opera, *The Pearlfishers*, was produced in 1863. His most famous work is the opera *Carmen*, which was first performed in 1875, just before his death. He also wrote songs, piano music, and orchestral works.

Black Prince, the, nickname of *Prince Edward* (1330–76). Prince of Wales, whose nickname probably derived from his black armour. He commanded the right wing at Crécy (1346) and in 1355 took over the English forces in Aquitaine, capturing the French king at Poitiers (1356). His later campaigns as Prince of Aquitaine, and the consequent taxation, caused the local nobility to transfer their allegiance to the French king. Edward returned to England in ill-health in 1371 and retired from public life.

Blake, William (1757–1827). British engraver, painter, and poet. He trained and worked as an engraver, writing poetry in his spare time at first. He later published books of engraved and illustrated poems, the best known of which are *Songs of Innocence* (1789) and *Songs of Experience* (1794). Some of his finest

Blake's Visions

Throughout his life Blake was subject to visions, the reality of which he never doubted. As a young child he once saw God peering at him through a window and a tree full of angels "bespangling every bough like stars" at Peckham Rye. Later, he would startle visitors by talking about the subjects of his extraordinary paintings as if they had been really present to him as he drew. His 'sitters' included figures from British history, biblical prophets and patriarchs, and, on one occasion, the ghost of a flea. Unsurprisingly, many of his contemporaries concluded that Blake was a little touched. He, however, remained defiant:

I mock thee not, though I by thee am mockéd
Thou call'st me Madman, but I call thee Blockhead.

('To Flaxman')

illustrations can be found in *The Book of Job* (1826). As his poetry became increasingly complex and symbolic, his designs developed an imaginative style that was to influence the romantic art of the 19th century.

Blériot, Louis (1872–1936). French aviator, the first man to fly across the English Channel. He conducted experiments with gliders and biplanes and subsequently developed his own powered monoplane. The record flight took place on 25 July 1909, when he flew from Calais to Dover in 37 minutes using his small 24 horse-power monoplane. This achievement played a significant role in the development of aviation and impressed governments all over the world with the importance of this new means of travel. During World

War I Blériot built planes for the French government and made important innovations in aircraft design.

Boadicea, Latin name of *Boudicca* (d. 61 AD). Queen of the Iceni, a British tribe of East Anglia. Her husband King Prasutagus had allied himself with the Roman invaders, but after his death imperial officials annexed his lands and ill-treated Boadicea and her daughters. She roused her own and neighbouring peoples in revolt, routed the Roman troops and sacked Colchester, London, and St Albans. Overwhelmed by the main Roman army, she poisoned herself to avoid capture.

Boccaccio, Giovanni (1313–75). Italian writer. Boccaccio was the illegitimate son of a merchant and embarked on a career in commerce before turning to story writing in verse and prose. His early life was spent in Florence and Naples. In 1350 he met Petrarch, whose biography he had written, and the two became close friends. Boccaccio's most influential work was the *Decameron*, probably written between 1348 and 1353, a collection of stories that range from earthy farcical tales to tragedies.

Bogart, Humphrey, full name *Humphrey De Forest Bogart* (1899–1957). US actor. He is famous for his portrayal of the tough guy in such films as *San Quentin* (1937) and *The Maltese Falcon* (1942). In *The Big Sleep* (1946) he starred with Lauren Bacall, who became his fourth wife. Notable later films include *The African Queen* (1951) and *The Caine Mutiny* (1954). He is remembered for his husky drawl and the catchphrase "Play it again,

> ❝ For all his outward toughness, insolence, braggadocio, and contempt...there came through a kind of sadness, loneliness, and heartbreak (all of which were very part of Bogie the man). I always felt sorry for him — sorry that he had imposed upon himself the facade of the character with which he had become identified.
>
> Edward G. Robinson on
> Humphrey Bogart ❞

Sam", which is in fact a misquote from the film *Casablanca* (1942).

Bohr, Niels (1885–1962). Danish physicist. Bohr studied in Copenhagen, where he later became professor of physics and director of the Institute of Theoretical Physics. While working in Britain he developed a new model for the structure of the atom; for this and for work on the emission of spectra he was awarded the Nobel Prize for physics in 1922. During World War II he fled from the Nazis to the US, where he worked on the atom bomb. His son **Aage Bohr** (1922–   ), also a scientist, shared the Nobel Prize for physics (1975) for his work on atomic theory.

Bolivar, Simon (1783–1830). South American soldier and statesman, who liberated six South American republics from Spain. A descendant of wealthy Spanish colonists in Venezuela, he returned from a visit to Europe (1804–07) inspired with revolutionary fervour. Despite many setbacks his forces set free New Granada (Colombia) in 1819 and Venezuela in 1821, and Bolivar set himself up as president. By 1825 Spanish rule in South America had ended, and Upper Peru was named Bolivia in Bolivar's honour. His dictatorial attempts to settle the civil disturbances that followed, during which he barely escaped assassination, ended in failure. He was forced to resign the presidency in 1830 and died of tuberculosis shortly afterwards.

Booth, William (1829–1912). British founder of the Salvation Army. The son of a Nottingham builder, he underwent a religious conversion at 15, first becoming a Methodist and later an independent revivalist preacher. In 1847 he moved to London and established the Christian Mission, later known as the Salvation Army, in Whitechapel. It was dedicated to religious and social work among the most poverty-stricken people. *In Darkest England and the Way Out* (1890) set out Booth's plans for rehabilitating the poor. Although Booth's emotional revivalistic approach was at first distrusted, the Salvation Army spread to the US, Australia, and other countries and its social rescue work gradually came to be appreciated and supported. In 1904 Booth was received by King Edward VII, who encouraged his work. The Salvation Army remains a thriving charity to this day.

Borg, Björn (1956–   ). Swedish tennis player. He won the French Open Championship in 1974, 1975, 1978, and

1979 and is the only man to have won the Wimbledon singles title five years running (1976–80). He was noted for his cool unemotional approach to the game.

Borges, Jorge Luis (1899–1986). Argentinian writer, best known for his complex and paradoxical stories. Born in Buenos Aires, Borges spent much of his youth in Europe, where he began to write poetry. After returning to Argentina he published short stories and journalism while working as a librarian; he was dismissed from this employment in 1946, for his opposition to the dictator Perón. Despite having lost his sight, he was appointed director of the National Library following Perón's fall in 1955. His international reputation rests mainly on the highly original stories published in *Fictions* (1944; 1966) and *The Aleph* (1949; 1970). He is regarded as the founder of the style known as 'magical realism', in which fantastic events are described in a realistic style.

Borgia, Cesare (1476–1507). Italian nobleman, the illegitimate son of Rodrigo de Borgia, who was Pope Alexander VI. Cesare became a cardinal at the age of 17, and succeeded his brother-in-law as papal captain-general. A brilliant soldier, he regained the central Italian states for the papacy but was dismissed by Pope Julius II. Borgia had a reputation for treachery and murder, but was also a patron of Leonardo da Vinci. He was the model for the ruthless administrator depicted by Machiavelli in *The Prince*. His sister, **Lucrezia Borgia** (1480–1519), was married for the first time when she was only 12 years old. She subsequently married three more times. Her third husband was assassinated by

> ❛ He was, by his twenty-seventh
> year, the most feared, hated,
> and envied man of his day,
> courted by the rulers of France,
> Spain, and the Empire…At
> thirty-one he was dead, dying
> in an ambush in northern
> Spain as violently and
> spectacularly as he had lived.
> Sarah Bradford,
> *Cesare Borgia, his Life
> and Times* (1967) ❜

her father and brother and in 1501 she married Alfonso, Duke of Ferrara. The Ferrara court became famous as a centre of culture, the poet Ariosto and the painter Titian being amongst those who received patronage there. More recent research has suggested that Lucrezia's reputation for cruelty and other crimes was unfounded.

Borodin, Alexander (1833–87). Russian composer. He trained as a doctor and was assistant professor of chemistry at St Petersburg medical academy; he later founded a school of medicine for women. All his musical composition was done in his spare time, as relaxation. His music has a typically Russian character. His best-known works are the unfinished opera *Prince Igor*, which contains the 'Polovtsian Dances', and the symphonic sketch *In the Steppes of Central Asia* (1880).

Bosch, Hieronymus (c. 1450–1516). Dutch painter. He is famous for his detailed colourful paintings of fantastic scenes, intended to satirize the foolish or evil aspects of human nature. Such works as *The Garden of Earthly Delights* and *The Seven Deadly Sins* abound with tiny figures of peasants, devils, and monsters. Bosch's style changed in his later works, such as *The Prodigal Son*, when he began to concentrate on 'close-ups' of one or two central figures.

Boswell, James (1740–95). Scottish biographer and diarist. A qualified lawyer, he met Samuel Johnson in 1763 and their friendship lasted until Johnson's death in 1784. His poetry and plays are undistinguished, his major achievement being *The Life of Samuel Johnson* (1791). His unpublished diaries, which are noted for their sexual frankness, were discovered in Ireland in the 1920s and 1930s.

> **❝** You have but two topics,
> yourself and me, and I'm
> sick of both.
> Samuel Johnson to
> James Boswell, in
> Boswell's *London Journal* **❞**

Botham, Ian (1955–   ). British cricketer. He made his county debut in 1974 and his Test debut three years later. Although his attacking style as both a bowler and a batsman made him a popular favourite, he was frequently involved in controversy. He held a record number of Test wickets (1986–88) and scored over 3000 runs in Test matches before retiring in 1993.

Botticelli, Sandro, real name *Sandro Filipepi* (c. 1445–1510). Italian painter. The nickname 'Botticelli', meaning 'little barrel', was first given to his elder brother. His style ranges from strong realistic painting, as in *St Sebastian* (1473), to more emotional and mystical work. His best-known paintings are the graceful mythological *Primavera* (1478), an allegorical representation of spring, and *The Birth of Venus* (c. 1485). He also painted some of the frescoes in the Sistine Chapel. He broke with his patrons, the Medicis, after the execution of the revolutionary priest Savanorola (1498), and his subsequent works were more sombre and religious.

Bowie, David, real name *David Jones* (1947–   ). British rock singer and songwriter, noted for his many changes of style and image. Bowie began to perform in pop bands while still in his teens and also trained as a mime artist. After enjoying his first hit with 'Space Oddity' (1969), he became a major star with the albums *The Rise and Fall of Ziggy Stardust* (1972) and *Aladdin Sane* (1973), which established his bizarre androgynous image. His later albums range from the experimental *Heroes* (1977), recorded in Berlin, to the more mainstream *Let's Dance* (1983) and the eclectic *Outside* (1995). He has also acted in a number of films, notably *The Man Who Fell to Earth* (1975), and exhibited his paintings.

Boyle, Robert (1627–91). English chemist, born in Ireland. Boyle studied chemistry and anatomy and in 1654 established a laboratory at Oxford, where he and Robert Hooke invented an air pump. His experiments with gases led to the formulation of Boyle's law, that at a constant temperature the volume of a quantity of gas is inversely proportional to its pressure. Boyle also developed tests for acidity and constructed a hermetically sealed thermometer. He is regarded as the originator of the 'experimental method'.

Bradman, Sir Donald (1908–). Australian cricketer. Principally a batsman, he played for New South Wales, South Australia, and Australia (1928–48), making 117 centuries in 338 first-class innings and achieving an overall average of 95.14 runs per innings (the world record). His record score of 452 not out in one innings remained unbroken for 29 years.

Brahe, Tycho (1546–1601). Danish astronomer. Brahe developed a passionate interest in astronomy after witnessing the total eclipse of the sun on 25 August 1560. His own observations revealed the inaccuracy of existing astronomical tables and the prevailing

Brahe's Nose

Having lost his nose in a duel while a student in Rostock, Brahe wore a large artificial one made of silver and gold. The astronomer liked people to feel it and his rivals suggested that he used it as an instrument in his observations. Amongst his other oddities, Brahe kept a hunchbacked fool named Jeppe, whom he is said to have rescued from being roasted alive by a band of mercenaries. According to some, he regarded the fool's half-witted utterances as a form of oracle.

Aristotelian conception of the heavens. In 1576 King Frederick II of Denmark granted Brahe an income and the use of an island near Copenhagen, where he built an observatory called Uranienborg. Here he made the most accurate observations possible without a telescope and calculated the length of the year to within one second. In 1597 he settled in Prague, where he met Johannes Kepler, who later used Brahe's observations as the basis for his laws of planetary motion.

Brahms, Johannes (1833–97). German composer. He came from a poor family and was working as a music teacher when he met the Hungarian violinist Eduard Reményi and toured with him (1853). During the concert tour he met Schumann and his wife Clara, who encouraged him to begin composing. Brahms fell in love with Clara, and after Schumann's death in 1856 they remained close friends. His works include the popular *Hungarian Dances* (1873), inspired by his association with Reményi, four symphonies (1876–85), and the choral work *A German Requiem* (1868).

Braille, Louis (1809–52). French teacher of the blind and inventor of the Braille alphabet. Braille blinded himself with a knife at the age of three while cutting a piece of leather. Despite his handicap he became a proficient musician and in 1819 went to Paris, where he attended the National Institute for Blind Youth. From 1828 he taught there and devised a method of representing letters by groups of dots embossed in cardboard, which could be read with the fingers. Braille's system has since been applied to non-Roman scripts and to music and mathematics.

Brancusi, Constantin

Brancusi, Constantin (1876–1957). Romanian abstract sculptor. Born into a peasant family, he learnt the craft of woodcarving before beginning formal studies in sculpture. From 1904 he lived in Paris. His work became increasingly abstract, and he simplified figures to basic egg shapes or cylinders, as in *The Kiss* (1910) and *Torso of a Young Man* (1917). In 1927 the US customs charged duty on his bronze *Bird in Space*, classing it as a piece of metal rather than as a work of art, but their decision was later overruled.

Brando, Marlon (1924–   ). US film actor. His career began in the theatre, where he was an outstanding success as the violent Stanley Kowalsky in Tennessee Williams's *A Streetcar Named Desire* (filmed in 1951). The leading practitioner of 'Method' acting, he has been most successful in portraying inarticulate but very masculine heroes. His best-known films include *On the Waterfront* and *The Wild One* (both 1954), and *The Godfather* and *Last Tango in Paris* (both 1972). Since the later 1970s Brando has appeared in few major roles; his more recent films include *A Dry White Season* (1989) and *Don Juan de Marco* (1995). At the same time his private life has been overshadowed by tragedy: in 1989

> ❝ As an actor, he is a genius, and even when he's dull, he's still much better than most actors at the top of their form. But he has preserved the mentality of an adolescent.
>
> Burt Reynolds on Marlon Brando ❞

Brando's son Christian was arrested for the murder of the boyfriend of his half-sister, who later committed suicide. He published his autobiography in 1994.

Brecht, Bertolt (1898–1956). German dramatist and poet. He served in the Medical Corps in World War I but later abandoned medicine for the theatre. The play *Drums in the Night* (1923) won immediate acclaim. From 1924 he lived in the left-wing intellectual circles of Berlin and in the late 1920s became a Marxist. With the composer Kurt Weill he wrote successful musical dramas, including *The Threepenny Opera* (1928). Brecht left Germany when the Nazis came to power and spent some time in Scandinavia and the US before returning to Germany in 1947. From 1949 he directed the Berliner Ensemble, the theatre company he had founded in East Berlin. His plays include *The Life of Galileo* (1943) and *The Caucasian Chalk Circle* (1949).

Brezhnev, Leonid Ilyich (1906–82). Soviet statesman. A qualified land surveyor and metallurgist, he served as a political officer in the Red Army during World War II. He succeeded Khrushchev as first secretary of the Communist party in 1964 and became president of the Soviet Union in 1977. His rule is now remembered as a period of stagnation and repression. The so-called 'Brezhnev Doctrine' authorized the Soviet Union to intervene in its satellite states to defend communism.

Britten, Benjamin (1913–76). British composer. He studied music under the composer Frank Bridge and later at the Royal College of Music, London. In the 1930s Britten wrote music for plays, films, and radio, and for the poems of W. H. Auden. He wrote the operetta *Paul Bunyan* (1941), with libretto by Auden, during his stay in the US (1939–42). His operas *Peter Grimes* (1945) and *The Rape of Lucretia* (1946) brought fame in Britain, as a result of which he helped to found the English Opera Group and the annual Aldeburgh Festival (1947). He also wrote songs for his companion Peter Pears, who performed in many of his operas. His other well-known compositions include *The Young Person's Guide to the Orchestra* (1945), the comic opera *Billy Budd* (1951), and the choral work *War Requiem* (1962). He was awarded a life peerage in 1976.

Brontë sisters. A family of British novelists, **Charlotte** (1816–55), **Emily Jane** (1818–48), and **Anne** (1820–49). The daughters of a clergyman, they had a lonely upbringing at Haworth on the Yorkshire moors, with their brother **Branwell** (1817–48). As children they wrote stories set in the the fantasy worlds of Angria and Gondal, which influenced their later work, notably that of Emily. Charlotte went to Brussels in 1842 to train as a teacher. In 1845 she discovered some poems secretly written by Emily and in 1846 the three sisters published a book of poetry under the pseudonyms of *Currer*, *Ellis*, and *Acton Bell*. Charlotte's masterpiece is the novel *Jane Eyre*, a powerful love story. In 1854 she married her father's curate but her tragic death the following year cut short their happy married life. Although Emily was one of the most original Romantic poets, she is best remembered for her novel *Wuthering Heights* (1847), dealing with the violent and unfulfilled love of the elemental Heathcliff for Catherine Earnshaw. Anne published two rather less dramatic novels, *Agnes Grey* (1845) and *The Tenant of Wildfell Hall* (1848). Branwell wasted his literary talents; he was dismissed from his railway clerkship for negligence and became an opium addict. Branwell, Emily, and Anne all died of consumption within two years of each other.

Brown, Sir Arthur Whitten (1886–1948). Scottish aviator. During World War I he served in the Royal Flying Corps. In June 1919 he and Captain John Alcock made the first ever crossing of the Atlantic Ocean by aeroplane. Flying from Newfoundland to County Galway in Ireland in a Vickers-Vimy biplane, they made the crossing in just over 16 hours. They received a £10,000 prize from the *Daily Mail* and were both knighted. Later that year Alcock was killed in a flying accident near Rouen.

Brown, Capability, nickname of *Lancelot Brown* (1715–83). British landscape gardener. He started work as a kitchen gardener but his extensive schemes for landscape improvement soon won him important patronage. Brown popularized the English style of garden, which uses the natural landscape, as opposed to the geometric French style. When viewing a garden to be improved, he would often say that the place had 'capabilities', hence his nickname. Kew Gardens and the grounds of Blenheim Palace are famous examples of his work.

Brown, Jim, full name *James Nathaniel Brown* (1936–   ). US Black American football player. At Syracuse University, Brown showed outstanding promise in boxing, basketball, and baseball as well as football. From 1957 to 1965 he played as a fullback for the Cleveland Browns; during his nine professional seasons he scored 126 touchdowns and set a series of records for running with the ball. After his retirement he appeared in a number of action movies and campaigned for the advancement of Black people in the business world.

Brown, John (1800–59). US anti-slavery militant. A White man, Brown settled in a Negro community with his family in 1849. He organized armed raids on supporters of slavery, believing that he had a divine mission to kill them. He was eventually hanged for murder, conspiracy, and treason after an attack on the government arsenal at Harper's Ferry, West Virginia (1859), in which 15 people were killed. After his death he was regarded as a martyr of the anti-slavery cause, being remembered in the song 'John Brown's Body'.

> ❝ John Brown has loosened the
> roots of the slave system; it
> only breathes — it does not live
> — hereafter.
> Wendell Phillips, speaking at
> the funeral of John Brown ❞

Browning, Elizabeth Barrett (1806–61). British poet. She was educated at home and began writing while still very young. An injury to her spine in a childhood riding accident made her a semi-invalid. In 1845 she met Robert Browning and became engaged to him. Her over-protective father disapproved of the marriage, so they married in secret and fled to Italy (1846), where they lived until her death. *Sonnets from the Portuguese* (1847) are love poems to Robert, who nicknamed her "my Portuguese". Her greatest work was the narrative poem *Aurora Leigh* (1856). Her husband **Robert Browning** (1812–89) was one of the leading poets of the Victorian age. In his poetry he made use of the dramatic monologue, in which a real or imaginary character serves as a mouthpiece for the poet's thoughts. His longest work, *The Ring and the Book* (1868–69), is the story of a Renaissance murder told from several different points of view. His other poems include *The Pied Piper of Hamelin* and 'Home Thoughts from Abroad'.

Bruce, Robert the (1274–1329). King of Scotland from 1306, who led the Scots against the English and won Scottish independence. His grandfather had unsuccessfully claimed the throne of Scotland in 1290. In 1306, after the execution of the Scottish leader Sir William Wallace, Robert the Bruce was crowned King Robert I. Edward I at first defeated Robert's followers, but his successor, Edward II, was decisively defeated by Robert at the Battle of Bannockburn in 1314. A truce followed. In 1327 Edward III tried to defeat the Scots, but instead was forced to agree to the Treaty of Northampton (1328). This recognized the independence of Scotland and Robert's title as king.

Bruegel, Pieter (c. 1525–69). Flemish painter. He is particularly well known for his lively and detailed paintings of peasant life, peopled with tiny active figures, such as *Months* (1565). A vein of satirical humour is present in many of his works. His two sons, Pieter the Younger and Jan, were also painters.

Brummell, Beau, nickname of *George Brummell* (1778–1840). British gentleman of fashion. He became a friend of the Prince of Wales (later George IV) at Eton, and after a year at Oxford he was the acknowledged leader of the fashionable world. He finally quarrelled with the prince and his enormous gambling debts forced him to retreat to France, where he died in a lunatic asylum.

Brummel and the Prince

Beau Brummell was noted for his impudent wit. On one occasion he was walking with a friend in one of the London parks when the Prince of Wales rode past. The prince, who had recently quarrelled with Brummell, greeted the other man but cut Brummell dead. With the prince still in earshot, Brummell turned to his companion and said in a loud but nonchalant voice "Who's your fat friend?" The resulting feud split London's fashionable society and proved the beginning of Brummell's downfall.

Brunel, Isambard Kingdom (1806–59). British engineer. Brunel worked with his father, also an engineer, on a number of early experimental projects. His first important achievement was the design for the Clifton suspension bridge (1829) and in 1833 he became chief engineer to the Great Western Railway. He built over 1600 km of track and many notable railway bridges. Also active as a ship designer, Brunel built the *Great Western* (1837), which provided the first regular transatlantic service, the *Great Britain* (1843), the first ship to have an iron hull and a screw propeller, and the *Great Eastern* (1858), which laid the first transatlantic cable.

Brunelleschi, Filippo (1377–1446). Italian architect and sculptor of the early Renaissance. He trained as a goldsmith and sculptor and later became interested in mathematical perspective. He invented machines to enable the construction of the dome of Florence Cathedral (1420–36), one of his best-known works.

Brutus, Marcus Junius (c. 85–42 BC). Roman politician. Although he had constantly opposed Julius Caesar's policies and fought for the republicans in 49 BC, Caesar pardoned and promoted him. However, he remained loyal to the republican cause and eventually joined in the plot to kill Caesar. Caesar's murder did not result in the immediate restoration of the republic, however, and Brutus raised an army to fight Caesar's lieutenant Mark Antony. Following his defeat at Philippi in 42 BC Brutus committed suicide, which he considered to be the only honourable course of action.

Buddha, title of *Siddhartha Gautama* (c. 563–483 BC). The founder of Buddhism, whose title means 'enlightened one'. He was the son of a king of the warrior caste and grew up in his father's palace in southern Nepal. He married and spent his youthful days in luxury, protected from the harsh realities of life. At 29 he first became aware of pain and death and left his family and home in order to find a solution to these evils. While sitting under a tree (thereafter known as the Bodhi Tree), he attained enlightenment. He then travelled around northern India, teaching what he had learnt, and founded an order of monks. The doctrine of Buddhism teaches that man can overcome suffering by leading a virtuous life and thereby getting rid of the desires that cause suffering.

> ❲ Ye must leave righteous ways behind, not to speak of unrighteous ways.
> *Some Sayings of the Buddha* ❳

Buñuel, Luis (1900–83). Spanish film director. He worked in France in the 1920s and there collaborated with the surrealist painter Salvador Dali on *Un Chien andalou* (1928). Surrealism, anticlericalism, and an irreverent attitude towards conventional morality characterize his films, which include *Viridiana* (1961), *Belle de jour* (1966), *The Discreet Charm of the Bourgeosie* (1972), and *That Obscure Object of Desire* (1977).

Bunyan, John (1628–88). English religious writer. The son of a Bedfordshire tinker, he joined the Baptist Church in 1653 and later became a preacher. Puritan preaching was banned at the Restoration, and Bunyan was imprisoned for several years. The religious allegory *Pilgrim's Progress* (1678), his best-known work, was written during his imprisonment. After his release he continued preaching in Bedfordshire, often in disguise, and was sometimes forced into hiding.

Burgess, Guy Francis (1911–63). British spy. *See* Kim Philby.

Burghley, William Cecil, Lord (1520–98). English statesman. On Elizabeth I's accession to the throne (1558) he was made her sole secretary and in 1572 became Lord High Treasurer, a post he held until his death. As the queen's adviser he had considerable influence on Elizabethan policy. A firm believer in England's role as a leader of European Protestantism, Burghley was responsible for the execution of Mary, Queen of Scots, thus ensuring a Protestant succession.

Burke, Edmund (1729–97). British Whig statesman. He entered Parliament in 1765, where he soon became a powerful and eloquent speaker. He advocated reconciliation with the American colonies and, as an opponent of democracy, he was hostile to the French Revolution. He instigated the impeachment of Warren Hastings, the leading British administrator in India, a procedure that took eight years and ended in Hastings's acquittal. The death of Burke's only son shortly after his retirement in 1794 shattered the remaining years of his life.

Burns, Robert (1759–96). Scottish poet. He started work as a farmer but was not very successful. *Poems Chiefly in the Scottish Dialect* (1786) was intended to pay for his emigration to Jamaica but was so successful that he gave up the plan. Instead, he travelled around Scotland, collecting and improving traditional ballads. Weakened by overwork and heavy drinking, he died aged only 37 and is regarded as Scotland's national poet. Spontaneity, wit, and simplicity are features of his poetry; his best-known poems include 'Auld Lang Syne' and 'To a Mouse'.

> ❛ If you can imagine a Scotch commercial traveller in a Scotch commercial hotel leaning on the bar and calling the barmaid 'Dearie' then you will know the keynote of Burns's verse.
> A. E. Housman, unpublished essay ❜

Burroughs, William S(eward) (1914–   ). US novelist. After studying at Harvard, Burroughs lived a bohemian life in New York, where he made friends with Jack Kerouac, Allen Ginsberg, and other writers of the Beat Generation. By the mid 1940s he was a heroin addict. In 1951 he killed his wife in a bizarre shooting incident in Mexico. Burroughs's first novel, *Junkie* (1953), was followed by such experimental works as *The Naked Lunch* (1959) and *The Soft Machine* (1961). His later novels, which continue to explore themes of drug addiction, homosexual fantasy, and political paranoia include *The Place of Dead Roads* (1984) and *The Western Lands* (1988).

Burton, Richard (1925–84). Welsh actor. After some years with the Old Vic company, during which he played several Shakespearean leads, he went to Hollywood in 1952. Helped by his good looks and fine voice, he gradually won popularity as a film actor. In 1964 he married the actress Elizabeth Taylor after a highly publicized affair; the couple were later divorced, remarried, and divorced again. His films include *Look Back in Anger* (1959), *Cleopatra* (1962), *Anne of the Thousand Days* (1970), and a film version of Dylan Thomas's *Under Milk Wood* (1971).

Bush, George (1924–   ). US statesman; 41st president of the US (1989–93). The son of a wealthy Republican family, Bush worked in the oil industry before entering politics in the 1960s. He was director of the CIA (1976–77) and vice-president to Ronald Reagan (1981–89). As president, he was chiefly interested in foreign affairs. He negotiated major arms reductions with the Soviet Union and in 1990–91 responded to Iraq's invasion of Kuwait by assembling a US-led multinational force to fight the second Gulf War. Despite these successes, he failed to deal with the US's mounting economic problems, a factor that contributed to his defeat by Bill Clinton in the 1992 presidential elections.

Butler, Samuel (1835–1902). British novelist. He shocked his family by refusing to follow his father into the Church and in 1860 emigrated to New Zealand. Money earned from sheep-farming enabled him to return to Britain in 1864, and he achieved some success as a painter before turning to literature with the satire *Erewhon* (1872). His autobiographical novel *The*

Way of All Flesh (1903), which condemned his claustrophobic Victorian upbringing, was published after his death.

Byrd, William (1543–1623). English composer. An organist at Lincoln Cathedral (1563–72), he then became joint organist with his teacher, Thomas Tallis, at the Chapel Royal, London. Together they wrote *Piae Cantiones* (1575) for Elizabeth I. Although Byrd was a Roman Catholic he managed to retain the regard and patronage of the Queen. Known as the father of keyboard music, he wrote over 120 pieces for the virginals, as well as Catholic masses and motets, and Anglican services and verse anthems. He also composed three collections of songs.

Byron, Lord (1788–1824). British poet, born *George Gordon Noel*. He inherited his title in 1798 when the expected heir died. After travelling in Spain, Greece, and Albania, he achieved fame and popularity with the im-

❝ I am so changeable…such a strange *mélange* of good and evil, that it would be difficult to describe me. There are two sentiments to which I am constant – a strong love of liberty, and a detestation of cant, and neither is calculated to gain me friends.
Lord Byron in Lady Blessington, *Conversations with Lord Byron* (1832) ❞

mensely successful *Childe Harold's Pilgrimage* (1812). In 1816, having separated from his wife amidst much scandal, he left England for Europe and befriended Shelley in Geneva. During his stormy and restless life he had many love affairs, including one with Lady Caroline Lamb. His later works include the satirical *Don Juan* (1818–24). In 1823 he set off to fight for Greek independence from Turkey but, weakened by the long journey under bad conditions, he died of a fever soon after arriving.

C

Cabot, John (c. 1450–99). Italian explorer and navigator. A Venetian citizen, he went to England in 1484 to raise support for a voyage to Asia, and was finally sponsored by Henry VII in 1496. The following year Cabot sailed from Bristol and reached the Labrador coast of Newfoundland. A second expedition in 1498 unsuccessfully attempted to discover a westward route to Japan. His son **Sebastian Cabot** (1476–1557), also a navigator, became cartographer to Henry VIII. In 1525 he sailed to South America, hoping to find treasure. As governor of the English Merchant Adventurers he organized expeditions to search for the north-east passage to Asia and succeeded in establishing trade with Russia.

Cadbury, George (1839–1922). British Quaker businessman and philanthropist. George and his brother Richard (1835–99) rescued their father's cocoa and chocolate firm from economic collapse in 1861, and developed a number of schemes to improve the lives of their workpeople. After Richard's death George built Bourneville, a special village with parks and sports facilities for the community. His workers were the first to have holidays, pensions, and medical services. His work influenced town planning and social welfare both in Britain and abroad.

Caesar, (Gaius) Julius (100–44 BC). Roman general and statesman. Born into a patrician family, Caesar secured his alliance with the popular party by marrying Cornelia in 84. After Cornelia died in 68, Caesar married Pompeia, a relative to Pompey. He divorced Pompeia in 62 and three years later took his third wife, Calpurnia. Initially his career was mainly political; in 60 he formed a ruling triumvirate with Pompey and Crassus. Elected consul in 59, he made his military reputation with his campaigns in Gaul (58–50). He also invaded Britain twice, in 55 and 54, and became a popular hero. However in 50, following the death of Crassus, the triumvirate came to an end. Pompey became opposed to Caesar's ambitions and persuaded the Senate to ask Caesar to disband his armies. Caesar refused and invaded Italy in 49, crossing over the River Rubicon that separated his province from Italy. This was the start of the civil wars (49–45). Caesar defeated Pompey at Pharsalus (48), then spent some time in Alexandria with Cleopatra, who bore him a son. After his defeat of Pharnaces at Zela (47), where he uttered the famous words "Veni, vidi, vici" ("I came, I saw, I conquered"), he defeated the remnants of Pompey's forces and returned to Rome as dictator. During his dictatorship Caesar introduced a number of reforms, notably the Julian calendar, which forms the basis of our present calendar. Further reforms were prevented by his assassination in 44, on the Ides of March (15 March), by a group of republicans led by Brutus and Cassius. Caesar was also a distinguished orator and writer; his works include *Commentaries* on the Gallic and civil wars.

Caligula's Horse

The behaviour of the emperor Caligula was sometimes so bizarre as to raise doubts about his sanity. According to the Roman historian Suetonius, he was so fond of his horse Incitatus that he dressed him in rich clothes with a collar of precious stones and kept him in a house full of costly furniture. At the time of Caligula's death, he apparently intended to make the horse a consul.

Caligula, Gaius Caesar Augustus (12–41 AD). Roman emperor. The son of Germanicus Caesar and Agrippina the Elder, he succeeded the emperor Tiberius in 37. Although initially popular, he soon became hated for his extravagant, capricious, and tyrannical behaviour. He had many of his relatives executed or murdered, and is alleged to have expressed the wish that the Roman people had a single neck, so that he could sever it at a blow. He was assassinated.

Callaghan, James, Baron (1912–   ). British politician. Before World War II he was a tax officer in the Civil Service; he first entered politics as Labour MP for South Cardiff in 1945. Having served as chancellor of the exchequer (1964–67), home secretary (1967–70), and foreign secretary (1974–76), he became prime minister on Harold Wilson's resignation in 1976. His period in office was marked by strikes and economic difficulties. Following Labour's defeat in the general election of 1979, he resigned as party leader in 1980.

Callas, Maria (1923–77). US opera singer of Greek descent, born *Maria Kalogeropoulos* in New York. A coloratura soprano, she studied singing at the Athens Conservatoire and first appeared at the Opera in Athens in 1945; she later became one of the leading singers at La Scala, Milan, and gained world-wide fame for her passionate style.

Calvin, John (1509–64). French Protestant theologian and religious reformer. Having broken with the Catholic Church, he travelled to Basel in Switzerland. There in 1536 he completed his major work, *The Institutes of Christian Religion*, in which he argued for reforms based on the practice and teaching of the early Church. His theological ideas, known as Calvinism, were widely influential; his theory of Church government is the basis of Presbyterianism. His name is especially associated with Geneva, where, in 1541, he established a church state that was one of the most important citadels of the Reformation.

Campbell, Donald (1921–67). British world speed record breaker. Having broken the world land and water speed records in a car and a boat that were both called Bluebird, he was killed in an attempt to raise his water speed record of 442.08 km per hour (276.3 mph) on Coniston Water. His father, **Sir Malcolm Campbell** (1885–1949), was also a speed enthusiast. He broke the world land speed record nine times (which was itself a record) between 1924 and 1935 and the world water speed record in 1939.

Camus, Albert (1913–60). French novelist, dramatist, and essayist, a leader of existentialist thought. In the 1930s he studied philosophy in Algiers and became involved with the Algerian Workers' Theatre. During World War II he was an active member of the Resistance, editing the movement's daily paper *Combat*. His works include *The Outsider* (1942), *The Plague* (1947), a vivid account of the effects of the plague in a North African town, and the play *Caligula* (1944). He was awarded the Nobel Prize in 1957 and died in a car crash three years later.

> ❛ An intellectual is a man whose mind watches itself.
> Albert Camus *Notebooks*
> (1935–42)

> What is a rebel? A man who says no.
> Albert Camus, *The Rebel*
> (1953) ❜

Canaletto, real name *Giovanni Antonio Canal* (1697–1768). Italian painter. His precise and highly detailed cityscapes, such as *The Basin of San Marco* (c. 1730), were inspired by the architecture of Venice. The British consul, Joseph Smith, sent many of his works to Britain and as a result Canaletto was commissioned to paint English country houses and views of London. These included *Warwick Castle* (c. 1748) and *London: Whitehall and the Privy Garden* (c. 1751).

> ### Canute on the Seashore
> According to legend, Canute once exposed the flattery of his courtiers, who were continually harping on his greatness and power, by setting his throne at the edge of the sea and commanding the incoming tide not to wet his feet. Having demonstrated so clearly the limits of human power, he allegedly never wore his crown again. The story first appeared in a 12th-century chronicle.

Canute (c. 995–1035). King of England, Denmark, and Norway. With his father, Sweyn I, king of Denmark, he invaded England in 1013; the next year he succeeded his father as king of Anglo-Saxon Mercia and Northumbria. He soon extended his rule to the rest of England and in 1018 succeeded his brother as king of Denmark as well. He won the crown of Norway in 1030. He was a devout Christian and a popular ruler, but the union of the three countries did not continue after his death.

Capone, Al(phonso) (1899–1947). US gangster, the son of an Italian barber. Employed at 20 to work as a strong-arm man for a Chicago gangster, he subsequently went into the illegal drink business, making a profit of two million dollars a year. Despite his life of crime, no evidence could be found to convict him until 1931, when he was sentenced to ten years' imprisonment for evading income tax, a charge often used by the US police to convict known gangsters. Many of his enemies swore to kill him but none were successful and he died of apoplexy on his Palm Island Estate.

Caravaggio, nickname of *Michelangelo Merisi* (1573–1610). Italian painter, one of the most influential artists of the Baroque period. He spent most of his career in Rome, where he painted numerous altarpieces and other sacred works. His work is noted for its realistic depiction of the human face and its strong contrasts of light and dark, as in his *Supper at Emmaus*. Caravaggio was notorious for his wild temper and style of life. After killing a man during an argument over a tennis match, he spent the last four years of his life in exile in Naples, Malta, and Sicily.

Carlyle, Thomas (1795–1881). Scottish historian and essayist, the son of a stonemason. He abandoned his plans to become a Calvinist minister in favour of an intellectual life of writing and translating. His major work *The French Revolution* (1837) had to be rewritten after the manuscript was accidentally burned. Carlyle's other works include *Sartor Resartus* (1833) and a six-volume history of Frederick the Great.

Carnegie, Andrew (1835–1919). US industrialist and philanthropist, born in Scotland. As a young immigrant in the US, he started at the bottom in a railway company but rose rapidly and made shrewd investments. During the American Civil War he founded iron and steel firms and established trusts to use his money for the good of the community. He endowed over 1,000 libraries and founded universities and colleges, giving away 300 million dollars in his lifetime.

Carnot, Lazare Nicolas Marguerite (1753–1823). French revolutionary soldier. He reorganized the revolutionary armies and became known as the 'Organizer of Victory' for the numerous military reforms he achieved in the early 1790s. In 1814 he emerged from retirement to aid Napoleon and successfully defended Antwerp. His son **Nicolas Léonard Sadi** (1796–1832), an army engineer and physicist, did research into heat. His 'Carnot principle' of heat engines was eventually incorporated into the theory of thermodynamics.

Carroll, Lewis, pen-name of *the Reverend Charles Lutwidge Dodgson* (1832–98). British writer for children. He became a lecturer in mathematics at Christ Church College, Oxford, in 1854. He was very fond of children, having none of his own, and wrote *Alice's Adventures in Wonderland* (1865) for Alice Liddell, the daughter of a friend. It was followed by *Through the Looking Glass* (1871) and the nonsense poem *The Hunting of the Snark* (1876). He also published a number of mathematical works under his own name.

Carter, Jimmy, full name *James Earl Carter* (1924–   ). US statesman, 39th president of the US (1977–81). The son of a peanut farmer, he resigned as a navy physicist to take over the family business on his father's death in 1953. He entered politics in 1960 and from 1970 to 1974 was governor of Georgia. In 1976 he defeated Gerald Ford in the presidential election and became the first Southern president since the American Civil War. His main achievement in office was a peace treaty between Egypt and Israel (1979). Since his defeat by

Ronald Reagan in the 1980 presidential elections he has re-emerged as a respected international negotiator.

Cartier-Bresson, Henri (1908–). French photographer. Born near Paris, Cartier-Bresson studied painting before turning to photography in 1931. He soon developed his famous technique of taking spontaneous photographs of everyday scenes using a small handheld camera. After the war, during which he worked with the Resistance, he helped to found the Magnum Photos agency in 1947. His photojournalism has appeared in magazines all over the world, while his portraits and travel photography have been published in a series of books. More recently he has returned to painting.

Caruso, Enrico (1873–1921). Italian operatic tenor, one of the earliest recording artists. After successes in Italy and Russia he made his London debut in 1902 at Covent Garden in *Rigoletto*. In 1903 he became leading artist at the Metropolitan Opera House, New York. A small chubby man with a flashing smile, he was known as the 'Man with the Orchid-lined Voice'.

> ❝ The beaming smile, lit by flashing white teeth, radiated an urchin exuberance and *joie de vivre*. Only Caruso would dare to go before the Metropolitan curtain, pat his stomach and implore the audience to go home "because I'm so hungry and want my supper".
> Stanley Johnson, *Caruso* ❞

Casals, Pablo (1876–1973). Spanish cellist, conductor, and composer. In 1895 he became leading cellist at the Paris Opera. He played in a classical trio and as a soloist before founding and conducting the Barcelona Orchestra (1919–20). After the Spanish Civil War he settled in Prades, France, where he founded a festival of classical chamber music. He is widely regarded as the finest cellist of all time.

Casanova, Giovanni Giacomo (1725–98). Italian adventurer and libertine. Having been expelled from a Venetian seminary, he became a violinist, a soldier, and a preacher. On returning to Venice in 1755 he was imprisoned for sorcery but made a daring escape. He subsequently travelled all over Europe, meeting such famous people as Voltaire and Frederick the Great. He served as a Venetian spy for a short time and spent his final years in Bohemia. His vivid and racy *Memoirs*, detailing his amorous exploits, were not published in an unexpurgated form until 1960.

Castro, Fidel (1926–   ). Cuban statesman and socialist revolutionary. As a boy Castro threatened to burn down the family home unless his parents sent him to school. As a result he graduated in law in 1950. He subsequently organized a campaign against the Batista dictatorship, the 26th of July Movement, and following an unsuccessful revolt (1956) escaped to the mountains with his 11 surviving supporters, including Che Guevara. The movement gradually regained strength until in 1959, with an army of 5,000, he was able to overthrow Batista. Castro then became premier and adopted a radical socialist policy. Despite fierce antagonism from the US in the 1960s and afterwards he remained in power. However, the collapse of communism in the late 1980s has left his regime increasingly isolated.

Catherine II, known as *Catherine the Great* (1729–96). Empress of Russia. The daughter of a German prince, she married the Russian Grand Duke Peter, later Tsar Peter III, in 1762. Because of physical weakness and signs of madness, the tsar was deposed after six months and Catherine ruled alone as empress. Although her love affairs were the subject of gossip throughout Europe, she was an able and enlightened despot, who successfully extended Russian territory and raised national prestige. She was also a generous patron of science and literature, which flourished during her reign.

> ❛ Standing, as I do, in view of
> God and eternity, I realize that
> patriotism is not enough. I
> must have no hatred or
> bitterness towards anyone.
>   Edith Cavell, on the eve of
>   her execution ❜

Cavell, Edith (1865–1915). British nurse and wartime heroine. During World War I she ran a nursing institute in Brussels that served as a refuge for over 200 Allied soldiers escaping to the neutral Netherlands. She was arrested, tried, and sentenced to death by the Germans and shot three days later.

Cavour, Count Camillo Benso di (1810–61). Italian statesman, born into an old aristocratic family of Piedmont. As a young man he travelled widely in Europe and developed strong liberal views. He was prime minister of Piedmont (1852–59; 1860–61) and campaigned for Italian unity, seeking French and British sympathy for his cause by sending troops to fight in the Crimean War. With French support he liberated Italy from Austrian domination (1859); a year later, following Garibaldi's successful campaign against the Neapolitan monarchy, he succeeded in unifying Italy under Victor Emmanuel II and the House of Savoy.

Caxton, William (c. 1422–91). The first English printer. Originally a merchant, Caxton learned the art of printing in Cologne in 1470–72. He set up his first printing press in Bruges and in 1476 returned to London, where he began printing in Westminster. The first book printed in English was *Sayings of the Philosophers* (1477). Caxton went on to print Chaucer's *The Canterbury Tales*, Malory's *Morte d'Arthur* and many other books, some of which were illustrated with woodcuts. He also translated and revised texts for printing.

Ceauçescu, Nicolae (1918–89). Romanian dictator. The son of a peasant, he worked in factories from the age of 11 and joined an illegal communist movement. He was twice imprisoned for his political activities (1936–38; 1940–44). After the communists took power in 1945 he rose steadily through the party ranks to become effective ruler of the country in 1965. He took the title president of Romania in 1974. His rule was marked by disastrous economic policies and the repression of all dissent; in foreign affairs he maintained Romania's independence of the Soviet Union. He was finally deposed in a violent revolution in December 1989; he and his wife Elena were executed by firing squad on Christmas Day.

Cellini, Benvenuto (1500–71). Florentine goldsmith, engraver, and sculptor. His *Autobiography* (1558–62) describes his tumultuous career. He was expelled from Florence in 1523 for brawling, and later from Rome for embezzling jewels from the papal mint. He lived at the French court from 1540 to 1545, where he made the famous gold salt cellar and the sculpture *Nymph of Fontainebleau* for Francis I. On his return to Florence he worked for Cosimo de' Medici. His sculptures include

Cellini's Saltcellar

The saltcellar created by Benvenuto Cellini for Francis I of France is one of the most famous artefacts of the Renaissance. One may imagine the surprise of guests at the king's table when confronted by this tiny but intricate masterpiece. The saltcellar, worked in gold and enamel, depicts the "marriage of the earth and the sea", a marriage that by implication resulted in the salt it contained. According to Cellini's *Autobiography* the king declared it to be "a hundred times more divine a thing than I have ever dreamed of". The saltcellar is now kept in Vienna.

the bronze *Perseus* (1545–54) and the marble statue *Apollo and Hyacinth.*

Cervantes, Miguel de (1547–1616). Spanish novelist, poet, and dramatist, creator of Don Quixote. He served as a soldier in Italy and lost the use of his left hand at the battle of Lepanto (1571). He was held prisoner in Algiers for five years, where he worked as slave until he was ransomed by his family in 1580. He began writing in 1585, enjoying his first major success with *Don Quixote* (1605), the tale of an impoverished gentleman who imagines he is a knight and rides about the country on chivalrous exploits. Cervantes wrote a second part in 1615 and also wrote plays and short stories.

Cézanne, Paul (1839–1906). French postimpressionist painter. He was to have followed his father's profession of banking but became interested in painting and went to Paris in 1861. There he met his old schoolfriend Emile Zola, and was introduced to the painter Camille Pissarro. At first he was influenced by the impressionists but later broke away from them. He was interested in structure and form and used planes of strong colour to create an illusion of depth. His works include landscapes, such as *Mountains in Provence* (1878–80), still-lifes, such as *Still-life with a Teapot* (1899), and portraits.

Chain, Sir Ernst Boris (1906–79). British biochemist, born in Germany. Educated in Berlin, Chain left Germany in 1933 owing to the rise of Hitler and came to work in England. At Oxford he came across Sir Alexander Fleming's work on penicillin. He drew it to the attention of Sir Howard Florey and together they isolated penicillin, which was used extensively in treating casualties of World War II. Chain, Florey, and Fleming were awarded the Nobel Prize in 1945.

Chaliapin, Fyodor Ivanovich (1873–1938). Russian operatic bass. Born into a peasant family, he joined a church choir and studied singing. He later became a member of a Moscow opera company and appeared in Milan, New York, and London, leaving Russia after the Revolution. He was most famous for his interpretations of roles in Mussorgsky's *Boris Godunov*, Mozart's *Don Giovanni*, and Rossini's *Barber of Seville*.

> Well, he seemed such a nice old gentleman; I thought I would give him my autograph.
> Attributed to Adolf Hitler, on Neville Chamberlain's visit to Germany in September 1938

> Chamberlain saw foreign policy through the wrong end of a municipal drainpipe.
> Attributed to both Winston Churchill and David Lloyd George

Chamberlain, Joseph (1836–1914). British statesman. Having made his fortune from his Birmingham screwmaking business, he was able to retire at 38 and devote himself to politics. As mayor of Birmingham, his radical reforms brought him to national prominence and he became known as the "gas-and-water socialist". He entered Parliament in 1876 as a Liberal but resigned over the issue of Home Rule for Ireland and subsequently led the Liberal Unionists. His monocle and orchid made him a popular subject for cartoonists. He was forced to retire from public life following a stroke in 1906. His son **Neville Chamberlain** (1869–1940) was also a politician, who first entered the House of Commons as a Conservative MP in 1918. He became prime minister in 1937 and is remembered for his attempts to placate Hitler immediately before World War II. On his return from his third visit to Germany in September 1938 he brandished a signed undertaking from Hitler and was welcomed as a hero for having avoid war and announced that he had brought back "peace with honour". However, Germany's invasion of Poland forced him to declare war on 3 September 1939. He resigned as prime minister in 1940, and died six months later.

Chanel, Coco, nickname of *Gabrielle Bonheur Chanel* (1883–1971). French dress designer. In the 1920s she made her name by glamorizing workers' clothes and school uniforms and introducing the 'little black dress'. She also ran perfume laboratories, producing the highly successful Chanel No. 5. She had an eventful social life, mixing with the rich and famous, and is the subject of the musical *Coco* (1969).

Chaplin, Charlie, full name *Sir Charles Spencer Chaplin* (1889–1977). British film comedian, director, and producer. Chaplin appeared as a child actor in music halls and in several stage plays before going to the US in

1910. The hard times he experienced as a child are reflected in the poignant humour of some of his films. He made his first films in 1913 for the Keystone Company and established the image of the little tramp – moustache, bowler hat, baggy trousers, walking stick, and flat-footed walk – that soon became famous throughout the world. Chaplin made numerous silent films and from 1920 began producing his own feature-length films, including *The Gold Rush* (1924), *Modern Times* (1936), *The Great Dictator* (1940), and *Limelight* (1952). He was knighted in 1975.

Charlemagne (c. 742–814). King of the Franks and Roman emperor. In the 770s he came to the aid of the pope and defeated the Lombards in Italy. He also conquered the pagan Saxons in Germany, who then accepted Christianity. His expedition against the Moors in Spain is recounted in a famous 12th-century French poem, the *Chanson de Roland*, which concerns the heroic death of one of his nobles. During the Christmas mass in Rome in 800, Pope Leo III crowned him emperor (without his advance knowledge), inaugurating the Holy Roman Empire. As emperor Charlemagne reformed the law, the economy, and church organization; he also greatly encouraged learning, religion, and culture. For this reason the latter part of his reign is known as the Carolingian Renaissance.

Charles, Prince (1948–   ). Prince of Wales, heir apparent to the throne of the United Kingdom. The eldest son of Elizabeth II, he was educated at Gordonstoun school and Cambridge University. He was invested as Prince of Wales in 1969 and spent five years in the Royal Navy (1971–76) before taking up full-time royal duties. In 1981 he married Lady Diana Spencer (1961–), daughter of the eighth Earl Spencer. As Princess of Wales, Diana became a hugely popular figure and one of the most photographed women of all time. They have two children, Prince William (1982–) and Prince Henry (1984–). The couple separated in 1992, amidst rumours and accusations that did much to harm the image of the monarchy. Prince Charles is known for his controversial views on modern architecture and his concern for environmental issues.

Charles I (1600–49). King of Britain and Ireland from 1625, son of James I. His firm belief that as king he ruled by divine right led to a breakdown in his relations with Parliament and eventually to civil war. He dissolved Parliament and attempted to rule without it. In 1640 he was forced to convene Parliament, which took the opportunity to assert its exclusive right to raise taxes. Charles declared war on Parliament in 1642 but suffered decisive defeats at Marston Moor (1644) and Naseby (1645). In 1649 he was tried and condemned for treason and was beheaded outside the Banqueting Hall in Whitehall. Despite his failure as a king, Charles's blatantly unjust trial led him to be hailed as a martyr after his execution.

Charles II (1630–85). King of Britain and Ireland from 1660, son of Charles I. After Oliver Cromwell's death, Parliament invited Charles to return from exile in France and he was crowned in 1661. His reign is known as the Restoration. Like his father he had financial difficulties, but he retained a working relationship with

---

Charles II Answers a Critic

Because of his rather lazy and pleasure-loving character, Charles II was frequently satirized by the poets of the day, notably the Earl of Rochester. On one occasion Rochester wrote the following verse on the door of the king's bedroom:

Here lies our sovereign lord the king
Whose promise none relies on;
He never said a foolish thing
Nor ever did a wise one.

Charles replied with the witty observation: "This is very true, for my words are my own, and my actions are those of my ministers".

Parliament during most of his reign and managed to arrange financial subsidies from Louis XIV. He was interested in science and was patron of the Royal Society, chartered in 1663. His personal charm helped him to remain a popular figure. He had a number of mistresses, the most famous of whom was the actress Nell Gwyn.

Charles V (1500–58). Holy Roman Emperor (1519–56). His vast empire included Spain and all its possessions, the Netherlands, Burgundy, Milan, Naples, Sicily, Sardinia, and Austria. His reign was constantly troubled by wars with other European rulers, by the religious conflicts of the Reformation, and by the threat of invasion by Ottoman Turks. He fought a series of wars against Francis I of France, who finally took Burgundy.

The Turks twice besieged Vienna but Charles was unable to defeat them decisively because of other pressures. He also failed to reconcile or defeat the German Protestant princes and was eventually forced to accept their demands. Exhausted by these problems, he abdicated and spent the two final years of his life in a Spanish monastery. He was succeeded by his son Philip as king of Spain and by his brother Ferdinand as Holy Roman Emperor.

Charles Edward Stuart, known as *Bonnie Prince Charlie* (1720–88). The 'Young Pretender' to the throne of England and Scotland, grandson of James II of England. In 1745 he landed in the Hebrides and headed a Jacobite rebellion. With an army of 2000 Highlanders he entered Edinburgh and went on to invade England, reaching as far south as Derby. However, he was forced to retreat to Scotland, where he was defeated at Culloden Moor (1746). He then hid in the Scottish Highlands, with a reward of £30,000 for his capture, before escaping to France. He was aided in his escape by Flora Macdonald, who disguised him as her Irish maidservant.

Chaucer, Geoffrey (c. 1340–1400). English poet. He came from a fairly prosperous family and held various government offices, including a post in the customs office. He is best known for *The Canterbury Tales*, a richly varied series of stories told by pilgrims on their way to Canterbury, and the narrative poem *Troilus and Criseyde*. These two masterpieces were the first major works of English poetry. As no books were printed in

England before 1476, none of Chaucer's works was published in his lifetime.

> ❝ As he is the father of English poetry, so I hold him in the same degree of veneration as the Grecians held Homer, or the Romans Virgil. He is a perpetual fountain of good sense, learned in all sciences, and therefore speaks properly on all subjects. As he knew what to say, so he knows also when to leave off...
>
> John Dryden on Geoffrey Chaucer, *Preface to the Fables* (1700) ❞

Chekhov, Anton (1860–1904). Russian dramatist and short-story writer. The son of a grocer, Chekhov helped to support his family by publishing humorous articles while studying medicine in Moscow. His writing later became more serious and he began to write short stories for literary journals. He practised medicine until 1898, when he moved to Yalta, hoping the climate would relieve his tuberculosis. There he wrote his great plays, including *The Seagull* (1896; revised 1904), *Three Sisters* (1901), and *The Cherry Orchard* (1904).

Chesterton, G(ilbert) K(eith) (1874–1936). British novelist and essayist, who became a Roman Catholic in 1922. His best-known works include the anti-imperialist novel *The Napoleon of Notting Hill* (1904), *The Man Who was Thursday* (1908), and a popular series of detective stories featuring the priest Father Brown. His enormous girth, piping voice, and absentminded manner were often lampooned.

Chiang Kai-Shek (1887–1975). Chinese soldier and statesman. He became active in the revolutions of 1911 that established the Chinese republic. As military leader of the republic he attacked the northern warlords, whom he defeated in 1928, and strove for the unification of China. His less successful campaigns against the communists, temporarily halted by the Japanese occupation (1937–45), ended in Chiang's defeat and withdrawal to Taiwan, where he retained the office of president until his death.

Chirac, Jacques René (1932–). French politician; president (1995–). Chirac was born in Paris and educated at the Ecole Nationale d'Administration. A Gaullist, he was first elected to the National Assembly in 1967. He was appointed prime minister in 1974 but resigned two years later owing to differences with President Giscard d'Estaing. He was again prime minister under President Mitterand (1986–88) and a long-serving mayor of Paris (1977–95). As president he aroused widespread anger with his decision to resume French nuclear testing in the Pacific. In late 1995 proposed cuts in welfare spending led to the worst public unrest since 1968.

Chomsky, Noam (1928–). US linguist and political writer. He became professor of modern languages and linguistics at the Massachusetts Institute of Technology (1961) and visited Britain to lecture at Oxford in 1969. His linguistic theories are set out in such works as *Syntactic Structures* (1957). Chomsky's ideas on grammar have had a most important influence on the study of language. A leading opponent of US involvement in the Vietnam War, he has continued his critique of US foreign policy in such books as *Chronicles of Dissent* (1992).

Chopin, Frédéric (1810–49). Polish composer and pianist. A child prodigy, he studied the piano and composition at the Warsaw Conservatory. In 1831 he settled in France, where he met the composers Berlioz and Liszt, leaders of the Romantic school. He befriended the novelist George Sand and lived with her in Majorca (1838–39) and later in France. After the 1848 revolution he visited Britain and played before Queen Victoria, despite suffering from tuberculosis. His health worsened and he died the following year. Chopin was influenced by Polish folk music and Italian opera. Most of his compositions are for solo piano; they include mazurkas, nocturnes, sonatas, preludes, waltzes, and polonaises.

Christie, Agatha (1891–1976). British writer of detective stories, born *Agatha Miller*. Her first novel, *The Mysterious Affair at Styles* (1920), was written while she was nursing in a wartime hospital. A prolific writer, she owed much of her enormous success to the appeal of her two detectives, Hercule Poirot and Miss Marple. The element of surprise is an important feature of all her stories, *The Murder of Roger Ackroyd* (1926) being

---

The Christie Disappearance

In December 1926 the private life of Agatha Christie, Britain's 'Queen of Crime', created its own authentic mystery. For some weeks the famous novelist disappeared from view, leading to a major police hunt and mounting public concern. She was eventually found staying in a health spa under a false name but was quite unable to explain how she had got there. The incident has never been satisfactorily explained: while the cynical regarded it as a publicity stunt, others have linked it to stress caused by her failing marriage (she divorced Archibald Christie in 1928).

---

particularly famous for its unexpected ending. *The Mousetrap* (1952) is the world's longest continually running play. In 1971 she was appointed DBE.

Churchill, Sir Winston (1874–1965). British statesman, who led Britain to victory during World War II. He became a Conservative MP in 1900 but later joined the Liberals. Appointed first lord of the Admiralty in 1911, he mobilized the navy on the eve of World War I without waiting for official Cabinet authority. He was chancellor of the exchequer during the General Strike (1926) and became first lord of the Admiralty again at the outbreak of World War II. On Chamberlain's resignation (1940), he was appointed prime minister. His stirring speeches, together with his famous cigar and V-for-victory sign, inspired the country during the war. Having achieved his 'grand alliance' between the USSR, Britain, and the US, he was finally able to announce Germany's surrender on 8 May 1945. His Conservative party was defeated in 1945 but he later returned as prime minister (1951–55). He was also a prolific writer, winning the Nobel Prize for literature in 1953. His major works include *The Second World War* (1948–54).

> **❝** I have never accepted what many people have kindly said, namely that I inspired the nation. It was the nation and the races dwelling all round the globe that had the lion heart. I had the luck to be called upon to give the roar.
>
> Winston Churchill on himself,
> 80th Birthday Speech,
> November 1954 **❞**

Cicero, Marcus Tullius (106–43 BC). Roman lawyer, orator, and statesman. He was elected consul in 63, when he defeated a revolution led by Catiline. Once the emergency was over his supporters deserted him; he was later exiled for executing the rebels without trial. He returned in 57 but retired from public life during Caesar's dictatorship. After Caesar's death he published the *Philippics*, a series of speeches attacking Mark Antony, who had him put to death. Cicero's writings on philosophy and political theory played an important part in the development of Latin literature. Nearly

1000 of his letters survive; these contain references to his family and provide an interesting picture of his personal life.

Cid, El, original name *Rodrigo Diaz de Vivar* (c. 1043–99). Spanish nobleman and legendary hero. From his brilliant military exploits both for and against the Moorish rulers of southern Spain he earned the title 'El Cid' ('The Lord'). Many legends gathered around his name, and he became a prominent character in Spanish romance and drama. Over 200 ballads celebrating his achievements have survived.

Clapton, Eric (1945–   ). British rock guitarist, singer, and songwriter. He studied at art school before taking up the guitar at 17. After playing with various groups, he found his first real success when he formed the group Cream in 1966. Each of the group's albums sold more than a million copies in the US. The group split up in 1968 and Clapton subsequently formed the group Derek and the Dominoes, with whom he recorded the album *Layla* (1970). During the 1970s his career was affected by drug addiction but he later came back to enjoy even greater success with such albums as *Journeyman* (1986) and *Unplugged* (1992).

Claudius, full name *Tiberius Claudius Drusus Nero Germanicus* (10 BC–AD 54). Roman emperor. He was considered unfit for public life because of physical deformity and, it was thought, mental infirmity. However, soldiers looting the palace after the emperor Caligula's murder in 41 found him hiding and proclaimed him emperor, thinking they would have more power through his weakness. Claudius ordered and took part in the invasion of Britain (43). For much of his reign he was dominated by his third wife Messalina, whose influence made him unpopular with the nobility. He was poisoned by his fourth wife, his niece Agrippina, the mother of Nero.

Cleopatra (69–30 BC). Egyptian queen, famous for her beauty. Of Greek descent, she became joint ruler with her brother Ptolemy XIII at 17 but lost power two years later. Julius Caesar re-established her and as his mistress she bore him a son, nicknamed Caesarion, and went with him to Rome. Following Caesar's death (44) she returned to Egypt, later captivating Mark Antony, who became her lover. This union was highly unpopular in Rome and provoked Octavian to declare war. Antony and Cleopatra were defeated at the Battle of Actium (31) and on receiving a false report of Cleopatra's death Antony killed himself. She in turn committed suicide, allegedly by a snake bite.

> **❝** If Cleopatra's nose had been shorter the whole face of the earth would have changed.
> Blaise Pascal, *Pensées* (1670) **❞**

Clinton, Bill, full name *William Jefferson Clinton* (1946–   ). US politician, 42nd president of the US (1993–   ). Born in Hope, Arkansas, Clinton studied at Yale Law School and became a successful lawyer. He subsequently entered politics and served five terms as governor of Arkansas (1979–81, 1983–92). In 1992 he defeated George Bush in presidential elections to become the first Democrat president for 12 years. Although he had campaigned on domestic issues, once in office he found himself preoccupied with problems in Somalia, Haiti, and Bosnia. His plans for a national health-care programme, formulated largely by his wife Hilary (1947–   ), failed to pass into law. Following mid-term elections in 1994, he was faced with a Republican majority in both houses of Congress.

Clive, Robert (1725–74). British soldier and founder of the British Empire in India. Initially a clerk with the East India Company in Madras (1744), he showed brilliant leadership as a volunteer officer against the French and helped to establish British power in India (1746–51). In 1755 he took command of the Madras army and recaptured Calcutta, where 146 British prisoners had been shut up in the 'black hole' by the Nawab of Bengal. Clive's victory at Plassey finished the campaign and in 1765 he became governor of Bengal. However, he had made enemies in England and was threatened with impeachment on his return there. Although acquitted of the charges against him, he is believed to have committed suicide as a result.

Cocteau, Jean (1889–1963). French poet, writer, painter, and dramatist, who also wrote and directed several films. He was involved in many modern movements in the arts and supported the composers known as Les Six (Darius Milhaud, François Poulenc, and others). He collaborated with Picasso, Diaghilev, and other well-known names in producing ballets and wrote a number of poetic dramas, including *Oedipus* and *The*

Infernal Machine. His films, which are surrealistic in style, include *Beauty and the Beast* (1946) and *Orpheus* (1950). Cocteau also wrote a number of novels and over 20 volumes of poetry and essays; in 1957 he painted the interior of the St Pierre Chapel at Villefranche.

Coleridge, Samuel Taylor (1772–1834). British poet and critic. After various unsuccessful enterprises, he met William Wordsworth in 1795 and together they published *Lyrical Ballads* (1798). This includes Coleridge's best-known poem, *The Rime of the Ancient Mariner*, a supernatural tale of the disasters that befall the crew of a ship when one of its members kills an albatross. By 1802 Coleridge was addicted to opium and had almost stopped writing poetry. He turned instead to lecturing and writing on literature and philosophy in such works as *Biographia Literaria* (1817).

> He was a mighty poet and
> A subtle-souled psychologist;
> All things he seemed to understand
> Of old or new, on sea or land,
> Save his own soul, which was a mist.
> Charles Lamb, 'Coleridge'

Columbus, Christopher (1451–1506). Italian explorer, popularly regarded as the discoverer of America. He maintained that the earth was round and that Asia could be reached by sailing westward. In 1492 the king and queen of Spain agreed to finance his voyage of exploration and he set sail with three ships, the *Santa Maria*, the *Niña* and the *Pinta*. He reached Dominica and Cuba and called them the West Indies, thinking that they were part of Asia. He later explored the Central and South American mainland and many more of the Caribbean islands, where he set up rich trading posts.

Confucius, Chinese name *K'ung-Fu-Tzu* (551–479 BC). Chinese philosopher, whose doctrine of enlightened responsible rule has influenced governments throughout the Far East. He taught that only concern for humanity, talent, and education qualified men for public office, birth being unimportant. Throughout his life Confucius tried unsuccessfully to obtain an administrative post where he could apply these principles, which were later made famous by his disciples and such publications as the *Confucian Analects*. His doctrine formed the foundation of the classical Chinese administrative system.

Congreve and the Duchess

During his later years Congreve enjoyed a close relationship with Henrietta, the second duchess of Marlborough. He was widely believed to be the father of her second daughter. When he died, the playwright left almost all his estate to Henrietta, who used her influence to arrange his burial in Westminster Abbey. According to some accounts, the duchess was so distraught by his loss that she had a small automaton made exactly to resemble him. Each day this would be brought to her table, where it would bow and nod as if in response to her conversation.

Congreve, William (1670–1729). English dramatist of the Restoration era, brought up in Ireland. He wrote several highly successful comedies, including the satirical *Love for Love* (1695). After the failure of *The Way of the World* (1700), now considered his best work, he gave up the theatre. He died in a carriage accident and is buried in Westminster Abbey (*see box*).

Conrad, Joseph (1857–1924). British novelist, born *Józef Teodor Konrad Korzeniowski* in Poland. An orphan, he served as a sailor in merchant ships from the age of 17, taught himself English, and took British nationality in 1886. His career as a writer began with the novel *Almayer's Folly* (1895). His later novels, which draw on his experiences at sea and his wide travels, include *Lord Jim* (1900), *Heart of Darkness* (1902), *Nostromo* (1904), and *The Secret Agent* (1907).

Constable, John (1776–1837). British painter, the son of a miller. He studied at the Royal Academy schools and first exhibited at the Academy in 1802. His works usually depict scenes from the English countryside and reflect the influence of the Dutch 17th-century landscape artists. His most famous paintings include *Dedham Vale* (1802), *Flatford Mill on the River Stour* (1817), and *The Hay-wain* (1821), which received instant acclaim at the Paris Salon. In 1816 Constable finally married Mary Bicknell, whose relatives had opposed the marriage for many years. An inheritance of £20,000 in 1828 enabled Constable to devote himself entirely to landscape painting.

Constantine the Great (c. AD 280–337). Roman emperor, who established Christianity as the official imperial religion. He succeeded his father, Constantius Chlorus, as emperor of the West in 306; after defeating all his rivals in a series of civil wars, he became sole emperor in 325. In 313, having seen a heavenly vision of the cross before a battle, Constantine was converted to Christianity. From then on he favoured Christians and became increasingly severe towards pagans. He founded Constantinople, formerly Byzantium, as the capital of the Christian empire (324).

Cook, James (1728–79). British navigator and explorer. In 1768 he captained the *Endeavour* on an expedition to the Pacific, during which he sailed round New Zealand and New Guinea and explored the east coast of Australia. In 1772 he sailed around Antarctica, discovering several Pacific Islands. One of the outstanding features of both voyages was the good health of the crew, whom Cook fed on a diet including fresh vegetables and fruit to prevent scurvy, a common disease amongst sailors at that time. On his third voyage, in which he hoped to find a passage joining the Atlantic and Pacific Oceans, Cook was killed by Hawaiian islanders when he tried to recover a stolen boat.

Copernicus, Nicolaus (1473–1543). Polish astronomer. His theory that the earth revolves on its axis and that the sun, not the earth, is the centre of the planetary system was the result of 30 years of research, and was fully described in his book *Concerning the Revolution of Celestial Bodies* (1543). The astronomers Kepler, Galileo, and Newton developed and expanded Copernicus's theory, which he was reluctant to publish in his lifetime. Though the initial reaction of the Catholic Church was favourable, Copernicus's book was subsequently banned until the 18th century.

> ❛ An upstart astrologer who strove to show that the earth revolves, not the heaven or firmament, the sun and the moon. This fool wishes to reverse the entire science of astronomy; but sacred scriptures tell us that Joshua commanded the sun to stand still, not the earth.
> Martin Luther on Nicolaus Copernicus ❜

Copland, Aaron (1900–90). US composer, pianist, and conductor. Born in New York to Russian-Jewish immigrants, Copland learned the piano from his sister. He later studied in Paris under Nadia Boulanger (1921–24) and developed an interest in the musical avant-garde. On his return to the US he composed a series of complex large-scale works including his *Symphonic Ode* (1929). During the 1930s and 1940s, however, he set out to develop a more accessible style, incorporating folk melodies and Latin-American rhythms into a number of his works. His best-known compositions include *El Salón México* (1936) and the ballet scores *Billy the Kid* (1938) and *Appalachian Spring* (1944). He also wrote film music and numerous pieces for the piano. Copland was a tireless advocate of contemporary music who did much to encourage its appreciation by a wider public.

Coppola, Francis Ford (1939–   ). US film director, writer, and producer. Born to Italian parents in Detroit, Coppola began his film career working on low-budget horror movies. He achieved his first real success with the screenplay for *Patton* (1970), which won an Oscar. Further acclaim followed with *The Godfather* (1972), a gangster epic that Coppola directed and co-wrote, and *The Godfather, Part II* (1974). His later films include *Apocalypse Now* (1979), a complex film about the Vietnam War, *The Cotton Club* (1984), one of Hollywood's most notorious flops, *The Godfather, Part III* (1990), and *Bram Stoker's Dracula* (1992).

Corot, Jean-Baptiste-Camille (1796–1875). French painter. He worked as a linen draper before turning to painting at the age of 26; his works received little acclaim until about 1856. His early landscapes are painted in the classical style, using strong colours, as in *Bridge at Narni* (1826–27), which he painted after his first visit to Italy (1825). On later visits he became interested in the effects of light and developed the use of subtle hazy colours. All his work was sketched from nature, including his portraits and large-scale landscapes, such as *The Church of Marissel* (1866) and *The Bridge of Nantes* (1868–70).

Correggio (1494–1534). Italian Renaissance painter, born *Antonio Allegri* and named after his birthplace, Correggio, near Parma. He is famous for his soft voluptuous style and advanced use of perspective, as seen in his paintings of mythological subjects, such as *Venus, Mercury and Cupid* and *Antiope Asleep* (c. 1525). His other works include frescoes on the ceiling of the Convent of San Paolo (c. 1519), the dome of San Giovanni Evangelista (1520–23) in Parma, and the religious painting *The Mystic Marriage of St Catherine* (c. 1526).

Cortes, Hernando (1485–1547). Spanish conqueror of Mexico. He settled as a farmer in Santo Domingo in 1504. Sent to explore Mexico in 1519, he marched inland, using force and diplomacy to overcome all opposition. He finally reached the capital (now Mexico City) and was welcomed by the Aztec emperor Montezuma as the reincarnation of a Mexican deity. However, Montezuma was killed during a revolt against the invaders and Cortes was forced to leave. In 1521 he returned and conquered the whole country after a siege of several months during which 50,000 Mexicans died from famine and the plague, and was appointed captain-general at Mexico in 1522.

Coulomb, Charles Augustin de (1736–1806). French scientist. Coulomb investigated electrical and magnetic attraction by means of the torsion balance, which he invented. He formulated Coulomb's Law, which states that the force between two electric charges is proportional to the product of the charges and inversely proportional to the square of the distance between them. The coulomb, a unit of electric charge, was named after him.

Coward, Sir Noël (1899–1973). British actor, playwright, and composer. Having appeared in his first play at the age of 12, he became famous as a playwright for his witty and satiric view of the interwar years. His first successful play, *The Vortex* (1924), was followed by the popular comedy *Hay Fever* (1925). His most popular musical, *Bitter Sweet* (1929), was successful in both London and New York. Among his films is the classic *Brief Encounter* (1945), which he wrote and produced. He was knighted in 1970.

Cranmer, Thomas (1489–1556). English churchman. Having been appointed Archbishop of Canterbury by Henry VIII in 1532, he served the king loyally and was responsible for annulling his marriage to Catherine of Aragon. He also presided at the coronation of Anne Boleyn. Cranmer supported the translation of the Bible into English and supervised the publication of the Anglican prayer books of 1549 and 1552. On the death of Edward VI, he supported the claim of the Protestant Lady Jane Grey to the crown. When the Catholic Mary

Cranmer's Hand

During his last imprisonment, Cranmer was induced to sign a recantation of his Protestant beliefs in order to escape execution as a heretic. However, when he was taken to a church in Oxford and told to make his recantation public, he refused, thereby sealing his fate. On being brought to the stake, Cranmer defiantly held his right hand, the one that had signed the recantation, in the rising flames, so that it might burn before the rest of his body.

became queen, he was convicted of treason and heresy and was burnt at the stake in Oxford.

Crazy Horse, Indian name *Ta-Sunko-Witko* (c. 1842–77). Sioux Indian chief. A member of the Oglala tribe, he emerged as a leader of his people in their resistance to White encroachment in the 1860s. In 1876 he helped to lead a surprise attack on General George Crook and his forces in Rosebud Valley, Montana, forcing them to withdraw. He then joined Sitting Bull in the massacre of Lt-Col. George Custer's forces at Little Big Horn. His people weakened by hunger, he finally surrendered in May 1877. He was killed a few months later, apparently while trying to escape from prison.

Crick, Francis (1916–   ). British biochemist. *See* James **Watson**.

Croesus (d. c. 546 BC). King of Lydia in Asia Minor, whose friendliness and generosity towards his Greek subjects made him a popular overlord. His great wealth, gained from his gold mines and from trade, gave rise to the saying "as rich as Croesus". According to legend, Croesus was condemned to death by the conquering Cyrus of Persia, but was saved from being burnt alive by a miraculous rainstorm.

Cromwell, Oliver (1599–1658). English general and statesman. He entered Parliament in 1628 and distinguished himself as a military leader during the civil war. His strongly disciplined force, the Ironsides, secured victory over the royalists at Marston Moor (1644) and provided the model for the parliamentary army.

A devout Puritan, Cromwell was convinced that the execution of Charles I was predestined by God and led the commission that condemned the king to death. From 1653 until his death he ruled England, Scotland, and Ireland under the title of Lord Protector. He was buried in Westminster Abbey but at the Restoration his body was disinterred and hanged at Tyburn.

> ❛ A devotee of law, he was forced to be often lawless; a civilian to the core, he had to maintain himself by the sword; with a passion to construct, his task was chiefly to destroy...
> John Buchan,
> *Oliver Cromwell* ❜

Cromwell, Thomas (c. 1485–1540). English statesman, created Earl of Essex in 1540. He rose to prominence following the fall of Cardinal Wolsey and entered the service of Henry VIII in 1530. As principal adviser to the king he played a major role in the Restoration and the dissolution of the monasteries. He persuaded Henry to marry Anne of Cleves to secure a German alliance. The marriage failed, however, and led to Cromwell's downfall. He was accused of treason and executed.

Crosby, Bing (1904–77). US singer, born *Harry Crosby*. His showbusiness career began while he was still at school, when he played the drums for a rhythm band.

He subsequently became the most famous of the crooners of the 1930s, selling nearly 300 million records containing some 3000 different titles. His 'White Christmas', written by Irving Berlin, stood for many years the best-selling record of all time. He made several films, notably *Going My Way* (1944) and the series of 'Road' films, in which he co-starred with the comedian Bob Hope.

Curie, Marie (1867–1934). Polish physicist. Born *Marie Sklodovska*, she married her teacher, the French physicist **Pierre Curie** (1859–1906), in 1895. Together they undertook research into radioactivity and succeeded in discovering and isolating the new elements radium and polonium from pitchblende ore. The Curies were awarded the Nobel Prize for physics in 1903 for the discovery of radioactivity. After Pierre's death in a road accident in 1906, Marie succeeded him as professor of physics at the University of Paris. She continued to work on radioactivity and on the medical application of radiation. In 1911 she was awarded a second Nobel Prize for the discovery of radium and plutonium. The radiation to which she was exposed in her research work finally caused her death. The Curies' first daughter **Irène Joliot-Curie** (1897–1956) worked with her mother at the Radium Institute; in 1935 she and her husband Jean-Frédéric (1900–58) were awarded the Nobel Prize for their discovery of artificial radiation.

Custer, George Armstrong (1839–76). US soldier. Despite his poor achievements at West Point military academy, he showed such brilliance as a cavalry officer during the American Civil War that he was placed at the head of a cavalry brigade in the final campaign. As commander of the 7th Cavalry Regiment, he crushed the Cheyenne Indians in 1868. In 1876, while campaigning against the Sioux Indians led by Sitting Bull, Custer discovered an enemy encampment near the Little Big Horn River and attacked it against orders. In the battle, known as 'Custer's Last Stand', he was killed along with his 264 men.

Cyrano de Bergerac (1619–55). French author and soldier. He was famous as a duellist and fought over 1000 duels, reputedly on account of his long nose. A highly original writer, he produced plays, novels, and political pamphlets. His fantastic novel *Voyages to the Moon and the Sun* (1656–62) anticipated such writers as Swift and Voltaire. He also forecast such discoveries as the atomic structure of matter, aviation, and the gramophone.

Cyrus (c. 590–529 BC). King of Persia. By usurping the Median king's leadership of Iran (549), he founded the Persian Empire, which he enlarged until it extended from the Aegean Sea to Afghanistan. Under his humane and tolerant rule, the exiled Jews in Babylonia were restored to Palestine (537). Cyrus died fighting in central Asia; his tomb is still visible near Pasargadae in Iran.

D

Daguerre, Louis Jacques Monde (1787–1851). French inventor of the daguerrotype, an early photographic process. A successful painter of panoramic views, he began work on the production of single positive photographic images with J. N. Niepce in 1829. Daguerre eventually succeeded in producing such images by exposing an iodized silver plate and developing and fixing the image produced. As the first practical form of photography, the daguerrotype was much used for portraits from the 1830s to the 1850s.

Daimler, Gottlieb (1834–1900). German mechanical engineer. He constructed one of the first internal combustion engines, which he applied successfully to a bicycle and a four-wheeled vehicle, the world's first motorcycle and car. In 1890 he set up the Daimler Motor Company, which built the first Mercedes car in 1899.

Dali, Salvador (1904–89). Spanish painter. He studied at the Academy of Fine Arts in Madrid but was expelled because of his bizarre behaviour. After studying the works of Sigmund Freud, he went to Paris and joined the Surrealists, a group of artists whose aim was to express the subconscious mind in their paintings. His interest in photographic realism is expressed both in his paintings and in his work with the director Luis Buñuel in the films *Un Chien Andalou* (1928) and *L'Age d'or* (1930). Such nightmarish paintings as *The Persistence of Memory* (1931) and *Premonition of Civil War* (1936) reveal his preoccupation with dream symbolism. In 1938, after rejoining the Catholic Church, he began to paint religious subjects. These paintings were denounced by the Surrealists and in 1940 Dali went to live in the US. He returned to Spain in 1955. His last years were spent as a bedridden recluse.

> 6 There is only one difference
> between a madman and me.
> I am not mad.
> Salvador Dali, *The American*
> July 1956 9

Dalton, John (1766–1844). British chemist. His early work was in the fields of meteorology and colour blindness. In 1801 he published the results of his researches into gases, including the law of partial pressures. This law states that the total pressure exerted by a mixture of gases is equal to the sum of the pressures of the component gases. Dalton also developed the atomic theory of matter and attempted to calculate the atomic weights of elements.

Dante, full name *Dante Alighieri* (1265–1321). Italian poet, son of a Florentine nobleman. At the age of nine he met Beatrice and his infatuation with her lasted until her death in 1290, despite her marriage to another. His earliest poems were sonnets, followed by the

Vita Nuova (c. 1293), a collection of lyrics interspersed with prose, inspired by his love for Beatrice. Following political upheavals in Florence, Dante was condemned to death in 1302 and was forced to live in exile. In 1308 he began work on the epic poem *The Divine Comedy*, in which he describes his journey from Hell to Paradise in the three sections *Inferno, Purgatory,* and *Paradise.*

Danton, Georges-Jacques (1759–94). French revolutionary leader. He led the rising of 1792, which overthrew Louis XVI and the monarchy, and was effectively head of the revolutionary government. However, he was unable to end the Reign of Terror, in which many people who were considered to be enemies of the revolution were guillotined, and he was himself tried and executed. One of the most controversial figures of the French Revolution, Danton has been regarded both as an outstanding orator and statesman and as a corrupt political opportunist.

Darius I (550–486 BC). King of Persia. After seizing the throne in 522, Darius organized the Persian Empire, dividing it into a number of semi-independent provinces and establishing a regular taxation system. In 513 he invaded Europe and penetrated north of the Danube. Between 499 and 494 he put down a revolt among his Greek subjects. His attempt to punish the Athenians for assisting the rebels was unsuccessful and he was defeated at Marathon (490).

Darwin, Charles (1809–82). British naturalist. At university Darwin studied first medicine and then theology, but he abandoned both to pursue his consuming interest – natural history. In 1831 he accepted the post of ship's naturalist on a voyage to South America and the Pacific in HMS *Beagle*. He returned in 1836 and spent the next 20 years using the information collected on the voyage to formulate his theory of evolution; his famous book *On the Origin of Species by Means of Natural Selection* was published in 1859. Darwin believed that living species were not created individually but developed over a long period of time, from ancestors similar to them, in a struggle for existence that resulted in the survival of the fittest. This view was in direct opposition to the established ideas of the day, based implicitly on the word of the Bible, and Darwin's book aroused much controversy. Many people refused to accept that man had evolved from ape-like ancestors and was not divinely created. Darwin subsequently published several other books, including *The Descent of Man* (1871), and his theory gradually gained acceptance. The influence of the Church,

> ❛ I do not see that Darwin's supreme service to his fellow men was his demonstration of evolution...Darwin's supreme service was that he won for man absolute freedom in the study of the laws of nature.
>
> H. F. Osborn, *Impressions of Great Naturalists* ❜

however, was strong enough to prevent his receiving any official honours from the state during his lifetime.

Davis, Bette, full name *Ruth Elizabeth Davis* (1908–89). US actress, best known for playing neurotic, intense, or menacing roles. She made her film debut in *The Bad Sister* (1931) and established her reputation in such melodramas as *Of Human Bondage* (1934). Other notable films included *Dangerous* (1935) and *Jezebel* (1938), both of which earned her Oscars, *The Little Foxes* (1941), and the classic *All About Eve* (1950). She later made a comeback playing strong-willed elderly women in such films as *Whatever Happened to Baby Jane?* (1962) and *The Whales of August* (1987).

Davis, Miles (1926–91). US jazz trumpeter, composer, and bandleader. Born into a middle-class Black family, he studied music at the Juillard School in New York. He began recording in 1945 and in the 1950s pioneered the style known as 'cool jazz'; he also became a heroin addict during this period. His most influential recordings included *Kind of Blue* (1959) and *Bitches Brew* (1969), which divided jazz fans by incorporating elements of rock music. After a serious car crash in 1972 he suffered from frequent ill-health but continued to tour widely.

Davy, Sir Humphrey (1778–1829). British chemist. In 1802 he became professor of chemistry at the Royal Institution in London. As the result of experiments in electrolysis he discovered the elements sodium and potassium. In 1812 he was knighted and visited the continent, where he met the scientists Ampère and

Humboldt. After his return to England, he invented the miners' safety lamp, in which the flame was screened to prevent it igniting the dangerous methane gas known as firedamp. He later became president of the Royal Society. Davy also wrote poetry as a means of relaxation from his scientific work.

The Famous Scientist

During his lifetime, Sir Humphrey Davy became easily the most celebrated scientist of the day. His fame was by no means confined to Britain: on one occasion a letter from Italy bearing only the enigmatic inscription 'SIROMFREDEVI, LONDRA' was successfully delivered to his home. Nor was it limited to the educated classes. Strolling through the streets of London one night, Davy encountered a man charging a penny a time to peer at the moon through a telescope. When Davy offered his penny, the showman, recognizing his illustrious client, remarked loftily that he could by no means accept payment from a "brother philosopher".

Dean, James, stage name of *James Byron* (1931–55). US actor, whose moody performances and early death have made him a lasting symbol of youthful rebellion. Dean studied at the University of California and appeared in a few small parts before signing with Warner Brothers in 1954. His fame rests on his starring roles in three films; *East of Eden* (1955), *Rebel Without a Cause* (1955), in which he played a sensitive delinquent, and *Giant* (1956). He was killed in a car crash a week after completing the last of these.

Debussy, Claude (1862–1918). French composer. He studied piano and composition at the Paris Conservatoire and won the Grand Prix de Rome in 1884. His style of composition bears many similarities to that of the French impressionist painters. Amongst his best-known works are *Prélude à l'après-midi d'un faune* (1894) and *Clair de lune*, part of the *Suite Bergamasque* (1890–1905). His other works, often based on poems, include the orchestral *Nocturnes* (1899), the opera *Pelléas and Mélisande* (1902), and the symphonic sketches *La Mer* (1905).

Defoe, Daniel (1660–1731). British novelist and journalist, the son of a London butcher. In 1703 he published a political satire that led to his imprisonment for 15 months in Newgate jail. He then became a government spy. Defoe published more than 200 volumes altogether, but is now remembered chiefly for his novels *Robinson Crusoe* (1719), based on the story of Alexander Selkirk, a Scottish sailor marooned for five years on a desert island, and *Moll Flanders* (1722).

Degas, Edgar (1834–1917). French impressionist painter and sculptor, born *Edgar de Gas*. He studied at the School of Fine Arts in Paris and his early paintings, such as *Spartan Girls and Boys Exercising* (1860), reflect his classical training. Influenced by photography and Japanese prints, he became interested in portraying movement and the effects of light. His best-known works often depict dancers or racehorses; these include the paintings *At the Races* (1869–72) and *Dancers* (1899) and the bronze statuette *Fourteen-Year-Old Dancer* (c. 1880). He became blind in later years.

De Gaulle, Charles (1890–1970). French soldier and statesman. In World War I he was severely wounded and became a prisoner of war. During World War II he led the Free French forces in Britain after the fall of France. He became president of the provisional government in 1945 but resigned the next year. After a period of retirement he became first president of the new Fifth Republic in 1958 and was re-elected in 1965. As president he ended French colonial rule in Algeria and withdrew French forces from NATO in 1966. Although his Gaullist party successfully quelled a revolt of students and workers in 1968, and won the elections of that year by a large majority, De Gaulle himself resigned after being defeated in a referendum on constitutional reform in 1969.

> ❛ Intelligent – brilliant –
> resourceful – he spoils his
> undoubted talents by his
> excessive assurance, his
> contempt for other people's
> point of view, and his
> attitude of a king in exile.
> Report of a French
> military college on
> Charles de Gaulle, 1922 ❜

De Havilland, Sir Geoffrey (1882–1965). British aircraft designer. He built his first aeroplane in 1908 and during World War I designed and tested several fighter and bomber aircraft. He subsequently formed his own company, which produced the famous two-seater Moth and, in World War II, the all-purpose Mosquito. De Havilland was knighted in 1944. After the war he developed the Vampire and the Comet, two of the first jet-propelled aircraft.

de Klerk, F(rederik) W(illem) (1936–   ) South African statesman, president (1989–94). De Klerk practised as a lawyer before entering South Africa's House of Assembly in 1972. He became leader of the National Party and state president following the resignation of P. W. Botha in 1989. As president, de Klerk showed an unexpected readiness to dismantle South Africa's apartheid system. He freed Nelson Mandela and other leaders of the outlawed ANC (1990), ended classification by race (1991), and signed a new constitution (1993). Following multiracial elections in 1994, he was replaced as president by Mandela, becoming a deputy president. De Klerk and Mandela were jointly awarded the Nobel Prize for peace in 1993.

Delacroix, Eugène (1798–1863). French Romantic painter, whose striking personality was reflected in his works. Influenced by English artists, Delacroix rejected the classical style that dominated French art at the time. His paintings *Massacre at Chios* (1824) and *Death of Sardanapalus* (1827) were condemned for their brilliant colouring and violent subject matter. In 1832 he visited North Africa and, inspired by the exotic scenery, produced paintings such as *Algerian Women* (1834). In the late 1830s he gained official recognition and was commissioned to paint murals, including the one at the Palace of Versailles (c. 1837).

De La Mare, Walter (1875–1956). British poet and novelist, whose works have an atmosphere of gentle mystery. A relative of Robert Browning, he wrote poetry for both children and adults, including *Songs of Childhood* (1902) and *The Listeners* (1912). He also wrote the fantasy novel *Memoirs of a Midget* (1921).

Delius, Frederick (1862–1934). British composer of German origin. He worked as a traveller for his father's firm of wool merchants before going to study music in Liepzig, where he met Edvard Greig. In 1888 he moved to France, where he married the artist Jelka Rosen in 1901. His compositions include the opera *A Village Romeo and Juliet* (1900–01) and the choral and orchestral works *Sea Drift* (1903) and *Requiem* (1914–16). From 1925 he was blind and paralysed but continued to compose with the aid of a friend who transcribed his music for him.

Delors, Jacques (1925–   ). French politician and economist. After graduating from the University of Paris in 1945, Delors became a head of department at the Banque de France, a position he held until 1962. Thereafter he worked mainly as a public servant, taking a special interest in economic affairs. A socialist, he was elected to the European parliament in 1979. As president of the European Commission (1985–94) he formulated the Delors Plan for greater European Union and was a leading architect of the Maastricht Treaty (1992). He was appointed to the Légion d'honneur in 1992.

De Mille, Cecil B(lount) (1881–1959). US film producer and director. The son of a playwright, he worked as an actor-manager in the theatre before entering the film business with Jesse L. Lasky and Samuel Goldwyn. His *The Squaw Man* (1914) was the first film made in Hollywood. Later films range from sex comedies to the grandiose biblical epics for which he is best known. These include *King of Kings* (1927) and *The Ten Commandments* (1956).

> ❛ His success was a world success, and he enjoyed every minute of it…He kept sex, sadism, patriotism, real estate, religion and public relations dancing in midair like jugglers' balls for fifty years.
>
> Agnes de Mille on her uncle Cecil B. de Mille in *Speak to Me, Dance with Me* ❜

Demosthenes (384–322 BC). Greek orator and statesman, who fought for Greek liberty against the imperialist ambitions of King Philip II of Macedonia. He made his first speech in court on his coming of age, when he successfully prosecuted his guardians for squandering his inheritance. In preparing himself to speak, Demosthenes is said to have practised with pebbles in his mouth to improve his diction. Although he hoped to form an anti-Macedonian alliance with Athens at its centre, Philip's victory at Chaeronea (338) silenced Demosthenes until the death of Philip's son,

Alexander the Great, in 323. His final attempt to rally Greece against Alexander's successors failed and he took poison to avoid execution.

Deng Xiao Ping (1904–   ). Chinese politician. The son of wealthy parents, he became a full-time worker for the Chinese Communist Party in 1927. He subsequently served in the civil war against the Nationalists and took part in the 'long march' led by Mao-Tse-Tung (1934–35). After the communist takeover in 1949, he rose steadily through the party ranks but fell from favour during the Cultural Revolution (1966–69) and again in 1976. Following Mao's death he became vice chairman of the central committee and vice premier to Hua Guo Feng (1920–   ). Although not officially recognized as leader, he emerged as the dominant force in Chinese politics after Hua's fall in 1982. Under his direction China pursued a policy of economic liberalization combined with severe repression of political dissent. Deng's attempts to improve relations with the West suffered a major setback following the Chinese army's massacre of protesting students in Tianamen Square, Beijing, in 1989. Despite his official retirement in that year he continues to dominate policy making.

De Niro, Robert (1943–   ). US actor, best-known for playing sensitive but inarticulate tough-guys. He began to appear in films in the mid 1960s but first achieved prominence in Martin Scorsese's *Mean Streets* (1973). He subsequently starred in a further six films by Scorsese, including *Taxi Driver* (1976), *Raging Bull* (1980), which earned him the Oscar for Best Actor, and *GoodFellas* (1990). His other films include *The Godfather, Part II*

(1974) and *Mary Shelley's Frankenstein* (1994). A leading exponent of Method acting, De Niro is famous for his arduous preparation for each role and his ability to disguise his appearance.

De Quincey, Thomas (1785–1859). British essayist. As a youth he ran away from his school in Manchester and lived in poverty in London for a time. He later became a close friend of Coleridge and Wordsworth, and rented Wordsworth's former Lake District home for some years. From 1820 he supported himself by journalism, soon acquiring a reputation for his writings on German literature and political economy. An opium addict from 1813, his *Confessions of an English Opium-Eater* (1822) made him famous.

Derrida, Jacques (1930–   ). French philosopher and literary critic. Born in Algeria, he studied philosophy at the Ecole Normale Supérieure and at Harvard. He is the originator of the complex theory known as deconstruction, which regards all literary and philosophical texts as undermined by their own contradictions. These ideas, expounded in such books as *Of Grammatology* and *Writing and Difference* (both 1967), have become highly influential, although some have criticized them as obscure and nihilistic. Later publications include *Ghosts of Marx* (1993). Derrida has taught widely in France and the US.

Descartes, René (1596–1650). French mathematician and philosopher. His philosophy is founded upon the only certainties he could find – his own existence ("I think, therefore I am") and the existence of God. His mathematical achievements include the invention of co-ordinate geometry. In 1649 Descartes visited the Swedish court, where Queen Christina insisted on having mathematics lessons from him at five o'clock each morning. He contracted pneumonia as a result and died the following year.

Descartes's Robot

According to one of his early biographers, the philosopher Descartes once constructed a robot in the guise of a young woman. This he took with him on his later travels. During one sea crossing, however, the captain of the ship was moved to peer into the chest in which the automaton lay hidden. When the lifelike form began to stir and move, the captain reacted with terror, concluding that it must be a device of the devil. The chest was immediately sealed and flung into the sea.

Dewar, Sir James (1842–1923). Scottish chemist and physicist. He became a professor at Cambridge University in 1875 and at the Royal Institution, London, in 1877. His researches into low-temperature phenomena enabled him to produce liquid hydrogen and oxygen and solid hydrogen. The liquefied gases were stored in vacuum flasks, which Dewar invented, using the absorbent qualities of charcoal to create the necessary vacuum.

Diaghilev, Sergei Pavlovich (1872–1929). Russian ballet impresario and founder of the Ballets Russes. His company, which introduced Russian ballet to western Europe, was formed in Paris in 1909 and won international fame for its often sensational productions. Diaghilev's genius was in bringing together outstanding artists, composers, choreographers, and dancers, including Picasso, Cocteau, Ravel, Stravinsky, Pavlova, and Nijinsky. The results influenced ballet companies throughout the world. Among Diaghilev's most famous productions are Stravinsky's *Firebird* (1910), *Petrushka* (1911), and *The Rite of Spring* (1913).

Diana, Princess (1961–   ). Princess of Wales. *See* Prince **Charles**.

Dickens, Charles (1812–70). British novelist. After his father was imprisoned for debt, the 12-year-old Dickens worked for a time in a blacking factory. He worked tremendously hard to teach himself shorthand and became a reporter. In 1833 his first published piece appeared, under the pen-name *Boz. The Pickwick Papers* (1837) brought him overnight fame, which never diminished. As editor of the periodicals *Household Words* and *All the Year Round*, he encouraged other writers, including Mrs Gaskell. His novels, many of which reflect his childhood experience of poverty and protest against social injustice, were bestsellers. They include *Oliver Twist* (1837–39), *The Old Curiosity Shop* (1841), *David Copperfield* (1850), and *Great Expectations* (1860–61). Dickens gave very successful public readings from his works in Britain and the US, even after a stroke left him lame in 1865. His unsatisfactory married life ended in separation in 1858, when he left his wife and ten children. He died from overwork, leaving *The Mystery of Edwin Drood* (1870) unfinished.

Dickinson, Emily (1830–86). US poet. The daughter of a lawyer, she spent most of her life in seclusion with her Calvinist family in Amherst, Massachusetts. She wrote over 1700 poems, most of which are short visionary lyrics on themes of love, death, religion, and the natural world. Her style is intense and highly idiosyncratic. Although she only published a handful of poems in her lifetime, she is now regarded as one of the greatest US writers. She also wrote numerous letters.

> ❜ I am small, like the Wren,
> and my Hair is bold, like the
> chestnut Bur, and my eyes like
> the Sherry in the Glass, that
> the guest leaves.
> Emily Dickinson on herself,
> undated letter ❜

Diderot, Denis (1713–84). French philosopher, who with Voltaire helped to create the Enlightenment, the French movement that attempted to replace orthodox views with scientific enquiry. His first two philosophical works were condemned for atheism and he was imprisoned for three months. From 1745 to 1772 he edited and contributed to the pioneering 28-volume *Encyclopedia* (1751–72). Diderot also wrote scholarly works, essays, and translations, as well as philosophical novels, such as *Rameau's Nephew* (written 1761–64; published 1821).

Diesel, Rudolf (1858–1913). German engineer, born in Paris, who invented the diesel engine. Such engines burn heavy oil mixed with air that is heated to the ignition temperature of the oil by compression. Diesel completed the first working model in 1893, although this exploded and nearly killed him. In 1897, after further work on the design, he produced a single-cylinder internal-combustion engine that proved very successful and is now used in road, rail, and marine transport. In 1913 Diesel disappeared on a Channel crossing and his body was never found.

Dietrich, Marlene, original name *Maria Magdalena von Losch* (1901–92). German film actress and singer, who lived in the US from 1930. After becoming famous in the role of a dance-hall entertainer in the film *The Blue Angel* (1930), she went to Hollywood and made a number of films that established her glamorous image. These include *Blonde Venus* (1932), *Witness for the Prosecution* (1957), and *Judgment at Nuremberg* (1961). During World War II she made hundreds of personal appearances before Allied troops, usually singing 'Lili Marlene', the song especially associated with her. In the 1950s and 1960s she remained one of the best-known cabaret entertainers in the world.

DiMaggio, Joe, full name *Joseph Paul DiMaggio* (1914–   ). US baseball player, considered one of the game's greatest heroes. Famous for his quiet charisma, he was often nicknamed 'Joltin' Joe' or 'the Yankee Clipper'. DiMaggio, who was born in Martinez, California, began to play minor-league baseball in San Francisco. In the later 1930s he became famous as an outstanding hitter and outfielder with the New York Yankees; the team won nine World Series titles during his 13 seasons on the side (he lost three seasons to World War II). After his retirement in 1951 he worked in public relations and on television. He married the film actress Marilyn Monroe in 1954 but the marriage lasted only nine months. His brothers Vincent DiMaggio and Dominic DiMaggio were also professional baseball players.

Diogenes (c. 400–320 BC). Greek philosopher, who rejected conventional behaviour in the search for simplicity and self-sufficiency. A number of stories are attached to his name. One of these alleges that he was found using a lantern in broad daylight to search for an honest man. His life of poverty, sleeping in public buildings, and begging for food, earned him

---

Diogenes and Alexander

When Alexander the Great was in Corinth, he made a point of visiting the famous Diogenes, who at that time was living in a tub in the outskirts of the city. The great king found the philosopher lying in the sun and humbly asked if there was anything he wanted. "Yes," snapped back Diogenes, "I want you to stand out of my sun." Although Alexander's retainers mocked the philosopher as a madman, the king himself was impressed: "If I were not Alexander," he said, "I should wish to be Diogenes."

---

the nickname of 'Cyon' (the Greek word for 'dog') and his followers were called 'Cynics'.

Dior, Christian (1905–57). French fashion designer. Dior opened his fashion house in 1947 with the very successful 'New Look'. With its natural waistlines and long full skirts this new style rejected the wartime austerity caused by shortage of material and brought back femininity and glamour. He later created the H and A lines, which also had worldwide success.

Disney, Walt(er) (1901–66). US producer of cartoon films. Originally a commercial artist, Disney made his first Mickey Mouse film in 1928 and went on to produce a series of animated shorts called 'Silly Symphonies'. In the 1930s he created other famous animal characters, such as Donald Duck, Pluto, and Goofy, and produced the first film in full Technicolor (1932). His earlier feature-length films, including *Snow White and the Seven Dwarfs* (1937), *Fantasia* (1940), and *Bambi* (1942), surpass many of his later productions, which were aimed almost exclusively at children. He also produced a number of live-action films, including *Treasure Island* (1950), and a series of wildlife films entitled 'True-Life Adventures'. During his life Disney was awarded a record 48 Oscars as well as over 900 honours and citations from all over the world. The Disney company continues to produce highly successful animated and live-action films, including *Beauty and the Beast* (1991), *The Lion King* (1994), and *The Santa Claus* (1995). The company also runs amusement parks populated with his best-known characters in California ('Disneyland'), Florida ('Disney World'), and France ('Euro Disney').

Disraeli, Benjamin (1804–81). British statesman and author, created *Earl of Beaconsfield* in 1876. Although he was born the son of a Jew, his father's quarrel with the synagogue resulted in his being baptized a Christian at the age of 13. His dandified appearance, conceit, and good looks soon made their mark on Victorian society. After several unsuccessful attempts he entered Parliament in 1837 but was howled down during his maiden speech. However, he went on to become an outstanding politician and is regarded as having consolidated the policies of the modern Conservative party. He served twice as prime minister (1868 and 1874–80) and was Queen Victoria's favourite minister. He wrote many novels, including *Vivian Grey* (1826) and *Sibyl* (1845), as well as political pamphlets and satires.

Gladstone and Disraeli

A story told by Princess Marie Louise, Queen Victoria's granddaughter, vividly illustrates the differences of personality and approach between Disraeli and his greatest rival. Having dined one evening with Gladstone and the following night with Disraeli, a young lady was asked to compare the two men. "When I left the table after sitting next to Mr Gladstone," she replied, "I thought he was the cleverest man in England. But after sitting next to Mr Disraeli I thought I was the cleverest woman in England."

Domingo, Placido (1941–   ). Spanish tenor. Domingo was brought up in Mexico, where he studied music and singing. Initially a baritone, he took his first major tenor role in 1960 and made his New York debut six years later. Since the early 1970s he has been in constant demand in the world's great opera houses. He has also starred in several films, including *Carmen* (1985). In 1990 he reached a huge international audience when he appeared with Luciano Pavarotti and José Carreras at a televised concert in Rome to mark the World Cup.

Dominic, St (1170–1221). Spanish founder of the Dominican order of preaching friars. He began preaching to heretics in France in 1203, having been sent there on a mission by Pope Innocent III. His new order was authorized by the pope in 1218 and a female order established in 1221. One of the rules of the order, the rule of poverty, was so strict that the monks were unable to possess houses or lands and were thus forced to become beggars. By the time of Dominic's death, his order had spread throughout western Europe. He was canonized in 1234.

Donatello, full name *Donato di Niccolo* (1386–1466). Italian sculptor. He trained in Florence, where he became a leader of the new Renaissance style and the most influential artist of the 15th century. From 1443 to 1453 he lived in Padua, where he produced the equestrian statue of Gattamelata and the altar in St Anthony's church. His other famous works include the nude statue *David*.

Donne, John (1572–1631). English metaphysical poet. He was barred from certain employments because he was brought up a Catholic. After a reckless youth he served with the Earl of Essex, becoming secretary to Sir Thomas Egerton in 1598. Donne's secret marriage in 1601 to Egerton's niece, Ann More, led to his imprisonment for a short time. In 1614 he was ordained an Anglican priest and in 1621 he became dean of St Paul's, where he won great renown as a preacher. Neither his love lyrics, written when he was a young man, nor his later religious poetry were published in his lifetime.

Dostoyevsky, Fyodor (1821–81). Russian novelist. At 16 he entered military engineering school, but later resigned his commission in order to write. *Poor Folk* (1846) was a minor success. In 1849 Dostoyevsky was condemned to death as a revolutionary but reprieved at the last moment and sent to Siberia for four years hard labour, during which his tendency to epilepsy increased. During the 1860s he fell into debt but his first major novels, *Crime and Punishment* (1866) and *The Idiot* (1868–69), enabled him to pay off some of his creditors. After *The Possessed* (1871–72) and *The Brothers Karamazov* (1879–80), Dostoyevsky was recognized as one of the greatest Russian writers of the age.

Doyle, Sir Arthur Conan (1859–1930). Scottish novelist and creator of Sherlock Holmes, the detective whose powers of deduction enabled him to solve the most complicated crimes. The character of Holmes was inspired by a surgeon at Edinburgh University, where Doyle studied medicine. He practised as a doctor until 1890 and again in the Boer War. The first Holmes novel,

A Study in Scarlet, appeared in 1887 and a number of short stories followed. The character of Holmes soon became extremely popular, although Doyle would have preferred to be remembered for his historical novels. He was knighted in 1902.

Drake, Sir Francis (c. 1540–96). English admiral, the first Briton to sail round the world. After making his name and his fortune in battles against the Spanish, he voyaged round the world in the *Golden Hind* (1577–80). Although he set off with four other ships, they became separated and he was left to complete the voyage alone. He was knighted on his return and became mayor of Plymouth in 1582. He was admiral of the fleet that stormed Cadiz in 1587 and a year later he led the attack on the Spanish Armada.

Dreyfus, Alfred (1859–1935). French army officer of Jewish birth. Found guilty in 1894 of espionage for Germany, he was condemned to life imprisonment on Devil's Island. The real traitor, Major Esterhazy, was acquitted. The blatant anti-Semitism of these verdicts caused violent controversy and after the suicide of an officer who had falsified important evidence, Dreyfus was returned to France for retrial (1899). One of his supporters was the French writer Zola. Dreyfus was found guilty again but pardoned; he was not proclaimed innocent until 1906. Subsequently he fought in World War I and was appointed to the Legion of Honour in 1919.

Dryden, John (1631–1700). English poet, dramatist, and critic. His works for the stage include both comic dramas and heroic tragedies such as *All for Love* (1677). In 1668 he was appointed Poet Laureate; his principal poetic works were translations and satires such as *Absalom and Achitophel* (1681). Dryden was converted to Roman Catholicism in 1685, when the Catholic James II came to the throne. As a result, he lost the laureateship when James was succeeded by the Protestants William and Mary in 1688. His last major work was his Virgil translation of 1697.

> ❢ His mind was of a slovenly character – fond of splendour, but indifferent to neatness. Hence most of his writings exhibit the sluttish magnificence of a Russian noble, all vermin diamonds, dirty linen, and inestimable sables.
>
> Lord Macaulay on John Dryden,
> *Edinburgh Review*
> January 1828 ❢

Dumas, Alexandre (1802–70). French novelist and dramatist, known as *Dumas père*. He frequently worked with such collaborators as August Maquet, who researched the background for his famous historical novels *The Three Musketeers* and *The Count of Monte Cristo* (both 1844). Between 1844 and 1854 he produced more than 24 novels and stories. His illegitimate son **Alexandre** (1824–95), known as *Dumas fils*, was also a novelist and dramatist. His best-known work was the play *The Lady of the Camelias* (1848), the tragic story of a famous French courtesan, which Verdi adapted as the opera *La Traviata* in 1853.

Duns Scotus, John (c. 1265–1308). Scottish philosopher, known as the *Subtle Doctor*. He became a Franciscan monk and lectured at Oxford, Paris, and Cologne, where he died prematurely. Duns Scotus criticized the philosophy of Aquinas for being too theoretical, maintaining that theology should depend on practical faith, not on speculation.

Du Pré, Jacqueline (1945–87). British cellist. Born in the Channel Islands, she studied the cello in London and subsequently with Paul Tortelier and Mstislav Rostropovich. Having made her concert debut at the age of 16, she went on to perform with principal orchestras all over the world. She earned a great reputation, particularly for her performance of Elgar's cello concerto, and in 1967 married the pianist Daniel Barenboim. In 1973 multiple sclerosis forced her to give up her performing career, but she continued to teach the cello.

Dürer, Albrecht (1471–1528). German painter and engraver. Dürer was the son of a goldsmith, from whom he probably learned the art of precise detailed drawing. At the age of 13 he produced the first known self-portrait, drawn from his reflection in a mirror. After a lengthy training and much travel in the Netherlands, Germany, and Italy, he opened a workshop in Nuremberg in 1495. His many paintings include *The Adoration of the Magi* (1504) and *The Martyrdom of St Bartholomew*. His interest in technical problems together with his sensitive realism made him the leading German painter of his day. After 1515 Dürer worked for the emperor Maximilian and in 1520 he became court painter to Charles V.

Dvořák, Antonin (1841–1904). Czech composer. He began composing in the 1860s and in 1875 was awarded a grant to work in Vienna. There he met Brahms, who greatly encouraged him in his career. His *Moravian Duets* (1876) and *Slavonic Dances* (1878) show the influence of native folk music and earned him world acclaim. He visited England and the US and became artistic director of the New York Conservatory in 1892. Here he wrote the last of his nine symphonies, *From the New World* (1893). He also composed religious music, such as *Stabat Mater* (1883), and operas, including *Russalka* (1900).

Dylan, Bob (1941–   ). US singer and songwriter. Born *Robert Zimmerman*, he is thought to have taken his new surname from the poet Dylan Thomas. He started singing in New York folk clubs and released his first record in 1962. He is best known for his classics of the 1960s, including the political songs 'Blowing in the Wind' and 'The Times They are A-Changin'', as well as the rock-influenced 'Like a Rolling Stone'. The complex lyrics of such songs as 'Mr Tambourine Man' were acclaimed by critics. By the early 1970s his voice and style had mellowed and his songs became less angry. His later albums include *Blood on the Tracks* (1975), *Desire* (1976), *Slow Train Coming* (1979), which reveals his conversion to Christianity, *Oh Mercy* (1989), and *World Gone Wrong* (1994).

E

Eastman, George (1854–1932). US inventor of the Kodak roll film camera. Eastman developed a process for making dry photographic plates in 1880 and subsequently pioneered the use of transparent photographic film. The first Kodak camera was marketed in 1888; the company also provided a developing and printing service and Eastman acquired a virtual monopoly of popular mass-market photography. In 1924 he gave half of his fortune to educational beneficiaries.

Edison, Thomas Alva (1847–1931). US inventor. Largely self-taught, Edison set up his first laboratory at the age of ten. At 12 he was printing his own newspaper, on board a railway train. His interest in telegraphy led to a number of important developments, including a new stock ticker for the New York stock market. He used the money from this invention to finance future research, inventing the phonograph in 1877 and the electric light bulb in 1878. He also introduced one of the first cinematographs and improved Alexander Bell's telephone by means of the carbon transmitter, which increased the volume of the signal. During his career he took out more than 1000 patents.

Edward I (1239–1307). King of England from 1272, son of Henry III. During his reign he worked out a series of statutes designed to strengthen government and remove abuses. He also brought the administrative system to maturity and furthered the development of Parliament. By 1282 all of Wales was brought under English domination. He also attempted to subjugate Scotland, but was not successful because of the powerful leadership of Wallace and Bruce.

Edward VII (1841–1910). King of Great Britain and Ireland, eldest son of Queen Victoria. After the death of Prince Albert in 1861, Victoria retired from public life for some years and Prince Edward carried out routine royal duties. In 1863 he married Princess Alexandra of Denmark. He travelled to Canada and the US, India, and Egypt. A prominent figure in society and a notorious womanizer, he became extremely popular but was not allowed to play a role in political affairs while Queen Victoria lived. He succeeded to the throne in 1901, at the age of 60.

Edward VIII (1894–1972). King of Great Britain and Northern Ireland. He succeeded to the throne on the death of his father, George V, in January 1936. However, his proposed marriage to a US divorcee, Mrs

6 I have found it impossible to carry the heavy burden of responsibility and to discharge my duties as king as I would wish to do without the help of the woman I love.
Edward VIII, abdication broadcast 11 December 1936 9

Wallis Simpson, forced him to abdicate in December 1936 before being crowned, in order to avoid a constitutional crisis. He was subsequently created duke of Windsor and married Mrs Simpson, spending most of the rest of his life in France with brief visits to Britain.

Edward the Confessor (c. 1004–66). King of England from 1043. The second son of Ethelred the Unready, he grew up in Normandy. He devoted much of his time to religion, from which he gained his nickname. Edward showed favouritism towards the Normans and was alleged to have promised the throne of England to William of Normandy. He later also promised it to Harold, son of the earl of Essex, and the two rival claims were resolved at the Battle of Hastings (1066), when Harold was killed. He was canonized in 1161.

Ehrlich, Paul (1854–1915). German bacteriologist. After obtaining his medical degree at Leipzig (1878), Ehrlich worked with Emil Adolf von Behring to find a cure for diphtheria. In 1892 he succeeded in producing a serum that was active against diphtheria, using antibodies formed by animals inoculated against the disease. After this Ehrlich concentrated on finding chemical stains that could be used to destroy disease-causing germs. He succeeded in discovering one, trypan red, which killed the parasites causing sleeping sickness. His major achievement, however, was the discovery of a compound, called salvarsan, that destroyed syphilis germs. This major breakthrough was announced to the world in 1910. Ehrlich received a Nobel Prize in 1908.

Eiffel, Alexandre-Gustave (1832–1923). French engineer. Eiffel specialized in metal construction, building a number of iron bridges as well as the huge locks for the Panama Canal. For the Paris centennial exhibition of 1889 Eiffel designed and built the three-stage Eiffel Tower on the Champ-de-Mars; the tower, which stands 300 m high, took two years to complete and cost £260,000. Eiffel acquired the nickname 'magician of iron', and was made an officer of the Légion d'Honneur. He later conducted a number of aerodynamic experiments from the tower.

> ❝ A keen amateur violinist, Einstein sometimes played in a string quartet for relaxation. Although he greatly enjoyed these sessions, some of his fellow musicians had misgivings about his abilities. "He's alright," commented one of them, "but I wish he'd learn to count." ❞

Einstein, Albert (1879–1955). US physicist, of German birth. He studied in Switzerland, becoming a Swiss citizen in 1901. In 1905, while working in the Berne Patent Office, he published four highly original scientific papers: the special theory of relativity, the theory of Brownian motion, the photon theory of light, and a paper on molecular dimensions. These were followed in 1916 by his general theory of relativity (which was verified in 1919). Einstein's work had a profound effect on science, superseding Newton's theories and setting the stage for the new era of modern physics. He was awarded the Nobel Prize for physics in 1921. On Hitler's rise to power, being Jewish, he left Europe for the US and became a professor at the Institute for Advanced Study in Princeton. In 1939, worried by reports that German scientists were developing nuclear weapons, Einstein was persuaded to write to President Roosevelt. He took no part, however, in the US production of the atom bomb that resulted from his warning, although the bomb itself depends on the principle of the equivalence of mass and energy that forms part of his special theory of relativity.

Eisenhower, Dwight D(avid) (1890–1969). US general and 34th president of the US. Having graduated from the US Military Academy at West Point in 1915, he commanded a tank training centre in World War I. During World War II he was rapidly promoted, becoming chief of the Allied forces in North Africa (1942–43) and supreme commander of the Allied invasion of Europe (1944). He was nicknamed 'Ike' by his men. Elected US president in 1952, he was re-elected for a second term in 1956. A Republican, Eisenhower presided over important advances in civil rights and attempted to revitalize the economy. Internationally, his presidency was dominated by the continuing Cold War with the Soviet Union. He retired in 1960.

Eisenstein, Sergei Mikhailovich (1898–1948). Russian film director. In the 1920s he pioneered new techniques of film editing, producing a number of films noted for their beautifully composed scenes and vivid images. *Battleship Potemkin* (1925) and *October (Ten Days that Shook the World)* (1927) deal with contemporary political themes relating to the Russian Revolution. By contrast *Alexander Nevsky* (1938), which includes a battle on a frozen lake, and *Ivan the Terrible* (in two parts, 1944–46) are epic dramas based on Russian history.

Elgar, Sir Edward (1857–1934). British composer. Self-taught, he played in local orchestras and settled in Malvern after an unsuccessful period in London (1889–91). His *Enigma Variations* (1899), an orchestral work based on an unheard theme, brought worldwide acclaim. Elgar played a major role in the revival of English choral music, particularly with his oratorio *The Dream of Gerontius* (1900). Other compositions include two symphonies, a violin concerto (1911), a cello concerto (1919), and the *Pomp and Circumstance* marches (1901–07, 1930), the first of which contains the tune 'Land of Hope and Glory'. Elgar was knighted in 1904.

Eliot, George, pen-name of *Mary Ann Evans* (1819–80). British novelist. After her mother's death in 1836, she kept house for her father until he died. In 1849 she moved to London and became an editor on the *Westminster Review*. She lived with the journalist George Henry Lewes, who was separated from his wife, from 1854 until his death in 1878. He encouraged her to write fiction, and she made her name with *Adam Bede* (1859). *The Mill on the Floss* (1860) followed, and *Middlemarch* (1871) was her greatest success. All three novels were set in her native Warwickshire. In 1880 she married an old friend, John Walter Cross, but died later that year.

Eliot, T(homas) S(tearns) (1888–1965). British poet, dramatist, and critic, born in the US. He studied philosophy at Harvard, and Oxford, where he met the poet Ezra Pound. On taking up residence in London he worked as a teacher and a bank clerk before becoming a director of a London publishing house. The poetry collection *Prufrock and Other Observations* (1917) made his name in literary circles, and *The Waste Land* (1922), a powerful exposé of the disillusionment of modern city life, confirmed him as a major poet. After living in England for some years he took British nationality in 1928 and announced his conversion to Anglo-Catholicism. His later poetry includes *Four Quartets* (1943) and the light verse in *Old Possum's Book of Practical Cats* (1939). He also contributed to the revival of verse drama in the theatre with such plays as *Murder in the Cathedral* (1935), based on the assassination of St Thomas Becket, and *The Cocktail Party* (1949). Eliot was awarded the Nobel Prize in 1948.

Elizabeth I (1533–1603). Queen of England from 1558, regarded as one of the greatest English sovereigns. The daughter of Henry VIII and Anne Boleyn, she led a hazardous early life during which both her mother and her stepmother, Catherine Howard, were executed. Well educated and of striking appearance, she succeeded to the throne at the age of 25. Despite many marriage plans made on her behalf, and flirtations with men, notably the earls of Leicester and Essex, she never married and became known as the 'Virgin

Queen'. Elizabeth re-established Protestantism but remained tolerant towards Catholics until her excommunication by the pope. A series of Catholic plots aiming to replace her with Mary, Queen of Scots ended with Mary's execution (1587). The defeat of the Spanish Armada (1588) was one of the most notable events of her reign; there was also considerable progress in exploration, colonization, and discovery.

Elizabeth II (1926–). Queen of Great Britain and Northern Ireland. In 1947 she married her third cousin Philip Mountbatten (1921–), who was created Duke of Edinburgh before the marriage. She succeeded her father George VI to the throne in 1952 and has four children. **Charles** (1948–) was created Prince of Wales in 1958. **Anne** (1950–), a noted horsewoman, was granted the title Princess Royal by the Queen in 1987. Their younger brothers are **Andrew**, Duke of York (1960–), and **Edward** (1964–). In addition to her royal duties, she has brought particular dedication to her role as head of the Commonwealth. Despite the declining popularity of the Royal Family in the 1990s, she remains a highly respected figure.

> ❛ A very pleasant middle to upper class lady, with a talkative retired Navy husband.
>
> Malcolm Muggeridge on
> Queen Elizabeth II,
> *Saturday Evening Post* ❜

Ellington, Duke, nickname of *Edward Kennedy Ellington* (1899–1974). US jazz pianist, bandleader, and composer. A Black, he started to work as a nightclub pianist while still in his teens. By the late 1920s he had moved from Washington, DC, to New York, where he began to assemble his own orchestra. Some of these musicians remained with him for over 30 years. Ellington's compositions range from the popular 'Mood Indigo' and 'Sophisticated Lady' to extended suites and tone-poems. He owed his nickname to his urbane manners and elegant dress.

Emerson, Ralph Waldo (1803–82). US philosopher, essayist, and poet. He resigned from his pulpit at the Second Unitarian Church in Boston in 1832. After visiting Europe he settled at Concord, Massachusetts, where he lived until his death. His writings, including *The Conduct of Life* (1860), affirm the importance of the individual and preach a romantically idealist philosophy of social reform.

Engels, Friedrich (1820–95). German philosopher and economist, a co-founder of Marxism. He was a member of a left-wing youth group in Berlin and met Karl Marx in 1844. He took an interest in the conditions of the workers at his father's cotton mill in Manchester, leading to his first major work, *The Condition of the Working Class in England* (1845). He collaborated with Marx on such works as *The German Ideology* (1845) and *The Communist Manifesto* (1848). They returned to England together after the failure of the 1848 revolution and Engels went back to work at the Manchester mill, supporting the Marx family from his earnings.

After Marx's death, Engels edited and completed the second and third volumes of *Das Kapital* (1885 and 1894).

Epicurus (341–270 BC). Greek philosopher. He settled in Athens in 306 and founded a philosophical community known as 'the Garden', from the place where he taught. Epicurus maintained that since the universe was entirely material, mankind should abandon traditional religion and pursue happiness by leading a quiet life of philosophical contemplation. Although the word 'Epicurean' has come to mean 'freely indulging in pleasure', Epicurus himself maintained that pleasure was simply "freedom from pain and fear".

Epstein, Sir Jacob (1880–1959). British sculptor, born in the US. His sculptures were expressionist in style, seeking to represent emotion rather than conventional form; as a result, many were controversial in their time. They include *Night and Day* (1928), *Lazarus* (New College, Oxford, 1949) and *Christ in Majesty* (Llandaff Cathedral, 1959). He also produced portrait busts of eminent people such as Einstein and Vaughan Williams.

> ❝ They are a form of statuary which no careful father would wish his daughter, or no discerning young man his fiancée, to see.
> *Evening Standard and St James Gazette* on Epstein's sculptures, 1908. ❞

Erasmus, Desiderius (c. 1466–1536). Dutch Humanist scholar, the illegitimate son of the priest Rogerius Gerardus. Erasmus himself adopted his Latin-Greek Christian name Desiderius which means 'beloved'. Ordained in 1492, he found monastic life irksome and spent much of his life travelling and studying. His satirical work *The Praise of Folly* (1509) was written in England for his friend Sir Thomas More. He is known for his Latin correspondence and for his edition of the Greek version of the New Testament (1516).

Ethelred II, known as *Ethelred the Unready* (c. 968–1016). King of England, whose nickname meant 'lacking in foresight'. Unable to prevent a Danish invasion, he tried to buy peace from the Danes with tributes, called Danegeld. In 1002 a large-scale massacre of the Danes, ordered by Ethelred, provoked further invasions and in 1013 Sweyn of Denmark was accepted as king of England. Ethelred was forced to flee but returned on Sweyn's death (1014). He died during Canute's invasion of England (1015–16).

Euclid (fl. c. 300 BC). Greek mathematician. All that is known of his life is that he taught mathematics at Alexandria in Egypt during the reign of Ptolemy I. Euclid wrote and compiled a number of works on mathematics, the most famous of which is the geometrical treatise called the *Elements*. His works, which remained unknown in Europe until over 1000 years after his death, subsequently became standard school textbooks; they were still used as such in the 20th century. According to the Greek philosopher Proclus, when asked by Ptolemy if geometry could be learned other than by studying the *Elements*, Euclid replied "There is no royal road to geometry".

Euripides (c. 485–406 BC). Greek tragic dramatist. Noted for his psychological realism, he broke away from the traditions of earlier dramatists by portraying legendary heroes as ordinary men and women. Nineteen of his plays survive, including *Alcestis* (438), *Medea* (431), which was criticized for its sympathetic treatment of the heroine, and *Trojan Women* (415). In 408 he was exiled to Macedonia, where he wrote his last and best known work, the *Bacchae* (406).

Euripides and the Oracle

According to tradition, Euripides was trained as an athlete by his family after an oracle prophesied that he would win contests as an adult. He later won five victories at the Dionysia, an annual drama festival held in Athens. Another highly dubious legend has it that Euripides foretold the manner of his own death in his last unfinished play, *The Bacchae*. Shortly after writing the famous scene in which Pentheus, king of Thebes, is torn apart by frenzied women, Euripides (it is said) suffered a similar fate from a pack of wild dogs.

Evans, Dame Edith (1888–1976). British actress. She played in many different types of drama, including Shakespeare and Restoration comedies, but is best remembered for her brilliant comic performance (1939) as Lady Bracknell in Wilde's *The Importance of Being Earnest*. She later repeated this role in the film version (1953).

F

Fabergé, Peter Carl (1846–1920). Russian goldsmith. Having inherited his father's jewellery business in 1870, he designed and created flowers, animals, and human figures in gold and enamel. These earned him a commission from Tsar Alexander III (1884) for gold Easter eggs. His workshops in St Petersburg and Moscow continued to produce these intricate masterpieces until the Revolution.

Fangio, Juan-Manuel (1911–95). Argentinian motor-racing driver. Fangio began his motor-racing career in South American competitions with a car he had built himself. He was the world Grand Prix champion a record five times (1952; 1954–57) – all the more remarkable as he only began racing in Europe in 1949 and retired in 1958.

Faraday, Michael (1791–1867). British chemist and physicist. He became assistant to Sir Humphrey Davy in 1813 and succeeded him as professor at the Royal Institution in 1833. Faraday's experiments with electricity and magnetism led to the discovery that an electric current is induced in a circuit that is moved relative to a magnetic field. This discovery led to the principle of the dynamo and the electric motor. Faraday was the first person to liquidize a gas by pressure; he also discovered the phenomena of electrolysis and the rotary polarization of light when passed through an electric field.

Faulkner, William (1897–1962). US novelist. He joined the Canadian Air Force in 1918, and later took various jobs, including painting and carpentry. His novels present a vivid picture of life in the Deep South of the US. *The Sound and the Fury* (1929) was well reviewed but failed to sell, and Faulkner wrote *As I Lay Dying* (1930) and *Sanctuary* (1931) while working as a night-fireman at a power station. *Light in August* (1933) followed, and by this time Faulkner had established himself as a writer. He also wrote Hollywood scripts, and won the Nobel Prize in 1949.

> ❛ A desperate disease requires
> a dangerous remedy.
> Guy Fawkes to King James I,
> 6 November 1605 ❜

Fawkes, Guy (1570–1606). English conspirator in the Gunpowder Plot. Angered by James I's oppression of Catholics, Fawkes conspired with several others to blow up the House of Lords while the king was there. On 4 November 1605, Fawkes was discovered in the cellar with the gunpowder that was to be set alight the following day. He was arrested and condemned to death, and after severe torture revealed the names of his fellow conspirators. The Gunpowder Plot is commemorated in Britain each year on 5 November, when effigies of Guy Fawkes are burnt.

Fellini, Federico (1920–93). Italian film director. Originally a cartoonist and writer, from the 1950s he directed a number of highly influential and imaginative films, including *La Dolce Vita* (1959), a portrait of the frivolous lives of a group of fashionable Romans. *8* (1963), a fantasy autobiography, was so named because at this stage in his life Fellini had made eight and a half films. Later films include *Fellini Satyricon* (1969), a version of a tale by the classical Latin writer Petronius, and *Ginger and Fred* (1986). He was awarded a special Oscar for his lifetime achievement in 1993.

Ferdinand (1452–1516). First king of Spain. He married **Isabella of Castile** (1451–1504) in 1469 and the couple were proclaimed joint sovereigns of Castile in 1474. When Ferdinand also succeeded to the throne of Aragon (1479) the two great kingdoms were united. Ferdinand's reign is notable for the introduction of the Spanish Inquisition (1480) and for Columbus's discovery of America.

Fermi, Enrico (1901–54). US physicist, born in Italy. He discovered neutron-induced radioactivity (1934–37) while working at the University of Rome and was awarded the Nobel Prize for physics in 1938. Disliking Italy's Fascist regime and having a Jewish wife, he did not return to Italy after receiving the prize in Sweden, travelling instead to the US with his family. There he was engaged in the Manhattan Project (1942) to produce the first atom bomb. In December 1942 he built the world's first atomic pile in the squash courts of Chicago University. This was a simple nuclear reactor in which a controlled chain reaction took place. In

1954 the annual Fermi Awards for outstanding work in nuclear physics were established in his honour.

The Nuclear Age is Announced

The world's first controlled nuclear chain reaction began at 2.20 p.m. on 2 December 1942 and lasted 28 minutes. This momentous breakthrough had been achieved by the Italian-born physicist Enrico Fermi, using an atomic pile consisting of graphite blocks packed with several tons of uranium. Immediately afterwards Fermi's collaborator, the US physicist Arthur Compton, made a call to Harvard University's Office of Scientific Research and Development. "The Italian navigator", he announced, "has reached the New World." Fermi went on to play a central role in the creation of the atomic bomb.

Fielding, Henry (1707–54). British novelist. For some years he managed a theatre company, writing the plays himself. In 1740 he became a barrister but continued to write for and edit journals. His first novel was the burlesque *Joseph Andrews* (1742). His best-known work is the satirical comedy *Tom Jones* (1749), in which spirit and honesty are shown to be more important than conventional morals. Fielding sailed to Portugal for his health in 1754 but died soon after arriving.

Fields, Gracie, real name *Grace Stansfield* (1898–1979). British singer and film actress. Born in Rochdale,

Fitzgerald, F(rancis) Scott

Lancashire, she first made her name in a touring revue (1918–25). Her songs, mainly sentimental ballads and comic numbers such as 'The Biggest Aspidistra in the World' were extremely popular, as were her film musicals of the 1930s. Between 1928 and 1957 she took part in eight royal command performances. Having been made a DBE in 1979, she died a few months later in Capri, which had been her home for many years.

Fitzgerald, F(rancis) Scott (1896–1940). US novelist. He published his first novel in 1920 the same year that he married Zelda Sayre. In 1924 they emigrated to France, where Fitzgerald wrote his highly acclaimed novel of US life in the 'roaring twenties', *The Great Gatsby* (1925). Zelda became mentally ill in the 1930s and Fitzgerald became an alcoholic. His next major novel, *Tender is the Night*, did not appear until 1934. In 1937 he moved to Hollywood to write film scripts.

Flaubert, Gustave (1821–80). French novelist. The son of a surgeon, he began writing stories while still at school. After some years in Paris, he returned to his native Rouen in 1846. His masterpiece *Madame Bovary* (1857), the story of an idealistic young woman's vain search for happiness through a series of unsuccessful love affairs, was condemned for immorality, but Flaubert was eventually acquitted of the charges made against him. His other works include the mystical *Salammbô* (1862), *Sentimental Education* (1870), and the short stories *Three Tales* (1877). All his works were meticulously documented; his obsession with realism and stylistic perfection is revealed in his correspondence with his mistress Louise Colet and other friends.

Fleming, Sir Alexander (1881–1955). Scottish bacteriologist, who discovered penicillin. Fleming came from a poor family and worked in London as a shipping clerk when his father died. However, he won a scholarship to study medicine at London University and obtained his degree in 1908. He became interested in germs and in 1928 was appointed professor of bacteriology. In the same year, during the course of his researches, he left a dish of staphylococcus bacteria uncovered and this became contaminated by a mould. Fleming noticed that the germs around each area of mould had dissolved. He identified the mould as *Penicillium notatum* and called the substance that killed the germs penicillin. He also found that penicillin destroyed some bacteria but not others. During World War II, when new drugs were needed to treat wounded soldiers, penicillin was isolated by Howard Florey and Ernst Chain and became the first effective antibiotic. For his work Fleming was knighted in 1944 and received the Nobel Prize in 1945.

Flynn, Errol (1909–59). US actor, born in Tasmania, Australia, noted for his devil-may-care image and scandalous private life. After a varied and adventurous youth, Flynn arrived in Hollywood in 1934, where he found instant success in *Captain Blood* (1935). His other famous roles included the title character in *The*

> ❛ To the Walter Mittys of the world he was all the heroes in one magnificent sexy animal package.
> Jack L. Warner on Errol Flynn ❜

Fonda, Henry

Adventures of Robin Hood (1938) and George Custer in *They Died with Their Boots On* (1941). Away from the screen, Flynn enjoyed a wild lifestyle characterized by drinking, brawling, and innumerable sexual conquests. In 1942 he was tried and acquitted of having underage sex with two teenage admirers. From the late 1940s his popularity declined and he became an alcoholic.

Fonda, Henry (1905–82). US film actor best known for his many roles as an honest and soft-spoken hero. His films include several for the director John Ford, notably *The Grapes of Wrath* (1940) and *My Darling Clementine* (1946). His other films include the courtroom drama *Twelve Angry Men* (1957), *Madigan* (1968), and *On Golden Pond* (1981), which earned him his only Oscar. His daughter **Jane** (1937–   ) is also an actress. Her films include *Cat Ballou* (1965), *Barbarella* (1968), *Klute* (1971), for which she won an Oscar, *Julia* (1977), and *Old Gringo* (1989). An outspoken supporter of left-wing causes in the late 1960s and 1970s, she later became better known for her exercise books and videos.

Fonteyn, Dame Margot (1919–91). British ballerina. Born *Margaret Hookham*, she made her debut in 1934, becoming a leading dancer in classical roles at the Sadler's Wells Ballet. She also performed in many contemporary ballets by the British choreographer Frederick Ashton, eventually becoming prima ballerina of the Royal Ballet. In the 1960s she danced frequently with Rudolf Nureyev; their partnership in such classics as *Giselle* is considered one of the most memorable in the history of ballet. She married Roberto Arias, Panamanian ambassador to Britain, in 1955. She later retired to Panama to look after his health.

Ford, Harrison (1942–   ). US film actor, famous for his action-adventure roles of the 1980s and 1990s. Although he made his film debut as early as 1966, Ford failed to break out of minor parts and gave up acting for carpentry in 1970. He returned to the screen a few years later, finally achieving stardom in the science-fiction epic *Star Wars* (1977); sequels followed in 1980 and 1983. He also starred as Indiana Jones in Steven Spielberg's fantasy adventure *Raiders of the Lost Ark* (1981) and its two sequels (1984 and 1989). Other notable films include *Blade Runner* (1982), *Witness* (1985), *Presumed Innocent* (1990), and *Clear and Present Danger* (1994). In the mid 1990s it was calculated that Ford had been the star in six of the ten most successful films in cinema history.

Ford, Henry (1863–1947). US motor-car manufacturer. Ford was the first industrialist to make cars for the mass market. A mechanic by training, he set up the Ford Motor Company in 1903. From 1909 to 1927 the famous Model T Ford was sold all over the world and factories were established in many other countries. In 1940 Ford built a large bomber aircraft factory at Willow Run. His empire continued to grow and he was succeeded as president of the company by his son and grandson.

Forster, E(dward) M(organ) (1879–1970). British novelist. His travels in Italy and India strongly influenced his novels, which explore cultural contrasts. His works

151

include *Where Angels Fear to Tread* (1905) and *A Room With a View* (1908), both of which have an Italian setting, and *Howards End* (1910). After completing his masterpiece, *A Passage to India* (1924), he gave up writing fiction to lecture on literary and political subjects. *Aspects of the Novel* (1927) is a collection of his lectures. Several of his novels were made into successful films in the 1980s and 1990s.

Fox, George (1624–91). English founder of the Society of Friends (the Quakers). The son of a weaver, he was largely self-educated. In 1642 he rejected the established Church and began to travel the country, preaching and establishing congregations. Fox and his followers were repeatedly imprisoned for blasphemy and persecuted until the Toleration Act of 1689. At one of his trials Fox told the judge that he should quake at the name of the Lord, a remark that gave rise to the nickname 'Quakers'. Fox's *Journal* was posthumously published in 1694.

Francis of Assisi, St, real name *Francesco di Bernardone* (c. 1182–1226). Italian founder of the Franciscan order of friars. After a vision in 1205, he abandoned his military career and his wealthy family for a life of poverty and prayer. He began to preach in 1208 and the following year received papal approval for his new order. This grew from a brotherhood of 11 in 1210 to over 5000 in 1219. In 1224 he received the stigmata, the five wounds of Christ, during a mystical experience. Francis is now mainly remembered for his affinity with wild animals and birds. He was canonized in 1228.

Franco, Francisco (1892–1975). Spanish dictator. He entered the army at the age of 14, served in Morocco, and became chief of staff in 1935. From Morocco he organized the military uprising that led to the Spanish Civil War; he later took over the leadership of the rebel forces on the death of the original leader, General Sanjurjo. Within three years the Republican forces were crushed and Franco became head of state (1939). He ruled as a dictator, becoming gradually more liberal as Spain's prosperity grew in the 1960s and 1970s. He arranged for Prince Juan Carlos (1938–), the royal heir to the throne, to become king of Spain after his death.

Franklin, Benjamin (1706–90). US scientist and statesman. Franklin began his career as a printer and journalist, from which he made sufficient money to devote the latter part of his life to science. In 1746 he performed an experiment in which lightning struck a kite and an electrical spark was discharged through a key attached on the end of the line. This showed that lightning was an electrical phenomenon and led to the invention of the lightning conductor. Franklin also discovered the course of the Gulf Stream, a warm ocean current in the Atlantic. He became involved in politics first as the representative for Pennsylvania in England and subsequently in France as spokesman for the Thirteen Colonies during the American War of Independence. He contributed to the drafting of both the Declaration of Independence and the US Constitution. His autobiography was first published in 1781.

> The body of
> Benjamin Franklin, printer,
> (Like the cover of an old book,
> Its contents worn out,
> And stripped of its lettering and gilding)
> Lies here, food for worms!
> Yet the work itself shall not be lost,
> For it will, as he believed, appear once more
> In a new
> And more beautiful edition,
> Corrected and amended
> By its Author!
>
> Benjamin Franklin, suggested
> epitaph for himself

Frederick I (c. 1123–90). Holy Roman Emperor, known as *Barbarossa* ('redbeard'). He succeeded his father as duke of Swabia and was crowned emperor in Rome in 1155. During a struggle against the pope (1159–77) he was excommunicated and decisively defeated in the battle of Legnano (1176). He drowned while on the Third Crusade to free Jerusalem.

Frederick II, known as *Frederick the Great* (1712–86). King of Prussia. As a boy he was forced to undergo military training by his father, Frederick William I, and was threatened with death when he tried to escape to France. He succeeded his father as king in 1740, inheriting his well-disciplined army, and immediately attacked Austria, securing Silesia in 1745. During the Seven Years War against the Austrians (1756–63) his military genius made Prussia a major European power. At home he encouraged agriculture, industry, and trade and improved education. He was also a great patron of the arts and culture.

Freud, Sigmund (1856–1939). Austrian psychiatrist who founded psychoanalysis, a method of treating mental disorders by inducing the patient to bring repressed feelings and memories into consciousness. Rejecting hypnosis, he encouraged his patients to talk freely about their thoughts, dreams, and childhood memories. He shocked the public by claiming that adult behaviour is strongly influenced by sexual experiences and desires in early childhood. His *The Interpretation of Dreams* (1900) and *The Psychopathology of Everyday Life* (1901) set out the basis of his theories. In 1938 Freud left Vienna to escape the Nazi occupation and went to London, where he died the following year. Sigmund Freud's grandson, the painter **Lucian Freud** (1922–   ), travelled to Britain and became a British citizen in the 1930s. He is noted especially for his portraits and nudes, most of which are painted in a harshly realistic style.

Friedman, Milton (1912–   ). US economist, a leading proponent of monetarism. Friedman carried out economic research for various government bureaus before becoming professor of economics at Chicago University (1948–82). He is well known for his theory that control of the money supply is the best cure for inflation and his advocacy of free markets with minimal government intervention. In the 1980s these ideas had a major influence on economic policy in both the US and Britain. His publications include *Capitalism and*

Freedom (1962), *Money Mischief* (1992), and (with his wife Rose Friedman) *Free to Choose* (1980).

Froebel, Friedrich (1782–1852). German educator. Although he had had little formal education himself, he taught for six years. During this time he developed such strong ideas about how children should be educated that he started his own school in 1816. A second, founded in 1840, was the first of the many 'kindergartens' that now exist all over the world.

Frost, Robert (Lee) (1874–1963). US poet. From the age of ten Frost was brought up in New England, a region that would provide him with lifelong inspiration. As a young man he worked in menial jobs and showed few signs of literary talent; he did not begin to write seriously until a visit to Britain in 1912–15, when he met a number of contemporary poets. His first collection,

The Poet's Business

Having finished a particularly good meal, Robert Frost and his dining companions went out onto the balcony to look at the sunset. "Oh, Mr Frost," gushed a young woman, "Isn't it a beautiful sunset!" "I never discuss business after dinner" replied the poet.

On another occasion Frost, who had just read one of his poems, was asked to explain it. "What do you want me to do?" he drawled, "Say it over again in worser English?"

A Boy's Will, appeared in 1913. Following his return to the US, Frost found a large and appreciative audience with such volumes as *Mountain Interval* (1916) and *New Hampshire* (1923). The deceptive simplicity of such poems as 'Stopping by Woods on a Snowy Evening' made him one of the most popular of modern poets. For the rest of his life he combined poetry with farming and lecturing at universities.

Fry, Elizabeth (1780–1845). British prison reformer, born *Elizabeth Gurney*. She was ordained as a Quaker preacher in 1811. In 1813 she visited Newgate prison and, horrified by conditions there, began to campaign for prison reform. She formed an association for female prisoners in 1817 and subsequently visited gaols in northern England and Scotland with her brother Joseph, publishing an influential report in 1819. She later campaigned for improvements in the treatment of prisoners and the insane throughout Europe.

Fuchs, Klaus (1911–88). German physicist and spy. As a young man he studied at Kiel University and became a member of the Communist party. In 1933 he went to Britain to escape the Nazis and was interned as a German citizen at the beginning of World War II. On his release he became involved in nuclear research for the Allies, taking British citizenship in 1942. Sent to the US to work on the atomic bomb in 1944, he was appointed head of Harwell Atomic Energy Research Station on his return to Britain at the end of the war. He was imprisoned in 1950 for passing information to the Russians; after his release in 1959 he became an East German citizen.

Fuchs, Sir Vivian (1908–   ). British geologist and explorer. He studied at Cambridge and went on several field trips abroad as a geologist. In 1957 he led the British Commonwealth Trans-Antarctic Expedition, with Sir Edmund Hillary. The expedition took four months to cross to the Pole, and mapped large areas of previously unexplored territory. He was knighted on his return in 1958. His autobiography, *A Time to Speak*, was published in 1990.

G

Gable, Clark (1901–60). US film actor, for many years the most popular leading man in Hollywood. He first appeared in major roles in the 1930s, when his numerous films included *Strange Interlude* (1932), *It Happened One Night* (1934), and *Mutiny on the Bounty* (1935). Perhaps his most famous role was as the unsentimental Rhett Butler in *Gone with the Wind* (1939). In 1945 Gable returned to the screen after four years' service in World War II but never regained his former pre-eminence. He died of a heart attack after completing *The Misfits* (1960). His third wife was the actress Carole Lombard (1908–42).

Gaddafi, Mu'ammer Muhammad al (1942–   ). Libyan soldier and politician. The son of nomads, Gaddafi joined the Libyan army in 1962 and formed a radical Arab nationalist organization among his fellow officers. Following his failure to receive a promotion, he led a successful coup in 1969 and declared the Libyan Arab Republic. As chairman of the Revolutionary Council, he promoted himself to colonel and took charge of the country's political and military affairs. He took the title of president in 1977. Widely regarded as a dangerous maverick, Gaddafi has backed terrorist campaigns in Israel and various Western countries in pursuit of his dream of Arab unity. In 1986 US planes bombed Tripoli in retaliation, killing Gaddafi's adopted daughter. He caused controversy again in 1995, when he began to expel thousands of Palestinian refugees from Libya.

Gagarin, Yuri (1934–68). Russian cosmonaut, the first man to travel in space. He came from a peasant family and went to flying school in 1955. Within a year he was piloting jets and in 1960 he started training as a cosmonaut. His historic spaceflight in *Vostok I* took place on 12 April 1961 and consisted of a single orbit of the earth. This proved that man could survive the mental and physical stresses of space travel. He died in an air crash and the town of his birth was renamed Gagarin in his memory.

Gainsborough, Thomas (1727–88). British painter of portraits and landscapes. After an apprenticeship in London, he set up as a portrait painter in Ipswich

---

Reconciliation

Thomas Gainsborough was noted for his extreme good nature and his generosity towards other artists. However, he was known to be on bad terms with his principal rival for royal patronage, Sir Joshua Reynolds, whose versatility he envied ("Damn him," Gainsborough once exclaimed, "how various he is!"). On discovering a tumour on his neck, Gainsborough realized that he was dying and calmly prepared for the end. He made a point of calling Reynolds to his bedside and the rivals were reconciled. Smiling, Gainsborough remarked "We are all going to heaven and Van Dyck is of the company."

(1752). His moves to Bath (1760) and London (1774) brought him more fashionable sitters, including Dr Johnson, Sheridan, and the royal family. He was a founder member of the Royal Academy, but withdrew after a quarrel about the hanging of a painting in 1784. About 750 of his portraits, a few finished landscapes, and many landscape drawings survive.

Galileo, full name *Galileo Galilei* (1564–1642). Italian astronomer and physicist. From observing a swinging lamp in Pisa Cathedral he made the discovery that a pendulum swings at a constant rate. He is said to have deduced the laws governing falling bodies by dropping objects off the Leaning Tower of Pisa. One of these laws states that all falling bodies descend at the same speed, whatever their size, and this discovery made him unpopular with contemporary scientists. He also improved the telescope and was the first person to use it for astronomical observations. For upholding the Copernican System against the established Ptolemaic System Galileo was convicted of heresy by Pope Urban VIII. Although Galileo was forced to recant his belief that the earth moved around the sun, he is supposed to have remarked "But it moves for all that".

Galvani, Luigi (1737–98). Italian anatomist. He lectured in medicine at the University of Bologna and was appointed professor of anatomy there in 1775. In 1771 he noticed that the muscles of dissected frogs' legs twitched not only in response to an electric current but also when in contact with two different metals. He thought that this was due to 'animal electricity' within the muscle itself, but was later proved wrong. In spite of this, his name was used in associated terminology; the electricity generated between two metals was called galvanic electricity and an instrument invented in 1820 for detecting electric current was called a galvanometer.

Gama, Vasco da (1460–1524). Portuguese navigator. A favourite at the Portuguese court, he was chosen by Manuel I to command an expedition to India. He sailed round the Cape of Good Hope, opening up a maritime route from Western Europe to Asia, and established a settlement at Calicut in India (1497–99). In 1502 he founded a colony in Mozambique and returned to Calicut to make commercial treaties. Appointed Portuguese Viceroy in India, he made a final voyage to India in 1524 and died at Cochin.

Gandhi, Indira (1917–84). Indian stateswoman. The daughter of Jawaharlal Nehru, she received a university education and was active in the Congress Party from 1938. She married Feroze Gandhi, who was not related to the Mahatma, in 1942. After her father's death in 1964 she became minister of information and then prime minister (1966). Although she was praised for her handling of foreign affairs, a series of economic and political crises led her to introduce a repressive state of emergency (1975); she also tried to control population growth by enforced sterilization. The unpopularity of these measures caused her to lose the general election in 1977. On being re-elected in 1979 she was faced by mounting religious violence, especially by Sikh extremists. After ordering the army to attack Sikh militants at the Golden Temple in Amritsar (1984), she was murdered by her own Sikh bodyguard. Her elder son **Rajiv Gandhi** (1944–91) succeeded her as prime minister and leader of the Congress Party (Mrs Gandhi's favourite son, Sanjay, had died in a plane crash in 1980). Continuing religious violence led him to resign as prime minister in 1989. Rajiv's assassination two years later while campaigning for re-election brought an end to the dynasty founded by Nehru, which had dominated Indian politics since the country was partitioned in 1947.

Gandhi's Poverty

By the 1930s Mahatma Gandhi had become a world-famous figure who was frequently seen alongside international leaders and other dignitaries. Nevertheless, he insisted on maintaining an extremely austere lifestyle, wearing the clothes of the poorest Indian peasants and generally staying in the slum areas of the cities he visited. In particular, he made a point of consorting with Untouchables, the oppressed outcasts of Indian society. To some sceptics, there was always something rather theatrical about Gandhi's poverty. Lord Mountbatten, the last British viceroy, once had to meet Gandhi at a railway station. As was his custom, Gandhi travelled without bodyguards or entourage in one of the crowded carriages reserved for Untouchables. Somewhat alarmed, Mountbatten asked one of Gandhi's colleagues whether this did not pose serious problems of security. He was solemnly assured that all the Untouchables in Gandhi's carriage had been carefully chosen and vetted by the authorities. "You would never guess how much it costs us to keep this old man in poverty" Mountbatten was told.

Gandhi, Mohandas, known as *Mahatma Gandhi* (1869–1948). Indian political and religious leader, a key figure in India's struggle for home rule. A Hindu, he was regarded as a prophet by many Indians and his nickname 'Mahatma' means 'the Great Soul'. Gandhi originally trained as a lawyer but in 1893 he gave up his £5,000 a year legal practice in Bombay to live on £1 a week campaigning against unfair treatment of Indians in South Africa. Back in India, he used similar methods of non-violent non-cooperation, including hunger strikes, as a means of achieving reform. He was assassinated by a Hindu extremist, offended by Gandhi's campaign for friendship between the Muslims and Hindus, in the year after India's independence.

Garbo, Greta, original name *Greta Gustafson* (1905–90). Swedish film actress. Having begun her film career in Sweden and Germany, she went to Hollywood in the 1920s, where she soon gained a reputation as the most beautiful actress of the silent screen. Her later talking films included *Queen Christina* (1933), *Anna Karenina* (1935), *Camille* (1936), and *Ninotchka* (1939). After retiring from acting in the 1940s she avoided all publicity, living in seclusion in New York until her death.

García Lorca, Federico (1898–1936). Spanish poet and dramatist. A native of Andalusia, he abandoned his musical studies for literature and published his first book of poems in 1921. His style became more contemporary after he went to New York for a year in 1929. On his return to Spain he founded a theatre company, for which he wrote the plays *Blood Wedding* (1933) and *The House of Bernarda Alba* (1936). He was murdered by fascist troops during the Spanish Civil War.

García Marquez, Gabriel (1928–   ). Colombian novelist and writer. Although he was brought up in poverty in a remote jungle village, García Marquez was able to study law at university. From 1948 he worked as a journalist, a career that took him to Europe, Cuba, and the US. He published his first book of stories in 1955 and the major novel *In Evil Hour* in 1962. Unpopular with the Colombian government because of his left-wing views, he spent the 1960s and 1970s abroad. His complex masterpiece *One Hundred Years of Solitude* appeared in 1967 and was heralded as a landmark in South American literature. Following the award of the Nobel Prize in 1982, he returned to Colombia on the personal invitation of the president. Subsequent works include *Love in a Time of Cholera* (1985) and *The General in His Labyrinth* (1989).

Garibaldi, Giuseppe (1807–82). Italian patriot and guerrilla leader. Accused of treason for his political activities in 1934, he was forced to flee from Italy to avoid the death penalty and went to South America. There he eloped with a beautiful Creole girl, Anita Riveira de Silva, and fought in the wars of national liberation. On his return to Italy he became a leading figure in the Risorgimento, a movement that aimed to unite the country, and fought against both Austria and France (1848–49; 1859). With his '1000 Volunteers', nicknamed the 'Redshirts', he conquered Sicily and Naples, an important step towards the unification of Italy (1860). He also made two attempts to free Rome from papal rule (1862; 1867) but was unsuccessful on both occasions.

Garland, Judy (1922–69). US singer and film actress. Born *Frances Gumm*, she first appeared on stage when she was three years old and made her first film when she was 14. Her fame as a juvenile star was assured with her performance as the farm girl Dorothy in *The Wizard of Oz* (1939), in which she sang her famous song, 'Over the Rainbow'. She subsequently appeared in a number of musical films, including *Meet Me in St Louis* (1944) and *Easter Parade* (1948). Despite problems with alcohol and drugs in her later years, she continued to make films and give highly successful concerts before devoted audiences. Her daughter, **Liza Minnelli** (1946–   ), is also a film actress and singer, perhaps best known for her award-winning performance in the musical film *Cabaret* (1972).

> There wasn't a damn thing she couldn't do — except look after herself.
> Bing Crosby on Judy Garland

Garrick, David (1717–79). British actor. He studied briefly under Dr Johnson and went with him to London in 1737. Garrick became famous for his tragic roles in Shakespeare's *Hamlet*, *Macbeth*, and especially *King Lear*. His natural and unaffected style was completely new in his day and revolutionized English acting. He enjoyed uninterrupted success in both tragic and comic roles, and was a distinguished manager of the Drury Lane Theatre for 30 years (from 1747). The

Garrick Theatre and the Garrick Club in London were both named in his honour.

Gates, Bill, full name *William Henry Gates III* (1955–). US businessman and creator of computer software. Gates was born and brought up in Seattle. At the age of 14 he founded a computer programming company with three friends; within a year they had earned $20,000 by selling their traffic-counting system to local governments. In 1975 he dropped out of his law course at Harvard to found the Microsoft Software company in Redmond, Washington. Gates's domination of the emerging computer industry began in 1980–81, when he devised an operating system and licensed it to IBM. MS-DOS (Microsoft Disk Operating System) became the standard operating system for nearly all IBM and IBM-compatible personal computers. During the 1980s Microsoft also cornered the market in more specialized software. When the company went public in 1986, Gates became a multimillionaire at the age of 31. Five years later he was ranked as the world's richest man. In the 1990s Gates made a fresh fortune from sales of Windows, a system that enables a computer to be operated with on-screen symbols rather than complex keyboard commands. A revised version was launched amid huge publicity in 1995.

Gauguin, Paul (1848–1903). French post-impressionist painter. Having abandoned his family and his banking career to devote himself to painting in 1881, he led a bohemian life in Paris, Martinique, and Brittany. After a disastrous collaboration with Van Gogh in Arles, he left Europe (1891) to live the simple life in Tahiti and the Marquesas Islands, where he died. Gauguin was much influenced by the art of the primitive people amongst whom he had chosen to make his home and painted some of his finest pictures in Polynesia. His symbolism in such paintings as *Nevermore*, together with his revolutionary use of pure unmixed colour exerted a great influence on 20th-century art.

Gay-Lussac, Joseph Louis (1778–1850). French chemist and physicist. In 1802 he demonstrated that all gases expand by the same fraction of their volume for the same increase in temperature. Subsequent researches with Alexander von Humboldt led to the discovery that water is composed of hydrogen and oxygen in the ratio 2:1; from this he formulated the law of volumes in 1808. Gay-Lussac also researched the properties of potassium and discovered the element boron.

Gehrig, Lou, full name *Henry Louis Gehrig* (1903–41). US baseball player, one of the greatest hitters in the history of the game. He attended Columbia University before joining the New York Yankees in 1925. During his 14 seasons with the team he established a series of batting records and played in 2130 consecutive games – an achievement that has never been equalled. He left the game with a career total of 1990 runs batted in, including 493 home runs. His early death was caused by a form of sclerosis, now often known as Lou Gehrig's disease.

Genet, Jean (1910–86). French novelist and playwright. The unwanted son of a prostitute, he fell into a life of petty crime and spent much of his youth in reform school and prison. His first novel, *Our Lady of the Flowers* (1944), was written in prison and brought Genet to the attention of Sartre and other literary figures. Like *The Miracle of the Rose* (1946) and *The Thief's Journal* (1949), it is a lyrical account of crime and prostitution based largely on Genet's own experiences. From the later 1940s Genet also wrote for the theatre. Such plays as *The Maids* (1946), *The Balcony* (1956), and *The Blacks* (1959) combined poetry and ritual with violent attacks on accepted moral values.

Genghis Khan, title, meaning 'universal ruler', given to *Temujan* (c. 1162–1227). As leader of the Mongol nomads of central Asia, he showed great skill in the organization and leadership of his warrior horsemen, and subdued China and all Asia north of the Himalayas. The policy of wholesale massacre that he maintained during his invasion of India, Iran, and southern Russia gave him a reputation for systematic brutality. He died after falling from a horse.

George III (1738–1820). King of Great Britain and Ireland. Having succeeded his grandfather George II in 1760, he married Charlotte of Mecklenburg-Strelitz the following year. He was blamed by the Whigs for the political instabilities of the 1760s and accused of trying to influence Parliament through corrupt 'king's friends'. During his reign the American colonies were lost and Britain fought the Napoleonic wars. After a breakdown in 1788 he suffered increasingly from fits of madness. By 1811 he was acknowledged to be insane and his son (later George IV) became regent.

George IV (1762–1830). King of Great Britain and Ireland; previously prince regent (1811–20) during the insanity of his father George III. He is quoted as saying that he had become "rather too fond of women and wine" before the age of 17. After a succession of mistresses, he met Maria Fitzherbert, a beautiful Catholic widow, whom he secretly married in 1785. This marriage was invalid, lacking the king's consent, and George married Princess Caroline of Brunswick in 1795 (in return for a settlement of his debts). They separated the following year. On his accession to the throne in 1820 he attempted to divorce Caroline, but as public sympathy was firmly with her he abandoned his project for fear of civil unrest.

> ❝ This delightful, blissful, wise, pleasurable, honourable, virtuous, true and immortal Prince was a violator of his word, a libertine over head and ears in debt and disgrace, a despiser of domestic ties, the companion of gamblers and demi-reps, a man who has just closed half a century without one single claim on the gratitude of his country or the respect of posterity.
>
> Leigh Hunt on the Prince Regent, *The Examiner* 22 March 1812. For writing this piece Hunt was imprisoned for two years. ❞

George V (1865–1936). King of Great Britain and Northern Ireland. The second son of Edward VII, he served in the navy until the death of his brother (1892) made him heir to the throne. He married Mary of Teck in 1893 and succeeded to the throne in 1910. With World War I he renounced all German titles and the royal house became known as Windsor. He visited the Western Front several times and took an active part in war policy, gaining considerable public respect. In 1932 he broadcast the first Christmas message to the nation, a tradition continued to the present day.

George VI (1895–1952). King of Great Britain and Northern Ireland. He married Lady Elizabeth Bowes-Lyon (now the Queen Mother) in 1923, their two children being Elizabeth (Queen Elizabeth II) and Margaret. George was proclaimed king on the abdication of his brother, Edward VIII. He was respected for his strong sense of duty, his family life, and for his courage in coping with ill-health and a stammer.

Geronimo (1829–1908). Apache Indian leader. One of about 4000 Apaches who were forced to move to a reservation in central Arizona in 1874, he subsequently led them in a campaign against the white settlers. In 1885, together with over 100 Apaches, he jumped the reservation. After 15 months on the run Geronimo surrendered in 1886 on condition that his fellow Apaches should be allowed to return to their homes.

Gershwin, George (1898–1937). US composer, born *Jacob Gershvin*. His first popular song, 'Swanee' (1919), was followed by the Broadway musical *Lady Be Good*

(1924). This was the first of a number of musicals that Gershwin wrote with his lyricist brother **Ira Gershwin** (1896–1983). His other compositions, most of which display a sophisticated jazz style, include *Rhapsody in Blue* (1924) for piano and orchestra, the tone poem *An American in Paris* (1928), and the Black folk opera *Porgy and Bess* (1935).

Gibbon, Edward (1737–94) British historian, noted for his formal polished style and rationalist outlook. Gibbon attended Oxford University but proved an undistinguished scholar. At 16 he shocked his family by converting to Catholicism and was sent off to Switzerland, where he reconverted. During this period abroad he began the serious study of history. After his return to England he served for several years in the army and entered Parliament in 1774. The first volume of his monumental *Decline and Fall of the Roman Empire* appeared in 1776, provoking some criticism with its attitude to the early Christians. In 1783 he retired to Lausanne to complete the work, publishing the final volumes five years later. His *Memoirs* appeared posthumously in 1796.

Gide, André (1869–1951). French novelist. Although he married in 1895, he led an active homosexual life after 1893. He made his reputation as a critic, co-founding the influential *New French Review* in 1908. Throughout his life he was torn between puritan and pagan instincts, a conflict that is reflected in his novels, which include *Strait is the Gate* (1909), *The Vatican Swindle* (1914), and *The Counterfeiters* (1926). He is also remembered for his *Journals* of the years 1889–1949. He was awarded the Nobel Prize in 1947.

Gielgud, Sir John (1904–   ). British actor and theatre director. He made his stage debut at the Old Vic at the age of 17. Several years later he became famous for his Shakespearean performances at the same theatre; his *Hamlet* broke box-office records in both London and New York. In 1958 he appeared alone in the international success *Ages of Man*, in which he recited passages from Shakespeare. He has also appeared in numerous comic parts, in several modern plays, and in films, notably as the valet Hobson in the comedy *Arthur* (1981) and as the title character in *Prospero's Books* (1991).

Gilbert, Sir W(illiam) S(chwenk) (1836–1911). British humorist and librettist. A barrister by profession, Gilbert became well known for his humorous verse,

---

A Prophecy Fulfilled

Although a notoriously brusque and irritable man, W. S. Gilbert liked nothing better than to sit peacefully in his garden at Harrow Weald, near London, and to look out over the adjoining lake. He often told friends that he expected to die in these surroundings one warm summer afternoon. This prophecy would be fulfilled, but not in the manner he expected. On 29 May 1911 Gilbert was in the garden when he noticed a young woman struggling to keep afloat in the lake. Although 75 years old, Gilbert plunged in to save her. The shock of the cold water was too much for the humorist, who suffered a fatal heart attack.

---

collected and published in 1869 as *The Bab Ballads*. In 1871 he met the composer Sir Arthur Sullivan, the first successful result of their collaboration being the comic opera *Trial by Jury* (1875). Sullivan's tuneful and light-hearted music provided the perfect match for Gilbert's witty and satirical verse. Subsequent major successes included *HMS Pinafore* (1878), *The Pirates of Penzance* (1879), and *The Mikado* (1885). The personal relationship between Gilbert and Sullivan was often stormy, owing to their very different temperaments; they had a famous quarrel over the price of a new carpet for the Savoy Theatre. Their last two operas, *Utopia Limited* (1893) and *The Grand Duke* (1896), were less successful.

Giotto (c. 1267–1337). Florentine painter. In 1296 he began the frescoes in the Church of St Francis at Assisi. Subsequently he worked in many other Italian cities. He became official architect of Florence in 1334 and master of the cathedral there. His pictures display action, movement, and narrative power, marking the transition from Gothic formalism to the realism of the Renaissance.

Gladstone, W(illiam) E(wart) (1809–98). British statesman. He entered Parliament in 1832 as a Tory, publishing his controversial book *The State in its Relations with the Church* in 1838. Having shifted his allegiance to the Liberal party, he served as chancellor of the exchequer (1852–55; 1859–66). He was prime minister four times between 1868 and 1894 and, with Disraeli, dominated politics in the late Victorian age. A great moralist, he tried to apply his own strict Christian principles to government and was known as a master of debate

> **‘** Posterity will do justice to that unprincipled maniac Gladstone — extraordinary mixture of envy, vindictiveness, hypocrisy, and superstition; and with one commanding characteristic — whether Prime Minister, or Leader of Opposition, whether preaching, praying, speechifying or scribbling — never a gentleman!
>
> Benjamin Disraeli on W. S. Gladstone **’**

(Queen Victoria once complained that he used to address her as if she were a public meeting). His achievements included parliamentary reform and two Irish Land Acts; however, his Irish Home Rule Bill was twice defeated and he resigned in 1894.

Gluck, Christoph (1714–87). German operatic composer. He studied in Prague and Vienna and later visited Italy, where his early operas were produced. In 1749 he settled in Vienna and, influenced by the librettist Calzabigi, began composing in a more natural style, in which the music reflected the plot and characters. His 'reform' operas include *Orfeo ed Euridice* (1762), *Alceste* (1767), and the French opera *Iphigénie en Tauride* (1779).

Godard, Jean-Luc (1930–   ). French film director, a leading figure in the New Wave of the late 1950s and

1960s. The son of a doctor, Godard began to write for the influential film magazine *Cahiers du Cinéma* in the 1950s. Here he met the future directors Claude Chabrol and François Truffaut, both of whom assisted him with his first feature *A bout de souffle* (*Breathless*; 1959). The new techniques of shooting and editing explored here were further developed in such films as *Contempt* (1963) and *Alphaville* (1965). Godard's work of the late 1960s and 1970s became still more uncompromising, reflecting his conversion to Maoist politics. After some years of willing obscurity, he returned to more mainstream film-making with such movies as *Suave qui peut* (*Slow Motion*; 1980), *Hail Mary* (1984), a controversial updating of the Nativity story, and *Nouvelle vague* (1990). His work has been widely influential.

Goebbels, Joseph (1897–1945). German Nazi politician. In 1926 Hitler appointed him Nazi party leader in Berlin; following the Nazi takeover in 1933, he became minister of public enlightenment and propaganda. As such he had total control over the press, literature, radio, films, and theatre for Nazi propaganda purposes. As World War II drew to a close, he remained with Hitler in his besieged bunker in Berlin. On the capture of that city, Goebbels committed suicide, together with his wife and six children.

Goering, Hermann (1893–1946). German Nazi politician. An ace fighter pilot in World War I and an early supporter of Hitler, he became minister for air and the interior under the Nazi regime. In World War II he commanded the Luftwaffe and controlled the German war economy. He was sentenced to death for war crimes at Nuremberg, but committed suicide shortly before his execution.

Goethe, Johann Wolfgang von (1749–1832). German poet, novelist, and dramatist. During the period of literary ferment known as the *Sturm-und-Drang* ('storm and stress') movement, Goethe created a sensation throughout Europe with the epistolary novel *The Sorrows of Young Werther* (1774). At much the same time he began work on *Faust*, which was to be his greatest achievement. In 1775 he moved to Weimar, where he later directed the court theatre (1791–1817). A major turning point in Goethe's life was his visit to Italy in 1786–88, which led him to renounce romanticism in favour of a more classical outlook. His friendship with Friedrich Schiller stimulated him to complete Part I of *Faust* (1808). His later works include the novel *Elective Affinities* (1808–09) and Part II of *Faust* (1832).

Goldsmith, Oliver (1730–74). Irish poet, novelist, and dramatist. A friend of Samuel Johnson, he spent most of his life in poverty. He rose to fame with a series of newspaper articles but enjoyed his greatest success with the comedy *She Stoops to Conquer* (1773). He is also remembered for the poem *The Deserted Village* (1770) and his novel *The Vicar of Wakefield* (1766).

Goldwyn, Samuel, original name *Schmuel Gelbfisz* (c. 1879–1974). US film producer, born in Warsaw. He came to Hollywood in 1910 and produced an enormous number of films, mostly for his own companies. He helped to create the reputation of many stars, including Gary Cooper and David Niven. His comic blunders with English phrases were celebrated and he is credited with many ludicrous expressions, such as "Anyone who goes to a psychiatrist needs to have his head examined".

Gorbachov, Mikhail (Sergeevich) (1931–). Soviet statesman; as leader of the Soviet Union (1985–91) he introduced social and economic reforms and was largely responsible for ending the Cold War. Born into a peasant family, he studied law before becoming an agricultural organizer for the Communist party. His dynamic personality soon made its mark and he was appointed to the Politburo while still in his forties . After becoming general secretary, he embarked on a radical programme summarized in the watchwords *glasnost* (openness) and *perestroika* (restructuring). In practice this meant greater accountability, toleration of dissident opinions, and the introduction of free-market elements in the economy. He agreed major arms-limitation treaties with the US (1987; 1990) and accepted the collapse of communist regimes throughout eastern Europe in 1989. Despite his popularity in the West, Gorbachov found fewer admirers in the Soviet Union, where his attempts to implement reform within the framework of state socialism antagonized many liberals, as well as the communist old-guard. His economic policies also caused considerable hardship. In August 1991 he was overthrown in a coup led by communist hardliners and held under house arrest. Although the coup collapsed and Gorbachov was reinstated, his authority never recovered. He resigned in December 1991, following his failure to prevent the break-up of the Soviet Union into its constituent republics.

Gordon, Charles George (1833–85). British general. In 1858, after service in the Crimea and Armenia, he was posted to China, where his successful command won him the nickname of 'Chinese Gordon'. As governor of the Sudan, then under Egyptian rule, he worked strenuously to suppress rebels and slavers until 1880. He returned there in 1884 to evacuate the country, threatened by the rebellious followers of the Sudanese sheik Mahdi, and was trapped in Khartoum. After ten months' siege, the city was captured and Gordon killed, just two days before the arrival of relief forces.

Gorky, Maxim, pen-name of *Alexei Peshkov* (1868–1936). Russian novelist, short-story writer, and playwright. His early life of terrible poverty is described in the trilogy *Childhood* (1913–14), *In the World* (1915–16), and *My Universities* (1923). Exiled for his support of the 1905 Revolution, he lived in Italy from 1906, where he suffered from tuberculosis. He returned to Russia in 1928 and became the first president of the Soviet Writers' Union in 1934. Nizhny Novgorod, the town where he was born, was renamed Gorky in 1932 but reverted to its original name in 1991.

Goya, Francisco José (1746–1828). Spanish painter and etcher, whose work had a profound influence on 19th-century French painting. His cartoons for the royal tapestry factory and his lively portraits won the king's approval, and he became a court painter in 1789. In 1792 a severe illness made him deaf, and his work became increasingly personal and original. The etchings *Los Caprichos* (1793–98) satirize the Church, while the macabre series of etchings *The*

Disasters of War (1810–14) and the paintings *2 May* and *3 May 1808* (1814) record the atrocities committed by French troops when Napoleon invaded Spain. Goya visited Paris in 1824 and then settled in Bordeaux, where he died.

Grace, W(illiam) G(ilbert) (1848–1915). English cricketer. Grace was playing for Gloucestershire by the age of 16. An outstanding all-rounder, he became captain of England and contributed greatly to the development of the modern game. By 1895 he had scored 100 centuries. During his career he scored 54,896 runs and took 2876 wickets; he was also the first player to score 2000 runs in a single season.

Dr Grace

The cricketer W. G. Grace was by profession a country doctor, although it seems a very bad one. He took ten years to qualify and during the summer months was rarely available to his patients, for obvious reasons. On one occasion a sick man presented himself at Grace's surgery and asked if the doctor was in. "Of course he's in," replied Grace's assistant, "he's only been batting since Monday lunchtime." On another occasion a worried young woman accosted him with the news that her twins were both running high temperatures. "Contact me at the ground if they reach 210 for two" he growled. Despite this neglect of his duties, Grace died a wealthy man thanks to the large sums he made from the sport (although he was officially an amateur). It is, in fact, difficult to deny that this greatest of sporting heroes was also idle, money-grubbing, and dishonest, "a cheat both on and off the cricket field".

Grahame, Kenneth (1859–1932). Scottish writer for children. He worked in the Bank of England for most of his life. His dislike of busy city life is reflected in the peaceful rural setting of *The Wind in the Willows* (1908), which was written for his only son.

Grant, Cary, stage name of *Archibald Leach* (1904–86). US film actor, born in Britain. After making his Hollywood debut in 1933, he appeared as the sophisticated leading man in numerous films, especially comedies and thrillers. These included *The Philadelphia Story* (1940), *Arsenic and Old Lace* (1944), and several films for Alfred Hitchcock, notably *North by Northwest* (1959).

Grant, Ulysses S(impson) (1822–85). US general and statesman; 18th president of the US (1869–77). Grant trained at the West Point Academy and fought in the Mexican War (1842–44) as a young lieutenant. During the US Civil War he proved himself a resourceful and determined general and was appointed supreme commander of the Federal (northern) armies in 1864. His policy of battering the Confederates into submission at whatever cost to his own troops earned him the nicknames 'Unconditional Surrender' Grant and 'Butcher' Grant. As Republican president he continued with the policy of Reconstruction, by which the southern states were reintegrated with the Union, fought inflation, and made an unsuccessful attempt to annex the Dominican Republic. Following his retirement he lived in some poverty and was obliged to sell his military memorabilia.

Grappelli, Stephane (1908–   ). French jazz violinist. Originally a classical musician, he changed direction after meeting Django Reinhardt in 1931; the two men founded the quintet of the Hot Club of France (1934) and recorded 'Lime House Blues' (1935). During World War II he lived in Britain, playing in night clubs; he returned to Paris in 1946. From the late 1950s he toured, mainly in Europe. His recordings include 'Viper's Dream' (1937) and 'Just One of Those Things' (1973), recorded at the Montreux Jazz Festival.

Grass, Günter (1927–   ). German novelist and writer. Grass was brought up in Danzig (now Gdańsk in Poland) and became a keen member of the Hitler Youth after Germany's annexation of that city. His later disillusion with Nazism helped to form the liberal and sceptical outlook seen in his work. In the 1950s he trained as a graphic artist and began to publish poetry with the backing of Gruppe 47, an important literary group. He found fame with his first novel, *The Tin Drum* (1958), a satirical fantasy based on modern German history. During the 1960s he became a prominent social commentator and campaigned for the Social Democrats. Later novels include *The Flounder* (1977), *The Rat* (1986), and *Toad Croaks* (1992). In the 1990s he provoked much criticism with his outspoken opposition to German unification.

Graves, Robert (1895–1985). British poet and novelist. He published three volumes of poetry during his military service in World War I. His popular autobiography, *Goodbye to All That* (1929), was also based on his wartime experiences. The novels of ancient Rome,

I, Claudius and its sequel *Claudius the God*, were published in 1934. He also published translations and editions of Greek myths. He lived in Majorca from 1929 and was professor of poetry at Oxford from 1961 to 1966.

Gray, Thomas (1716–71). British poet who led a quiet scholarly life, mainly at Cambridge. He is known chiefly for his *Elegy Written in a Country Churchyard* (1751). Twenty years later he was buried in the country churchyard of the poem, at Stoke Poges in Buckinghamshire.

> ❛ I would rather have written
> that poem [Gray's *Elegy*]
> than take Quebec.
> Remark attributed to General
> James Wolfe, on the night before
> he was killed at Quebec ❜

Greco, El, real name *Domenikos Theotokopoulos* (1541–1614). Spanish painter, sculptor, and architect, born in Crete. He worked in Venice, possibly studying under Titian, and Rome, where he was influenced by Michelangelo's work. In the 1570s he settled in Toledo, Spain, and was commissioned to design altarpieces. His paintings, mostly of religious subjects, are characterized by elongated figures and the use of brilliant colours. They include *Burial of Count Orgaz* (1586) and *Assumption* (1613). His work aroused hostile criticism in his lifetime.

Greene, Graham (1904–91). British novelist and writer. A Roman Catholic convert, he travelled extensively and worked as a journalist and a film critic. He divided his work into 'entertainments', such as the spy-thriller *The Third Man* (1949), and serious novels that reflect religious and moral concerns, including *Brighton Rock* (1938), *The Power and the Glory* (1940), and *The Heart of the Matter* (1948). As a narrative writer, Greene was much influenced by film techniques and wrote film scripts for a number of his novels, including *Our Man in Havana* (1960).

Gregory I, St (c. 540–604). Italian pope. In 572 he achieved the highest civilian office in Rome, that of urban prefect, but resigned two years later and donated his inheritance to establish monasteries. Elected pope in 590, he initiated reforms in the Church and established missions in England (596). He was canonized on his death.

Grieg, Edvard (1843–1907). Norwegian composer. The son of a diplomat, he studied at Leipzig and Copenhagen, where he met the Norwegian Romantic composer Nordraak. Through him, Grieg came to appreciate Norwegian folk music, which inspired works such as *Norwegian Dances* and *Lyric Pieces* (1867–1901) for piano. He toured Europe as a pianist and conductor and met Liszt and Ibsen in Rome (1869–70). His most famous compositions are the incidental music to Ibsen's *Peer Gynt* (1876) and his piano concerto (1868). Grieg spent much of his later life in a house on the Troldhaugen fjord in Norway.

Griffith, D(avid) W(ark) (1875–1948). US film director, who greatly influenced the development of cinema in the 1910s. He has been credited with developing many basic film techniques, including the use of close-ups and flash-backs. The son of a former Confederate soldier, he worked as an actor and journalist before becoming interested in the new art of cinema. From 1908 he wrote and directed hundreds of short films for the Biograph company and in 1915 released his masterpiece *The Birth of a Nation*. This three-hour epic of the Civil War proved a huge critical and commercial success but was widely condemned for its racism. In reply to his critics Griffith made *Intolerance* (1916), a technically brilliant film that failed at the box office. Subsequent films, such as *Broken Blossoms* (1919) and *Way Down East* (1920), were less remarkable and he found no further work after the coming of sound.

> I made them *see*, didn't I...I changed everything.
> Remember how small the world was before I came along...I brought it all to life. I moved the whole world onto a twenty-foot screen. I was a greater discoverer than Columbus.
> D. W. Griffith in Adela Rogers St Johns, *The Honeycomb*

Grimaldi, Joseph (1779–1837). British clown. The son of an Italian actor, he first performed at the age of two as a child dancer at Sadler's Wells. He later transformed the traditional role of the clown, inventing many new jokes. A performer of the greatest skill, he was at once a singer, acrobat, dancer, actor, and pantomimist. The clown has been called 'Joey' in his honour ever since.

Grimm, Jakob Ludwig (1785–1863) and his brother **Wilhelm Karl** (1786–1859). German scholars. Their famous collection of folk-tales, many of which had never been written down before, was published in three volumes (1812–13). These include such stories as 'Rumpelstiltskin' and 'Little Red Riding Hood'. The collection became the basis of the study of German folklore, as well as a popular children's book. Both Jakob and Wilhelm became professors at Göttingen and Berlin. Jakob's *German Grammar* was one of the greatest language studies of the age.

Gropius, Walter (1883–1969). US architect, born in Berlin. He studied architecture in Munich and Berlin and founded the Bauhaus school of architecture in Weimar (1919). In 1925 the Bauhaus moved to Dessau, where Gropius designed the school building. He later worked in Britain (1936), designing schools and factories with Maxwell Fry, and taught at Harvard (1937–52). His buildings include the Harvard Graduate Center (1950) and the US Embassy, Athens (1960).

Grotius, Hugo (1583–1645). Dutch political philosopher. He was active in Netherlands politics and arrested as a republican in 1618. Sentenced to life imprisonment, he escaped to France with the aid of his wife in 1620. His important and influential book on international law, published in 1625, used the concepts of natural law and the Social Contract as a rational foundation for a legal system. He also wrote a history of the Netherlands.

Guevara, Che, real name *Ernesto Guevara* (1928–67). Argentinian revolutionary. A qualified doctor, he left Argentina in 1953 because of his opposition to the dictator Perón. He became a communist after seeing the poverty in many South American countries and fought under Fidel Castro in the Cuban Revolution (1956–59). Although he became a government minister there, he later disappeared to resume his guerrilla activities. He was eventually captured and shot by the army in Bolivia while training a guerrilla group there. His dedication and death made him a hero among young Western revolutionaries in the late 1960s and 1970s.

Guggenheim, Meyer (1828–1905). US industrialist, born in Switzerland. In 1847 he went to the US and by 1901 he dominated the mining industry there. Of his seven sons, **Daniel** (1856–1930) established the Daniel and Florence Guggenheim Foundation for the promotion of "the well-being of mankind" (1924) and founded a school of aeronautics at New York University (1925). **Simon** (1867–1941) established a foundation to assist artists and scholars, while **Solomon** (1861–1949) founded the Guggenheim Museum of Art in New York City.

Guinness, Sir Alec (1914–   ). British stage and screen actor. Having first appeared on stage in 1934, Guinness gained recognition for distinguished performances in Shakespearean roles, especially for his modern-dress *Hamlet* (1938). Among later stage successes were his portrayal of T. E. Lawrence in Rattigan's *Ross* (1960).

Guinness is also known as a highly versatile screen comedian, as in *Kind Hearts and Coronets* (1949), in which he played eight members of a family, and *The Ladykillers* (1955). Other films include *Bridge on the River Kwai* (1957), for which he won an Oscar, and *A Passage to India* (1984). His best remembered television role was as the spymaster Smiley in *Tinker, Tailor, Soldier, Spy* (1979) and *Smiley's People* (1981–82). He was knighted in 1959.

> **❝** The outstanding poet of anonymity.
> Sir Peter Ustinov on Sir Alec Guinness **❞**

Gutenberg, Johannes (c. 1390–1468). German printer, who invented a method of printing from movable metal type. He worked initially with goldsmiths in Strasbourg but had financial troubles and formed his own printing business. The first printed Bible (1455) is attributed to him. His method has only really been superseded in the 20th century, with the development of lithographic printing, phototypesetting, and computer technology.

Gwyn, Nell, full name *Eleanor Gwyn* (1651–87). English actress. As a child she sold oranges to the theatre-goers at Drury Lane Theatre, making her first appearance on stage at the age of 15. A successful actress, she was admired by the poet Dryden, who wrote a number of parts for her. In 1669 she became the mistress of Charles II, and eventually bore him two sons. The king remained devoted to her all his life and on his

---

The Protestant Whore

Nell Gwyn was much loved for her high spirits and ready wit. In 1675 she visited Oxford, where Charles II was staying. The crowd, believing her to be the Duchess of Portsmouth, Charles's hated Catholic mistress, surrounded her coach and began to shout and jeer. Understanding the situation at once, Nell leaned out of the window and good-humouredly remarked "Pray, good people, be civil: I am the *Protestant* whore". This produced roars of laughter and applause and she was allowed to continue on her journey.

---

deathbed said, "Let not poor Nellie starve." According to tradition, she was responsible for the founding of the Royal Hospital, Chelsea.

H

Habsburg. Chief royal family of Europe from the 5th to the 20th centuries. Its name derived from the 11th-century ancestral castle on the River Aare in what is now Switzerland. Rudolf, Count of Habsburg, became Holy Roman Emperor in 1273 and under him Austria became a hereditary possession. From 1438 to 1806, excluding 1740–45, all the Holy Roman Emperors came from the Habsburg house. Under Emperor Charles V the Spanish crown was acquired by the Habsburgs (1516). Their domains were divided, Spain passing to Charles's son, Philip II, and the Austrian possessions to his brother, Ferdinand I. The Spanish line died out in 1700 but the Austrian Habsburgs became emperors of Austria in 1804 and of Austria-Hungary in 1848. They were deposed after World War I.

Hadrian, full name *Publius Aelius Hadrianus* (76–138 AD). Roman emperor from 117, selected by his predecessor Trajan. His rule was chiefly remarkable for his personal tours of the Empire and for his building projects, notably at Athens. He also ordered the construction of a number of defences, including Hadrian's Wall in northern England.

Hahn, Otto (1879–1969). German chemist. He discovered a new radioactive substance called radiothorium and a new radioactive element called protactinium. In 1938 he observed the bombardment of uranium by neutrons and realized that the uranium atoms were splitting to produce radioactive atoms of the lighter element, barium. The process was later named nuclear fission and Hahn was awarded the Nobel Prize for chemistry in 1944.

Haig, Douglas, Earl (1861–1928). British field marshal. The son of a landed Scottish family, Haig trained at Sandhurst and served in the Sudan, South Africa, and India. During World War I he commanded a corps in France before being made commander-in-chief of British forces in December 1915. The following year he directed a slow war of attrition along the Somme, resulting in appalling losses; similar tactics were used at Paschendaele in 1917. Despite criticism from Lloyd George and others he kept his position, mainly because of his connections with the Royal Family. Under the supreme command of General Foch, Haig led the final victorious attack on German positions in 1918. After the war he helped to found the British Legion, which cares for ex-servicemen and their families. His

> ❛ Every position must be held to the last man: there must be no retirement. With our backs to the wall, and believing in the justice of our cause, each one of us must fight on to the end.
> Field Marshal Haig, order to British troops 12 April 1918 ❜

reputation was damaged by papers published after his death, which revealed him as an ambitious intriguer.

Haile Selassie I, former name *Ras Tafari Makonnen* (1891–1975). Emperor of Ethiopia, who succeeded the empress Zauditu on her death in 1930. He heroically led the resistance to the Italian invasion (1935) but went into exile the following year in Britain. He returned to power in 1941 but was deposed in a military coup (1974) and died in captivity. Adherents of the Rastafarian religion regard him as the human incarnation of God.

Halley, Edmund (1656–1742). English astronomer. Halley's first important work was a star catalogue of the Southern Hemisphere. In 1684 he met Newton and encouraged him to write *Principia*, a study of the laws of planetary motion. Halley also produced the first meteorological map of the world and the first magnetic chart. In 1705 he published *A Synopsis of the Astronomy of Comets*, in which he accurately predicted the return of a comet previously seen in 1531, 1607, and 1682. The comet, now known as Halley's Comet, last appeared in 1986.

Hals, Frans (c. 1581–1666). Dutch painter of Flemish descent. One of the greatest 17th-century portrait painters, he studied with Van Mander in Haarlem, where he spent most of his life. His early group portraits, particularly *The Banquet of the Officers of the St George Militia Company* (1616) show a lively informal style that is also evident in his single figures. His best-known portrait is probably *The Laughing Cavalier* (1624). Hals's later works, including *Regents of the St Elizabeth*

Hospital (1641), are more sombre and profound, particularly those painted in his old age, when he was destitute.

Hammerstein II, Oscar (1895–1960). US librettist. The grandson of the impresario Oscar Hammerstein, he worked with the composer Rudolf Friml on *Rose Marie* (1924) and Jerome Kern on *Show Boat* (1927), which includes the song 'Ol' Man River'. His famous partnership with Richard Rodgers produced such famous musicals as *Oklahoma!* (1943), *Carousel* (1945), and *The Sound of Music* (1959).

Handel, George Frederick (1685–1759). German composer and musician, who spent most of his working life in Britain. After studying in Halle he produced his early operas in Hamburg and Italy, where he had great success. Following a brief period as musical director at the Hanoverian court (1710), he visited Britain and settled there in 1712. Handel is best known for his oratorios, including *Israel in Egypt* (1738) and the *Messiah* (1741), which was composed in only 21 days. His other works include the orchestral *Water Music* (1717), chamber music, and organ concertos.

Hannibal (247–c. 183 BC). Carthaginian general. After the death of his brother-in-law Hasdrubal, Hannibal was made commander-in-chief of the Carthaginian army at 26. During the second Punic War against the Romans, Hannibal led 40,000 men, with horses and 38 elephants, over the snows of the Alps to invade northern Italy. The Romans did not expect him to take such a hazardous route, and he had a major victory at Lake

Trasimeno (217). However, he failed to attack Rome itself and was driven out. After the Carthaginian treaty with Rome, Hannibal was threatened with betrayal to the Romans and escaped to Bithynia, where he poisoned himself.

Hardie, (James) Keir (1856–1915). Scottish socialist. An illegitimate child, he began work in the coal mines at the age of ten. His mother later married an active trade unionist. Hardie became secretary of the Scottish Miners' Federation in 1886 and was chief founder of the Independent Labour Party (ILP) in 1893. Regarded as the founder of the modern Labour party, Hardie is remembered for his pacifism, especially in his opposition to the Boer War, and his campaigns for the poor and unemployed.

Hardy, Oliver (1892–1957). US actor. *See* Stan **Laurel**.

Hardy, Thomas (1840–1928). British novelist and poet. The son of a Dorset builder, he was educated locally and became an architect. Most of his novels are set in Wessex, an area of southwest England that includes his native Dorset. Although Hardy became popular with *Far from the Madding Crowd* (1874), his later novels, including *Tess of the D'Urbervilles* (1891) and the fatalistic *Jude the Obscure* (1895), were bitterly attacked by reviewers because they outraged contemporary morals. As a result he abandoned fiction and published several volumes of poetry, which contained both new poems and some written years earlier. *The Dynasts* (1904–08) is an epic verse-drama. Despite the adverse reactions he

---

Hardy and the Critics

On its first appearance Hardy's *Jude the Obscure* (1895) caused a furore with its frank discussion of sexual relationships outside marriage and its attacks on social intolerance. The *Pall Mall Gazette* dismissed the novel as "dirt, drivel and damnation" and one bishop burnt the book in public — "presumably", Hardy observed, "in regret at not being able to burn me." Hardy should not have been entirely surprised at this reception. *The Return of the Native* had provoked accusations of decadence "in the French manner", while *Tess of the D'Urbervilles* only appeared in serial form after the author agreed to make certain changes. Chief among these was a scene in which Angel Clare carries Tess and her friends in his arms across a flooded lane. At the editor's insistence, Tess and her companions were transported by wheelbarrow. The reception of *Jude* was a major factor in Hardy's decision to confine himself to poetry in future. It was Hardy who once remarked: "If Galileo had said in verse that the world moved, the Inquisition might have let him alone."

---

was awarded an OM in 1910 and was buried in Westminster Abbey.

Hargreaves, James (d. 1778). British spinner and inventor. In 1764 he invented a hand-powered machine that could operate eight spindles mechanically. This he named the spinning 'jenny' after his daughter. The invention aroused hostility among other spinners, a group of whom destroyed many of the machines. Hargreaves moved to Nottingham in 1768 where he set up a small but successful spinning mill.

Harold II (c. 1020–66). The last Anglo-Saxon king of England. The son of Earl Godwin, he was recognized as heir to the throne by Edward the Confessor, but had earlier promised to support William of Normandy's claim to the throne. On Edward's death (1066), Harold was immediately crowned and William prepared to invade England. Harold defeated and killed his brother Tostig of Northumberland and Harald Hardrada, King of Norway, who had invaded northern England, at Stamford Bridge. A few days later William landed with his Norman invaders and Harold was killed at the Battle of Hastings, shot in the eye with an arrow.

Harun ar-Rashid (766–809 AD). Caliph of Baghdad. He held military commands against the Byzantine Empire from the age of 14, and succeeded his brother as caliph in 786. His encouragement of trade and industry made Baghdad prosperous, while the brilliant culture of his court is reflected in the tales of *The Thousand and One Nights*.

Harvey, William (1578–1657). English physician. Harvey was educated at Cambridge and Padua, where he was taught by Fabricius and influenced by Galileo. He returned to England after obtaining his degree (1602), set up his practice and became court physician to James I and Charles I. His prime interest, however, was in medical research and he dissected many species of animals. By examining the heart and blood vessels, he concluded that blood circulated around the body, from the heart to the arteries and veins and then back to the heart. He published his results in *On the Motions of the Heart and Blood* (1628). Harvey's ideas were

> ❛ He was the first Englishman of
> whom we know enough to say
> that he was definitely what we
> now mean by a 'scientific
> man'. He viewed the problems
> of life as we view them; he
> observed the facts as we
> observe them; he experimented
> as we experiment and he
> reasoned as we reason.
> Sir Wilmot Herrington on William
> Harvey, *St Bartholomew's
> Hospital Journal* 1928 ❜

ridiculed at first, since they disproved the established views of Galen, but by the end of his life he had achieved the recognition that his work deserved.

Hastings, Warren (1732–1818). First British governor-general of India. Hastings went to India at the age of 17 and quickly rose in importance. In 1772 he became governor of Bengal and two years later he was appointed governor-general of India. Although an able administrator, he aroused some opposition and on his resignation and return to Britain (1785) he was impeached for corruption and cruelty (1788). The trial dragged on for seven years, at the end of which he was acquitted.

Havel, Václav (1936–   ). Czech statesman, playwright, and essayist. Having been prevented from studying drama because of his anti-communist background, Havel began his career as a stagehand. By the mid 1960s he was writing such absurdist plays as *The Garden*

Party (1963) and *The Memorandum* (1965) for Prague's Theatre on the Balustrade. Following the Soviet-led invasion of 1968 his work was banned in Czechoslovakia; such later plays as *Largo Desolato* (1983) and *Temptation* (1985) were, however, well received in the West. For his continuing dissident activities Havel was imprisoned in 1979–83 and again in 1989, becoming the chief figurehead of opposition to the communist regime. After the fall of communism in November 1989, Havel was elected president of Czechoslovakia. Having failed to prevent the break-up of the country he resigned that position in 1992, becoming president of the new Czech Republic the following year. He has continued to publish volumes of political and moral essays, such as *Summer Meditations* (1992).

Hawking, Stephen W(illiam) (1942–). British theoretical phycisist. Since graduating from Oxford University in the mid 1960s he has held a variety of posts at Cambridge, including Lucasian professor of mathematics (from 1979). He has worked mainly in the field of general relativity and the theory of black holes. In 1974 he demonstrated that black holes – celestial bodies that have undergone total gravitational collapse – emit particles. Hawking has for many years suffered from a progressive nervous disease that has confined him to a wheelchair and necessitated the use of a speech synthesizer. His publications include *A Brief History of Time* (1988), which became a worldwide bestseller, and *Black Holes and Baby Universes* (1993).

Haydn, (Franz) Josef (1732–1809). Austrian composer. The son of a poor wheelwright, he became a choirboy at St Stephen's cathedral, Vienna, and later worked as a music teacher and accompanist. In 1766 he became director of music to the Hungarian Prince Esterházy, at whose court he composed some of his 104 symphonies, including the *Farewell* (1772) and the *Paris* set (1786). After the prince's death (1790), Haydn made two visits to London (1791–92; 1794–95), where he wrote the 12 *London* symphonies, including the *Surprise* (1791), and several piano sonatas. After his return to Vienna, Haydn composed masses and oratorios, such as *The Creation* (1798) and *The Seasons* (1801).

A Musical Farewell

Haydn was for many years musical director to Prince Miklós József Esterházy at the family castle of Esterháza. Unfortunately, this castle was situated in a remote part of rural Hungary and the Prince's musicians found long periods of service there, away from their wives and families, very irksome. Haydn's Symphony no. 5, known as the *Farewell*, was composed during one such period. In the last movement of this work, the instruments of the orchestra are silenced one by one until the music dies away completely. At the first performance, each player followed the completion of his part by blowing out his candle and quietly leaving the orchestra. When the last notes ceased, Prince Esterházy was left facing a dark empty stage. Taking the hint, he immediately granted his musicians a holiday.

Hayek, Friedrich (August von) (1899–1992). British economist, born in Austria. After graduating from the University of Vienna in 1921, Hayek carried out economic research for the Austrian government. From the 1930s onwards he held a series of professorships in Britain, the US, and Germany. He became famous outside academic circles with his book *The Road to Serfdom* (1944), which argues passionately for an absolutely free market as the only guarantor of individual liberty. This position was further developed in such publications as *Law, Legislation and Liberty* (1973–79). Hayek's ideas had a major influence on the social and economic policies of the Thatcher and Reagan governments in the 1980s.

Hazlitt, William (1778–1830). British essayist. He gave up his early intention to become a Unitarian minister like his father, and instead studied painting. Later he turned to freelance journalism and criticism; his *Characters of Shakespeare's Plays* was published in 1817. He is remembered for his lectures and essays on authors and literature, which were collected into such volumes as *Table Talk* (1821), and his radical journalism. He spent the last years of his life in poverty and illness.

Heaney, Seamus (1939–   ). Irish poet and critic. The son of farmers in Northern Ireland, he was educated in Belfast and began to publish in the 1960s. While such early collections as *Death of a Naturalist* (1966) explore his rural upbringing and family history, later poems, such as those in *North* (1975), *Field Work* (1979), and *Station Island* (1984) deal with complex themes from Irish history and culture. He became an Irish citizen in 1972. A respected critic, he was appointed professor of poetry at Oxford University in 1989. Recent publications include the bestselling poetry volume *Seeing Things*

(1991) and the essays in *The Redress of Poetry* (1995). Heaney was awarded the Nobel prize in 1995.

Heath, Sir Edward (1916–   ). British Conservative politician; prime minister (1970–74). He served as Lord Privy Seal (1960–63) and president of the Board of Trade (1963–64) before succeeding Sir Alec Douglas-Home as leader of the Conservative party in 1965. As prime minister he successfully negotiated Britain's entry into the European Economic Community (1973). Nevertheless, confrontations with the striking miners and other trade unions led to his defeat in the general elections of 1974. The following year Margaret Thatcher succeeded him as leader of the Conservative party. He was a critic of Thatcher's policies in the 1980s and remains an outspoken advocate of European integration. A keen sailor, Heath captained the yacht *Morning Cloud* to win the Admiral's Cup in 1971.

Hegel, Georg Wilhelm Friedrich (1770–1831). German philosopher. He was professor of philosophy at the universities of Heidelberg (1817–18) and Berlin (1818–31). His famous doctrine of the 'dialectic' – that a statement and its denial (thesis and antithesis) contain a greater amount of truth in combination (synthesis) than when considered separately – was taken over and modified by Marx. Hegel's imprecise thought and defence of authoritarianism have caused his doctrines to be severely criticized by modern philosophers.

Heidegger, Martin (1889–1976). German philosopher, a pioneer of existentialist thought. The son of a sexton, he originally intended to become a Roman Catholic priest. In the 1920s he studied under Edmund Husserl at the University of Freiburg, where he later became professor of philosophy (1928–45). Heidegger's major work *Being and Time* appeared in 1927; in it he explored such concepts as being, nothingness, and human choice in highly abstract terms. Owing to his support for the Nazi regime, he was removed from his post after World War II and spent the rest of his life working in isolation. His writings had a profound effect on such post-war philosophers as Jean-Paul Sartre.

Heine, Heinrich (1797–1856). German Jewish poet. The poems in his *Book of Songs* (1827), some of which were set to music by Schumann, made his reputation. From 1831 Heine lived in Paris, where he wrote mainly prose; the satirical and liberal nature of these writings led to their publication being banned in Germany. *New Poems* (1844) marked his return to poetry. From 1848 he suffered from spinal paralysis and was bedridden. Heine's

Heine's Marriage

In 1841 Heine married his mistress, Eugénie Mirat, an assistant in a Paris shoeshop. This liaison puzzled many of Heine's friends, as Eugénie was vain and silly as well as being totally uneducated. Although the poet sacrificed his social and financial position to marry Eugénie, he was by no means blind to her faults. When he died he left her all his worldly goods on the condition that she remarried. That way, he said, at least one man would regret his death.

marriage to his mistress Eugénie Mirat alienated him from his family, who tried to cut off his annuity and destroyed the bulk of his memoirs after his death.

Heisenberg, Werner Karl (1901–76). German physicist. In 1927 he invented a mathematical system, called matrix mechanics, to explain the structure of the hydrogen atom in terms of Planck's quantum theory. In the same year he announced his uncertainty principle, which has had a profound effect on both physics and philosophy. In 1932 he was awarded a Nobel Prize. Heisenberg was one of the few scientists to remain in Germany during the Nazi period, when he headed Hitler's unsuccessful attempt to make an atom bomb.

Helpmann, Sir Robert (1909–86). Australian ballet dancer, choreographer, and actor. He was the principal male dancer of the Sadler's Wells Ballet (1933–50) and the choreographer of *Miracle in the Gorbals* (1944) and other ballets. One of his greatest roles as a dancer was Dr Coppelius in *Coppelia* (1940). He also acted in a number of Shakespearean roles and appeared in several films, including *The Tales of Hoffmann* (1950) and *The Quiller Memorandum* (1966).

Hemingway, Ernest (1899–1961). US novelist. He became a reporter on leaving school and served with the Red Cross in World War I. The book with which he made his name as a writer, *A Farewell to Arms* (1929), was based on his wartime experiences. Later works reflect his interest in the cultures of Africa, Spain, and Cuba, and his enthusiasm for big-game hunting and bullfighting. *For Whom the Bell Tolls* (1940) is a story of the Spanish Civil War, which Hemingway witnessed as a war correspondent. He was also an accredited correspondent during World War II. He was awarded the Nobel Prize in 1954. Always subject to depression, he committed suicide by shooting himself.

Hendrix, Jimi, full name *James Marshall Hendrix* (1942–70). Black US rock guitarist. A self-taught musician, he was influenced by the blues singers B. B. King and Muddy Waters. He travelled to Britain in 1966 and formed the group the Jimi Hendrix Experience, which played at several pop festivals including Woodstock (1969) and the Isle of Wight (1970). His stage act was spectacular and controversial, while his records, which include 'Hey Joe' (1967), 'Purple Haze' (1967), and the album *Electric Ladyland* (1968), are characterized by his innovative use of the electric guitar. He died as a result of a barbiturate overdose.

Henry II (1133–89). King of England. The grandson of Henry I, he inherited considerable lands in France and enlarged these through his marriage to Eleanor of Aquitaine (1152). Having persuaded King Stephen to make him heir to the English throne, he was crowned in 1154 and at once strengthened and restored royal authority. However, his attempt to confine the limits of Church power brought him into conflict with Thomas Becket, and ended with Becket's murder.

Henry IV, known as *Henry of Navarre* (1553–1610). King of France. He was educated as a Calvinist and after 1569 was recognized as the leader of the Huguenots, the French Calvinists. Although he succeeded to the French throne in 1589, it took a further ten years of religious wars to establish his position. He was converted to Catholicism in 1593 but signed the Edict of Nantes (1598) granting freedom of worship to Protestants. He married Marie de' Medici in 1600, after his first marriage was annulled. He was assassinated by a religious fanatic.

Henry V (1387–1422). King of England. He succeeded his father, Henry IV of England, in 1413. He went to France to claim the French throne and secured a decisive victory over the French at Agincourt (1415). Following his marriage to Catherine of Valois he was recognized as heir to the French throne by her father, Charles VI, but died of dysentery two years later.

Wild Prince Hal

According to legend, Henry V led a wild and riotous life as Prince of Wales before reforming to become an ideal king. Shakespeare added to the legend by presenting 'Hal' as a close companion of the rascally Falstaff. One famous but unreliable tale concerns Hal's arrest for disorderly conduct and his subsequent appearance before Sir William Gascoigne, who sent him to prison. After Henry's coronation he supposedly rewarded the judge by having him appointed chief justice.

In fact, the real Prince Henry was anything but the irresponsible character depicted by Shakespeare and others. Indeed, by the time he became king in 1413, he already had extensive experience of warfare and government: from 1406 he commanded the war in Wales against Owen Glendower and he headed the royal council in 1410 and 1411.

Henry VII (1457–1509). King of England. The sole surviving claimant to the English throne from the house of Lancaster, he fled to Brittany for safety in 1471. He invaded England in 1485 and, having killed Richard III at the Battle of Bosworth, claimed the throne. On his marriage to Elizabeth of York (1486) the houses of Lancaster and York were united and the Tudor dynasty founded. As king he crushed the independence of the nobility, extracting great wealth from them that was later inherited by his son, Henry VIII.

Henry VIII (1491–1547). King of England. He succeeded his father Henry VII in 1509 and the same year married Catherine of Aragon, the widow of his elder brother

> 6 The crimes and cruelties of this Prince were too numerous to be mentioned...and nothing can be said in his vindication, but that his abolishing religious houses and leaving them to the ruinous depredations of time has been of infinite use to the landscape of England in general, which probably was a principal motive for his doing it, since otherwise why should a man who was of no religion himself be at so much trouble to abolish one which had for ages been established in the kingdom?
>
> Jane Austen on Henry VIII,
> *The History of England* 9

Arthur. In the early years of his reign he was handsome, accomplished, and active in foreign affairs. However, his policy was dominated during the 1520s by his anxiety to end his marriage to Catherine, because of his love for Anne Boleyn and his desire for a male heir. Unable to obtain papal consent for an annulment, Henry proclaimed himself Head of the English Church (1534) and began the dissolution of the monasteries. He subsequently married Anne but had her beheaded for alleged adultery just two years later. His third wife, Jane Seymour, died in childbirth (1537), while his marriage to Anne of Cleves (1540) lasted just a few weeks before being annulled. His fifth wife Catherine Howard was also beheaded for adultery (1542); in 1543 Henry married Catherine Parr, who survived him.

Henry the Navigator (1394–1460). Portuguese prince. Although he made no voyages himself, he directed and promoted exploration and colonization of hitherto unexplored lands, including the west coast of Africa, the Azores, and Madeira. He set up an observatory and a school of navigation and financed many of the early voyages himself.

Hepburn, Katharine (1907–   ). US actress. A graduate of Bryn Mawr college, she made her stage debut in 1928 and her first film in 1932. She co-starred with Spencer Tracy in *State of the Union* (1948) and many other films of the 1940s; the partnership was successfully revived in *Guess Who's Coming to Dinner* (1967). Her other major films include *The African Queen* (1951), with Humphrey Bogart, *The Lion in Winter* (1968), in which she played Eleanor of Aquitaine, and *On Golden*

Pond (1981). Hepburn has won a record four Oscars as Best Actress, as well as 13 nominations.

Hereward the Wake (fl. 1070). English chieftain and hero. A Lincolnshire landowner, he led the Anglo-Saxon rebellion against William the Conqueror (1070–71). Although William captured Hereward's stronghold on the Isle of Ely (1071), Hereward managed to escape across the marshes with a handful of companions. His subsequent fate is unknown.

Herod (73–04 BC). King of Judaea under the Romans from 37. Although he had the temple at Jerusalem rebuilt, many Jews resented his introduction of Greek culture into Jerusalem. He was an efficient and able ruler, but is remembered for his tyrannical and bloodthirsty deeds, particularly his alleged decision to kill all the male infants in Bethlehem in his attempt to destroy Jesus Christ.

Herodotus (c. 484–c. 425 BC). Greek historian, often called the 'father of history'. He spent his early life in Halicarnassus but was banished from that city for political reasons and moved to Samos. After a period in Athens he moved to a Greek colony in Italy, where he died. His great work is an account of the wars between Greece and Persia in nine books. Apart from the lively narrative, this contains much interesting material on the geography and customs of the region gathered from Herodotus's own travels. He is regarded as the first historian to research his subject thoroughly and to subject his sources to critical examination.

Hesse, Hermann (1877–1962). German novelist. He was at first destined for the priesthood but was unhappy at his seminary and ran away. After some years working as a bookseller, he turned to freelance writing in 1904. A conscientious objector in World War I, Hesse lived in Switzerland after 1914. His novels, which explore mystical or psychoanalytical themes, include *Steppenwolf* (1927) and *The Glass Bead Game* (1943). He won the Nobel Prize in 1946.

Heyerdahl, Thor (1914–   ). Norwegian anthropologist and ethnologist. In 1947 he sailed from Peru to Polynesia on the balsa-wood raft *Kon-Tiki*, proving that the Pre-Incans could have made this journey. In a similar experiment, the *Ra* expedition (1969–70), he sailed a papyrus reed boat from Morocco to Central America. In 1977–78 Heyerdahl sailed from Iraq to the Horn of Africa, later burning his reed boat *Tigris* in protest at the wars raging in the region. In the late 1980s he led a series of archaeological expeditions to Easter Island.

Hillary and Tenzing

Hillary's dramatic photograph of Tenzing Norgay on the summit of Everest was published in newspapers all round the globe. Why, he was sometimes asked, was there no equivalent picture of himself? Hillary replied by pointing to Tenzing's inexperience with the camera: "As far as I knew, he had never taken a photograph before, and the summit of Everest was hardly the place to show him how." Both men always refused to say which of them stood on the summit first, insisting that the final assault was a true collaborative effort.

Hillary, Sir Edmund (1919–). New Zealand mountaineer and explorer. In 1953 he joined Colonel John Hunt's expedition to Mount Everest and on 29 May, with the Sherpa Tenzing Norgay, he was the first to reach the summit. After an expedition to the South Pole (1958) with Sir Vivian Fuchs, he led expeditions to the Himalayas (1961–64) and up the River Ganges (1977). From 1984 to 1989 he was New Zealand's high commissioner to India, Bangladesh, and Nepal. He was knighted in 1953 (*see box*).

Himmler, Heinrich (1900–45). German Nazi leader, chief of the Gestapo. A former poultry farmer, he was appointed leader of the SS, Hitler's personal bodyguard, in 1929. From 1934 he organized the Gestapo and had control over the police forces of the whole Reich. During World War II, as Hitler's effective second-in-command, he was responsible for organizing the mass murders of Jews in the concentration camps. He was captured by the Allies in 1945 but committed suicide by taking poison from a phial hidden in his mouth.

Hippocrates (c. 460–377 BC). Greek physician, whose name became associated with a number of medical writings (the Hippocratic Collection). The Collection contains works on all aspects of medicine, including directions for treatment to restore the balance of the fluids or four bodily 'humours', the disturbance of which was thought to cause disease. The 'Hippocratic Oath' a code of ethics defining a physician's relationship with his patient, survives to this day.

Hirohito (1901–89). Emperor of Japan. The 124th direct descendant of Jimmu, the legendary first emperor of Japan, he succeeded his father Yoshihito to the throne in 1926. Following the surrender of Japan in World War II he accepted a new constitution, renouncing claims to imperial divinity and accepting more limited powers. The precise nature of his role during the war remains a matter of controversy. He visited Europe in 1971 and in 1974 made a tour of the US. Hirohito, who was also an eminent botanist and zoologist, was succeeded on his death by his son Akihito (1933–).

Hitchcock, Sir Alfred (1899–1980). British film director. He directed many films in Britain, including *The Thirty-Nine Steps* (1935), before going to Hollywood in 1940. Hitchcock is generally acknowledged to be the master of cinematic suspense, as in such thrillers as *Dial M for Murder* (1954), *Psycho* (1960), and *The Birds* (1963). His fleeting appearances in each of his films, in a very minor role or as an extra, have become a trademark. Hitchcock also produced two popular suspense series for television. He was knighted shortly before his death.

Hitler, Adolf (1889–1945). German dictator, whose thirst for power led to World War II and the deaths of some 30 million people. The son of a customs officer, he spent his early years in poverty. After becoming president of the Nazi party in 1921 he made an unsuccessful attempt to overthrow the government at Munich (1923). During his imprisonment for this offence he began writing *Mein Kampf*, which stated his nationalistic beliefs and his hatred of Jews. Made chancellor of

Germany in 1933, Hitler transformed the country into a totalitarian state and took the title of 'Führer' (1934). He began a campaign to restore German power in Europe and started a fanatical persecution of the Jews. Ultimately about 12 million people, roughly half of them Jewish, died in Hitler's concentration and labour camps. In 1937 he annexed Austria and in 1938 overran Czechoslovakia; his invasion of Poland in September 1939 precipitated World War II. A failed assassination attempt, a bomb explosion organized by several high-ranking officers, led to a purge in which thousands were executed (1944). Eventually, knowing that German defeat was inevitable, Hitler retreated to his bunker in Berlin. There he married his mistress Eva Braun on 29 April 1945; the following day they are believed to have committed suicide together. Their bodies were burned.

> 6 I go the way that Providence dictates with the assurance of a sleepwalker.
> Adolf Hitler, speech 26 September 1938 9

Hobbes, Thomas (1588–1679). English philosopher. Hobbes was born in Malmesbury, Wiltshire, and educated at Oxford University. For much of his life he worked as a private tutor, his pupils including the Prince of Wales (later Charles II) in the 1640s. He knew many leading thinkers of the day, including Bacon, Galileo, and Descartes. His principal work *Leviathan* (1651; 1668) applies the principles of scientific materialism to the study of man in society. Hobbes argues that man is inherently selfish and driven by his appetites; because of this, public order needs to be imposed by an absolute ruler. In accordance with these views he supported Cromwell during the Interregnum and the monarchy after the Restoration.

Ho Chi Minh, original name *Nguyen That Thank* (1890–1969). Vietnamese political leader. During his early years he worked as a seaman and as a labourer in France. After studying in Moscow, he founded the Indochinese Communist party in 1930 and led the Viet Minh guerrillas against the Japanese from 1941. The subsequent Indochinese War against the French (1946–54) left him in control of northern Vietnam. Following the partition of the country he became president of North Vietnam in 1954. He continued the guerrilla struggle to unite Vietnam in the 1950s and 1960s. The southern capital of Saigon was renamed Ho Chi Minh City after its fall to communist guerrillas in 1975.

Hockney, David (1937–   ). British artist, photographer, and designer. Hockney was born in Bradford and began to attract attention while still a student at the Royal College of Art (1959–62). During the 1960s his witty drawings and portraits caused him to be associated with the British Pop Art movement. His earlier works include the series of etchings *A Rake's Progress* (1963) and the group portrait *Mr and Mrs Clark and Percy* (1971). Since the mid 1970s he has lived mainly in California. His works from this period include numerous paintings of swimmers and swimming pools and a series of photographic collages. He is also well known for his designs for plays and operas. A major retrospective of his drawings opened in London in 1995.

Hogarth, William (1697–1764). British painter and engraver. After serving his apprenticeship to a silversmith, he began to engrave book illustrations. He then studied painting at St Martin's Lane Academy and became an oil painter. In the 1730s Hogarth began a series of paintings satirizing contemporary society, including *A Harlot's Progress* (1732), *A Rake's Progress* (1735), and *Marriage à la Mode* (1745), from which he also made engravings. The Copyright Act (1735) was passed to prevent imitation of these works, which proved very popular. Hogarth also painted portraits, including the *Shrimp Girl*. His treatise *The Analysis of Beauty* (1753), in which he criticized the art establishment, aroused much controversy.

Hokusai, Katsushika (1760–1849). Japanese painter and engraver. He was taught by Shunshō, a print designer, and is famous for his coloured woodcuts, used extensively in book illustrations. His simplified design is best shown in landscapes such as *The Amusements of the Eastern Capital* (1799) and *The 36 Views of Mount Fuji* (1823–29). His work influenced late 19th-century European painters.

Holbein the Younger, Hans (c. 1497–1543). German painter and designer. After studying in the studio of his father, Hans Holbein the Elder, he moved to Basel, Switzerland (1515), and began painting portraits, such as *Erasmus* (1517). Holbein then settled in England, where he worked for Sir Thomas More (1526–28) before becoming court painter to Henry VIII. His later portraits include *The Ambassadors* (1533) and *Anne of Cleves* (1539/40). Holbein died of the plague in London. Holbein's great skill in portrait painting lay in his technique of drawing the eye away from the garments and surroundings of his subjects and focusing attention on their facial characteristics.

Holliday, Billie (1915–59), stage name of *Eleonora Fagan Holliday*. Black US jazz singer. Born and brought up in poverty, Holliday worked in a brothel until her late teens. After escaping, she sang in Harlem nightclubs and began to make records in the mid 1930s. Her performances are remarkable for their subtle phrasing, which creates effects of great poignancy. International fame arrived in the 1940s and 1950s, when she appeared in films, on television, and in prestigious concerts in the US and Europe. By this time, however, she was addicted to the heroin that eventually killed her. She published an autobiography, *Lady Sings the Blues*, in 1956.

Holst, Gustav (1874–1934). British composer of Swedish descent. Educated at the Royal College of Music, he later taught there and at St Paul's Girls' School and Morley College, London. His knowledge of Sanskrit inspired the chamber opera *Savitri* (1908) and a series of choral hymns. A friend of Vaughan Williams, he was interested in English folk songs and the Tudor composers and wrote much choral music, including *The Hymn of Jesus* and *The Ode to Death*. Holst's best-known compositions are the orchestral suite *The Planets* (1916) and *Egdon Heath* (1927), another orchestral work.

Homer (before 700 BC). The traditional author of the *Iliad* and the *Odyssey*, the earliest works of Greek literature. The *Iliad* tells of the Trojan War while the *Odyssey* recounts the travels of Odysseus – both stories that had been handed down by word of mouth from generation to generation. Homer is said to have been a blind minstrel from the island of Chios.

Hoover, J(ohn) Edgar (1895–1972). US lawyer and administrator, who directed the FBI from 1924 until his death. After taking his master's degree in law (1917), Hoover entered the Department of Justice as an attorney. He became assistant director of the FBI in 1921 and director three years later. In the 1920s and 1930s Hoover fought organized crime by establishing fingerprint files and crime detection laboratories; he also implemented major administrative reforms. Later, the emphasis shifted to the detection of Nazi and then communist spy rings. Although widely regarded as a national hero in his lifetime, Hoover has since been accused of using his immense personal power for political ends. In particular, he is accused of using illegal

> ❝ As an administrator, he was an erratic unchallengeable czar, banishing agents...on whimsy, terrorizing them with torrents of implausible rules, insisting on conformity of thought as well as dress...A shrewd bureaucratic genius who cared less about crime than about perpetuating his crime-busting image. ❞
> *Time* 22 December 1975

methods to subvert the civil rights movement of the 1960s.

Hope, Bob, stage name of *Leslie Townes Hope* (1903–). US film comedian. Born in Britain, he was taken to the US as a child of three. He appeared in many Hollywood films from 1938 onwards and became famous for his rapid-fire wisecracks and deadpan expression. *The Road to Singapore* (1940) began the popular 'Road' series of comedies, in which he starred with Bing Crosby and Dorothy Lamour. He presided at the annual presentation of the Academy Awards for some 40 years.

Hopkins, Sir Anthony (1937–). British film and stage actor. Born in South Wales, Hopkins trained at RADA and made his stage debut in 1960. His first film was *The Lion in Winter* (1968). During the 1970s and 1980s he worked mainly in US television. International stardom came late, with his performance as a serial killer in *The Silence of the Lambs* (1991), a role that earned him an Oscar. He was knighted the following year. His other films include *The Bounty* (1984), *Howard's End* (1992), and *Shadowlands* (1994), in which he played the writer C. S. Lewis.

Hopkins, Gerard Manley (1844–89). British poet. He became a Roman Catholic at Oxford in 1866 and was ordained as a Jesuit priest in 1877. Although he burnt all his early poems when he began to train for the priesthood, he started to write again in 1875. Subsequently he sent his poems to his friend Robert Bridges, who collected them into a posthumous edition, *Poems* (1918). With their unconventional rhythms and diction, such poems as 'The Wreck of the Deutschland' influenced many younger poets in the 1920s and 1930s.

Horace, full name *Quintus Horatius Flaccus* (65–08 BC). Roman poet. Although an ex-slave, his father gave him an upper-class education. Having served in Brutus's army, Horace was deprived of his property after Brutus's defeat at Philippi. His friend Virgil brought his early writings to the notice of Augustus's minister Maecenas, who was greatly impressed by his work. Under his generous patronage Horace wrote his *Satires* (35–30) and *Epistles* (20–13), as well as the Greek-inspired lyric poems *Odes* (23 and 13).

Horowitz, Vladimir (1904–89). Russian pianist. A student at Kiev Conservatory, he performed acclaimed recitals in Leningrad (1924), followed by extensive tours of Europe and the US. In 1933 he married the daughter of the conductor Toscanini and in 1944 became a naturalized US citizen.

Houdini, Harry, original name *Erich Weiss* (1874–1926). US illusionist and escapologist, born in Budapest. He won an international reputation for his daring escapes from handcuffs, straitjackets, locked trunks, ropes, and chains. Many of his performances took place under water or in similarly dangerous circumstances. He also escaped from several prisons, to the dismay of the prison authorities who had challenged him to make the attempt. Having claimed to be invulnerable to blows from the fist, he died as a result of a punch delivered before he had time to tense his muscles to resist the blow.

> ❬ He hurled at the universe a challenge to bind, fetter, or confine him…He triumphed over manacles and prison cells, the wet-sheet packs of insane asylums, webs of fish net, iron boxes bolted shut…His skill and daring finally fused deeply with the unconscious wish of Everyman; to escape from chains and leg irons, gibbets and coffins…by magic.
> William Lindsay Gresham,
> *Houdini* ❭

Howard, John (1726–90). British prison reformer. On his way to Lisbon in 1755 he was captured by the French and imprisoned. This experience led him to campaign for penal reform and an improvement in prison conditions. He was appointed High Sheriff of Bedfordshire (1773) and wrote *State of Prisons in England and Wales, with an Account of some Foreign Prisons* (1777).

Hudson, Henry (d. 1611). English explorer and navigator. On his first two voyages, in 1607 and 1608, Hudson reached Spitzbergen and Novaya Zemlya. In 1609 he attempted to find a north-west passage to China and Japan and reached Canada at the mouth of the Hudson river. On a return voyage in 1610 Hudson explored the vast area of Hudson's Bay, but his crew mutinied and left him and eight others to die in an open boat. Although Hudson's attempts to establish shorter trading routes to the East via America were unsuccessful, he greatly increased European knowledge of the geography of North America and the Arctic.

Hughes, Ted (1930–). British poet and writer. Hughes was born in Yorkshire and educated at Oxford University. There he met the poet Sylvia Plath, whom he married in 1956; she committed suicide seven years later. Hughes made his reputation with the powerful, sometimes savage, poems about the natural world in *The Hawk in the Rain* (1957) and other early volumes. Later collections include *Crow* (1970), *Moortown* (1979), and *Flowers and Insects* (1987). His writings for children have also proved popular. In 1984 he was appointed poet laureate, a position he has used to campaign on environmental issues. His *Collected Poems* appeared in 1995.

Hugo, Victor (1802–85). French Romantic poet, novelist, and dramatist, the son of a Napoleonic general. His earliest publications were poems but he made his name with the Romantic drama *Hernani* (1830). The poems *Autumn Leaves* (1831) and the novel *The Hunchback of Notre Dame* (1831) confirmed his success. Juliette Drouet, the courtesan who was Hugo's mistress for 50 years, appeared in his play *Lucrèce Borgia* (1833). After the 1848 Revolution Hugo was elected deputy for Paris but he fled at the establishment of the Second Empire in 1851. *Les Misérables* (1862), one of his best-known novels, was written in exile in the Channel Islands. He returned to France as a national hero at the fall of the Second Empire in 1870 and received a state funeral in 1885.

Hume, David (1711–76). Scottish philosopher. Having studied law and commerce, he went to France at 23 to write his *Treatise of Human Nature* (1739), an unusually witty book for a philosopher. Hume argued that there can be no knowledge that is not gained by the senses, and therefore no true knowledge of the 'self'. Although Hume's extreme scepticism and atheism debarred him from academic life, he filled several diplomatic and literary posts. He also wrote a well-known *History of England*.

Hussein, Saddam (1937–   ). Iraqi dictator. Born into a landless peasant family, Saddam became involved with the radical Ba'ath party as a young man. In 1959 he was implicated in the attempted murder of the Iraqi prime minister and fled to Egypt. After returning to Iraq in the early 1960s he was imprisoned for a further plot against the state but again escaped. In 1968 he played a leading role in the coup that brought the Ba'athists to power and became effective ruler of Iraq. He assumed absolute power in 1979, when he became president and head of the armed forces. Saddam's rule has been characterized by the violent repression of minorities, such as the Kurds, and the attempt to make Iraq the leading power in the region. This ambition led to a long but inconclusive war with Iran (1980–88). In 1990 he invaded Kuwait and refused to withdraw his armies, thus provoking the Gulf War of 1991, in which US-led multinational forces routed the Iraqi invaders. Despite this humiliating defeat, the collapse of the Iraqi economy, several regional uprisings, and the defection of leading supporters, Saddam has retained his grip on power.

Huxley, Aldous (1894–1963). British novelist and essayist. Almost blind from an eye disease, he made his reputation with such witty satirical novels as *Antic Hay* (1923). *Point Counter Point* (1928) contains a famous portrait of D. H. Lawrence. Huxley's best-known novel, *Brave New World* (1932), portrays a frightening future in which there is total control of human breeding and conditioning. Huxley later explored the use of drugs to achieve mystical experiences. His brother **Sir Julian Huxley** (1887–1975) was a scientist. He researched into ecology, ornithology, and hormones and held many academic posts, including the chair of zoology at King's College, London. His writings on biology made the subject accessible to a wide readership. He was the first director general of UNESCO and also worked on the development of the Regent's Park and Whipsnade zoos. Their grandfather **Thomas Huxley** (1825–95) was also a scientist. In 1846 he made a four-year voyage to the South Seas, where he studied and classified marine life. He published several important papers on his return and in 1854 became a lecturer at the School of Mines in London, an institution which he eventually

> 6 You could always tell by his conversation which volume of the *Encyclopaedia Britannica* he'd been reading. One day it would be Alps, Andes and Apennines, and the next it would he Himalayas and Hippocratic Oath.
> Bertrand Russell on Aldous Huxley 9

transformed into the Royal College of Science. Huxley became a friend of Charles Darwin, whose ideas on evolution he defended publicly to great effect. He was active as a writer, lecturer, and educationalist until his death and received honorary degrees from many countries.

Hypatia (c. 370–415 AD). Neoplatonist philosopher and mathematician. The daughter of the philosopher Theon, she lectured in Alexandria where she gained a reputation for learning, wisdom, and eloquence amongst both pagans and Christians. However, following the appointment of Cyril to the patriarchate of Alexandria in 410, tensions between these communities grew. Resenting her influence on the city prefect, Orestes, church leaders denounced Hypatia and she was seized by a Christian mob and lynched.

I

Ibn Saud, Abdul Aziz (1880–1953). King of Saudi Arabia. A member of an exiled ruling family, he began a conquest of central Arabia in 1902. That year he captured Riyadh and took control of Nejd, the former kingdom of his grandfather. He subsequently defeated his rival in Hejaz and annexed the kingdom (1924). In 1932 he unified his territories under the name of Saudi Arabia. The discovery of oil in the 1930s brought great wealth to the country and by the time of his death he was the most influential figure in the Middle East.

Ibsen, Henrik (1828–1906). Norwegian dramatist. His merchant father was ruined in 1836 and Ibsen left

> ❜ The majority never has right on its side. Never I say! That is one of the lies that a free thinking man is bound to rebel against.
>
> You should never have your best trousers on when you go out to fight for freedom and truth.
>
> Henrik Ibsen, *An Enemy of the People* (1882) ❜

home at 16. After gaining experience in theatrical production in Bergen, he directed the theatre of Christiania (now Oslo) from 1857 until its collapse five years later. In 1864 he moved to Rome, where he wrote the verse dramas *Brand* (1866) and *Peer Gynt* (1867), for which Grieg composed incidental music. *Pillars of Society* (1877) and *A Doll's House* (1879) marked the beginning of a period of social dramas, including *Ghosts* (1881) and *Hedda Gabler* (1890). In 1891 he returned as a celebrity to Norway. A stroke in 1900 rendered him a helpless invalid.

Ingres, Jean Auguste Dominique (1780–1867). French painter. He studied in David's studio in Paris and in 1801 won the Grand Prix de Rome with *The Envoys of Agamemnon*, painted in the neoclassical style. He worked and studied in Rome until 1820 and opened a large studio on his return to Paris. Ingres led the Classical school of painters while Delacroix was the leader of the Romantics. He is noted for his clarity of line, as shown in his portraits of the Rivière family (1805), and for the sensuality of his nude portraits, particularly *Grande Odalisque* (1814) and *The Turkish Bath* (1862).

Ionesco, Eugène (1912–94). French dramatist. Born in Romania, he lived in France from 1938 until his death. His plays, which include *The Bald Primadonna* (1950) and *The Chairs* (1952), are early examples of the Theatre of the Absurd. In *Rhinoceros* (1959), a satirical attack on conformity, all but one of the inhabitants of a town gradually turn into rhinoceroses. Later plays include *Journey Among the Dead* (1982).

Irving, Sir Henry, stage name of *John Henry Brodribb* (1838–1905). British actor and theatre manager. He became associated with the Lyceum Theatre in 1871 and in 1878 became its manager. His productions at the Lyceum, especially those in which he played Shakespearean roles, dominated the London stage until his death. Among his famous performances were his portrayal of Hamlet and his sympathetic interpretation of Shylock in *The Merchant of Venice*. He was the first actor to be knighted (1895) for his services to the theatre.

> ❟ His Hamlet was not Shakespeare's Hamlet, nor his Lear Shakespeare's Lear...he had no power of adapting himself to an author's conceptions: his conceptions were his own and they were all Irving.
>
> George Bernard Shaw, *Pen Portraits and Reviews* ❟

Ivan III, known as *Ivan the Great* (1440–1505). Russian ruler and Grand Prince of Moscow. He succeeded his father in 1462 and considerably extended his Muscovite territory. He finally freed Russia from her Tartar overlords (1480) by stopping payment of the customary tribute to the Golden Horde, the Mongol warriors of Batu Khan. He subsequently claimed the title of 'Ruler of all Russia', and is regarded by some as the first tsar.

Ivan IV, known as *Ivan the Terrible* (1530–84). Tsar of Russia. He became Grand Prince of Moscow in 1533 and was crowned tsar of all Russia in 1547 at the age of 17. As tsar, he followed a policy of expansion and consolidation, conquering Kazan, Astrakhan, and western Siberia. After the death of his first wife he became almost insanely tyrannical and was responsible for several ruthless massacres. These included the killing of his own son (1561). He subsequently married a further five times.

J

Jackson, Michael (1958–   ). US singer and songwriter. The youngest of the Jackson Five, a Black pop group consisting of five (later six) brothers, he sang on most of their hits of the 1970s. In 1979 he released the solo album *Off the Wall*, which became a bestseller. This was followed by the dance album *Thriller* (1983), his most successful record, and *Bad* (1987). Jackson is also well known for his eccentric and reclusive lifestyle. In 1993 his career was plunged into scandal when allegations that he had sexually abused a minor led to a police investigation. The case was withdrawn following payment of a multi-million-dollar settlement to the boy's family. In 1995 Jackson released *History*, a mixture of old hits and new songs.

Jackson, Thomas 'Stonewall' (1824–63). US general. He served in Mexico and taught artillery tactics at the Virginia Military Institute before joining the Confederate army in the American Civil War. He earned his nickname for his solid defence at the Battle of Bull Run (1861) and had further successes against Federal forces in the Shenandoah Valley and at Fredericksburg (1862). Fighting with General Lee at Chancellorsville, near Washington, Jackson was accidentally shot by his own men. He had his left arm amputated, but died ten days later.

James, Henry (1843–1916). US novelist. Born into a literary family in New York, he was a well-known reviewer and short-story writer by the age of 22. From 1876 he lived in Europe and in 1915 he became a British subject. His early novels include *The Portrait of a Lady* (1881). *The Turn of the Screw* (1898) is a supernatural tale of two children possessed by the evil souls of their former servants. James's style became more complex and symbolic in his later works, such as *The Golden Bowl* (1904). His experiments with drama were unsuccessful.

James, Jesse (1847–82). US outlaw. He formed the James gang with his brother Frank and took part in numerous train and bank robberies. A reward was offered for his capture and one of his gang murdered him to claim the reward. After his death he became a romantic hero of the Wild West.

James I (1566–1625). King of Britain and Ireland from 1603 and, as James VI, king of Scotland from 1567. He succeeded to the Scottish throne in infancy on the abdication of his mother, Mary, Queen of Scots. On the death of Elizabeth I (1603) he became the first Stuart king of England. He was generally unpopular with Parliament for his belief in the divine right of kings, his tendency to leave policy-making to his favourites, and his schemes for an alliance with Spain. An accomplished scholar, he wrote a book against smoking called *A Counterblast to Tobacco*. One of the major achievements of his reign was the Authorized Version of the Bible (1611).

4 July 1826

By a strange coincidence, Thomas Jefferson and his predecessor in office, John Adams, both died on the same day. Still more remarkably, this was 4 July 1826 – the 50th anniversary of the Declaration of Independence. It is said that Jefferson, realizing that his life was failing fast, repeatedly asked those around his bed for the date. On hearing that it was indeed the Fourth, he sighed and sank into a deep sleep. Later that afternoon John Adams recovered briefly from a coma to whisper his last words: "Thomas Jefferson lives." Jefferson had, in fact, died a few hours earlier.

Jefferson, Thomas (1743–1826). Third president of the US. As a member of the Virginia delegation at the meeting of the Continental Congress in Philadelphia, he was chief author of the Declaration of Independence (1776). He served as US minister in France (1785–89), secretary of state (1789–93), and vice president (1797–1801), before being elected president in 1801. His most notable achievement in office was the Louisiana Purchase (1803), which secured a vast territory for the US. After his retirement in 1809 he founded the University of Virginia.

Jeffreys, Judge, full title *George, first Baron Jeffreys* (c. 1645–89). Notorious English judge. He became widely known and hated as the merciless judge associated with the state trials of suspected Catholic conspirators against Charles II. During the 'Bloody Assizes' of 1685, following the Duke of Monmouth's unsuccessful rebellion against James II, Judge Jeffreys sentenced 320 people to death and several hundreds to be sold as slaves. Following James's flight overseas in 1688, Jeffreys attempted to escape the country disguised as a sailor but was recognized and arrested at Wapping, London. He died in the Tower of London.

Jenner, Edward (1749–1823). British physician. After obtaining his medical degree in 1792 Jenner started to experiment with possible cures for smallpox. In 1796 he removed some blister fluid from a milkmaid with cowpox (a disease similar to smallpox but much milder) and injected it into a boy. Two months later the boy was injected with smallpox but did not develop the disease. Jenner repeated this experiment in 1798 and published his findings, coining the word vaccination for the practice (from *vaccinia*, the Latin name for cowpox). After 70 of London's most respected surgeons signed a document stating their confidence in the discovery, vaccination spread throughout Britain and Europe. In Britain the number of deaths from smallpox was reduced by two thirds.

Jesus Christ (c. 4 BC–c. 29 AD). The founder of Christianity, one of the major religions of the world. According to biblical tradition he was born of the Virgin Mary in Bethlehem, and was brought up as a Jew. His public ministry began at the age of 30 and lasted only three years. He claimed to be the Son of God who could forgive sins, and authenticated this claim by performing miracles. Humility before God and love of one's neighbour were the essence of his teaching. The Jewish religious leaders feared his power and he was betrayed by one of his disciples, Judas, and brought to trial. Although it could not be proved that he had done anything wrong, he was crucified by the Roman authorities. Three days after his death, his followers claimed that he had risen from the tomb and had appeared physically on several occasions before ascending into heaven. The life and death of Christ have had a profound effect on millions of people throughout history.

Jinnah, Mohammed Ali (1876–1948). Indian Muslim politician. After studying law in England, Jinnah returned to India and entered politics in 1906. From 1934 he was elected annually as president of the Muslim League, in which role he pressed for the creation of an independent state for Indian Muslims. In 1947, when Pakistan came into existence, he was its first head of state.

Joan of Arc, St (1412–31). French heroine. The daughter of a farmer, from the age of 13 she heard voices and saw visions of saints, convincing her that her mission was to free France from the occupying English armies. In 1429 she travelled to Chinon, dressed as a man, to join the Dauphin, later Charles VII, the French heir to the throne. After leading the relief of Orleans, which had been besieged for seven months, she accompanied Charles to his coronation. In 1430 she was captured and tried before an ecclesiastical court on over 70 charges, including witchcraft and heresy. Found guilty, she was handed over to the English and burned at the stake in Rouen market place on 30 May 1431. She was canonized in 1920.

John (1167–1216). King of England, the youngest son of Henry II and Eleanor of Aquitaine. He tried unsuccessfully to seize power in 1193 while his brother, Richard I, was absent on the third Crusade. On Richard's death (1199) he was recognized as king in England but Anjou and Brittany supported the rival claim of his nephew, Arthur. John captured Arthur and is believed to have had him murdered. In 1215 a

> He was the very worst of all our kings...a faithless son, a treacherous brother, an ungrateful master; to his people a hated tyrant. Polluted with every crime that could disgrace a man, false to every obligation that should bind a king, he...yet failed in every design he undertook...In the whole view there is no redeeming trait...
> Bishop William Stubbs, *The Constitutional History of England*
> Unfortunately for his reputation, John was not a great benefactor to monasteries which kept chronicles.
> W. C. Warren, *King John*

number of barons rose in revolt against his tyranny and forced him to seal the Magna Carta, a document confirming their feudal rights.

John XXIII, original name *Angelo Giuseppe Roncalli* (1881–1963). Italian pope. The son of tenant farmers, he was ordained as a priest in 1900. In 1953 he was made a cardinal and appointed archbishop of Venice. When he was elected pope in 1958, Roncalli was 77 years old and few expected his reign to see major changes. However, within a year he had called the Second Vatican Council, the most important meeting of the Church in modern times. During its sessions (1962–65) the Council approved various measures to modernize and democratize the Church. Despite his age, John XXIII travelled widely and became a popular figure amongst non-Catholics as well as Catholics.

John, Elton, original name *Reginald Kenneth Dwight* (1947–   ). British rock singer, songwriter, and pianist. He began working as a pub pianist in 1964, earning £1 a night. In the mid 1960s he began his longstanding collaboration with the lyricist Bernie Taupin. His album *Elton John* (1970) was well received in the US and international success followed with *Don't Shoot Me, I'm Only the Piano Player* and *Goodbye Yellow Brick Road* (both 1973). He became well known for his flamboyant stage appearances and eccentric dress. Later hits include 'Sacrifice' (1990). An enormously wealthy man, he is president of Watford Football Club.

John Paul II, original name *Karol Wojtyla* (1920–   ). Polish pope. Ordained in 1946, he became bishop of Cracow in 1958 and archbishop in 1964. He was created cardinal in 1967. Elected pope in 1978, he took the name John Paul in honour of his immediate predecessor John Paul I, who died after only 33 days in office. The first non-Italian pope since 1522, he has travelled more widely than any of his predecessors. As pontiff he has spoken out on issues of human rights and social justice while opposing political activity by the clergy in Third World countries. He has rejected any relaxation of the Church's traditional teaching on contraception, homosexuality, and the maintenance of a celibate male priesthood.

Johns, Jasper (1930–   ). US painter, sculptor, and graphic artist, whose style anticipated the Pop art movement of the 1950s. After service in the US army, Johns settled in New York in 1952, where he supported himself by creating window displays for department stores. His works of this period, which include the well-known *Flags* series featuring different versions of the Stars and Stripes, are characterized by an impersonal treatment of familiar images. Other subjects treated in the same way include targets and numbers. From the late 1950s he created bronze sculptures that were exact replicas of such household objects as beer cans and electric lightbulbs. Johns has also acted as artistic adviser to the Merce Cunningham dance company.

Johnson, Amy (1903–41). British aviator. In 1930 she became the first woman to fly solo from London to Australia, and was awarded the CBE for her achievement. She also made record flights to Tokyo in 1931 and Cape

Town in 1932. Later that year she married her rival J. A. Mollison (1905–59); the two flew the Atlantic together in 1933, crashing on landing at Bridgeport, Connecticut, after a non-stop flight. The couple were divorced in 1938. In 1939 Amy Johnson became a ferry pilot with the Air Transport Auxiliary; in 1941 her plane disappeared over the Thames estuary and she was presumed dead.

Johnson, Samuel (1709–84). British poet, essayist, and lexicographer. The son of a bookseller, he made his reputation by the poem *London* (1738) and the magazine *The Rambler*, which he wrote single-handed from 1750 to 1752. His highly influential *Dictionary of the English Language* (1755) took eight years to write. In 1763 he met James Boswell, his biographer; many of his finest thoughts and sayings are to be found in Boswell's *Life of Samuel Johnson* (1791). Johnson edited

Samuel and Tetty

In 1735 Samuel Johnson married Elizabeth Porter (d. 1752), a widow considerably older than himself. The marriage appears to have been very happy until her later years, when 'Tetty' insisted on sleeping alone because of her failing health. This circumstance caused Johnson considerable vexation, underlying his assertion that "marriage has many pains but celibacy has no pleasures." Johnson is well-known for his refusal to come backstage at Garrick's theatre because "the silk stockings and white bosoms of your actresses excite my amorous propensities". When Tetty died, Johnson took off her wedding ring and wore it himself for the rest of his life.

all of Shakespeare's plays and the works of 52 English poets. The prefaces were issued separately as *Lives of the Poets* (1781). During his last years he was a semi-invalid, holding court for writers and conversationalists at his Fleet Street home. He is buried in Westminster Abbey.

John the Apostle, St (fl. 1st century AD). One of the 12 Apostles of Jesus Christ. He and his brother James, sons of a fisherman, were among Christ's first disciples and John became an authoritative figure in the early church. According to legend he was martyred and buried at Ephesus. Tradition identifies him as the author of three New Testament epistles, the fourth gospel, and the Book of Revelations.

John the Baptist, St (fl. 1st century AD). Jewish prophet. He spent some years in a monastic community in the desert before becoming known as a prophet, preaching the imminence of the Final Judgment. According to the New Testament he was a relative of Jesus Christ. His baptism of Christ marked the beginning of Jesus's ministry. Soon afterwards, John was arrested by Herod Antipas and beheaded at the request of Salome, Herod's stepdaughter. The early Christian Church took up his rite of baptism as a sacrament.

Jones, Inigo (1573–1652). English architect and stage designer. He visited Italy and was greatly influenced by Palladio's classical style of architecture. In 1605 he began to design scenery and costumes for court masques and later introduced the proscenium arch and movable scenery to England. As Surveyor to the

Crown (1615–42) he designed his best-known buildings, The Queen's House, Greenwich (1616–35) and the Banqueting Hall, Whitehall (1619–22). His other works include the portico of St Paul's Cathedral and the Piazza at Covent Garden.

Jonson, Ben (1572–1637). English dramatist and poet. As a youth he was apprenticed to a bricklayer but ran away to Flanders as a soldier. About 1595 he joined a London theatre company, first acting and then writing. In 1598 he killed an actor in a duel and narrowly escaped hanging. *Every Man in His Humour* (1598) was performed at the Globe with Shakespeare in the cast. *Volpone* (1606) and *The Alchemist* (1610) were also very successful. Jonson was popular at the court of James I, who engaged him to write masques, but was less favoured when Charles I became king in 1625. His later plays were unsuccessful. He is buried in Westminster Abbey.

Joplin, Scott (1868–1917). Black US ragtime composer and pianist. As a teenager he studied harmony and travelled round the Southern states playing in bars and brothels. Influenced by Black folk melodies, he played in the syncopated style called ragtime. Success came with the publication of 'Maple Leaf Rag' (1899) and 'The Entertainer' (1902). Joplin then moved to New York where he composed 'Fig Leaf Rag' (1908) and the ragtime opera *Treemonisha*, first performed in Harlem in 1915. He died in poverty in an asylum. In the 1970s his music enjoyed a popular revival, due partly to the use of 'The Entertainer' as the theme music for the film *The Sting* (1973).

Jordan, Michael (1963–   ). US basketball player, usually considered the greatest in the history of his sport. A Black, Jordan was born in Brooklyn, New York. Although he preferred baseball as a child, his height when full grown (1.98 m; 6ft 6in) helped him to excel at basketball during his college years. In 1984 he won a gold medal as part of the US Olympic team. He was subsequently recruited by the Chicago Bulls and remained with the team for the rest of his career. During his nine professional seasons he set numerous scoring records and became known as 'Air Jordan' for his remarkable leaping ability. In 1992 and 1993 he earned more money than any other US athlete, mainly through endorsements. He retired at the age of 30, while still at the peak of his abilities.

Joseph II (1741–90). Holy Roman Emperor. He succeeded his father Francis I in 1765, but gained real power only after the death of his mother, Maria Theresa, in 1780. He introduced many reforms in an unsuccessful bid to modernize the Austrian Habsburg lands. For his efforts he is considered to be one of the 18th century's 'enlightened despots'.

Joséphine (1763–1814). French empress, born *Marie Josèphe-Rose Tascher de la Pagerie* in Martinique. Widow of the vicomte de Beauharnais, she married Napoleon Bonaparte in 1796 and became empress in 1804. She had two children from her first marriage but was unable to give Napoleon a son. The marriage was annulled in 1810 and she retired to Malmaison near Paris.

Joyce, James (1882–1941). Irish novelist. After a Jesuit education he left Ireland in 1904 and never returned there to live. He travelled with Nora Barnacle but did not marry her until 1931. They lived at various times in Trieste, Zürich, and Paris. After writing *Dubliners* (1914), a collection of short stories, Joyce turned to the novel with the autobiographical *A Portrait of the Artist as a Young Man* (1916). His best-known work, *Ulysses*

> ❢ A dogged attempt to cover the universe with mud...a simplification of the human character in the interests of Hell.
> E. M. Forster on Joyce's *Ulysses*

> An anarchical production infamous in taste, in style, in everything.
> Edmund Gosse on *Ulysses*

> Nothing but old fags and cabbage stumps of quotations from the Bible and the rest, stewed in the juice of deliberate, journalistic dirty-mindedness.
> D. H. Lawrence on *Ulysses*

> The work of a queasy undergraduate scratching his pimples.
> Virginia Woolf on *Ulysses* ❢

(1922), took seven years to write and chronicles just 24 hours in the life of its hero. It was banned for obscenity for some years in Britain and the US but was published in Paris. In the novel Joyce used the 'stream of consciousness' technique to express the flow of thoughts and feelings of his central characters. In *Finnegans Wake* (1939), extracts of which were published from time to time in periodicals, Joyce used even more radical techniques. In later years he was nearly blind, despite many eye operations.

Jung, Carl (1875–1961). Swiss psychologist. Having initially collaborated with Freud, Jung soon developed his own ideas, disagreeing with Freud's emphasis on the sexual origins of mental disorders. He proposed and examined the difference between two personality types, 'extroverts' and 'introverts', and argued for the existence of a 'collective unconscious' consisting of symbols and ideas held by all people. His important writings include *Psychology of the Unconscious* (1912) and *Psychological Types* (1921).

Justinian, full name *Flavius Petrus Sabbatius Justinianus* (483–565 AD). Byzantine emperor from 527, whose codification of Roman law has influenced all subsequent legal systems. His building achievements included the church of Hagia Sophia at Constantinople, a masterpiece of Byzantine architecture. Justinian's foreign policy was less successful, his wars against Persia proving indecisive. His wife was the empress Theodora, a former actress.

K

Kafka, Franz (1883–1924). Austrian-Jewish novelist and short-story writer. A native of Prague, he worked as an insurance clerk while writing in his spare time. His novels, which reflect the torment and conflict of his personal life, include *Metamorphosis* (written 1915) and *The Trial* (written 1914). In 1917 he suffered a haemorrhage, marking the onset of the tuberculosis from which he died. His will asked that his works, so far unpublished, should be burnt after his death. However, his literary executor, the poet Max Brod, ignored Kafka's instructions and published them.

Kant, Immanuel (1724–1804). German philosopher. As a young man poverty prevented him from following an academic career; he worked as a private tutor for nine years before taking his degree in 1755. For the next 15 years he lectured on physics, gradually widening his field to take in logic, ethics, and metaphysics. He criticized the philosophy of Leibniz, which prevailed in German universities at that time. In 1770 he became professor of logic and metaphysics at Königsberg. International fame followed with a series of major works, including *Critique of Pure Reason* (1781; revised 1787).

Karpov, Anatoly (1951–). Russian chess player. He gained the world championship in 1975 when Bobby Fischer refused to agree to the conditions for the match. Karpov successfully defended the title against Viktor Korchnoi in 1978 and 1981. Their much-publicized matches were seen by some as a contest between East and West, Karpov being a resident of the Soviet Union and Korchnoi a defector. Karpov was defeated by Gary Kasparov in 1985, 1986, 1987, and 1990 but regained his title in 1993 (when Kasparov did not compete). He was a member of the Soviet parliament in 1989–91.

Kasparov, Gary, original name *Garri Weinstein* (1963–). Azerbaidzhani chess player, often considered the greatest master of modern times. Of Armenian-Jewish descent, he learned chess at the age of six and was an international grandmaster at 17. In 1984 he challenged Anatoly Karpov for the world title but the match was discontinued after 48 games without a result; he defeated Karpov in a rematch the following year, becoming the youngest ever world champion. Kasparov successfully defended his title against Karpov in 1986, 1987, and 1990. In 1993 Kasparov left FIDE, the official chess organization, and set up a rival body, the Professional Chess Association, with the British player Nigel Short. He has subsequently played a number of exhibition matches against computers.

Kaunda, Kenneth (1924–). Zambian politician; president (1964–91). He began his career as a teacher and entered politics in 1950. He formed his own political party, the Zambia African National Congress, in 1958 but it was declared illegal and he was imprisoned by the British. After his release (1960) he became leader of the United National Independence Party, which he led to electoral victory in 1964. Later that year he was confirmed as the first president of the independent republic of Zambia. As president Kaunda nationalized much of the economy and attempted to deal with the problem of tribal conflict; Zambia became a one-party state in 1972. In 1991 he was defeated in free elections. He retired the following year but returned to lead Zambia's main opposition party in 1995.

Keaton, Buster, stage name of *Joseph Francis Keaton* (1895–1966). US film comedian. The son of vaudeville entertainers, he began making silent films with 'Fattie' Arbuckle in the Keystone Kop series in 1917. One of the greatest comedians of the silent screen, he was outstanding for his stunts and famous for a face that remained deadpan in the most hair-raising of circumstances. His films include *The General* (1926) and *Steamboat Bill Junior* (1927).

Keats, John (1795–1821). British poet. His parents died before he was 15 and his guardians apprenticed him to a surgeon. He gave up surgery in 1817 to write poetry, but his first volume, *Poems* (1817), had little success. In the same year he met Fanny Brawne, and they soon became engaged but never married. Almost all his great poems, including the odes 'To a Nightingale', 'On a Grecian Urn', and 'To Melancholy', the narrative poem 'La Belle Dame Sans Merci', and 'Hyperion', were written within the year 1819–20. When he began to show symptoms of tuberculosis, of which his brother had

A Death Warrant

During 1818 Keats suffered a series of severe sore throats. With his early training as a doctor he was under no illusion as to the nature of his illness. His friend Charles Armitage Brown recorded the moment that Keats realized that he had definitely contracted tuberculosis (he had nursed his brother Tom until he died of the same disease in 1818): "On entering the cold sheets, before his head was on the pillow, he slightly coughed, and I heard him say, 'That is blood from my mouth.' I went towards him; he was examining a single drop of blood upon the sheet. 'Bring me the candle, Brown, and let me see this blood.' After regarding it steadfastly, he looked up in my face, with a calmness of countenance that I can never forget, and said, 'I know the colour of that blood; it is arterial blood; I cannot be deceived in that colour; that drop of blood is my death-warrant — I must die.'"

died, he sailed for Italy for his health (September 1820) but died shortly afterwards. He is buried in Rome.

Keller, Helen (1880–1968). US social worker. Although left blind and deaf by an illness at the age of 19 months, she learned to read, write, and speak with the help of her mentor, Anne Sullivan. She graduated from Radcliffe College, Cambridge, Massachusetts, in 1904. A determined and courageous woman, she travelled all over the world, giving lectures and campaigning for improvement in the teaching of the physically handicapped.

Kelvin, William Thomson, 1st Baron (1824–1907). Scottish scientist. Kelvin was professor of natural philosophy at

Glasgow University from 1846 to 1899. He undertook research into electricity, magnetism, heat, and elasticity, earning a knighthood (1866) for his work on the transmission of electric current in telegraph cables. His work in thermodynamics enabled him to define the absolute scale of temperature and the units of the scale were named after him. He was elevated to the peerage in 1892.

Kennedy, John Fitzgerald (1917–63). US statesman; 35th president of the US. A son of the millionaire Joseph P. Kennedy, he won distinction in the navy during World War II and entered politics as the Democratic representative for Massachusetts. In 1953 he married Jacqueline Lee Bouvier (1929–94), who married the Greek shipping millionaire Aristotle Onassis after Kennedy's death. Despite his youth, Kennedy ran for president in 1960 and beat Richard Nixon by a very narrow margin to become the first Catholic president. His successful demand for the withdrawal of Soviet missiles from Cuba (1962), and the signing of the Nuclear Test-Ban Treaty (1963) between the Soviet Union, Britain, and the US, are often considered the greatest achievements of his short term of office. On 22 November 1963, Kennedy was assassinated while driving through Dallas in an open car. He was being filmed for television at the time, and the event caused widespread shock throughout the world. His younger brothers **Robert** (1925–68) and **Edward** (1932–) have also been involved in US politics. Robert, who served as attorney general during the Kennedy administration, was assassinated in 1968 while campaigning for the presidential nomination. Edward has been a prominent liberal senator since 1962.

> ❝ In some ways John Fitzgerald Kennedy died just in time. He died in time to be remembered as he would like to be remembered, as ever-young, still victorious, struck down undefeated... The Kennedy Administration was approaching an impasse, certainly at home, quite possibly abroad, from which there seemed no escape.
>
> I. F. Stone, 'We All Had A Finger On That Trigger' ❞

Kenyatta, Jomo (c. 1891–1978). Kenyan statesman; president (1964–78). Born *Kamau Ngengi*, a member of the Kikuyu tribe, he was educated at a Scottish mission and later studied in London. In 1947 he became president of the Kenya African National Union, which campaigned for independence. He was subsequently accused of managing the Mau Mau terrorist uprising and was imprisoned by the British (1953–59). In 1963 he became prime minister of Kenya and on the country's independence (1964) was elected president, a position he held until his death.

Kepler, Johannes (1571–1630). German mathematician and astronomer. He became lecturer in astronomy at the University of Grätz in 1594 and two years later he joined Tycho Brahe at Prague. Kepler succeeded Brahe as imperial mathematician and deduced his three laws of planetary motion from Brahe's observations. Newton later proved Kepler's laws mathematically and used them as a basis for his laws of universal gravitation. Kepler also made important advances in the understanding of optics.

Keynes, John Maynard (1883–1946). British economist. He was a director of the Bank of England from 1941 and became governor of the International Monetary Fund shortly before his death. Among his influential writings are *The Economic Consequences of the Peace* (1919) and *The General Theory of Employment, Interest and Money* (1935); in the latter he put forward his revolutionary view that high levels of unemployment should be alleviated by increased government spending. 'Keynesianism' dominated economic policy in Britain from 1945 until the late 1970s.

Khomeini, Ayatollah, title of *Ruhollah Hendi* (1900–89). Iranian religious leader, who became the effective ruler of his country after the Islamic Revolution of 1979. Khomeini taught for many years at the theological school in Qom, writing numerous works on Islamic law. In 1964 he was forced to leave the country after criticizing the Westernizing regime of the shah. Working from France, he helped to orchestrate the Islamic Revolution that overthrew the shah in January 1979. On his return to Iran he was greeted as a saviour and became the most powerful figure in the new Islamic state. Khomeini outraged Western opinion with his support for the seizure of the US embassy (1979). He also presided over mass executions of dissidents in the 1980s and a long and futile war with Iraq (1980–88). International criticism was further aroused by his offer of a large reward to anyone who would kill the British author Salman Rushdie (1989). Since Khomeini's death, Iran's leaders have made cautious attempts to mend relations with the West.

Khruschev, Nikita Sergeyevich (1894–1971). Russian statesman. Born into a Ukrainian peasant family, he joined the Communist party in 1918. He became a member of the Politburo (the party's policy-making committee) in 1939 and was made first secretary of the party following Stalin's death in 1953. Over the next few years he followed a policy of 'destalinization', launching an attack on the reputation of the dead leader and releasing many of his victims. In 1958 he became premier. Although he maintained peaceful relations with the West he caused a serious rift with China leading to his enforced resignation in 1964.

Kierkegaard, Søren (1813–55). Danish religious philosopher. He studied theology and philosophy at Copenhagen and then spent several years in Berlin, where he wrote *Either/Or* (1843). Like most of his works, it was published under a pseudonym. Kierkegaard believed that the proof of God's existence could be found in man's personal relationship with Him, rather than in the Bible. Volumes such as *The Concept of Dread* (1844) have been regarded as the basis of modern existentialist philosophy.

King, Billie Jean (1943–   ). US tennis player, winner of a record 20 Wimbledon titles, including six in the singles. She also won the Australian (1968), French (1972) and US (1967; 1971–72; 1974) singles championships.

King, Martin Luther (1929–68). US Baptist minister and leader of the Black civil-rights movement. He took a PhD in theology before becoming a pastor in Montgomery, Alabama, in 1955. The civil-rights movement, which campaigned to end segregation, spread rapidly throughout the South and King, recognized as its leader, was twice imprisoned. In 1963 he organized a peaceful march on Washington, where his famous speech beginning 'I have a dream' was delivered to 200,000 people. Following the Civil Rights Act of 1964, which helped to end discrimination against Blacks, King was awarded the Nobel Peace Prize. From 1965 King took up the cause of poor whites and opposed US involvement in Vietnam. He was assassinated on a motel balcony in Memphis, Tennessee, by James Earl Ray, a white Southerner.

> ❛ I just want to do God's will. And he's allowed me to go up to the mountain. And I've looked over, and I've seen the promised land…So I'm happy tonight. I'm not worried about anything. I'm not fearing any man.
> Martin Luther King.
> In a speech 3 April 1968.
> He was assassinated the following day. ❜

Kingsley, Charles (1819–75). British novelist and poet. At Cambridge he joined the Christian Socialist movement, for whom he wrote essays and pamphlets; his early novels were also concerned with social problems of the period. His better-known novels include *Westward Ho!* (1855), set in Elizabethan times, and his classic children's story *The Water Babies* (1863), which attacks the exploitation of child labour. He was professor of modern history at Cambridge (1860–69) but resigned to become canon of Chester and, later, of Westminster.

Kipling, Rudyard (1865–1936). British poet and writer, author of *The Jungle Books* (1894–95) and *Just So Stories* (1902) for children and numerous short stories. Kipling was born in Bombay but brought up in England; a number of his works are set in India. He returned to India as a journalist but made his name in Britain with *Barrack-Room Ballads* (1892). His poetry, much of it written in soldiers' cockney dialect, won great popularity. However, on the death of Tennyson, Kipling refused the post of Poet Laureate. He was awarded the Nobel Prize in 1907. His other works include the novel *Kim* (1901).

Kissinger, Henry (1923–   ). US politician, born in Germany of Jewish parents. He emigrated to the US with his family in 1938 to escape the Nazi persecution of the Jews. He served in several advisory positions from 1955 to 1968, when Richard Nixon appointed him presidential assistant for national security affairs. Kissinger subsequently played a major role in negotiations to achieve peace in Vietnam, earning him a share in the

1973 Nobel Peace Prize. He served as secretary of state (1973–76) and in 1979 published his memoirs.

Kitchener, Horatio Herbert, Earl (1850–1916). British field marshal. His victory over the Mahdi at Omdurman (1898) ended the war in the Sudan. He also played a decisive role in the Boer War (1899–1902), with his anti-guerrilla tactics. In 1914 he was made secretary for war and used his popularity to raise the vast army that fought in World War I. He was drowned when the cruiser on which he was travelling sank near the Orkneys.

The *Hampshire* disaster

Despite his reputation as a national hero, Kitchener failed to impress his cabinet colleagues during his period as secretary for war. Lloyd George compared him to "one of those revolving lighthouses which radiate momentary gleams of revealing light…and then relapse into complete darkness". Other ministers were privately appalled by Kitchener's stubbornness and indecision, but accepted that it would be politically impossible to remove him. Eventually fate took a hand. On 5 June 1916 HMS *Hampshire*, with Kitchener on board, hit a German mine shortly after leaving Scapa Flow. On hearing the news of Kitchener's death, the press baron Northcliffe is said to have remarked excitedly "So Providence is on the side of the British Empire after all!"

Kohl, Helmut (1930–). German statesman; chancellor of West Germany (1982–90) and of Germany (1990–). The son of a conservative Roman Catholic family, Kohl joined the Christian Democratic Union as a teenager.

After taking a doctorate in political science (1958), he worked in regional politics for many years. He became chairman of the CDU in 1973 and stood unsuccessfully for the chancellorship three years later. On the fall of Helmut Schmidt's coalition in 1982 Kohl became chancellor; he retained the post after elections in 1983 and 1987. In office he has pursued free-market economic policies and shown a strong commitment to greater European integration. Following the reunion of Germany and his election as chancellor of the united country in 1990, he became one of the most powerful statesmen in the Western world.

Kruger, Paul (1825–1904). Boer statesman. Of Dutch descent, he went with his parents and other families on the 'great trek' from Cape Colony to settle north of the Orange River. A member of the Dutch Reformed Church of the Transvaal, he considered himself to be under special guidance and protection. Kruger served as president of the Transvaal four times (1883–98). During his last term of office his denial of civil rights to the Uitlanders (white immigrants to the Transvaal) and his opposition to British imperial interests led to the Boer War (1899–1902). He fled to Europe in 1899 and died in Switzerland.

Kublai Khan (1215–94). Mongol emperor of China, grandson of Genghis Khan. He succeeded his brother Mangu in 1259 and by 1279 had conquered the whole of China, ending the Sung dynasty. His attempts to extend his rule with invasions of Java and Japan were unsuccessful. He was also a patron of literature and established Buddhism as the state religion.

Kubrick, Stanley (1928–   ). US film director and scriptwriter. He worked as a magazine photographer and made documentary films before writing and directing *Paths of Glory* (1958), a distinguished film about World War I. His other films include *Lolita* (1962), *Dr Strangelove* (1964), the science-fiction epic *2001: A Space Odyssey* (1968), *The Shining* (1980), and *Full-Metal Jacket* (1987). *A Clockwork Orange* (1971) aroused some controversy, as it was feared that impressionable people might be led to imitate the scenes of horrific violence in the film. On the director's wishes, the film was withdrawn in Britain.

Kundera, Milan (1929–   ). Czech novelist and writer. From the late 1950s Kundera taught literature at the Prague Academy of Music and Dramatic Arts, while also publishing poetry and drama. The short stories in *Laughable Loves* (1963; 1965) and his first novel, *The Joke* (1967), were remarkable at the time for their irreverent style and sexual frankness. Following the crushing of Czech liberalism by the Soviet-led invasion of 1968, Kundera's books were banned and he lost his teaching posts. He emigrated to France in 1975, becoming a French citizen six years later. His other novels, most of which are mordant sex comedies that explore the private conduct of the Czechs under totalitarianism, include *Life is Elsewhere* (1975), *The Unbearable Lightness of Being* (1984), and *Immortality* (1991). These books have enjoyed a wide readership in the West.

Kurosawa, Akira (1910–   ). Japanese film director, whose work fuses Western and Eastern traditions. After some years working as an editor and screenwriter,

Kurosawa made his debut as a director with *Judo Saga* (1943). Although he made several accomplished films in the 1940s, it was *Rashomon* (1950), a complex tale set in medieval Japan, that established his international reputation. The film took first prize at the Venice Film Festival and became the first Japanese movie to achieve success in the West. His other films of the 1950s included *Ikiru* (1952), *The Seven Samurai* (1954), and *Throne of Blood* (1957), a Noh-style reworking of Shakespeare's *Macbeth*. The success of the adventures *Derzu Uzala* (1975) and *Kagemusha* (1980) enabled Kurosawa to raise the finance for *Ran* (1985), an epic reworking of the *King Lear* story that is usually considered his masterpiece. Subsequent films include *Dreams* (1990) and *Not Yet* (1993).

L

La Fontaine, Jean de (1621–95). French poet and writer of fables. He was employed for a time as master of waters and forests in Château-Thierry but from 1656 he lived in Paris, supported by a series of noble patrons. He is best known for his *Tales* (1664–74) and his *Fables* (1668–94), which are based on those attributed to Aesop.

Lamarck, Jean Baptiste de Monet, Chevalier de (1744–1829). French naturalist. Born into a family of impoverished aristocrats, Lamarck began his career as a soldier, serving in the Seven Years War. He resigned because of illness and went on to study medicine and natural history, becoming professor of invertebrate zoology at the Museum of Natural History, Paris, in 1793. In his *Zoological Philosophy* (1809) Lamarck put forward his theory of evolution by the inheritance of acquired characteristics. He maintained that a primitive antelope, for instance, by constantly stretching to feed on the leaves of trees, would gradually develop a longer neck and legs. These longer parts would be inherited by its offspring, and in the course of time these antelopes would develop into giraffes. Although Lamarck was the first biologist to propose a theory to explain how species change and develop, his theory was not accepted during his lifetime and he died blind and penniless. Though attempts have been made to revive it, Lamarckism has been generally rejected in favour of Charles Darwin's theory of evolution by natural selection. Lamarck also compiled the seven-volume *Natural History of Invertebrates* (1815–22).

Lamb, Charles (1775–1834). British essayist. After his education at Christ's Hospital, where he became a friend of S. T. Coleridge, Lamb worked as a clerk from 1792 until his retirement in 1825. In 1796 his sister Mary killed their mother and was declared insane. Apart from occasional periods spent in asylums, she

The Eccentric Elia

In his *Essays of Elia*, published between 1820 and 1823 in the *London Magazine*, Charles Lamb portrayed himself as a quaint eccentric with strong prejudices on many subjects. He adopted the pseudonym Elia, the name of an Italian clerk at the South Sea House in London, in order to avoid embarrassing his brother John, who worked for the same company. Lamb's many eccentricities included an immoderate addiction to gin, tobacco, and bad jokes (he once prayed that his last breath might be "drawn through a pipe and exhaled in a pun"). Not all his contemporaries found these habits endearing. The stern Thomas Carlyle, recalling the shadow of madness that hung over the Lamb family, wrote censoriously: "Charles Lamb I sincerely believe to be in some considerable degree insane. A more pitiful, ricketty, gasping, staggering, stammering Tom-fool I do not know... Besides, he is now a confirmed, shameless drunkard; *asks* vehemently for gin and water in strangers' houses...Poor Lamb! Poor England, when such a despicable abortion is named genius!"

lived with Lamb for the rest of his life and they adopted a daughter in 1823. Lamb worked with his sister on *Tales from Shakespeare* (1807), a retelling of the stories of Shakespeare's plays. He is best known for his *Essays* (1823), written under the pen-name *Elia*. His other publications included a selection of poetry by contemporaries of Shakespeare that did much to revive interest in Elizabethan literature.

Lang, Fritz (1890–1976). German film director, a pioneer of expressionism in the cinema. Among the outstanding films he made in Germany are *Metropolis* (1926), a terrifying picture of a futuristic slave state, and *M* (1931), the portrait of a child-murderer (played by Peter Lorre). Having attacked the Nazis in *The Testament of Dr Mabuse* (1932), he fled Germany after Hitler came to power. He worked in Hollywood from 1936 until 1958 and directed numerous films, mainly thrillers, including *Western Union* (1941), *The Ministry of Fear* (1944), and *The Big Heat* (1953).

Lao-tzu (fl. 6th century BC). Chinese philosopher, said to be the founder of Taoism and the author of the Taoist scripture *Tao-Te Ching*. Although there are legendary accounts of his life dating from the 2nd century AD, there is no historical evidence of his existence. One of these accounts alleges that Lao-tzu disappeared on a trip to the West.

Lara, Brian (1969–). West Indian cricketer. A left-handed batsman, Lara made an immediate impact on Test cricket on his debut in 1991 with his carefree fast-scoring style. In 1994 he achieved the highest-ever Test score with 375 against England, following this a few weeks later with 501 not out for Warwickshire against Durham, the highest-ever first-class score.

Larkin, Philip (1922–85). British poet and writer. Born in Coventry, he studied English literature at Oxford University, where he met his friend Kingsley Amis. He was librarian of Hull University from 1955 until his death. Larkin's first collection of poems, *The North Ship* (1945), shows the influence of Yeats. His later work is quite different, being characterized by an ironic colloquial style and a tone of wry pessimism. The collections *The Less Deceived* (1955), *The Whitsun Weddings* (1964), and *High Windows* (1974) established Larkin as the leading English poet of his generation. He also published two novels and a volume of essays on jazz. His *Collected Poems* appeared in 1988 and his *Selected Letters* in 1992.

La Rochefoucauld, François, Duc de (1613–80). French writer. He spent some 25 years in politics and war, participating in the Fronde uprising of 1648. His major work, *Maxims* (1665), consists of a collection of terse reflections on life and on moral issues; it was later revised to contain over 500 maxims. La Rochefoucauld died of the cumulative effects of gout.

Laurel, Stan (1890–1965) and **Hardy, Oliver** (1892–1957). US actors, partners in some of the best-known film comedies ever made. Laurel, the thin member of the pair, was born *Arthur Stanley Jefferson* in Britain. He went to the US and formed a partnership with his fat and domineering counterpart, Hardy, in 1926. They made more than 50 short comedies and many feature-length films. Their humour depended on skilfully contrived visual jokes, slapstick, and their own contrasting mannerisms and personalities. Their films include *Leave 'Em Laughing* (1928), *The Music Box* (1932), *Pack Up Your Troubles* (1932), and *Babes in Toyland* (1934).

Laver, Rod (1938–). Australian tennis player. He won the Wimbledon men's singles four times and became the only player to win the Grand Slam (the Australian, US, French, and Wimbledon championships) twice, in 1962 and 1969. Between these dates he was barred from Wimbledon for his professional status.

Lavoisier, Antoine Laurent (1743–94). French chemist. He investigated the phenomenon of burning and showed that it did not involve the release of phlogiston, a hypothetical substance, but that during combustion a part of common air, which he named oxygen, was consumed. His discovery of the composition of water, though not original, was the start of quantitative chemical analysis. A farmer-general of taxes, he was guillotined as an enemy of the people during the Revolution.

Lawrence, D(avid) H(erbert) (1885–1930). British novelist, poet, and dramatist. The son of a coal-miner, Lawrence was born and educated in Nottinghamshire, the setting of many of his works. He taught for a time but devoted himself to literature after the publication of his first novel, *The White Peacock* (1911). In 1912 he eloped to Germany with Frieda Weekley, whom he married after her divorce in 1914. They returned to Britain before the outbreak of World War I. The semi-autobiographical *Sons and Lovers* (1913) brought him considerable success. Frieda Lawrence's German nationality made the couple unpopular during World War I, and they were closely watched by police. Lawrence's novels describe human relationships and sexual desires with a frankness that led to *The Rainbow* (1915) being judged obscene. The whole edition was confiscated. There was a similar reaction to his subsequent novels; *Women in Love* (1921) had to be privately printed in New York, while *Lady Chatterley's Lover* (1928) was banned for many years. Lawrence's other works include short stories, travel books, plays, and criticism.

> ❛ One of the great denouncers, the great missionaries the English send to themselves to tell them they are crass, gross, lost, dead, mad and addicted to unnatural vice. I suppose it is a good thing that these chaps continue to roll up, though in this case I wonder whether as much silly conduct has not been encouraged as heartless conduct deterred.
>
> Kingsley Amis on D. H. Lawrence, *What Became of Jane Austen?* (1970) ❜

Lawrence, T(homas) E(dward), known as *Lawrence of Arabia* (1888–1935). British soldier, writer, and scholar. After studying history at Oxford, he worked in Syria on archaeological excavations for the British Museum.

In World War I he encouraged the Arabs in their revolt against Turkey (an ally of Germany). Living as one of them, Lawrence himself led many Arab attacks on Turkish supply trains and against Turkish forces. He related his exploits in *The Seven Pillars of Wisdom* (1926). Anxious to avoid hero-worship, he enlisted in the RAF and then the Royal Tank Corps under assumed names. He died at 46 in a motorcycle accident near his home in Dorset. A colourful but enigmatic figure, Lawrence caught the imagination of the British public and his life has prompted numerous biographies.

Lean, Sir David (1908–91). British film director and screenwriter. Having begun his career as a studio tea boy, Lean later became a respected film editor. During World War II he collaborated with Noël Coward on several films, including the classic romance *Brief Encounter* (1945). He then made his international reputation with the Dickens adaptation *Great Expectations* (1946). During the 1950s and 1960s Lean directed a series of spectacular big-budget epics that pleased critics and audiences alike; *The Bridge on the River Kwai* (1957) was followed by *Lawrence of Arabia* (1962) and *Doctor Zhivago* (1965). By contrast *Ryan's Daughter* (1970) was poorly received. After a break of 14 years, Lean returned to directing with *A Passage to India* (1984), a successful adaptation of the Forster novel.

Le Corbusier, original name *Charles-Édouard Jeanneret* (1887–1965). Swiss-born French architect. He began his career as an engraver and painter but later grew interested in the design problems arising out of industrial and urban developments. He believed that a house should be designed according to its function, as a "machine for living in". His works include the large block of flats in Marseilles called the Unité d'Habitation. He also drafted the town plans for a number of important cities, and put forward his theories in various books. He is considered to be one of the most influential of 20th-century architects.

> 6 It is well that war is so terrible; else we would grow too fond of it.
> Remark attributed to General Robert E. Lee, after the battle of Fredericksburg (1862) 9

Lee, Robert E(dward) (1807–70). US general. He fought in the Mexican War (1846–48) before commanding the Confederate Army of North Virginia in the US Civil War (1861–65). He inflicted a number of defeats on the Federal forces of General Grant and protected the important towns of Richmond and Petersburg. Defeated at Gettysburg (1863), he continued his brilliant defensive operations but was forced to surrender at Appomattox Court House (1865). As a defeated hero he helped to rebuild the nation's confidence after the War and became president of Washington College at Lexington in Virginia.

Lee Kwan Yu (1923–). Singaporean statesman; prime minister (1959–90). The son of wealthy Chinese parents, Lee studied law at Cambridge University before returning to Singapore, where he worked in the trade union movement. He founded the centrist People's

Action Party in 1954, was elected to parliament a year later, and helped to negotiate Singapore's self-governing status in 1959. As prime minister he led Singapore into the Federation of Malaysia in 1963 and out again in 1965, when the country became an independent republic. During his long period in office, Singapore made remarkable economic progress, thanks largely to Lee's policy of encouraging foreign investment. His regime attracted some criticism for its authoritarianism and intolerance of opposition.

Leibniz, Gottfried (1646–1716). German philosopher and mathematician. Having qualified as a lawyer in 1666, he entered the court of the elector of Mainz and worked on political missions. A meeting with Christian Huygens in Paris rekindled his interest in mathematics; the invention of a calculating machine and a new form of calculus are amongst his achievements in this field. He entered the service of the duke of Brunswick-Luneburg in 1676, and in 1685 he became the official historian of the House of Brunswick. His philosophical works include *Theodicy* (1710) and *Monadology* (1714), in which he puts forward his optimistic philosophy that this is the best of all possible worlds.

Lenin, Vladimir Ilyich, original name *Vladimir Ulyanov* (1870–1924). Russian revolutionary and Marxist theoretician. His eldest brother was hanged (1887) for an assassination attempt on Tsar Alexander III. Banished to Siberia for revolutionary activities in 1895, he formed the Bolsheviks (Russian Communist Party) in 1903, three years after his release. When the Russian Revolution broke out in 1917 he returned to Russia from

Switzerland and, partnered by Trotsky, led the Bolsheviks in the October Revolution. Following the civil war (1918–20) the Soviet Union was established, with Lenin as its first leader. He had been instrumental in forming the Comintern (the Communist International Organization) in 1919. In 1922 he fell ill and a bullet he had received in an assassination attempt (1918) was removed from his neck. He recovered but remained an invalid and later suffered several strokes. His classics of political theory include *What is to be Done?* (1902) and *Imperialism* (1917).

Leonardo da Vinci (1452–1519). Italian artist, scientist, and engineer. He trained as a painter in Florence and his few surviving works include the *Mona Lisa* (now in the Louvre, Paris) and the fresco *The Last Supper* (in Milan). Living mainly in Milan and Florence, he also worked as a military engineer and made copious notes on his investigations of architecture, anatomy, biology, military and civil engineering, mathematics, and music. The most famous collection of his notes, which includes drawings of a tank, a helicopter, and a submarine, is the *Atlantic Codex* in Windsor Castle.

Lesseps, Ferdinand de (1805–94). French diplomat and engineer, who promoted the building of the Suez and Panama Canals. He served as a consul in various foreign cities, including Cairo, where he became interested in plans for the Suez Canal. He was subsequently allowed to raise the money necessary and to supervise the construction of the canal (1859–69). In 1880 he headed the Panama Canal Company, but this became bankrupt within ten years, before the canal was finished. De Lesseps was subsequently charged with breach of trust over his running of this scheme. He was sentenced to five years' imprisonment in 1892 but was too ill to leave his bed and died two years later at home.

Lévi-Strauss, Claude (1908–   ). French anthropologist, a pioneer of the intellectual approach known as structuralism. After his studies at the Sorbonne he taught sociology in São Paolo, Brazil, and undertook several expeditions to study the Amazon Indians. He subsequently worked in New York and Paris, becoming professor of anthropology at the Collège de France in 1960. In his studies Lévi-Strauss interpreted complex anthropological data in terms of a few basic structural models – such as binary oppositions and hierarchies – that he considered to underlie all human thinking. This approach, which he adapted from modern linguistics, later proved highly influential throughout the humanities. Lévi-Strauss's works include *The Elementary Structures of Kinship* (1949) and *Mythologies* (1964–71). He was appointed to the Légion d'honneur in 1991.

Lincoln, Abraham (1809–65). US statesman; 16th president of the US. Born in a log cabin in Kentucky, he was entirely self-educated. After working as a lawyer, he sat in Congress and later joined the new Republican party (1856). In 1860 he was elected president on an anti-slavery ticket. His term of office was occupied by the civil war against the Southern slave states that had withdrawn from the Union following his election. Just five days after the Union victory, he was

---

> ### Lincoln the Emancipator
>
> On 1 January 1863 the Emancipation Proclamation, which officially freed all the slaves in the Southern states, was put before Lincoln for the presidential signature. While the secretary of state and other officials waited in hushed anticipation, Lincoln paused, took up his pen, paused, and put it down again. He then repeated the operation still more slowly. Eventually he looked up and addressed his colleagues; "I have been shaking hands since nine o'clock this morning, and my right arm is almost paralysed. If my name ever goes into history, it will be for this act, and my whole soul is in it. If my hand trembles when I sign the Proclamation, all who examine the document hereafter will say, 'He hesitated.'" He then picked up the pen for a third time and slowly and deliberately wrote his signature.

shot at Ford's Theatre, Washington DC, by the little-known actor John Wilkes Booth, who wished to avenge the defeat of the South. Lincoln died in hospital the next day and was subsequently regarded as both a martyr and a hero.

Lindbergh, Charles (1902–74). US aviator. He became an airmail pilot in 1926 and the following year made the first solo transatlantic flight (from New York to Paris) in his monoplane *Spirit of St Louis*. In 1932 his two-year-old son was kidnapped and murdered. This led to new legislation against kidnapping, nicknamed the 'Lindbergh Law'. Lindbergh later made a number of speeches recommending US neutrality in World War II, provoking criticism from President Roosevelt.

Linnaeus, Carolus (1707–78). Swedish botanist, born *Carl Linné*, who established a system for naming and classifying plants and animals that is still used today. While a lecturer in botany at the University of Uppsala, he travelled extensively in north-west Europe, discovering many new species of plants. In 1735 he published his *Systema Naturae*, in which he classified living things in a methodical way. He also assigned two Latin names to each organism – one for its genus and the other for its species. Thus Linnaeus gave the human species the name *Homo sapiens*. Linnaeus's work provided a valuable basis for the work of later biologists. His books and collections are kept at the Linnaean Society, founded in London in 1788 in his honour.

Lister, Joseph (1827–1912). British surgeon. Making use of Louis Pasteur's discovery that infections could be caused by germs carried in the air, he founded antiseptic surgery in 1865 by sterilizing wounds and surgical instruments with carbolic acid. He thereby reduced the deaths after amputation in his Glasgow hospital by two thirds. His methods were very soon adopted elsewhere.

Liszt, Franz (1811–86). Hungarian composer, pianist, and conductor. Before he was 20 he had established an international reputation as a virtuoso pianist. He wrote many celebrated works for the piano, including two concertos and 20 Hungarian rhapsodies. Many of his compositions for the piano were of the utmost difficulty and were written both to expand the technique of the instrument and to display the composer's phenomenal powers as a performer. His daughter, Cosima, married Richard Wagner. In 1865 Liszt took minor religious orders in the Roman Catholic Church. His later compositions include masses and a requiem.

Livingstone, David (1813–73). Scottish missionary and explorer. He studied medicine and in 1840 was ordained as a missionary. The following year he went to southern Africa and began a series of expeditions. These included the crossing of the Kalahari desert and the discovery of the Zambezi River (1851) and Victoria Falls (1855). He married Mary Moffat, the daughter of

> ‘ When Mr Stanley entered Ujiji pm Nov 3 1871 with the procession of his servants he found a crowd of people in the street attracted by his approach. In the centre of a group of Arabs, to the left hand, he perceived a pale, grey-bearded white man, dressed in a shirt or jacket of red serge, with trousers, and wearing on his head a naval cap with a gold band. "Dr Livingstone, I presume," said Mr Stanley in accosting him with the calmness of an ordinary greeting at first sight, as he might have done in New York or London.
> *Illustrated London News*
> 9 November 1872 ’

the missionary Robert Moffat, in 1844. She died in 1862, during his expedition to Lake Malawi (formerly Nyasa). Livingstone then began his search for the source of the Nile. Feared lost in 1871, he was found by the explorer Stanley near Lake Tanganyika, but died while continuing his search. He published a number of books and journals, including *The Zambezi and Its Tributaries* (1865), in which he protested against slavery.

Livy, full name *Titus Livius* (c. 59 BC–17 AD). Roman historian. About one quarter of his massive history of Rome survives, describing the early history of the city and her wars against Hannibal, Macedonia, and Syria. His swift narrative and vivid characterization make his work interesting to read and he is considered one of the greatest Roman historians.

Lloyd George, David (1863–1945). Welsh Liberal statesman. After a poor childhood he became a solicitor and in 1890 was elected MP for Caernarvon Boroughs, a seat he held for 54 years. He supported Welsh nationalism and through his wit and persuasiveness became a prominent figure in the House of Commons. He was also notorious for his many affairs with women. As chancellor of the exchequer (1908–15) he introduced health insurance and old-age pensions, laying the foundations of the Welfare State. Later, as prime minister (1916–22), he saw Britain through World War I. After his coalition government fell he never regained his former dominance in British politics.

Lloyd Webber, Sir Andrew (1948–   ). British popular composer. His first musical was *Joseph and the Amazing*

Technicolour Dreamcoat (1968), written to be performed by children. This work marked the beginning of his collaboration with the librettist Tim Rice, which continued with the highly successful musicals *Jesus Christ Superstar* (1970) and *Evita* (1978). Lloyd Webber then used a series of different librettists for *Cats* (1981), based on poems by T. S. Eliot, *Starlight Express* (1984), *The Phantom of the Opera* (1987), and *Sunset Boulevard* (1993). In 1993 he had five shows running simultaneously in London's West End. He has also composed *Variations* (1977), an instrumental work for cello and rock band, and a *Requiem* (1985).

Locke, John (1632–1704). British philosopher. Medicine and experimental science were his early interests and he joined the Royal Society in 1668. In 1667 Lord Shaftesbury appointed Locke as his physician and their association lasted until Shaftesbury's death in 1683. Locke's major works are *An Essay Concerning Human Understanding* (1690), which argued influentially that all human knowledge originates in sense impressions, and

> ❛ No one has yet succeeded in inventing a philosophy at once credible and self-consistent. Locke aimed at credibility, and achieved it at the expense of consistency. Most of the great philosophers have done the opposite.
> Bertrand Russell, *History of Western Philosophy* (1945) ❜

Two Treatises on Government (1690), a statement of Whig theory.

Longfellow, Henry Wadsworth (1807–82). US poet. He was professor of modern languages at Bowdoin and Harvard from 1829 to 1854, when he gave up teaching to concentrate on writing. His works, which were popular in both Europe and the US, include *Ballads and Other Poems* (1841), containing the poem 'The Wreck of the Hesperus', and the long narrative work *The Song of Hiawatha* (1855).

Louis IX, St (1214–70). King of France. He became king at the age of 12 under the regency of his mother, Blanche of Castile. During his personal rule he strengthened royal authority and encouraged learning and the arts. In 1248 he embarked on the Seventh Crusade, in which he suffered defeat and capture before returning to France. He went on another crusade in 1269 but died of fever the following year. Famous for his piety in his lifetime, he was canonized by Pope Boniface VIII in 1297.

Louis XIV (1638–1715). King of France from 1643, known as the *Sun King* for the glorious nature of his rule. The son of Louis XIII and Anne of Austria, he became king at the age of five; his minister Cardinal Mazarin held power until Louis assumed total responsibility for ruling France in 1661. Under his minister Colbert he developed the economy and increased trade. The army was also strengthened and Louis engaged in several wars, extending the French borders and securing the Spanish throne for his grandson. He also patronized the arts and was responsible for the building of the magnificent palace at Versailles. Louis had a series of mistresses and many children. Following the death of his first wife, Maria Theresa, he secretly married the pious Madame de Maintenon, a former mistress.

Louis XV (1710–74). King of France. He succeeded to the throne at only five years of age and during his minority the country was administered by the Duc d'Orléans and Cardinal Fleury. Following Fleury's death (1744), Louis attempted to rule alone but was dominated by his mistresses, especially Madame de Pompadour, to whom he gave away large sums of his country's money. His reign saw defeat in the Seven Years' War (1756–63) and left France on the verge of bankruptcy, paving the way for the French Revolution.

Louis XVI (1754–93). King of France from 1774. He married Marie Antoinette in 1770 and succeeded to the

---

A Royal Diarist

On 14 July 1789 an armed mob seized the Bastille, a royal prison in Paris that had come to symbolize the oppressive nature of Bourbon rule. This date is traditionally seen as the beginning of the French Revolution. Oblivious of these developments, Louis XVI spent the whole day hunting in the woods near Versailles. So it was, that on this epochal day in his country's history, Louis could write the notorious diary entry: "July 14: Nothing."

---

throne when France was virtually bankrupt. Dominated by his wife, he failed to bring in large-scale reforms to improve the financial situation. In 1789 the National Assembly was formed and the French Revolution began. The Palace of Versailles was attacked and Louis and his family were moved out. Public opinion was generally sympathetic to the royal family until Louis's escape attempt (1791). He was captured at Varennes and held prisoner before being tried for treason and guillotined.

Louis, Joe, full name *Joseph Louis Barrow* (1914–81). US boxer. World heavyweight champion from 1937 to 1949, a record reign, he earned the nickname 'The Brown Bomber' for his ability to win by an early knockout with either hand. He retired while still champion but shortage of funds forced him to resume his career in 1950. He was only ever beaten three times.

Lowell, Robert (1917–77). US poet. The son of a distinguished New England family, Lowell studied at Harvard and Kenyon College, Ohio. In 1940 he converted to Roman Catholicism (a faith he later abandoned). During World War II religious objections to the bombing of civilians led him to refuse the draft, a stance that resulted in his imprisonment. Lowell's early poems, collected in such volumes as *Lord Weary's Castle* (1946), show the influence of the Metaphysical poets in their compressed formal style. With *Life Studies* (1959), however, his art took a radically different turn; the poems are more loosely written and deal with aspects of his turbulent personal life, including the episodes of madness that periodically afflicted him. This 'confessional' approach had a great influence on young US poets. Lowell's later work includes a volume of translations, *Imitations* (1961), *For the Union Dead* (1964), and *Notebook* (1969).

Loyola, St Ignatius of (1491–1556). Spanish founder of the Society of Jesus (the Jesuits). A wound sustained in 1521 ended his military career and he turned to religion after reading the Bible during his recovery. The *Spiritual Exercises* (written 1522–35) were begun during a period of self-imposed austerity. After a pilgrimage to Jerusalem in 1523–24 he was tried for heresy but acquitted. Ordained in 1537, he obtained papal approval for his new order in 1540; the Jesuits subsequently became a leading force in the Counter-Reformation. Loyola established schools, organized missions, and directed the Jesuits until his death. He was canonized in 1622.

Lucretius, full name *Titus Lucretius Carus* (c. 94–55 BC). Roman poet. In his poem *On the Nature of Things* he puts forward the materialist philosophy of Epicurus, arguing that fear of the gods is the chief obstacle to human happiness. He is said to have committed suicide in a fit of madness.

Luke, St (fl. 1st century AD). Author of the third Gospel and the *Acts of the Apostles*. A doctor, he accompanied St Paul on part of his second and third missionary journeys. In his New Testament books Luke affirms that Christ is the saviour of all men and traces the progress of this belief in the growth of the early Church. He is also the patron saint of doctors.

Lumière, Auguste (1862–1954) and his brother **Louis** (1864–1948). French cinema pioneers. The brothers' father, Antoine Lumière, was a manufacturer of photographic paper and film. In 1894 Louis saw an exhibition of Thomas Edison's Kinetoscope, a peepshow machine that showed moving pictures to one viewer at a time. He at once had the idea of projecting images from an intermittently moving film roll onto a large screen for paying audiences. The brothers patented their Cinématographe, a combined camera-projector, in February 1895 and on 28 December gave what is considered the first public cinema show at the Grand Café in Paris. Their short documentary films were soon being shown to amazed audiences all around the world. Despite this important achievement, however, the brothers failed to realize the commercial and artistic potential of their invention. Both soon abandoned film-making for other areas of research.

> ❝ This invention is not for sale, but if it were it would ruin you. It can be exploited for a while as a scientific curiosity; beyond that it has no commercial future.
> Antoine Lumière, rejecting the attempts of a rival film-maker to buy a Cinématographe ❞

Luther, Martin (1483–1546). German leader of the Protestant Reformation. The son of a miner, he became an Augustinian monk, was ordained as a priest (1507), and taught at the University of Wittenberg. In 1517 he launched an attack on the sale of Indulgences and nailed a list of his objections, known as the 95 theses, to the door of Wittenberg church. These criticisms found wide support in Germany and Luther gradually broadened his denunciation of abuses and certain traditional teachings of the Church. He defended his views before the Emperor Charles V at the Diet of Worms (1521). Despite attempts at reconciliation, the opposing sides grew further apart. Luther was excommunicated for publicly burning a papal edict against him in 1521 and four years later married a former nun. After taking part in the drafting of the Augsburg Confession (1530), a statement of Lutheran beliefs, he gradually left the leadership of the Reformation to others. The most important of his many religious writings is his translation of the Bible, which established the German language in its modern form. Lutheranism is now the principal form of Protestantism in Germany and the national religion in the Scandinavian countries, with over 80 million members throughout the world.

M

McAdam, John (1756–1836). Scottish inventor. He experimented with road construction in Ayreshire, Cornwall, and Bristol and developed a method that used a raised core of large rocks with drainage ditches at each side, covered with a surface of small stones bound with gravel. This technique, called 'macadamizing' after its inventor, has been widely adopted. Tar or asphalt is used to bind and smooth the surface in modern road-making. McAdam became surveyor-general of roads in 1827.

MacArthur, Douglas (1880–1964). US general. The son of a US governor of the Philippines, he trained at West Point and served in World War I. He was later chief of staff to the US army (1930–35). In 1941 he was recalled from retirement to lead the defence of the Philippines against the Japanese. Although forced to withdraw, he reconquered the islands in 1944–45 and was appointed commander of all US army forces in the Pacific. He accepted the Japanese surrender in September 1945 and headed the occupying forces in Japan until 1950. With the outbreak of the Korean War in 1950, he was appointed commander of the UN troops defending South Korea against North Korean forces backed by communist China. His wish to extend the war by bombing China provoked his dismissal by President

Truman. Although a brilliant strategist, MacArthur was considered arrogant and self-willed by many colleagues and superiors.

Macaulay, Lord Thomas Babington (1800–59). British historian, poet, and statesman. A Whig and an opponent of slavery from his youth, he served as an MP from 1830 to 1853 and held important government and colonial offices. His publications include essays and speeches, *The Lays of Ancient Rome* (1842), and a five-volume *History of England* (1849–61). This is probably the most popular historical work ever written. Today it is regarded as a brilliant but somewhat biased work, strongly reflecting Macaulay's Whig views. Palmerston raised him to the peerage in 1857, with the title Baron Macaulay of Rothley.

The Eloquent Macaulay

Thomas Macaulay was famous for the unceasing flow of his conversation, which gave his interlocutors little or no chance to get a word in. His fellow historian Thomas Carlyle once remarked that "Macaulay was well for a while, but one wouldn't *live* under Niagara". Still more sharply, Sydney Smith commented on the change in Macaulay's manner after a visit to India: "His enemies might perhaps have said before...that he talked rather too much: but now he has occasional flashes of silence that make his conversation perfectly delightful".

McCarthy, Joseph (1908–57). US Republican politician. He caused a nationwide sensation in 1950 with his allegations that there were 205 communists working in the State Department. His witch-hunt against communism was termed 'McCarthyism', and caused a large number of people, most of whom were innocent, to lose their jobs and their reputations. In 1954 he was censured by his colleagues in the Senate and was unable to regain power.

Macdonald, (James) Ramsay (1866–1937). British statesman. He joined the Independent Labour party in 1894, soon after its foundation, and became an MP in 1906. Having become party leader in 1911, he was forced to resign this position after opposing Britain's entry into World War I. He regained the leadership (1922) and in 1924 became prime minister of the first British Labour government, which fell later that year. He returned to office in 1929 and from 1931 served as prime minister in the mainly Conservative 'National' government, having split with the Labour party he had helped to found. He retired from office in 1935.

McEnroe, John (Patrick) (1959–   ). US tennis player. The 18-year-old McEnroe came to prominence when he reached the semi-finals on his first Wimbledon appearance (1977). He went on to take the Wimbledon singles title in 1981, 1983, and 1984, and the US Open in 1979, 1980, 1981, and 1984. He also won numerous doubles titles, usually with the US player Peter Fleming. Despite these successes, McEnroe was notorious for his temperamental behaviour on court, which resulted in a number of fines. In 1986 he married the US film actress Tatum O'Neal.

Machiavelli, Niccolo (1469–1527). Italian writer and politician. By the age of 29 he held important government posts and travelled as a diplomat in Europe. When the Medicis came to power Machiavelli was suspected of conspiracy against them and imprisoned for a time, but later held office again. His best-known work *The Prince* (written 1513) puts forward his political ideal of a united Italy governed by a powerful ruler. In it he justifies acts of treachery and tyranny by the ruler as being necessary to maintain authority over the people. His other works include his *Discourses* (1519) on political history, a history of Florence, and a satirical comedy entitled *Mandragola* (1520).

Maclean, Donald (1913–83). British spy. *See* Kim **Philby**.

Macmillan, Harold (1894–1986). British Conservative statesman. A member of a family of publishers, he was educated at Eton and served in World War I. He entered parliament in 1924 and was a much praised housing minister (1951–54). As chancellor of the exchequer (1955–57) he introduced premium bonds. In 1957 he succeeded Anthony Eden as prime minister at a time when the Conservative party was divided over the Suez Crisis. In the 1959 general election he led the party to victory with the slogan "you've never had it so good". He resigned in 1963 because of ill-health and retired from politics a year later. In his later years he criticized many of the social and economic policies of Margaret Thatcher. He was created Earl of Stockton in

1984. His memoirs include *Winds of Change* (1966) and *Riding the Storm* (1971).

Madonna, full name *Madonna Louise Veronica Ciccone* (1958–   ). US singer and film actress. Born into an Italian family, she trained as a dancer and began to record in the early 1980s. The song 'Holiday' became a US hit in 1983. With her striking looks, skilful use of the new medium of video, and talent for self-publicity, she rose to international stardom in 1985–86, when the album *Like a Virgin* became a million seller. Her success continued with such hits as 'Like a Prayer' (1989) and 'Justify My Love' (1991), making her the best-selling female performer of all time. In the 1990s her stage performances became more sexually explicit and she published a controversial book of erotic photographs, *Sex* (1992). Sales of recent releases, such as *Bedtime Stories* (1995), suggest that her immense popularity may be waning.

Magellan, Ferdinand (c. 1480–1521). Portuguese explorer. Between 1505 and 1516 he carried out various expeditions to Africa and India for the Portuguese crown. In 1519, with the backing of Spain, he set out on an expedition to discover a route to the Spice Islands (Moluccas) by sailing west. Having crossed the Atlantic, he passed through the straits now named after him to enter the Pacific. Despite severe hardships, one of his five ships reached the East Indies in 1521. Although Magellan himself was killed by hostile islanders, his ship, the *Victoria*, went on to complete the circumnavigation of the globe under Sebastián del Cano (1522).

Magritte, René (1898–1967). Belgian surrealist painter. When Magritte was 14 his mother committed suicide, a tragedy alluded to in a number of his works. After completing his artistic training in Brussels, he worked for several years designing wallpaper. In 1925 he adopted the surreal style that he would follow for the rest of his life and moved to the Paris area to be near the French Surrealists. He returned to Belgium in 1930. His work is famous for the way it makes familiar objects appear dream-like or menacing by placing them in incongruous surroundings. Certain images – most notably blank-faced men in bowler hats – recur again and again in his paintings. Magritte did not become internationally well known until the last 20 years of his life, when he received several important commissions to provide murals for public buildings.

Mahler, Gustav (1860–1911). Austrian composer and conductor. A German-speaking Jew, Mahler was born

Mahler on Vacation

Owing to his busy career as a conductor, Mahler did most of his composing during long summer vacations in the Austrian Alps. Despite his frail health, he swam tirelessly and took long mountain walks as well as working prodigiously on his music, much of which draws its inspiration from the landscape. On one occasion a visitor to his country retreat was told: "Don't bother looking at the view. I have already composed it".

in what is now the Czech Republic. After studies at the Vienna conservatory, he became the conductor of the Vienna Imperial Opera (1897–1907) and later of the New York Metropolitan Opera and the New York Philharmonic Orchestra. He wrote 10 large-scale symphonies, of which the fourth and fifth are perhaps best known, as well as numerous songs and song-cycles.

Mailer, Norman (1923–   ). US novelist and writer. Mailer studied at Harvard University and spent two years on active service during World War II. His wartime experiences provided the basis of his first novel, *The Naked and the Dead* (1948). A similar preoccupation with violence, male comradeship and personal integrity is apparent in his later novels, which include *The Deer Park* (1955), *An American Dream* (1965), *Ancient Evenings* (1983), *Tough Guys Don't Dance* (1984), and *Harlot's Ghost* (1991). His major non-fiction writings include *Why Are We in Vietnam?* (1967), *The Armies of the Night* (1968), about the anti-war movement, and *Marilyn* (1973), about the life of Marilyn Monroe. Many of his books blur the distinction between journalism and fiction, notably *The Executioner's Song* (1979), a fictionalized version of the life and death of Gary Gilmore, a real-life murderer, and *Oswald's Tale* (1995), about the assassin of President Kennedy.

Major, John (1943–   ). British Conservative politician; prime minister (1990–   ). Major was brought up in south London, the son of a circus performer turned small businessman. After various labouring jobs, he began a career in banking and served in local government. He entered parliament in 1979 and achieved his first ministerial position seven years later. In 1989–90 he became in swift succession foreign secretary, chancellor of the exchequer, and prime minister on the fall of Margaret Thatcher (November 1990). During the first months of his premiership he was faced with the international crisis that culminated in the Gulf War (1991). While continuing to pursue many of Thatcher's policies, he adopted a more conciliatory low-key style, notably in his dealings with Europe. Under his leadership, the Conservatives were unexpectedly returned to power in the general election of 1992. Subsequently, however, his government was weakened by disunity on European policy and a series of scandals, and Major himself became highly unpopular. In 1995 he took the unprecedented step of resigning the leadership of the Conservative party in order to force an election, which he won. The main achievement of his second administration was the beginning of exploratory peace talks in Northern Ireland, resulting in a ceasefire from 1994.

Mallarmé, Stéphane (1842–98). French Symbolist poet. Born in Paris, he made his living teaching English until 1871; he was also a frequent visitor to England. Important influences on his work included Edgar Allan Poe, some of whose poems he translated, and Baudelaire. In the 1860s he emerged as a leader of the Symbolist movement, which believed in the power of poetry to evoke a transcendental reality beyond the world of appearances. His poetry, which revels in word music and mysterious imagery, is famous for its obscurity. Mallarmé's best-known works include *Hérodiade* (1864), *L'Après-midi d'un faune* (1865), and his last poem, *Un Coup de dés jamais n'abolira le hasard*.

Malory, Sir Thomas (d. c. 1471). English poet, author of the *Morte d'Arthur*, the first prose version of the story of King Arthur and the Knights of the Round Table. Malory's identity is uncertain, but he is thought to have been born in Warwickshire and to have served at Calais before becoming an MP in 1442. He was arrested for theft and rape in 1451 and subsequently spent several periods in jail, the last for his support of the Lancastrians in the Wars of the Roses. *Morte d'Arthur*, written in jail, was not printed until 1485.

Mandela, Nelson (Rolihlahia) (1818–). South African politician; first Black president of his country (1994–). The son of a tribal chief, Mandela practised as a lawyer and was active in the African National Congress. After this organization was banned in 1960, he led a campaign of sabotage and guerrilla activity until 1962, when he was arrested and imprisoned. In 1964 he was retried and sentenced to life imprisonment for treason. After a long international campaign he was finally released in 1990, having by this time become an almost mythical symbol of resistance to apartheid. As vice-president and then president (from 1991) of the ANC, he led negotiations with the government of F. W. de Klerk and signed South Africa's new non-racial constitution (1993). That same year he was awarded the Nobel Peace Prize jointly with de Klerk. In 1994 he led the ANC to an overwhelming victory in the country's first multiracial elections. His wife **Winnie Mandela** (1934–) became an international figure during the campaign for Nelson's release. Following her conviction on charges relating to the abduction and assault of several youths, they separated in 1992; Nelson Mandela began divorce proceedings in 1995.

Manet, Édouard (1832–83). French painter, often regarded as the founder of impressionism. Manet abandoned his study of law and decided to become a painter after a voyage to Rio de Janeiro. In 1863 he exhibited paintings with Monet and Renoir; the beginning of French Impressionism is usually dated from this exhibition. Although his paintings, such as *The Absinthe Drinker* and *Déjeuner sur l'herbe*, were considered shocking at the time, they reflect Manet's admiration and study of old masters such as Velasquez.

> ❛ Is this drawing? Is this painting?
> Jules Castagnary, of Manet's
> ***Déjeuner sur l'herbe***

> This is a young man's practical joke...
> Louis Etienne, of the same ❜

Mann, Thomas (1875–1955). German novelist. After a reluctant and unsuccessful attempt at a business career, he studied at Munich. *Buddenbrooks* (1900), an epic family saga set in his native Lübeck, brought him fame, and was followed by such successes as *Death in Venice* (1912) and *The Magic Mountain* (1924). Having been deprived of German citizenship in 1936 after an attack on the Nazi regime, he emigrated to the US in 1938. His last novels include the tetralogy *Joseph and his Brothers* (1933–43), *Doktor Faustus* (1947), and the unfinished *Confessions of Felix Krull* (1955). He spent his last years in Switzerland. Mann was awarded the Nobel Prize in 1929.

Mantle, Mickey (1931–). US baseball player, a famous hitter who scored 536 home runs during his career. Having been trained by his father, a semiprofessional player, Mantle was recruited by the New York Yankees in 1951. During his 17 seasons with the team he frequently led the American League tables for runs scored and home runs. Mantle, who could bat powerfully with either arm, often appeared on the pitch heavily bandaged owing to the lasting effects of a youthful bone-tissue disease. After retiring as a player in 1968, he worked as a coach. In 1983 he was barred from working in professional baseball because he had taken a public-relations job with a casino. The ban was later lifted.

Mao Tse-Tung (1893–1976). Chinese communist leader, a founder member of the Chinese Communist party. In the 1920s Mao's guerrilla forces collaborated with the Nationalist party in their struggle against the warlords. Following a split with the Nationalists, he retreated from south-east China to Shensi in the 'Long March' (1934–35). On the formation of the communist People's Republic of China (1949) he became its chairman. Although he retired from this position in 1959 he remained in control of the country. He inspired the 'Great Leap Forward' in 1957 and the 'Cultural Revolution' (1966); during this turbulent and destructive period his 'little red book' of thoughts had great influence. His third wife, the actress Chiang Ching, became increasingly powerful in Mao's later years. Following his death she was arrested, together with other members of the 'Gang of Four', and accused of plotting against Mao's successor, Hua Guo-Feng.

> ❛ Our fathers were indeed wise. They invented printing, but not newspapers. They invented gunpowder, but used it only for fireworks. Finally, they invented the compass, but took care not to use it to discover America.
>
> Remark attributed to Mao Tse-Tung ❜

Maradona, Diego (1960–   ). Argentinian soccer player. Born in a shanty-town of Buenos Aires, he became famous as a child for his foot-juggling displays on television. He became a professional footballer at 15 and in 1982 was sold to Barcelona for a then-record fee. By this time he was widely known for his flamboyant skills and his temperamental behaviour. He was transferred to Napoli in 1984 and in 1986 led Argentina to victory in the World Cup (a triumph made possible by Maradona's notorious handballed goal against England in the quarter-final). In 1991 he was banned from world football for 18 months for using cocaine; a further ban was imposed in 1994 for his use of stimulants.

Marat, Jean-Paul (1743–93). French revolutionary. He practised medicine in Paris for a time but gave this up to become a revolutionary and to edit the radical journal *L'Ami du Peuple*. Having been elected to the National Convention in 1792 he helped bring about the fall from power of the Girondins, the moderate republicans, in 1793. Marat suffered from a skin disease and while taking one of his frequent medicinal baths he was stabbed to death by a Girondin fanatic, Charlotte Corday.

Marceau, Marcel (1923–   ). French mime. He is the best-known modern performer of mime, using only movement and formalized gestures to express character and tell a story. He became internationally famous as the white-faced clown character Bip, which he based on the traditional character of Pierrot.

Marconi, Guglielmo (1874–1937). Italian developer of radio telegraphy. He began research into the transmission of radio waves in 1894 and continued his experiments in Britain from 1896, achieving radio communication over 12 miles by 1897. Reaction to these advances was cool until 1899, when Marconi used radio to report on the Americas Cup Yacht Race. In 1909 he received the Nobel prize for physics. He sent the first radio message from Britain to Australia in 1918. During World War I he developed short-wave radio, initially for use in warfare. His discoveries were later applied to the transmission of signals over large distances at greatly increased power.

Maria Theresa (1717–80). Archduchess of Austria and queen of Hungary and Bohemia. The daughter of Charles VI, she succeeded to the Habsburg dominions on his death (1740) during the War of Austrian Succession (1740–48). As a woman she was unable to inherit his title, but secured this for her husband, Francis I, in 1745. On his death in 1765 their son Joseph II, one of 16 children, became Holy Roman Emperor. Maria Theresa proved herself to be a capable ruler and was a major figure in 18th-century Europe.

Marie Antoinette (1755–93). Queen of France. In 1770 she married the dauphin of France, who became Louis XVI in 1774. Her extravagant and frivolous way of life, which included romantically playing at being a milkmaid on an imitation farm at Versailles, made her unpopular, as did her interference in political affairs. When told that the people of Paris had no bread, Marie Antoinette is supposed to have said: "Let them eat cake". With the outbreak of the French Revolution she displayed both stubbornness and courage, exercising considerable influence over her weak-willed husband. In 1793, together with Louis, she was convicted of treason and guillotined.

> ❛ Courage! I have shown it for years; think you I shall lose it at the moment when my sufferings are to end?
> Marie Antoinette, remark on her way to the guillotine, 16 October 1793 ❜

Mark, St (fl. 1st century AD). New Testament figure. He accompanied Barnabas and St Paul on part of their first missionary journey but left them to return to Jerusalem. He is traditionally believed to be the compiler of the second Gospel, for which he may have drawn information from Peter, and to have founded the Christian Church in Alexandria.

Mark Antony, Latin name *Marcus Antonius* (c. 82–30 BC). Roman statesman and soldier. He served as a cavalry commander during the reign of Julius Caesar. After Caesar's assassination he roused the Roman people against Caesar's republican assassins, Brutus and Cassius, whom he defeated at Philippi (42). As the triumvir (joint ruler) responsible for Rome's eastern provinces, he became the lover of Cleopatra, the queen of Egypt. He quarrelled with his fellow triumvir Octavian, and joined forces with Cleopatra against him. After their defeat at Actium (31), they fled to Egypt and committed suicide.

Markova, Dame Alicia, stage name of *Lilian Alicia Marks* (1910–   ). British ballerina. She became prima ballerina of the Vic-Wells Ballet (1932–35) and subsequently danced with the Ballets Russes of Monte Carlo and several US companies. From 1970 she taught in the US. She is noted for her delicate interpretations of the classic roles in such ballets as *Giselle*, *Swan Lake*, and *Romeo and Juliet*.

Marley, Bob, full name *Robert Nesta Marley* (1945–80). Jamaican reggae singer, the first rock superstar to emerge from a developing country. Marley was born in St Anns, Jamaica, the illegitimate son of a senior naval officer. Having co-formed the Wailers reggae group in 1963, Marley soon emerged as their lead singer and chief songwriter. The group later found international acclaim with their albums *Catch a Fire* (1973) and *Natty Dread* (1975). Marley's songs, which preached Rastafarianism and anti-establishment politics, made him a controversial public figure in Jamaica; he survived an assassination attempt in 1975. Later albums, which achieved large sales in Europe and the US, included *Exodus* (1977) and *Uprising* (1980). Since his death from cancer he has been regarded as a national hero in Jamaica.

Marlborough, Duke of, born *John Churchill* (1650–1722). British general and statesman. At 15 he served as page to the duke of York (later James II), and advanced in his favour through his sister Arabella, who was the duke's mistress. He helped to put down Monmouth's rebellion against James II in 1685. Later, by supporting the successor to James's throne, William III, he became even more influential in government. His wife Sarah was a firm friend and confidante of the Princess Anne, and when Anne came to the throne he was made a duke. He led the British and allied armies against the French forces of Louis XIV in the War of the Spanish Succession (1701–14), winning notable victories at Blenheim (1704), Ramillies (1706), Oudenarde (1708), and Malplaquet (1709). However, because of a quarrel between the queen and the duchess of Marlborough, he was refused any military position or office on his return. He returned to favour under George I and was given the magnificent mansion and grounds of Blenheim Palace, near Woodstock in Oxfordshire.

Marlowe, Christopher (1564–93). English dramatist. The son of a shoemaker, he was educated at Cambridge

Death in Deptford

After four centuries the circumstances surrounding the death of Christopher Marlowe remain shrouded in mystery. It is now generally accepted that Marlowe was employed on missions abroad under Sir Francis Walsingham, the head of Elizabeth I's secret service. Arguably the playwright must have appeared a considerable security risk, being known for his atheism, homosexuality, and reckless character. On 30 May 1593 – at a time when he was under investigation by the Privy Council on suspicion of writing subversive pamphlets – Marlowe and four other men took a room for the evening at a tavern in Deptford, now a suburb in SE London. Two of the playwright's companions, Ingram Frizer and Robert Poley, are now known to have been government agents. After dinner a fight broke out during which Marlowe apparently attempted to kill Frizer: in the words of one contemporary account, Frizer "quickly perceyving it, so avoyded the thrust, that withal drawing out his dagger for his defence hee stabd this Marlowe into the eye, in such sort, that his braines comming out at the daggers point, hee shortly after dyed". At the subsequent enquiry Frizer alleged that the quarrel had broken out over a game of backgammon, evidence corroborated by the other two men present; another version of the story suggested that there had been an argument over the bill. However, many writers have since concluded that the murder was premeditated, perhaps in order to silence the freethinking playwright.

and from then until his death was employed as a government spy. By 1589 he was acting and writing plays in London. *Tamburlaine* (1590) was the first English play to be written in blank verse. His later works include *Edward II* (1594) and *Dr Faustus* (1604), the story of a man who sells his soul to the devil. In 1593 a warrant was issued for his arrest for atheism and immorality. Twelve days later he was killed during a tavern brawl in circumstances that remain mysterious.

Marvell, Andrew (1621–78). English poet. In his time he was best known as a political writer and pamphleteer, most of his poems being published after his death. He was Cromwell's Latin secretary from 1657, in which role he assisted the blind Milton, and MP for Hull from 1659. His poems include 'The Garden' and 'To His Coy Mistress'.

Marx, Karl (1818–83). German political theorist and economist, the founder of Marxism. He was a member of a left-wing movement in Berlin and in 1843 moved to Paris, where he met his friend and collaborator Friedrich Engels. He soon became well known in Socialist circles. *The Communist Manifesto* (1848) was commissioned by the London Communist League. It outlined the communist theory that the coming victory of the working classes would put an end to the class struggles of the past. After the unsuccessful 1848 revolution, Marx was expelled from Germany and took up residence in London, where he helped to organize the First International, a working men's association, in 1864. His major theoretical works, including *A Critique of Political Economy* (1859) and *Das Kapital* (1867; 1885–94), were not financially profitable, and the Marx family became dependent on the generosity of Engels. Marx is buried in Highgate cemetery, London.

Marx Brothers. A family of US film comedians. The three principal members of the team were **Groucho**, born *Julius Marx* (1890–1977); **Harpo**, born *Adolph Marx* (1888–1964); and **Chico**, born *Leonard Marx* (1886–79). **Zeppo**, born *Herbert Marx* (1901–79), appeared in the first five Marx Brothers' films as the romantic lead. Each brother had a distinctive image. Groucho was known for his rapid wisecracks, peculiar walk, painted moustache, and cigar. Harpo was a mute with a talent for harp-playing. Chico had an Italian accent and played the piano. Their films include *Animal Crackers* (1930), *Horse Feathers* (1932), and *A Night at the Opera* (1935).

Mary I, known as *Mary Tudor* (1516–58). Queen of England from 1553, the first woman to rule England in her own right. She was the eldest daughter of Henry VIII by Catherine of Aragon but following the annulment of their marriage was declared illegitimate. She succeeded Edward VI to the throne despite a conspiracy that had made Lady Jane Grey queen for just nine days. A staunch Roman Catholic, Mary married Philip II, king of Spain, thereby provoking a rebellion led by Sir Thomas Wyatt. Her systematic persecution of Protestants (1555), during which about 300 heretics were burnt at the stake, earned her the name of 'Bloody Mary'. During her reign the English lost the last of their possessions in France; according to tradition Mary said: "When I am dead and opened you shall find 'Calais' engraved on my heart". She died unpopular and childless.

Mary, Queen of Scots (1542–87). Queen of Scotland. She succeeded her father, James V of Scotland, when

> ❝ This may be truly said, that if a life of exile and misery, endured with almost saintly patience from the 15th June 1567 to the day of her death on the 8th February 1587 could atone for crimes and errors of the class attributed to her, no such penalty was ever more fully discharged than by Mary Stuart.
>
> Walter Scott *History of Scotland* (1829–30) ❞

only a week old and was brought up in France, where she later married Francis II. She returned to Scotland after his death in 1560, a Catholic queen of a Protestant country. She married her cousin, Henry Darnley, in 1565 but they soon quarrelled. Darnley was involved in the murder of Mary's secretary, Rizzio, and was himself murdered by a conspiracy in which Mary was believed to have had a part. Just three months later she married the earl of Bothwell, who had been accused of the murder. Rebellions in Scotland followed and Mary fled to England, where Elizabeth I had her imprisoned. After 18 years in prison she was finally executed, following numerous Catholic plots to place her on the English throne.

Matisse, Henri (1869–1954). French artist, a leading member of the Fauves, a group of painters active from 1905 to 1908. Their style, called Fauvism, distorted or simplified natural forms for the sake of design and pattern and employed lively pure colours. The style had great influence on subsequent modern painting. Matisse's skill with colour and decoration can be seen in the chapel he designed for the Dominicans at Vence, France (1949–51).

Matthew, St (fl. 1st century AD). New Testament figure, traditionally believed to be the author of the first Gospel. A tax collector by profession, he was among Christ's first disciples. St Matthew's Gospel gives a full account of Christ's ethical teaching and is particularly directed towards Jewish readers.

Matthews, Sir Stanley (1915–   ). English footballer with a reputation for expert dribbling. The son of a barber, he was recruited by Stoke City while still in his teens. He played as a winger for Stoke and then Blackpool until the age of 50 and appeared 54 times for England. He was knighted in 1965, the year of his retirement.

Maupassant, Guy de (1850–93). French short-story writer and novelist. During a ten-year period as a clerk in the civil service, he was encouraged and supervised in his writing by Flaubert, who was a family friend. Maupassant's first published story, 'Ball of Fat', brought him instant fame in 1880. His volumes of stories incude *Mademoiselle Fifi* (1882). He also six novels, notably *Bel-Ami* (1885), the story of a young man's adventures in fashionable Parisian society, and *The Two Brothers* (1888). Maupassant suffered from a nervous illness, brought on by syphilis, and was committed to an asylum in 1892.

Maxwell, James Clerk (1831–79). Scottish physicist. Maxwell worked out the mathematical basis of Faraday's theory of the relationship between electricity and magnetism. He also formulated an electromagnetic theory of light, believing that light, electricity, and magnetism were all phenomena of an all-pervasive substance called the 'ether'. Though the concept of the 'ether' was later abandoned, Maxwell's work led to major advances in science and technology. He also worked on the kinetic theory of gases and colour vision.

Mazzini, Guiseppe (1805–72). Italian political thinker and writer, committed to the unification of Italy as a republic. He joined a secret republican society, the Carbonari, but was betrayed and exiled to France in 1831. He spent many years in Switzerland, Britain, and France, where he plotted several unsuccessful uprisings in Italy. With the revolution of 1848 he returned to Italy and became head of the republican government in Rome until it was overthrown. The establishment of Italy as a unified kingdom (1861), rather than as a republic, was a great disappointment to him.

Medici family. Florentine mercantile family that ruled Florence for most of the period from 1434 to 1737. **Giovanni** (1360–1429) founded the wealth of the family and was succeeded by his son, **Cosimo** (1389–1464), who dominated the Florentine government and was a great patron of the arts and literature. He was succeeded by his son **Piero** (1416–69), who was virtually bedridden, and his grandson, **Lorenzo the Magnificent** (1449–92). Lorenzo was of great influence in Florence and his patronage was more lavish than his grandfather's. During his life Florence became the centre of Renaissance culture. His son **Giovanni** (1475–1521) became Pope Leo X (1513), while his daughter **Catherine** (1519–89) became queen of France on her marriage to Henry II (1533). A patron of the arts, she had considerable political influence, and was the mother of Francis II, Charles IX, and Henry III.

Meir, Golda (1898–1978). Israeli politician. Born in Kiev, she travelled with her family to the US in 1906. She became an active Zionist and emigrated with her husband to Palestine (1921), where they joined a kibbutz. She was active in the struggle for independence and a founder of the state of Israel in 1948. Subsequently she served as minister of labour (1949–56) and foreign minister (1956–66). As prime minister (1969–74) she saw Israel through the Arab-Israeli War (1973).

Melville, Herman (1819–91). US novelist. He joined a merchant ship as a cabin boy in 1839 and later served on a whaler and a frigate. His adventures at sea included desertion to escape brutal treatment by one ship's officers and involvement in a mutiny, for which he was imprisoned. These experiences influenced his first novel *Typee* (1846) and the story *Billy Budd* (unpublished until 1924). In 1850 he settled in Massachusetts, where he wrote his best-known novel *Moby Dick* (1851), the story of the mad Captain Ahab's obsessive pursuit of a white whale. The novel was unsuccessful at the time and Melville died almost unknown.

Melville the Storyteller

When reading his works out loud to friends, Herman Melville had an uncanny way of projecting himself into the incidents and characters of the story. "Normally he was not a man of noticeable appearance", wrote one witness, "but when the narrative inspiration was on him, he looked like all the things he was describing – savages, sea-captains...or the terrible Moby Dick himself". One one occasion he spent the evening entertaining Nathaniel Hawthorne and his wife with tales of life in the South Seas, depicting a Polynesian warrior by striding about the room wielding a heavy club. After he had gone Mrs Hawthorne said "Where is that club with which Mr Melville was laying about him so?" There was no sign of it; when they next saw Melville they asked about it. He told them that there had been no club, other than that produced in their own minds by his vivid descriptive skill.

Mendel, Gregor (1822–84). Austrian botanist, who discovered the basic principles of genetics. The son of a peasant, Mendel became a monk and lived at the Abbey of St Thomas in Brünn. He trained as a science teacher and maintained his early interest in botany, growing pea plants in the monastery garden in a series of experiments that lasted for eight years (1857–65). He concluded that characteristics such as tallness in pea plants were determined by pairs of factors (now known as genes), which were contributed equally by both parents and were inherited by the offspring. Mendel published his findings in 1865 but they aroused little enthusiasm. The importance of his work was not recognized until 1900, when it was rediscovered by

Hugo de Vries and other biologists working in the same field.

Mendeleyev, Dmitry Ivanovich (1834–1907). Russian chemist. His most important work was done on the classification of the elements into the periodic table. Elements were listed in increasing order of atomic weight and those with similar properties were grouped together. Mendeleyev left gaps for unknown elements, three of which were discovered within 20 years. He also worked on the properties of petroleum, the liquefaction of gases, and aeronautics.

Mendelssohn, Felix, full name *Jakob Ludwig Felix Mendelssohn-Bartholdy* (1809–47). German composer. By the age of 15 he had already written symphonies, operas, and numerous other pieces. His oratorios *St Paul* and *Elijah* were especially popular in Britain, which he visited several times. The overture *Fingal's Cave* was composed after a visit to Scotland. His other compositions include *Songs Without Words* for piano, incidental music to *A Midsummer Night's Dream*, and the *Italian Symphony*. Mendelssohn was also responsible for the great revival of interest in Bach's music.

Menuhin, Yehudi (1916–   ). British violinist, born in the US. A child prodigy, he made his first concert appearance with the San Francisco Symphony Orchestra at the age of seven. After a triumphant world tour at 18, he retired for two years to devote himself to further study. He has since given hundreds of concerts and won international acclaim. Since 1944 he has lived in Britain. He founded the Yehudi Menuhin School, a boarding school for young musicians, in Surrey in 1963. His numerous honours include being made a life peer and awarded the Légion d'honneur (1985).

Mercator, Gerardus (1512–94). Flemish cartographer, who constructed the first map of the world showing latitude and longitude by means of intersecting lines (1569). Based on what is now known as 'Mercator's projection', it enabled sailors to plot courses over long distances without adjusting compass readings. A skilled mathematician and engraver, Mercator was the first person to use the term 'atlas' to describe a collection of maps.

Metternich, Prince Clemens (1773–1859). Austrian statesman. Through his marriage to the granddaughter of the state chancellor Kaunitz (1795), Metternich was assured a high position at court. He served as minister of foreign affairs (1809–48) and negotiated the marriage of Napoleon to Marie Louise of Austria (1810). He was one of the leading figures at the Congress of Vienna (1814–15). During the revolution of 1848 he was forced to flee to Britain.

Michelangelo, full name *Michelagniolo di Lodovico Buonarroti Simoni* (1475–1564). Italian painter, sculptor, architect, and poet. One of the supreme geniuses of the Italian Renaissance, he grew up in Florence and

❝ He was a good sort of man, but didn't know how to paint.
El Greco on Michelangelo ❞

was encouraged as a youth by his patron, Lorenzo de' Medici. He lived in the Medici palace until Lorenzo's death in 1492. In 1496 he went to Rome, where he produced the famous sculpture of the *Pietà*. After returning to Florence in 1501, he sculpted the statue of *David* from a block of marble that other sculptors had found impossible to use. He was commissioned by Pope Julius II to paint the ceiling of the Sistine Chapel of the Vatican. This mural, based on Genesis, and the *Last Judgment* which he painted later on the wall of the chapel, are perhaps his best-known paintings. Michelangelo also designed the tomb of Pope Julius and the Medici sepulchral chapel in Florence. He became the chief architect of St Peter's in Rome and designed its dome. His poetry includes sonnets and madrigals.

Mies Van Der Rohe, Ludwig (1886–1969). US architect, born in Germany. With his friends Gropius and Le Corbusier, he is considered one of the founding fathers of modern architecture. In 1930 Mies became director of the influential German school of architecture and applied arts, the Bauhaus. An anti-Nazi, he emigrated to the US in 1937. He became famous for his functional designs using steel and glass. Among the many buildings he designed are the Seagram Building, New York, and the National Gallery, Berlin.

Mill, John Stuart (1806–73). Scottish philosopher and economist. The son of the economist James Mill, he is said to have been a child prodigy, reading Greek at the age of three. He established the Utilitarian Society in 1823 but moved away from strict utilitarianism to a more human philosophy after a nervous breakdown in 1827. His major writings include *Principles of Political Economy* (1848), *On Liberty* (1859), and *On the Subjection of Women* (1869). He became an MP in 1865, and lent valuable support to women's suffrage.

Millais, Sir John Everett (1829–96). British painter. His artistic talent developed early and at nine he won a silver medal from the London Society of Artists. With Holman Hunt and Dante Gabriel Rossetti he founded the Pre-Raphaelite Brotherhood in 1848. Some of his best and most famous paintings are perfect examples of Pre-Raphaelite style, for example *Christ in the House of his Parents* (1850) and *Ophelia* (1852). Millais adopted a popular sentimental style in his later pictures, such as *The Boyhood of Raleigh* (1870). His *Bubbles* became widely known from its use as an advertisement for Pears' soap. He was created a baronet in 1885 and elected president of the Royal Academy in 1896.

Miller, Arthur (1915–   ). US dramatist. His father was ruined during the Depression and Miller worked in a warehouse to pay for his studies at the University of Michigan. There he wrote his early plays, including *All My Sons* (1947). He was awarded the Pulitzer Prize in drama for *Death of a Salesman* (1949). In *The Crucible* (1953) he uses the setting of the 17th-century witch hunts in Salem to condemn all instances of minority persecution, particularly the anti-communist trials in the US at that time. He also wrote short stories and a screenplay for his second wife, Marilyn Monroe. Miller's more recent works include *The Ride Down Mt Morgan* (1991), *The Last Yankee* (1992), and the novel *Plain Girl* (1995).

Milne, A(lan) A(lexander)

Milne, A(lan) A(lexander) (1882–1956). British children's writer, the creator of Winnie-the-Pooh. He worked as a journalist before making his name with several plays. During this time he also wrote a number of poems for his son Christopher Robin, some of which featured Christopher Robin's toy bear Winnie-the-Pooh. These poems were later published in two volumes. Winnie-the-Pooh reappeared in the two collections of stories, *Winnie-the-Pooh* (1926) and *The House at Pooh Corner* (1928). All four books have had lasting success with children. *Toad of Toad Hall* (1929) is his adaptation for the stage of Kenneth Grahame's classic *The Wind in the Willows*.

Milton's Blindness

When Milton lost his sight he had no compunction over pressing his daughters into service as his secretaries, determined that his disability should not silence him. The unfortunate girls worked long hours, taking down much of *Paradise Lost* at their father's dictation as well as reading to him at length from works in Greek and Latin – languages of which they were almost entirely ignorant. Did the girls perhaps think of the celebrated line from their father's sonnet 'On his blindness' – "They also serve who only stand and wait"? After the Restoration, Milton was visited by the Duke of York (later James II), who suggested to the poet that his blindness was a divine punishment for having defended the execution of Charles I. Milton retorted: "If Your Highness thinks that misfortunes are the indexes of the wrath of heaven, what must you think of your father's tragical end? I have only lost my eyes – your father lost his head."

Milton, John (1608–74). English Puritan poet and prose-writer. His early poems include *Lycidas* (1637). During the 1640s he devoted himself to controversial writings on religious and political subjects. Several of his pamphlets were concerned with divorce, which Milton advocated, having separated from his first wife. He also held government offices under Cromwell, despite going blind in 1652. He was arrested at the Restoration but released after a short time. His two best-known works, the epic poem *Paradise Lost* (1667), based on the Old Testament story of the fall of man, and *Samson Agonistes* (1671), were dictated to his daughters in retirement.

Mitchell, Reginald Joseph (1895–1937). British aircraft designer. He joined the Supermarine Aviation Company in 1916 and became chief engineer in 1920. He designed many aircraft, including flying boats and racing planes, but is best remembered for the Spitfire, which played an important role in World War II, particularly in the Battle of Britain.

Mitterrand, François (1916–96). French statesman; president of France (1981–95). The son of a stationmaster, Mitterrand was raised in southwestern France and studied at the University of Paris. As a soldier during World War II, he was captured by the Germans but subsequently escaped (1941). He later worked briefly as an official for the Vichy government. After the war he was elected to the national assembly (1946) and held a series of ministerial posts. He stood unsuccessfully as the socialist candidate for the presidency in 1965 and 1974; his eventual victory in the elections of 1981 made him the

first socialist president for 35 years. As president he nationalized the French banking system and took a leading role in forming EC policy. From 1986 he was
obliged to share power with his right-wing prime minister, Jacques Chirac. He was re-elected in 1988 and
presided over lavish celebrations of the bicentenary of
the French Revolution the following year.

Modigliani, Amedeo (1884–1920). Italian painter and
sculptor. In 1906 he moved to Paris, where he studied
African and other primitive art. His early sculpture
and the elongated faces in his portraits show the influence of African masks. An alcoholic and a drug addict, he died of tuberculosis. The following day his
pregnant mistress committed suicide by jumping out
of a window.

Mohammed (c. 570–632). The founder of Islam, known
to his followers as 'The Prophet'. He was born at Mecca
and worked as a shepherd and caravan guide. From 595,
when he married a rich widow, he was able to devote
time to religious meditation. In about 616 he publicly
declared that he was the prophet of God, having had a
number of divine revelations. His teaching is contained
in the Koran, the sacred book of Islam, which Muslims
believe to be the definitive word of God. Owing to
persecution, Mohammed and his new followers were
forced to flee from Mecca to Medina in 622. The Islamic era and calendar are dated from the time of
this flight, which is known as the Hegira. Mohammed
defeated his opponents in several battles and returned
to Mecca in 630 as the acknowledged prophet of God.
He died and was buried at Medina.

Molière and the Béjarts

Throughout his career Molière was closely associated with a theatrical family called the Béjarts. As a young man he was much influenced by Madeleine Béjart, with whom he founded the ill-fated Illustre-Théâtre in 1643. Madeleine, who became Molière's mistress, later created many of the soubrette roles in his plays. In 1662, however, the playwright married Madeleine's much younger sister Armande. By this time Molière had many enemies, and jealous rivals were soon circulating rumours that Armande was in fact his own daughter by Madeleine. It was largely to silence this gossip that King Louis XIV stood godfather to the couple's first child. Sadly, the marriage proved less than happy; the character of the insincere Célimène in Molière's bitterest comedy, *The Misanthrope*, is thought to have been based on Armande.

Molière, pseudonym of *Jean-Baptiste Poquelin* (1622–73). French dramatist. The son of the royal upholsterer, he co-founded the Illustre-Théâtre, an unsuccessful theatre company, in 1643. From 1645 he worked with a touring troupe. In 1658 they moved to Paris, where Molière enjoyed his first success as a writer. The social comedy *Les Précieuses ridicules* (1659) attracted royal patronage for the company. Thereafter Molière wrote and performed in a series of comedies, including *Tartuffe* (1664), a satirical attack on religious hypocrisy, *The Misanthrope* (1666), and *Le Bourgeois Gentilhomme* (1670). Molière was frequently attacked for his biting social satire, and *Tartuffe* was banned for a time. He died after collapsing on stage in 1673.

Monet, Claude (1840–1926). French painter, the only impressionist to win international recognition in his lifetime. His paintings of gardens, boating scenes, and other landscapes emphasized subtle variations of light and atmosphere. Having retired to his house and garden at Giverny, on the Seine, he worked on his famous cycle of waterlily paintings from 1914 until his death.

Monroe, Marilyn, stage name of *Norma Jean Mortenson* (1926–62). US film actress, who became internationally famous as a sex symbol. She grew up in orphanages and married at the age of 14. Her second and third husbands were the baseball star Joe di Maggio and the playwright Arthur Miller. Although she enjoyed great success, her real acting talent was frustrated by her Hollywood image as a 'dumb blonde'. Her films include *The Seven-Year Itch* (1955), *Some Like it Hot* (1959), and *The Misfits* (1960). She died from an overdose of sleeping pills.

> ❛ I know people who say 'Hollywood broke her heart' and all that, but I don't believe it. She was very observant and tough-minded and appealing, but she had this bad judgment about things. She adored and trusted the wrong people... she had to challenge the gods at every turn, and eventually she lost.
> George Cukor on Marilyn Monroe, in Gavin Lambert, *On Cukor* ❜

Montaigne, Michel de (1533–92). French essayist. He dropped the family name, Eyquem, and adopted instead the name of the family estates. He practised law until 1570 and in 1581 became mayor of Bordeaux. He turned to writing after the death of his friend La Boétie and his subsequent unhappy marriage to Françoise de la Chassaigne. His *Essays* (1580; revised 1588) were published in three volumes, and consist of sceptical dissertations on various aspects of life and human nature.

Montana, Joe (1956–   ). US American football player. Montana grew up in the Pittsburgh area and showed early promise as an all-round athlete. Despite his small physique, he chose football rather than baseball, basketball, or athletics, in which he also excelled. In 1979 he was recruited by the San Francisco 49ers. Playing as a quarterback, he set a series of records for completed passes and became famous for his knack of saving the day in the last moments of a match. The 49ers took the NFL Superbowl title in 1982, 1985, and 1989. He moved to the Kansas City Chiefs in 1993.

Montesquieu, original name *Charles-Louis de Secondat* (1689–1755). French political philosopher. He inherited large estates in 1713 and the title Baron de Montesquieu in 1716. For a time he led a dissipated life in Parisian salons and court circles. The satirical *Persian Letters* (1721) brought him fame as a writer but his writing became more serious after a stay in England (1729–31). *The Spirit of Laws* (1748), an examination of the principles of government, is his major work.

Monteverdi, Claudio (1567–1643). Italian composer. He was born at Cremona and studied music in the cathedral there. From about 1591 to 1612 he was attached to the court of the dukes of Mantua, where he wrote his first two operas. The first of these, *Orfeo* (1607), is the first important opera ever written. Having been dismissed from Mantua, he lived in poverty until he was appointed musical director of St Mark's, Venice (1613), where he remained until his death. In 1633 he became a priest. Four of his operas survive, the best known being *The Coronation of Poppea* (1642). He also wrote many madrigals and much sacred music, including the *Vespers* (1610).

Montfort, Simon de (c. 1208–65). English statesman. He came to England from his native France in 1229 and successfully claimed the earldom of Leicester. One of Henry III's favourites, he became discontented with the king's misrule and led an uprising of nobles against him. He defeated Henry in battle at Lewes (1264) and effectively became ruler himself until killed at Evesham by the forces of Henry's son, Edward.

Montgolfier, Joseph Michel (1740–1810) and his brother **Jacques-Étienne** (1745–99). French balloonists. In 1782 Joseph Montgolfier experimented with a silk envelope, which he inflated and caused to rise with hot air from a fire. In June 1783 the brothers launched an elaborately decorated balloon with three animals as passengers. A later development that year was an oval-shaped balloon, with its own stove to provide hot air and a passenger gallery. In November 1783 the first manned ascent and the first free flight by balloon were made.

Montgomery, Bernard, Viscount (1887–1976). British field marshal. A bishop's son, he served with distinction in World War I. In 1940 he commanded a division that was evacuated from Dunkirk. At the head of the 8th Army in North Africa, he routed Rommel's Afrika Korps at the Battle of Alamein (1942). He commanded all Allied ground forces on D-Day (1944) and later received the German surrender on Lüneburg Heath (1945). He achieved popularity through mixing with the men he led, and was most commonly seen in battledress and a beret. After the war he commanded the British-occupied zone of Germany (1946–48) and was deputy supreme commander in Europe for NATO (1951–58).

Montrose, Marquess of, born *James Graham* (1612–50). Scottish general. He fought in the Covenanter army opposed to Charles I's imposition of Anglicanism on Presbyterian Scotland but in the Civil War changed sides, leading an army for Charles against the Presbyterians (1644–45). He had many resounding victories but was routed at Philiphaugh (1645) and fled to the Continent. He returned with a small army in 1650 to avenge Charles's execution but was defeated again and hanged.

Moon, Sun Myung (1920–   ). South Korean businessman and religious leader, founder of the Unification Church. Moon, a millionaire who established his fortune by making and selling weapons in the Korean

War, founded the Unification Church in 1954. The sect's doctrines include a fanatical opposition to the spread of 'world communism' and a belief in Moon as the second Messiah. The Church spread to the US in the early 1960s and is now active in many parts of the world, with some four million adherents. It has been accused of brainwashing its followers (the so-called 'Moonies') and of using them as virtual slave labour. In 1982 Moon, who has lived in the US since the early 1970s, was sentenced to 18 months in jail for conspiracy to evade taxes.

Moore, Henry (1898–1986). British sculptor and artist. He studied at the Royal College of Art and began producing sculpture in 1922. In his sculptures of the human figure he attempted to remain faithful to the nature of the block of wood or stone he was using as material; later works were cast in bronze. He was influenced by primitive art and by surrealist and abstract works. During World War II he acted as an official war artist and produced moving realistic drawings of the war's affect on civilians. He gained international recognition soon after the war. There were major exhibitions of his work in New York (1946), London (1968), and Florence (1972).

More, Sir Thomas (1478–1535). English statesman and humanist. He was a scholar of Greek and theology prior to studying law. His best-known literary work, *Utopia* (1516), describes an ideal state in which there is universal education and religious toleration. In 1529 he rose to the position of Lord Chancellor. However, he felt unable to support Henry VIII's decision to break

---

More on Marriage

For a great Christian idealist, Sir Thomas More had an unusually direct approach to the choice of marriage partners.
In his *Utopia* he argued that all prospective partners should
inspect each other naked before entering into a binding
contract. More unusually, he was prepared to put this pre-
cept into practice with his own daughters. When Sir William
Roper called on More early one morning to ask for the hand
of one of his daughters, the delighted father led his guest
to the girls' bedroom and whipped the sheet off their sleeping forms. The naked girls awoke and quickly turned onto
their stomachs. Sir William told More: "Now I have seen
both sides", and made his choice. The marriage was very
happy. As a young man More, too, had been faced with a
choice between two sisters. Although his inclination was towards the younger girl, a noted beauty, he feared that such
a choice would offend the older and plainer sister. Largely
out of compassion, he chose her instead — and enjoyed a
long and happy marriage.

---

away from papal authority in order to annul his marriage to Catherine of Aragon and resigned. His refusal
to recognize Henry as the head of the English Church
led to his execution. He was canonized in 1935.

Morris, William (1834–96). British craftsman, poet, and
socialist. Morris became an artist through the influence of Dante Gabriel Rossetti. In 1861 he set up the
firm of Morris and Co., which produced wallpapers,
tapestries, furniture, and stained glass. His poetry, designs, and socialist ideals reflected his interest in the
Middle Ages, which he regarded as a period when
work, craftsmanship, and art had been closely linked.

His romance *News from Nowhere* (1891) expressed his horror of industrialization. Morris was largely responsible for the revival of handicrafts in England and for a revolution in the arts of furnishing and house decoration.

Morrison, Toni, original name *Chloe Anthony Wofford* (1931–). US writer, whose works concentrate on the experience of Black women in the US. Morrison grew up in the Midwest and studied at Howard University and Cornell University. After several years of teaching, she began a successful career as a fiction editor. Her early novels *The Bluest Eye* (1970) and *Sula* (1973) were followed by *Song of Solomon* (1977), a poetic fantasy that brought her national acclaim. Later works include *Tar Baby* (1983), the Pulitzer Prize-winning *Beloved* (1987), and *Jazz* (1992). She was awarded the Nobel Prize in 1993.

Morse, Samuel (1791–1872). US inventor of the Morse Code. A keen artist, he studied painting in Britain from 1811 to 1815. He also became interested in electricity. He had the idea of a telegraph in 1832 and by 1838 he had built a prototype and devised the Morse Code for use on it. In 1843, with government sponsorship, he set up the first commercial line, between Washington and Baltimore. In the Morse Code each letter of the alphabet is represented by a series of dots and dashes, a dash being three times the length of a dot.

Mosley, Sir Oswald (1896–1980). British politician. He served in Parliament successively as a Conservative (1918–22), an Independent (1922–24), and a Labour member (1924–30). After unsuccessfully trying to form a socialist party in 1931, he founded the British Union of Fascists (1932). At the outbreak of World War II he was interned but was released in 1943 on health grounds. Following the war he resumed his fascist activities and founded the Union Movement.

Mountbatten of Burma, Louis, 1st Earl (1900–79). British naval commander, a greatgrandson of Queen Victoria. His father, Prince Louis of Battenberg, adopted the name of Mountbatten in 1917. Mountbatten served in the Royal Navy in both World Wars. As supreme commander for south-east Asia (1943–46) he successfully led the recapture of Burma from the Japanese. He then played a major part in the transfer of power to India and Pakistan, and their partition, as the last viceroy of India (1947). In 1979 he was murdered while on his annual holiday in Ireland, when his boat was blown up by a bomb planted by IRA terrorists.

Mozart, Wolfgang Amadeus (1756–91). Austrian composer. The son of a well-known violinist and composer, he was a musical prodigy and spent his childhood touring Europe and giving recitals with his father and sister. From 1770 to 1781 Mozart was master of the band at the court of the archbishop of Salzburg, who did not appreciate his genius and treated him like a servant. He married after leaving this post and spent most of the rest of his life in Vienna. Although many of his works were successful with the public, he was continually troubled by financial difficulties. He composed some 40 symphonies, 25 piano concertos, 25 string quartets, a number of operas, and many other works. His operas include *Don Giovanni* (1787), *Cosi fan tutte* (1790), and *The Magic Flute* (1791).

Munch, Edvard (1863–1944). Norwegian expressionist painter. Mainly self-taught as an artist, Munch travelled to Paris as a young man, where he came under the influence of Gauguin and Van Gogh. He adopted the powerful expressionist style of his mature works during a subsequent stay in Berlin. With their morbid subject matter, distorted forms, and use of primary colours, these works had a major influence on German art in the early 20th century. His most famous work is the anguished *The Scream* (1893). In 1910 he returned to settle in Norway, where he painted the murals for the festival hall in Oslo University (1913).

Murdoch, Rupert (1931–   ). US publisher and media mogul, born in Australia. The son of a journalist and publisher, Murdoch studied at Oxford and worked on the London *Daily Express* before returning home to manage the family newspapers (1952). Over the following years he acquired and transformed a series of titles, in each case boosting sales with a downmarket emphasis on scandal, sport, and populist politics. He became a major figure in British publishing by acquiring the *News of the World* (1969) and *The Sun* (1970), which became the country's best-selling daily. Owing to Murdoch's track record, there was much controversy when he also acquired *The Times* in 1981. In 1986 he led a technological revolution in British newspaper publishing when he moved production of *The Times* to a new high-tech plant without a union agreement. During the 1980s Murdoch became increasingly involved in radio, television, film, and book publishing. In 1985, the year he became a US citizen, he acquired the film studio 20th Century-Fox. He launched the satellite TV channel Sky (later British Sky Broadcasting) in 1989. Both Murdoch's influence on popular standards and the sheer extent of his media empire have provoked some concern.

> ❝ Fascism is a religion; the 20th century will be known in history as the century of Fascism.
>
> Benito Mussolini ❞

Mussolini, Benito (1883–1945). Italian dictator. The son of a blacksmith, he founded the Fascist Party in 1919, the members of which became known as the 'Blackshirts'. In 1922 Mussolini led the Blackshirts in the March on Rome, as a result of which he became prime minister. He subsequently established a fascist dictatorship, in which he became known as *Duce* (leader). At first Italians were impressed by his public-works programmes and his skill in negotiating the Lateran treaty with the Roman Catholic church (which created the Vatican City as a separate state). However, his invasion of Ethiopia in 1936 provoked worldwide protests. He drew Italy into World War II (1940) in alliance with Hitler, but the country suffered serious defeat. A revolt against him in 1943 ended his fascist regime but he was spectacularly rescued from imprisonment by German paratroopers. Later he and his mistress were shot by partisans while trying to flee the country.

Mussorgsky, Modest Petrovich (1839–81). Russian composer. He resigned an army commission in 1856 and worked as a clerk in the civil service, hoping to have more time to devote to music. His highly original works, many of which were left incomplete, made use of Russian folk music. Mussorgsky ruined his health by drinking and died in poverty. His masterpiece, the opera *Boris Godunov* (1869), became well known in a version revised by Rimsky-Korsakov but has since been produced in its original form. Other well-known works are the orchestral piece, *Night on the Bare Mountain*, and the piano suite *Pictures from an Exhibition*.

N

Nabokov, Vladimir (1899–1977). Russian novelist and critic. His aristocratic family fled Russia at the Revolution. After some years in Europe, Nabokov became professor of Russian and European literature at Cornell University in the US. His early works were written in Russian but from the 1940s he chose to write in English. *Lolita* (1955), the story of a middle-aged man's infatuation with a 12-year-old girl, brought him international fame, though some of this was due to the controversial subject of the novel. *Pale Fire* (1962) is

---

Nabokov's Pug

The writer Nabokov was also an expert lepidopterist, never happier than when he was collecting butterflies. He considered one of his greatest achievements to be the discovery of a new species of butterfly, Nabokov's Pug (*Eupithecia nabokovi*), in 1943. The discovery was made during one of his many collecting trips from a friend's house at Alta in Utah. Nabokov was well known for his single-minded concentration in pursuit of his prey. On one occasion he returned to Alta with the news that he had heard someone groaning in pain near a stream he had visited but had not broken off the chase to investigate. The body of a prospector was subsequently found at the spot, which was renamed Dead Man's Gulch.

---

perhaps his greatest work. He also published scholarly works on literature and entomology.

Namath, Joe, full name *Joseph William Namath* (1943–   ). US American footballer, considered one of the best passers in the history of the sport. Brought up in Beaver Falls, a steel-mill town in Pennsylvania, he played quarterback at the University of Alabama until 1964, when he was recruited by the New York Jets. In 1969 he was briefly obliged to resign from the team owing to the controversy aroused by his ownership of a Broadway nightclub. He continued with the Jets for a further seven seasons, during which he set numerous records for passing the ball. After one season with the Los Angeles Rams he retired in 1978. Namath is also well known to the US public for his appearances in commercials and in acting roles.

Nansen, Fridtjof (1861–1930). Norwegian polar explorer, scientist, and statesman. He successfully crossed Greenland in 1888 and five years later set off to explore the Arctic. He reached the North Pole in 1896 by letting his ship *Fram* drift north in the ice and continuing by dog sled. After his return Nansen became professor of zoology and subsequently oceanography at Oslo University. From 1906 to 1908 he was Norwegian ambassador to London. In 1922 he received the Nobel Peace Prize for his refugee relief work with the League of Nations.

Napoleon I, full name *Napoleon Bonaparte* (1769–1821). French general and emperor, one of Europe's greatest leaders. He entered the military school in Paris as a cadet in 1784 and rose to prominence during the French Revolution. He married Joséphine, widow of the Vicomte de Beauharnais, in 1769 and in the same year was put in command of the victorious Italian campaign (1796–97). In 1799 a coup established Napoleon as first consul and he effectively became a military dictator, assuming the title of emperor in 1804. He secured his greatest victory at the Battle of Austerlitz (1805) against Austria and Russia; following the Peace of Tilsit he ruled virtually the whole of continental Europe. Anxious for a male heir, he divorced Joséphine (1810) and married the Archduchess Marie Louise of Austria, who bore him a son a year later. His decline began with an unsuccessful campaign in Spain and his disastrous invasion of Russia (1812), during which about five sixths of his army perished on the retreat from Moscow. The other European nations united against him and the French were crushed at Leipzig (1814). Napoleon was exiled to Elba. Although he escaped and regained power for the 'Hundred Days', he was decisively defeated at Waterloo (1815). This time he was exiled to St Helena, where he died.

Nash, John (1752–1835). British architect. His most famous work was done in London for George IV's 'Metropolitan Improvement' schemes. He designed the Regent's Park terraces (1821–28) and later enlarged Buckingham Palace and designed Marble Arch as an entrance to the palace. Nash also remodelled Brighton Pavilion in an oriental style.

Nasser, Gamal Abdel (1918–70). Egyptian statesman. He served in the army until 1952, when he was one of the leaders of the coup that overthrew King Farouk. He became prime minister (1954), president of Egypt (1956), and president of the United Arab Republic (1958), a state created by the union of Egypt, Syria, and (subsequently) North Yemen. His nationalization of the Suez Canal in 1956 led to an abortive Anglo-French invasion of Egypt (the Suez crisis). During his presidency Egypt became an Islamic Arab state and the leading power in the Arab world.

Navratilova, Martina (1956–). US tennis player, born in Czechoslavia. She defected to the US in 1975 and became a citizen of that country in 1981. Her successes include nine Wimbledon singles titles (1978–79; 1982–87; 1990) and victories in the US Open and the French Championship. She has also been highly successful in doubles, winning eight grand slam titles with the US player Pam Shriver. By the mid 1980s she had become the highest-earning sportswoman of all time. Her records include an unbroken run of 74 wins. She retired in 1994.

Nebuchadnezzar II (c. 630–562 BC). King of Babylon from 605 BC. He widely extended Babylonian power, especially in Palestine and Syria, and his total destruction of Judah led to the deportation of many Jews to Babylon. During his reign Nebuchadnezzar had the city and temples of Babylon magnificently rebuilt, including the famous Hanging Gardens. The biblical story of his madness is probably not based on historical fact.

Nehru, Jawaharlal (1889–1964). Indian statesman; first prime minister of independent India (1957–64). A lawyer by training, he became committed to the cause of Indian independence during the 1910s. Between 1921 and 1945 he was imprisoned nine times by the British, serving a total of 13 years for his nationalist activities. As leader of the Congress party (from 1929), he was second only to Gandhi in the influence he had among his people. During his premiership he worked to build up India's industry and economy and maintained a policy of nonalignment. His daughter was the politician Indira Gandhi.

Nelson, Horatio, Viscount (1758–1805). British admiral. He joined his first ship at 12 and was a captain by the age of 20. He fought against the French at Genoa in 1795 and subsequently destroyed Napoleon's fleet at Aboukir Bay in Egypt (1798). In 1793 he met the wife of the British ambassador in Rome, Lady Emma Hamilton, who bore him a daughter in 1801. Nelson's naval service was continually interrupted by ill health. He lost the sight of his right eye in battle and his right arm was amputated after he was shot through the elbow. At the Battle of Copenhagen (1801) he ignored a signal ordering him to break off the action by putting his telescope to his blind eye and claiming not to see the signal. A superior Danish fleet was destroyed as a result. In 1805 he fought in the *Victory* against the French fleet of Admiral Villeneuve at the Battle of Trafalgar. Although the French were defeated, Nelson was mortally wounded by a sharpshooter at the height of the battle. The destruction of the French fleet at Trafalgar was a decisive factor in Britain's eventual victory in the Napoleonic Wars.

Nero, full name *Nero Claudius Caesar Drusus Germanicus* (37–68 AD). Roman emperor. His mother, Agrippina, secured the succession for him on the death of her second husband Claudius (54), excluding Britannicus, the rightful heir. Nero, who early displayed traits of cruelty, is believed to have arranged the deaths of Agrippina, Britannicus, his wife Octavia, and many others. The Great Fire of Rome (64) is often attributed to Nero, although modern historians do not consider him guilty of starting it; he himself accused the Christians of the crime and violently persecuted them. During a rebellion in 68 he was condemned to death by the senate but committed suicide before the sentence could be carried out.

The Great Artist

Nero's downfall was precipitated in part by his love of the theatre. Although acting was considered a scandalous profession at the time, Nero participated enthusiastically in plays and mimes and was inordinately proud of his abilities. He is said to have had the famous performer Paris put to death from sheer jealousy of his success. In 66 AD Nero went on a tour of Greece, during which he acted in a number of Greek plays. His portrayal of 'low' characters, such as pregnant women and slaves, is said to have disgusted many leading Romans far more than his evident cruelty and depravity. The loss of credibility this entailed was one factor in the revolts that led to his fall in 68. As he prepared to commit suicide, Nero watched the servants building his funeral pyre and sighed through his tears "How great an artist is lost here!"

Newcomen, Thomas (1663–1729). English engineer. In 1705 he patented a steam engine for pumping water out of mines, in which the actual pumping was done by atmospheric pressure rather than by the steam itself. It could therefore pump over greater heights and the mines could be sunk deeper. The first commercially successful steam engine was installed near Dudley Castle, Staffordshire, in 1712. In due course Newcomen's engine was superseded by one designed by Watt.

Newman, John Henry, Cardinal (1801–90). British churchman. He was ordained an Anglican priest and in 1827 was appointed vicar of St Mary's, Oxford. With other members of the university he started the Oxford or 'Tractarian' Movement in 1833. It attempted to revive Catholic traditions in the Church of England and took its name from *Tracts for the Times*, a series of articles on the subject. In 1845 Newman became a Roman Catholic. He was appointed rector of Dublin University in 1854 and created a cardinal in 1879. His best-known works are *The Idea of a University* (1854), his autobiography *Apologia pro vita sua* (1864), and the hymn 'Lead, Kindly Light'. In 1991 he was awarded the title 'Venerable', the first step towards canonization.

Newman, Paul (1925–). US film actor and director. He first appeared in films in the 1950s and has played a variety of heroes and antiheroes. His earlier films include *Cat on a Hot Tin Roof* (1959) and *Cool Hand Luke* (1967). His highly successful partnership with Robert Redford in *Butch Cassidy and the Sundance Kid* (1969) was revived in *The Sting* (1973). Later successes include

The Verdict (1982), *The Color of Money* (1986), which earned him an Oscar, and *Nobody's Fool* (1994). Newman is married to the actress Joanne Woodward, whom he has directed in several films. He has also created a highly successful range of food products.

Newton, Sir Isaac (1642–1727). English mathematician and scientist. After graduating from Trinity College, Cambridge, Newton privately studied the works of the leading scientists and mathematicians of his day. He formulated the rules of the calculus, the binomial theorem, and the law of gravity and demonstrated that white light is made up of rays of light of different colours. In 1667 he returned to Cambridge as a Fellow of Trinity College, becoming professor of mathematics in 1669. Although his work remained largely unpublished, in 1672 he was elected a Fellow of the Royal Society for his invention of the reflecting telescope and for his researches into light. In 1684, encouraged by Edmond Halley, Newton began writing *The Mathematical Principles of Natural Philosophy* (1687). This major work contained the law of universal gravitation, Newton's three laws of motion and many other important ideas that together formed the basis for the development of modern physics. Newton became Master of the Royal Mint in 1700 and president of the Royal Society in 1703. The publication of his *Optics* in 1704 provoked a long quarrel with Leibniz, each accusing the other of plagiarism. Newton was also a keen student of alchemy and wrote commentaries on the biblical books of Daniel and Revelation. Newton was knighted by Queen Anne in 1705, becoming the first person to be honoured in this way for scientific achievement.

> ❛ I don't know what I may
> seem to the world, but as to
> myself, I seem to have been
> only like a boy playing on the
> sea-shore and diverting
> myself in now and then
> finding a smoother pebble or
> a prettier shell than
> ordinary, whilst the great
> ocean of truth lay all
> undiscovered before me.
> Sir Isaac Newton of himself,
> in Joseph Spence,
> *Anecdotes* (1820) ❜

Nicholas II (1868–1918). Last tsar of Russia, the son of Alexander III, whom he succeeded in 1894. He married the German Princess Alexandra (1894), a woman of stronger character than his own. Unsuited by temperament to govern Russia, the tsar was ill at ease in public and clung obstinately to the belief that he ruled through divine right. Russia's disastrous defeat in the Japanese war (1904–05), leading to the 1905 revolution, forced him to agree to a new constitution. During World War I his involvement in the war left the country's government effectively with Alexandra, whose decisions and policies were considerably influenced by Rasputin. Following the Bolsheviks' seizure of power (1917) he was forced to abdicate and was shot with his wife and children at Ekaterinburg. In 1995 DNA testing established that a number of bones, which had been discovered four years earlier in a disused mineshaft, were those of Nicholas.

Nicklaus, Jack (1940–). US golfer, who won more major championships than any other player. Between 1959 and 1986 he was US amateur champion twice, US Open champion four times, British Open Champion three times, US Professional Golfers Association champion five times, and Masters champion five times – a total of 19 titles in 26 years.

Nietzsche, Friedrich (1844–1900). German philosopher. He was appointed a professor at Basel University in 1869 despite his lack of a doctorate. *The Birth of Tragedy* (1872) was his first book. Nietzsche resigned his professorship owing to ill-health in 1879 and devoted the next ten years to writing, living alone in rented rooms. The important works *Thus Spake Zarathustra* (1883–89) and *Beyond Good and Evil* (1886), in which he preached a total rejection of Christian values, only slowly attracted attention. In 1889 he collapsed with a mental breakdown and never fully recovered.

Nightingale, Florence (1820–1910). British nurse and hospital reformer. At the age of 34, during the Crimean War, she volunteered to take a party of nurses to work in the British military hospitals in Turkey. By hard work and determination she soon improved the appalling conditions there, reducing the death rate by 40 per cent; her custom of making a night round earned her the nickname 'The Lady with the Lamp'. She returned to Britain in 1856 to enormous public acclaim and devoted the rest of her life to improving the Army's medical service and developing civilian training for nurses and midwives. She founded the Nightingale School for Nurses, the first such school in the world, at St Thomas's Hospital, London. In 1907 she became the first woman to receive the Order of Merit.

Nijinsky, Vaslav (1890–1950). Russian ballet dancer and choreographer. His family was by tradition associated with dancing and he became a member of the Russian Imperial Ballet at the age of 18. After leaving Russia in 1911, he joined Diaghilev's company in France and rapidly gained an international reputation. His dancing was outstanding and he seemed to defy the law of gravity. As a choreographer he introduced new styles of dancing in ballets such as *L'Après-midi d'un faune* and *The Rite of Spring*. However, his mental instability forced him to retire from ballet in 1918.

Nixon, Richard M(ilhous) (1913–94). US politician; 37th president of the US. He served as vice-president (1952–60) under Eisenhower and was an unsuccessful candidate for the presidency in 1960. Following several political setbacks, he was elected president in 1969. In 1972 he became the first US president to visit communist China. After his re-election later that year he achieved the withdrawal of the US from the Vietnam War (1973). However, public support for Nixon crumbled during investigations into the so-called Watergate affair, which revealed that agents of Nixon's presidential campaign had broken into Democratic party headquarters to gain information. Threatened with impeachment for his tacit approval of the affair, Nixon resigned, being the first US president to do so.

> ❝ President Nixon's motto was,
> if two wrongs don't make a
> right, try three.
> Norman Cousins, *The Daily
> Telegraph* 17 July 1979 ❞

Nobel, Alfred Bernhard (1833–96). Swedish chemist and engineer. His research into the safe use of nitroglycerine led him to the development of dynamite, which contains nitroglycerine in a stable dry form that can be exploded by a detonator. Nobel left the bulk of his fortune to establish annual international awards, the Nobel Prizes, which are awarded for outstanding achievements in chemistry, physics, medicine, literature, peace, and economics.

Nolan, Sir Sidney (1917–91). Australian painter, whose works were inspired by Australian folklore and landscapes. Nolan was born in Melbourne, the son of a tram driver. Largely self-taught, he became a full-time painter in 1938 and gave an exhibition of abstracts in 1940. He painted his first Australian landscapes during army service in World War II and in 1946 became famous with his *Ned Kelly* series, which depict the outlaw in an intentionally naive style. He followed this success with a series based on the first explorers of the Australian interior. In the early 1950s he travelled widely in Europe and Africa. Despite settling in London in 1954, he continued to specialize in Australian subjects. He also designed for the stage and produced illustrations for books, including a volume of his own poetry. Nolan was knighted in 1981.

Nostradamus (1503–66). French astrologer and physician, also known as *Michel de Notredame*. His *Centuries* (1555), a collection of obscure prophecies, brought him fame and in 1560 he was appointed physician to Charles IX of France. The accuracy of his prophecies, one of which is supposed to predict the rise of Hitler, has been the subject of much debate.

Nuffield, William Richard Morris, Viscount (1877–1963). British industrialist and philanthropist. The son of a farm labourer, he started work at 15. He set up a bicycle repair shop, extending it to motorcycles and, later, to cars. In 1912 he founded the company Morris Motors Ltd at Cowley, near Oxford, producing his first Morris Oxford car in 1913. His business was successful and he concentrated on producing cars as cheaply as possible. The first MG sports car was produced in 1923. Following the merger of Morris Motors with the Austin Motor Company (1952), his company became the third largest car-manufacturer in the world. He gave much of his wealth to charity and founded Nuffield College, Oxford, and the Nuffield Foundation.

Nureyev, Rudolph (1938–93). Russian ballet dancer. A member of the Kirov Ballet of Leningrad, Nureyev sought political asylum in the West in 1961. He was soon acclaimed as one of the greatest of 20th-century dancers, being particularly admired for his performances with Dame Margot Fonteyn. He has been credited with re-establishing the importance of the male dancer in classical ballet. Nureyev became an Austrian citizen in 1982 and was director of the Paris Opéra Ballet from 1983 to 1989.

Nyerere, Julius (1922–). Tanzanian statesman; president (1962–85). After studying at Makerere College in Uganda and Edinburgh University he formed (1954) the Tanganyika African National Union to fight for Tanganyikan independence. When this was achieved, in 1960, Nyerere became chief minister, assuming the presidency in 1962. In 1964 the country changed its name to Tanzania, after union with Zanzibar. Nyerere ruled a one-party state until his retirement as president in 1985; he retired as party chairman in 1990.

O

Oates, Lawrence (1880–1912). British Antarctic explorer, a member of Scott's Antarctic expedition (1910–13). After reaching the South Pole, Oates was suffering from severe frostbite. Knowing that he would be a burden to his companions on the return journey, he walked out into a blizzard to die. Oates's last words were recorded in Scott's diary: "I am just going outside, and may be some time".

Oates, Titus (1649–1705). English clergyman and perjurer. He began obtaining money or other advantages by bringing false charges against people early in his career. Having converted to Roman Catholicism in 1677, he went to Spain and France, pretending to study for the priesthood. He returned to England and with an ally invented the 'popish plot', a supposed Jesuit conspiracy to murder Charles II. At least 35 innocent people were executed because of his false accusations. In 1685 he was convicted of perjury, flogged almost to death, and imprisoned. Although he was released in 1688, the House of Lords refused to quash his conviction.

O'Casey, Sean (1880–1964). Irish dramatist. Born to a poor Protestant family, O'Casey worked as a manual labourer and was entirely self-educated. He joined the paramilitary Irish Citizen Army but left disillusioned in 1914. His early plays, staged by the Abbey Theatre, Dublin, are mainly concerned with civil strife in Ireland, and include *Juno and the Paycock* (1924) and *The Plough and the Stars* (1926), set during the 1916 Easter Rising. Although many of his plays are set in times of crisis and war, O'Casey wrote some of the best comic scenes and dialogues in modern drama. After the Abbey rejected *The Silver Tassie* (1929), he left Ireland for Britain, where he married the Irish actress Eileen Carey Reynolds. He continued to write plays, as well as a six-volume autobiography.

Offenbach, Jacques (1819–80). French composer. Of German origin, he studied music in Paris and played in the orchestra of the Opéra-Comique. He later became a conductor at the Théâtre Française. In 1855 he opened a theatre of his own for which he wrote 90 operettas over a period of 30 years. His best-known light opera is *Orpheus in the Underworld* (1858). His only successful serious opera was *The Tales of Hoffmann* (1881), which was completed by another composer after his death.

Ohm, Georg Simon (1787–1854). German physicist. His experiments with electricity, while he was a professor at Cologne, led to his formulation of a rule now known as Ohm's law. This states that the current flowing through a conductor is directly proportional to its resistance. Ohm's discovery is the basis of much electrical and electronic theory; the unit of electrical resistance is named after him.

> ❝ Between good and great
> acting is fixed an inexorable
> gulf, which may be crossed
> only by the elect, ...Gielgud,
> seizing a parasol, crosses by
> tightrope; [Michael]
> Redgrave, with lunatic
> obstinacy, plunges into the
> torrent, usually sinking
> within yards of the opposite
> shore; Laurence Olivier pole
> vaults over, hair-raisingly,
> in a single animal leap.
> Kenneth Tynan ❞

Olivier, Laurence, Baron (1907–89). British actor. The son of a clergyman, he made his debut at 15 as Katherine in a boys' performance of *The Taming of the Shrew*. From the late 1930s onwards he was a regular performer with the Old Vic Company. He later became the founding director of the National Theatre (1962–73). Although he appeared in a wide range of roles, he was particularly associated with famous Shakespearean parts, such as Hamlet, Henry V, Richard III, Macbeth, and Romeo. He also directed films of the first three of these plays. His other roles included Archie Rice, hero of *The Entertainer* (1957), Berenger in Ionesco's *Rhinoceros* (1960), and Lord Marchmain in the television version of *Brideshead Revisited* (1981). His three wives included the actresses Vivien Leigh and Joan Plowright. He was made a life peer in 1970, the first actor to be so honoured.

Omar Khayyam (c. 1048–1122). Persian poet, astronomer, and mathematician, The son of a tent-maker, he was best known in Persia for his treatise on algebra and metaphysics and for his astronomical works. His fame in the Western world, however, rests on Edward Fitzgerald's free translation of a number of his poems as *The Rubáiyát of Omar Khayyam* (1859). This consists of a series of quatrains expressing a cynical and hedonistic view of life. Persian scholars have expressed doubts that all the verses attributed to Khayyam were written by him.

Onassis, Aristotle Socrates (1906–75). Greek shipping tycoon, who became one of the world's richest men. Onassis was born in Smyrna (now Izmir in Turkey), the son of a Greek merchant. When he was 16 Turkish hostility to Greeks caused the family to flee to Athens. A year later he set off to make his fortune in South America with only $60. Working from Buenos Aires, he built up a successful tobacco importing business before diversifying into other commodities; he was a dollar millionaire by his mid twenties. During the Depression, Onassis had the foresight to buy six freighters at a bargain price; these were to form the basis of the vast merchant fleet that he built up in the 1940s and 1950s. In 1956 Onassis sold his whaling ships to Japan and was awarded a contract to run the Greek national airline. With his fabulous wealth, glamorous lifestyle, and friendships with celebrities from all walks of life, Onassis became an internationally famous figure. In 1968 he married Jacqueline Bouvier Kennedy (1929–94), the widow of the assassinated US president.

O'Neill, Eugene (1888–1953). US dramatist. The son of touring actors, he worked as a seaman from 1907. In 1912 he developed tuberculosis and spent six months in a sanatorium; it was during this confinement that he began to write. He won growing recognition as a dramatist from 1916 onwards and was awarded the Nobel Prize in 1936. His plays, which are generally sombre and intense, include *Desire Under the Elms* (1924), the trilogy *Mourning Becomes Electra* (1931), *The Iceman Cometh* (1946), and *Long Day's Journey into Night* (1956), which is based on the unhappy experiences of his early life.

Oppenheimer, J(ulius) Robert (1904–67). US physicist. After graduating from Harvard University he did atomic research at the Cavendish Laboratory, Cambridge. He was chosen in 1943 to direct a new scientific laboratory for the Manhattan Project, which aimed to use nuclear energy for military purposes. This was established at Los Alamos, New Mexico, and produced the first atomic bomb. The first nuclear explosion took place on 16 July 1945, at Almogordo, New Mexico. Oppenheimer later opposed US development of the hydrogen bomb. He was accused of being a security risk during Joseph McCarthy's anti-communist witch-hunt, but was rehabilitated in 1963, when he received the Enrico Fermi Award from President Johnson.

> The physicists have known sin; and this is a knowledge which they cannot lose.
> J. Robert Oppenheimer, *Open Mind* (1955)

Orwell, George, penname of *Eric Blair* (1903–50). British novelist and writer. Born in India, he was educated at Eton and served with the police in Burma for five years. His determination to reject his privileged background and experience poverty inspired his early books *Down and Out in Paris and London* (1933) and *The Road to Wigan Pier* (1937). While fighting for the Republicans in the Spanish Civil War he developed a hatred for communist totalitarianism, which he attacks in the allegorical tale *Animal Farm* (1945). *Nineteen Eighty-Four* (1949) paints a horrific picture of a future state dominated by 'Big Brother' and reflects Orwell's mistrust of all political dogma. He died of tuberculosis.

Osborne, John (1929–94). British dramatist. After leaving university he worked for a time as an actor. His first play, *Look Back in Anger* (1956), depicts a dissatisfied young man rebelling against social privilege. It was the first of a number of plays written in the 1950s, whose authors were nicknamed 'angry young men'. Several notable English actors starred in Osborne's subsequent plays: Laurence Olivier in *The Entertainer* (1957), Albert Finney in *Luther* (1961), Nicol Williamson in *Inadmissable Evidence* (1964), and Paul Scofield in *The Hotel in Amsterdam* (1968). His last play, written after a long interval, was *Déjà Vu* (1992). He also wrote an Oscar-winning script for the film *Tom Jones* (1963) and two bitter volumes of autobiography (1981, 1991).

Otto I, known as *Otto the Great* (912–73). King of Germany and Holy Roman Emperor. He succeeded to the throne in 936 and deliberately used the bishops to strengthen his rule. He was crowned Holy Roman Emperor by Pope John XII (962), but subsequently had him deposed and elected a pope of his own choice. During his reign Otto had a constant struggle to control the powers of the German dukes whilst holding the invading Magyars at bay in eastern Europe.

Ovid, full name *Publius Ovidius Naso* (43 BC–17 AD). Roman poet. His love poems (16 BC) made him famous. He also wrote *Love-Letters of the Heroines* and the witty and immoral *Art of Love* (1 AD). His *Metamorphoses*, a collection of verse stories in 15 books, was unfinished when he was exiled in 8 AD. The reason for his exile is not known. The *Metamorphoses* were published posthumously, together with his letters from exile.

Ovid's Exile

The reasons why Ovid was suddenly exiled from Rome at the age of 50 have never been satisfactorily explained. He himself never revealed the cause of his banishment, apparently regarding it as too dangerous to mention. According to some, he had been discovered in an affair with Livia, the wife of the emperor Augustus; others conjecture that Ovid had somehow found out about the emperor's incest with his daughter Julia. Ovid spent his last years living on the Black Sea coast, writing a series of nostalgic elegies and verse epistles. These are full of the most extravagant flattery of Augustus, from whom he evidently hoped to obtain a pardon. When the emperor died, Ovid even consecrated a chapel to the new 'god'.

Owen, Robert (1771–1858). Welsh industrialist and reformer. In 1880 he became the co-owner of a mill at New Lanark, Scotland, where he introduced schemes to improve the conditions of the workers and their families. The community was visited by many other social reformers, who regarded it as a model for future experiments. Owen's attempts to establish co-operative communities elsewhere were less successful.

Owens, Jesse, full name *James Cleveland Owens* (1913–80). US Black athlete. Born in Alabama, the son of poor farmers, Owens showed remarkable athletic abilities from an early age. In May 1935, at an event in Michigan, he beat or equalled six world records during the space of an hour. The long-jump record he set that day was not beaten for 25 years. In 1936 he won four gold medals (100 metres, 200 metres, 4 × 100 metres relay, and long jump) at the Berlin Olympics, much to the displeasure of Hitler, who apparently left the stadium to avoid congratulating the Black athlete. After returning to the US, financial pressures obliged him to turn professional, thus ensuring his absence from major competition.

P

Paderewski, Ignace Jan (1860–1941). Polish pianist and statesman. He made his debut in Vienna in 1887 and over the next few years established himself internationally, especially as an interpreter of Chopin. During World War I he toured the US to raise funds for Polish war victims. In 1919 he became the first prime minister of free Poland but resigned the same year and returned to his musical career. Of his own compositions, only the *Minuet in G* is widely known.

Paganini, Niccolò (1782–1840). Italian violinist. He first appeared in public at the age of 11. After studying in Parma he made the first of many European tours and was soon hailed as the greatest violinist of his time. His incredible virtuosity and dark gaunt appearance gave rise to the story that he was in league with the devil. He composed numerous works for the violin and was also a brilliant guitarist.

Page, Sir Frederick Handley (1885–1962). British aeronautical pioneer. In World War I Page designed the Handley Page 0/400, the first twin-engine bomber. Between the wars the Handley Page company, founded in 1909, merged with Imperial Airways. During World War II Page designed the Harrow, Hampden, and

Halifax bombers. He also built the post-war Victor B2 bomber, armed with the Blue Steel missile.

Liberty

Benjamin Franklin once told Tom Paine, "Where liberty is, there is my country." Paine replied, "Where liberty is not, there is mine."

Paine, Tom (1737–1809). US political philosopher and writer. Born into a Quaker family in Thetford, Norfolk, Paine initially followed his father's trade of corset maker. In 1774 he emigrated to Philadelphia, where he began to write radical journalism. After the outbreak of the American Revolution (1775–83) he became famous with his pamphlet *Common Sense* (1776), which argued for immediate independence. Having returned to Britain in 1787, he published *The Rights of Man* (1791–92), a defence of the French Revolution. His call for a similar revolution in Britain led to his indictment for treason, forcing him to flee to France. As a member of the French National Convention (1792–93) he opposed the execution of Louis XVI and urged moderation. This led to his imprisonment during the Terror (1794–95). While in prison he completed *The Age of Reason* (1794–96), an attack on Christianity that alienated most of Paine's supporters in the US. He returned to America in 1802 but died in poverty and neglect.

Palestrina, Giovanni Pierluigi da (1525–94). Italian composer of sacred music. He was born in the town of

Palestrina, near Rome, and became organist and choirmaster there at the age of 18. In 1551 he went to Rome, where he became choirmaster of the Julian Chapel. Towards the end of his life he published many unaccompanied choral compositions, including masses, motets, hymns, and madrigals.

Palladio, Andrea (1508–80). Italian architect. Influenced by written descriptions of ancient Roman architecture, Palladio emphasized classical proportion and balance in his buildings. He designed many villas and palaces in his native Vicenza as well as several important churches in Venice. In 1570 he published *Four Books on Architecture*, a summary of his ideas and techniques. His writings later became the basis for the Palladian style of architecture throughout Europe.

Palmer, Arnold (1929–). US golfer. He won many championships, including the US amateur and Open, the Masters (1958, 1960, 1962, 1964), and the British Open (1961, 1962). His personality also increased the popularity of golf as a spectator sport.

Palmerston, Henry John Temple, Viscount (1784–1865). British statesman; foreign secretary (1830–34, 1835–41, 1846–51) and prime minister (1855–58, 1859–65). Although he entered parliament as a Tory (1807), he later crossed to the Whigs. As foreign secretary he secured the formation of an independent Belgium (1830). He first became prime minister in 1855, following the mismanagement of the Crimean War. With his bluff personality and nationalistic foreign policy he was known as "the most English minister who ever governed England" and was very popular with the public.

Pankhurst, Emmeline (1858–1928). British suffragette. She became concerned about women's rights and worked with her husband, the lawyer Richard Marsden Pankhurst, for the Married Women's Property Act. In 1903 she founded the Women's Social and Political Union with her daughters **Christabel** (1880–1958) and **Sylvia** (1882–1960); the campaign to obtain women's suffrage was launched three years later. From 1912 the suffragettes used militant methods, such as arson, window smashing, and bombing. In 1913 Mrs Pankhurst was arrested and imprisoned 12 times but released after going on hunger strikes. During World War I she broke off her campaign and toured the US and Russia. She died just a month before full women's suffrage was granted.

> ❝ We women suffragists have a great mission – the greatest mission the world has ever known. It is to free half the human race, and through that freedom to save the rest.
> Emmeline Pankhurst, speech October 1912 ❞

Park, Mungo (1771–1806). Scottish explorer. In 1795 he sailed to Gambia and travelled inland to explore the course of the Niger. On returning to Britain he described his adventures in *Travels in the Interior Districts of Africa* (1797). On a second expedition to the Niger (1805) he was attacked by natives and drowned.

Parker, Charlie (1920–55). US jazz saxophonist, bandleader, and composer, nicknamed *Bird*. Charlie Parker left school at 14 to immerse himself in the emerging Kansas City jazz scene. Over the next ten years he featured in various ensembles, including the Earl Hines big band, in which he played alongside the trumpeter Dizzy Gillespie. After moving to New York in the 1940s he worked as a freelance musician and led small bebop groups of his own. By the age of 25 he had become legendary as an improviser of extraordinary skill and fluency. With Gillespie, Miles Davis, and Thelonius Monk he was one of a handful of figures who revolutionized jazz in the immediate post-war years. An alcoholic and a heroin addict, he suffered from mental instability and died of his excesses at the early age of 34. His well-known compositions include 'Ornithology' and 'Now's the Time'.

Parnell, Charles Stewart (1846–91). Irish nationalist leader. As leader of the Irish Home Rule party from 1880, he organized obstructive tactics that caused chaos in Parliament. In 1881 he was imprisoned for inciting violence in Kilmainham, Ireland, while opposing the new land act. After a long inquiry he was cleared of complicity in the Phoenix Park Murders (1882). *The Times* later (1887) charged Parnell with involvement in crimes committed by the Land League but a long inquiry showed that the documents on which the charges had been based were forgeries. His involvement as co-respondent in the divorce of Katharine O'Shea, a colleague's wife, caused a scandal and ruined his career. He married Katharine in 1891.

Pascal, Blaise (1623–62). French mathematician, physicist, and religious philosopher. While only 17 he produced a highly successful mathematical treatise. He subsequently invented a mechanical adding machine to aid his father in his administrative work and from 1645 manufactured these to sell. During his studies of the application of pressure on contained fluids he invented the hydraulic press and syringe. He also formulated elementary laws of probability. Following a mystical experience in 1654, he retired to the Jansenist monastery at Port-Royal. There he wrote his celebrated *Provincial Letters* (1656–57), defending Jansenism, and his *Pensées* (1670), a series of profound aphorisms on human nature and religious belief.

Pasternak, Boris (1890–1960). Russian novelist and poet. From a cultured Jewish background, he made his name after the Russian Revolution as an avant-garde poet. During the 1930s he published translations of several Shakespearean tragedies. His major novel, *Doctor Zhivago*, was rejected by publishers in the Soviet Union for its political content but was published abroad in 1957. It won Pasternak the 1958 Nobel Prize but after the award was denounced as a "hostile political act" in the official publication of the Soviet Writers' Union and on Moscow radio he was obliged to decline it.

The real Lara

Lara, the beautiful and courageous heroine of Pasternak's *Doctor Zhivago*, was based largely on a real-life original, the writer's companion Olga Invinskaya (1912–95). The two met in October 1946 and became lovers some months later; Pasternak was 23 years her senior. Olga's life was almost as tragic and remarkable as that of Lara. By the time she met Pasternak she had already been widowed twice (her first husband committed suicide and her second was killed in World War II). In an attempt to put pressure on Pasternak, the authorities arrested her in 1950 on charges of being an accomplice to spying. She spent five years in a labour camp, having miscarried Pasternak's child as a result of her treatment. Although the couple were reunited for Pasternak's last years, she was arrested again after his death in 1960; this time, hoping to tarnish the international reputation of *Doctor Zhivago* and its author, the authorities accused her of dishonestly profiteering from the book's success in the West. Although she was released after a year, she was not rehabilitated until 1988. Her last years were spent in an unsuccessful attempt to regain Pasternak's love letters to her, which were seized at the time of her second arrest.

Pasteur, Louis (1822–95). French chemist. After completing some distinguished work on the optical activity of tartaric acid, Pasteur was appointed dean of the faculty of sciences at Lille University in 1854. Here he solved the problem of why wines and beers sour with age. By heating the wine to a temperature of 120°F he killed the yeast that caused the souring. This process, later called 'pasteurization', is now widely used not only for wines and beers but also for milk. Pasteur then began to study infectious diseases and came to the conclusion that they were transmitted from one person to another by the germs that caused them. Despite being partially paralysed by a stroke in 1868, he continued his work. In 1881 he made sheep immune to anthrax by inoculating them with anthrax germs that had been heated to reduce their virulence. Using similar methods, he inoculated animals against chicken cholera and rabies. His crowning achievement came in 1885, when he successfully treated a boy with rabies by means of weakened rabies germs. Pasteur's researches into the prevention of disease by inoculation led him to discover methods of treating the diseases of silkworms, which were of great commercial importance to the French silk industry. The Pasteur Institute, founded in 1888 to treat patients with rabies, is now a centre for biological research.

Patrick, St (c. 389–461 AD). Patron saint of Ireland. Patrick is believed to have been born in Wales. At 16 he was captured by a group of pirates who took him to Ireland as a slave. After six years he escaped, probably to Britain, but later returned to Ireland as a Christian missionary. Although opposed by the druids, he succeeded in converting many people and is believed to have founded the diocese of Armagh (c. 444), which became the centre of Irish Christianity. His feast day is 17 March.

Patton, George S(mith) (1885–1945). US general. After graduating from West Point in 1909, Patton saw active service in Mexico and in World War I. Between the wars he became one of the US army's leading advocates of the tank and the armoured car. In 1943 he led Allied ground forces in the invasion of Tunisia and then commanded the US 7th Army in the capture of Sardinia. Patton's aggressive character led him into trouble later that year, when he publicly struck a soldier whom he suspected of malingering. The soldier was suffering from severe shell shock. After a few months during which he received no further postings, Patton was put in command of the US 3rd Army after the Normandy landings. Although he often antagonized colleagues with his reckless style, Patton made remarkable progress through France and Germany in 1944–45. He died as a result of a car crash only a few weeks after the end of the war. His life is the subject of the film *Patton: Lust for Glory* (1970), starring George C. Scott.

Paul, St, original name *Saul* (d. c. 67 AD). New Testament figure. Brought up as a strict Jew and educated under the rabbi Gamaliel, he later directed the persecution of Christians. His encounter with the risen Christ on the road to Damascus converted him to Christianity. Paul carried out much of his teaching ministry, which was undertaken alongside his trade as a tent-maker, on his missionary journeys through Asia and into Europe. His letters form part of the New Testament and express in lasting form the implications of the Christian gospel.

Pavarotti, Luciano (1935–   ). Italian operatic tenor. The son of an amateur tenor, Pavarotti made his debut in 1961 as Rodolfo in Puccini's *La Bohème*, a role he repeated for his Covent Garden debut two years later. He toured Europe with the La Scala company in 1963–64 and Australia with Joan Sutherland in 1965. His US debut followed in 1968. By the 1990s Pavarotti's performances and recordings had established him as one of the most successful opera stars in the world. In 1990 he became popular with a much wider audience when he sang (with Placido Domingo and José Carreras) at a televised concert in Rome marking the World Cup. That same year his record of Puccini's 'Nessun Dorma' went to the top of the pop charts in Britain, helping to bring opera to a new mass audience. His records have continued to sell in quantities usually only associated with pop stars.

Pavlov, Ivan Petrovich (1849–1936). Russian physiologist, best known for his work on conditioned reflexes in dogs. Originally intended for the priesthood, Pavlov became interested in natural history and studied physiology at St Petersburg University. Here he did valuable work on the mechanism of digestion, for which he received a Nobel Prize in 1904. After this he began his famous experiments with dogs. A hungry dog will salivate at the sight of food. Pavlov rang a bell every time food was presented and found that eventually the dog salivated whenever the bell was rung, even in the absence of food. This is a conditioned reflex. His work led Pavlov to believe that all human mental activity was the result of conditioned reflexes. Though an outspoken anti-communist, Pavlov remained in the Soviet Union after the Russian Revolution and was given facilities to continue his researches.

Pavlova, Anna (1885–1931). Russian ballerina. Despite poverty and sickness as a child, she trained at the Ballet School in St Petersburg and became prima ballerina with the Russian Imperial Ballet in 1906. She danced with Diaghilev's company in 1909 but thereafter performed independently and toured with her own company. Her performances popularized classical Russian ballet in the West. She died of pneumonia brought on largely through overwork.

Payton, Walter (1954–). US American football player, regarded as the greatest running back in the history of the game. Payton was born in Columbia, Missouri, and graduated from Jackson State University. He was recruited by the Chicago Bears in 1975 and remained with the team for 12 seasons. During this period he set a series of records for running with the ball and for yardage gained by running and passing. He retired after the 1987 season.

Paz, Octavio (1914–). Mexican poet, writer, and diplomat. Paz was born and educated in Mexico City. As a young man, his Marxist views led him to fight on the Republican side in the Spanish Civil War. His earlier poetry, published in the 1930s and 1940s, shows the influence of surrealism. Later work, such as the famous long poem *Piedro del sol* (*Sun Stone*; 1957), is more metaphysical and reflective. Paz's work as a diplomat included postings in France and Japan and a period as Mexico's ambassador to India (1962–68). He has also written various critical and other prose works, notably *The Labyrinth of Solitude* (1950). The appearance of his *Collected Poems* (1989) was followed by the award of the Nobel Prize for literature in 1990.

An Unfortunate Manner

Although widely admired for his abilities, Peel was disliked in his own party for his aloofness and lack of social graces. One Irish MP compared his smile to "the silver plate on a coffin", while Disraeli, Peel's great enemy and eventual nemesis, compared him to a poker: "The only difference is that a poker gives off occasional signs of warmth." The lack of personal loyalty that Peel inspired was certainly one factor in his downfall during the Corn Law crisis of 1846.

Peel, Sir Robert (1788–1850). British statesman; home secretary (1822–27; 1828–30) and prime minister (1834–35; 1841–46). As home secretary he founded the London Metropolitan Police (1829), the members of which were nicknamed 'Peelers' or 'Bobbies' after him. His Tamworth Manifesto (1834) is regarded as having established the modern Conservative party. In 1846 he was responsible for the repeal of the Corn Laws, in opposition to the majority of his party, and he consequently fell from power. He died after being thrown from a horse.

Pelé, real name *Edson Arantes do Nascimento* (1940–   ). Brazilian footballer, regarded as one of the greatest players of all time. Born into a poor Black family, he played for the São Paulo team and Santos as inside left and goal scorer. He played for Brazil in four World

Cup competitions (1958–70), three of which Brazil won, and scored two goals in the 1958 final at the age of 17.

Penn, William (1644–1718). English Quaker and founder of Pennsylvania. Imprisoned several times for non-conformism, he was granted land in America by Charles II in payment of a debt to his father, Admiral Sir William Penn. In 1682 he founded the Quaker colony of Pennsylvania. On his first visit to the colony (1682–84), Penn insisted that the Indians be treated fairly and made treaties with them. As a result friendly relations were established between the new government and the Indians from the start. Penn promoted constitutional reforms, such as full religious tolerance and frequent elections.

Pepys, Samuel (1633–1703). English diarist. The son of a tailor, he held various public offices, principally at the Admiralty, where he introduced important naval reforms. He became an MP in 1679 but spent some

> ❝ Equally pleased with a watch, a coach, a piece of meat, a tune on the fiddle, or a fact in hydrostatics, Pepys was pleased yet more by the beauty, the worth, the mirth, or the mere scenic attitude in life of his fellow creatures. He shows himself throughout a sterling humanist.
> Robert Louis Stevenson, *Samuel Pepys* (1882) ❞

months in the Tower of London after a false accusation of treason. His famous diary, kept from 1659 to 1669, was written in a private code that remained unbroken until the 19th century. It contains valuable information about life in 17th-century London, including a description of the Great Fire of London in 1666.

Pericles (c. 495–429 BC) Greek statesman, considered to be the most influential of the 'golden age' in Athens (460–429 BC), when the Greek civilization was at its political and cultural zenith. His thoughtful detached character earned him the nickname 'the Olympian'. Aspiring to make Athens the cultural and intellectual centre of Greece, he initiated the construction of the magnificent buildings on the Acropolis in 447. In every year from 443 to his death he was elected general by popular vote. He fell from favour temporarily when the Peloponnesian War broke out in 431 but was reinstated before his death.

Perlman, Itzhak (1945–   ). Israeli violinist. The son of Polish emigré parents, Perlman contracted polio at the age of four. Despire this handicap, he was able to learn the violin and trained at the Juilliard School of Music in New York. He made his debut in that city in 1963. Famous as a virtuoso violinist, he is well known for his recitals with the pianist Vladimir Ashkenazy.

Perón, Juan Domingo (1895–1974). Argentinian political leader. As secretary of labour and welfare he gained support from the poorer workers, the *descamisados*. His mistress **Eva** (1922–52), popularly known as *Evita*, also rallied support for him. She was a film and radio actress renowned for her beauty and personal magnetism. The two were married in 1945 and Perón was elected president the following year. Following the death of Eva his popularity waned and he was overthrown in 1955. He was re-elected in 1973 but died a year later and was succeeded by his third wife, **Isabel** (1931–   ), who became the world's first woman president (1974–76).

Pestalozzi, Johann Heinrich (1746–1823). Swiss educational reformer. Inspired by Rousseau's educational theories, he started a school for poor children on his estate at Stanz. The school aimed to make the children self-reliant and able to think for themselves. Although the scheme failed, Pestalozzi gained valuable experience and set out his ideas in the novel *Leonard and Gertrude* (1781–87), which was widely read. His later schools were more successful and he greatly influenced the development of primary school education.

Pétain, (Henri) Philippe (1856–1951). French general and politician, head of the Vichy regime in unoccupied France (1941–42). The son of a peasant family, Pétain graduated from the St Cyr military academy in 1878. He later became an instructor at the École de Guerre (1888–1915). During World War I Pétain was promoted to general and became a national hero for his stubborn defence of Verdun (1916). He was commander-in-chief of French forces for most of 1917 (until replaced by Foch). After the war, Pétain served in high-ranking administrative posts and became minister of war in 1934. In the view of many historians, his old-fashioned defensive notions were a major factor in France's defeat in 1940. Having been appointed prime minister (1940) at the height of the crisis, he negotiated an armistice with Germany that left the north of the country occupied and the south (Vichy France) as a Nazi puppet state. Pétain then headed the administration in Vichy until the Germans invaded in 1942. Following the liberation he was sentenced to death for treason (1945). Owing to his advanced age and former reputation, this sentence was commuted to life imprisonment.

Peter, St (fl. 1st century AD). New Testament disciple of Christ, also known as *Simon Peter*. A fisherman, he was brought to Christ by his brother Andrew, and through his forceful and often impulsive character became a spokesman for the rest of the disciples. After the resurrection of Christ, Peter led the apostles in the early Church and was instrumental in opening the Church to Gentiles. According to ancient sources, Peter was martyred at Rome, probably during Nero's persecution of the Christians (64–67 AD). Two New Testament letters are attributed to him. His symbol is two crossed keys – signs of the authority granted to him by Jesus in Matthew 16:16–19 ("I will give you the keys of the kingdom of heaven").

Peter I, known as *Peter the Great* (1627–1725). Tsar and emperor of Russia. He became joint tsar with his elder but incompetent half-brother Ivan in 1682 and assumed full control of the government in 1689. Having disguised himself as a minor embassy official he visited Prussia, Hanover, and Amsterdam in 1697, gaining considerable information about the countries and spending some time working as a shipwright.

Peter and the Gardener

As part of his project to Westernize Russia, Peter the Great decreed in 1722 that if any nobleman beat or ill-treated his serfs he should be looked upon as insane and a guardian appointed to take care of his estate. However, Peter was himself a notoriously short-tempered man who on one occasion struck his gardener in a rage. Regarding this treatment as a matter of great shame, the gardener took to his bed and shortly afterwards died. Peter, hearing of this, exclaimed with tears in his eyes, "Alas! I have civilized my own subjects; I have conquered other nations; yet I have not been able to civilize or to conquer myself."

Following a visit to England (1698) he returned to Russia to follow a policy of reform and modernization along the lines of the Western cities he had visited. During the war with Sweden (1700–21) he gained a section of territory on which the new capital, St Petersburg, was founded (1703), giving Russia access to the Baltic Sea and "a window on Europe". He took the title of emperor in 1721.

Petrarch, real name *Francesco Petrarca* (1304–74). Italian humanist poet and scholar. His *Canzoniere* (begun 1342) is a collection of sonnets and odes addressed to Laura, about whom little is known. Petrarch met her in a church in 1327 but apparently never saw her again. Petrarch's sonnets had a great influence on the development of European poetry, especially on Chaucer in England. He also wrote a number of scholarly works in Latin.

Phidias (fl. 5th century BC). Greek sculptor, usually considered the greatest artist of the ancient world. An Athenian, he was commissioned by Pericles to supply a series of statues for the city and appointed superintendent of public works. He designed the sculptures on the walls of the Parthenon (the so-called Elgin Marbles) and himself executed a gold and ivory statue of Athena for the interior. His other works included a bronze statue of Athena on the Acropolis and a statue of Zeus at Olympia. He apparently fled from Athens after being accused of appropriating gold from a statue for himself and of carving his own features on a public sculpture.

Philby, Kim, real name *Harold Adrian Russell Philby* (1912–88). British diplomat and spy, associated with the Russian agents Guy Burgess and Donald Maclean. In 1933 Philby, a communist, became a Russian agent. He was recruited into British intelligence by Burgess in 1940. From 1949 to 1951 Philby was a high-ranking British diplomat in Washington and passed important information to the Soviet Union. In 1951 he helped Burgess and Maclean to escape to the Soviet Union. Philby came under suspicion himself but was cleared in 1955. In 1963 he fled to the Soviet Union and admitted·his activities in *My Secret War* (1968). A fourth member of the ring, Sir Anthony Blunt, Surveyor of the Queen's Pictures, was unmasked in 1979 and stripped of his knighthood. In 1991 John Cairncross admitted that he was the rumoured 'fifth man' in the ring.

Philip II (1527–98). King of Spain from 1556. Having succeeded to the throne on his father's abdication, he soon became the most powerful monarch in Europe. He championed Catholicism and made widespread use of the Inquisition against heretics. This religious intolerance provoked a major revolt in the Netherlands. Following the execution of Mary, Queen of Scots, he declared war on England and sent out the Armada (1588). Its destruction resulted in a decline in Spanish power. Philip married four times, his second wife being Mary I of England.

Piaf, Edith (1915–63). French singer, born *Edith Giovanna Gassion*. Her small stature earned her the nickname *Piaf*, which is Parisian slang for 'sparrow'. She toured with her father, an acrobat, and at 15 began singing in the streets of Paris. She later became a cabaret star and in 1945 acted in the play *Le Bel Indifferent*, which was written for her by Jean Cocteau. Her songs, which often reflect the miseries of her early life, include 'La Vie en Rose' (1945) and 'Non, Je Ne Regrette Rien'. She wrote the words and music of several of her famous songs and published an autobiography (1958). Her early death was caused by addiction to drugs and alcohol.

Piaget, Jean (1896–1980). Swiss psychologist. Having first studied biology, he became interested in the development of thought processes in the young. His experiments with his own children led him to describe the stages in which thought, perception, and language develop. An early and important work of his is *The Language and Thought of the Child* (1926).

Picasso, Pablo (1881–1973). Spanish painter and sculptor. After studying in Madrid he moved to Paris, where he painted the dancers, clowns, and acrobats of the city in his early 'Blue' and 'Rose' periods. He then evolved a new style called 'Cubism', in which he painted things as if they were being seen from several viewpoints simultaneously, as in the painting *Les Demoiselles d'Avignon* (1907). During the 1920s and 1930s Picasso's style evolved still further. The painting *Guernica* (1937) depicts in symbolic style the artist's horror at the death and destruction that took place during the Spanish Civil War. After World War II Picasso settled in the South of France, where he continued to produce large numbers of paintings, as well as sculpture and pottery. The most influential of 20th-century artists, he was also one of the most prolific; his works are in collections and galleries all over the world.

Responsibility

During World War II Picasso chose to remain in Nazi-occupied Paris. As a famous avant-garde artist known for his left-wing views, he suffered a certain amount of routine harassment but nothing worse. On one occasion a Gestapo officer visited Picasso's studio and noticed a photograph of *Guernica*, the artist's anguished response to the bombing of a Basque village by German planes. "Did you do that?" asked the Nazi. "No," replied Picasso, "you did."

Piccard, Auguste (1884–1962). Swiss physicist. A member of a famous family of scholars, scientists, and explorers, he pioneered stratosphere flights in a balloon to observe cosmic rays and other phenomena of the atmosphere. In this he was assisted by his twin brother **Jean Felix** (1884–1963), a chemist. Auguste completed a bathyscape (diving bell) in 1948 and descended over 3,000 m in it (1953). His son **Jacques** (1922–   ) descended to 10,917 m in his bathyscape *Trieste* in 1960.

Pickford, Mary, screen name of *Gladys Mary Smith* (1893–1979). US actress, one of the first internationally known stars of the cinema. Born in Canada, she began acting as a child and made her first film at the age of 16; the director, D. W. Griffith, paid her $5 a day. With her long ringlets and girlish charm, she went on to beguile international audiences in such films as *Rebecca of Sunnybrook Farm* (1917). Despite her image as the 'World's Sweetheart' she was known for her business acumen. In 1919 she founded United Artists with Griffith, Charlie Chaplin, and Douglas Fairbanks, whom she married the following year (they divorced in 1933). She remained at the pinnacle of the Hollywood aristocracy throughout the 1920s but found it difficult to break out of girlish roles. Her career did not long survive the coming of sound and she died a virtual recluse.

Pinter, Harold (1930–   ). British dramatist. The son of a Jewish tailor in the East End of London, he published poems and acted in repertory before turning to drama. His first full-length play *The Birthday Party* (1957) ran for only a week. It was *The Caretaker* (1960) that made his name and established his reputation for enigmatic drama with a strong suggestion of menace. His plays of the 1960s and 1970s included *The Homecoming* (1965) and *No Man's Land* (1975). During the 1980s he wrote mainly for the cinema and campaigned on political issues. *Moonlight* (1993) was his first major play for 15 years. Pinter has also written radio and television plays; his screenplays include *The Servant* (1962) and *The French Lieutenant's Woman* (1981).

Pirandello, Luigi (1867–1936). Italian dramatist and writer. The son of a mine owner, Pirandello was born in Sicily and studied in Rome and Bonn. Although family wealth enabled him to embark on a literary career in the 1890s, a mining disaster in 1903 reduced him and his wife to poverty. Shortly afterwards she began to show signs of insanity, leading to her eventual removal to an asylum. Pirandello was already known as a novelist and short-story writer when he turned to writing for the stage in 1910. His best-known play, *Six Characters in Search of an Author*, was premiered in Rome in 1921 and seen in London and New York the following year. The play is a paradoxical exploration of the nature of theatrical illusion. His other plays include the tragedy *Henry IV* (1922), which examines ideas of madness and sanity. Pirandello was awarded the Nobel Prize for literature in 1934. With their anti-naturalist style his plays had a major influence on later writers, especially on the Theatre of the Absurd.

Pitman, Sir Isaac (1813–97). British educator and inventor of a system of shorthand writing. The system, published as *The Stenographic Sound Hand*, was invented by Pitman in 1837. It was based on phonetic principles and Pitman founded the *Phonetic Journal* to promote it. His grandson **James** (1901–   ) invented a new alphabet to facilitate the learning of reading. Called the *Initial Teaching Alphabet*, it consists of 44 letters that can be used to spell words according to consistent phonetic rules.

Pitt, William, the Elder (1708–78). British statesman and orator; known as the 'Great Commoner', he was created earl of Chatham in 1766. Having entered Parliament in 1735 he formed a government at the beginning of the Seven Years War (1756–63), saying "I am sure I can save this country and nobody else can". He achieved brilliant success during the war with the military defeat of the French in Canada and India (1759). Pitt was forced to resign by George III (1761) but

After Austerlitz

The early death of William Pitt the Younger is thought to have been brought on by the strain of his responsibilities during the Napoleonic Wars. With Napoleon's victory over Russia and Austria at Austerlitz in December 1805, Pitt's political and military strategy was left in ruins. When brought news of the disaster, he is said to have pointed to a map of Europe hanging on the wall and remarked "Roll up that map; it will not be wanted these ten years." Napoleon remained master of continental Europe until 1814. Pitt never recovered from the blow of Austerlitz. His last words are supposed to have been either "Oh, my country! How I love my country!" or, more prosaically, "I think I could eat one of Bellamy's veal pies."

later formed a coalition government (1766–68). He suffered increasingly from ill health and bouts of insanity in his later years. His son, **William Pitt the Younger** (1759–1806), was also a statesman. A Tory, he became prime minister while only 24 and successfully reorganized the national finances. From 1793 Britain was drawn into war with revolutionary France, in which Pitt achieved little success. He secured the Union of Britain and Ireland in 1800 but resigned following George III's refusal to accept Catholic emancipation. During his second ministry (1804–06) he led Britain in the Napoleonic Wars. The defeat of the Allies by Napoleon at Austerlitz (1805) proved his death-blow.

Pius IX, original name *Giovanni Maria Mastai-Ferreti* (1792–1878). Roman Catholic churchman, pope from 1846. At first sympathetic to liberal and nationalist causes, he became steadily more reactionary after the revolution of 1848. Although the Church lost control of the Papal States and Rome, which were taken into the newly formed kingdom of Italy, Pius managed to increase its spiritual power. In 1854 he defined the dogma of the Immaculate Conception of the Virgin Mary and in 1870 he proclaimed the doctrine of papal infallibility. His 32-year pontificate was the longest in history.

Pizzaro, Francisco (1478–1541). Spanish adventurer. In 1530, under powers granted by Charles V of Spain, Pizarro led the expedition to Peru that conquered the Incas. He also founded Lima (1535), the present capital of Peru. Pizarro and his partner Almagro became rich from the spoils of their conquests, but the division of the gold caused a quarrel, and Pizarro was killed by the followers of Almagro.

Planck, Max (1858–1947). German physicist. He originated the quantum theory, upon which much of modern physics is based. While investigating black-body radiation he discovered that energy is emitted by bodies in separate amounts, which he called quanta. The ratio of the energy of a quantum to the frequency of the radiation was named Planck's constant in his honour. He received a Nobel Prize for this work in 1918. Remaining in Germany during the Nazi period, he attempted bravely but unsuccessfully to intercede with Hitler on behalf of Jewish scientists.

Plath, Sylvia (1932–63). US poet. Plath was born in Boston, Massachusetts, the daughter of a university professor. As an undergraduate at Smith College she showed early signs of literary brilliance but also suffered from severe depression, leading to a suicide attempt in 1953. She married the British poet Ted Hughes in 1956 and settled permanently in Britain three years later. Her first book of poems, *The Colossus*, was published in 1960. At the end of 1962 Hughes abandoned Plath and their two small children to live with another woman. The following months, the last of her life, were marked by an apparent mental breakdown accompanied by a burst of creativity. During this period she published her novel *The Bell Jar* (1963) and wrote most of the poems for which she is best known. In early 1963 she committed suicide by gassing herself; she was 30 years old. A first selection of the fearsomely intense poems written at the end of her life was published as *Ariel* (1965), which caused a literary sensation. Further poems appeared in the 1970s and in Plath's *Collected Poems* (1981), which won a Pulitzer prize.

Plato (429–347 BC). Greek philosopher. Disillusioned with politics, he became a fervent disciple of Socrates, who influenced his early writings. After the death of Socrates he travelled widely. Having returned to Athens in 387, he set up his Academy to prepare young men for public life through the study of mathematics and philosophy. He explained his teaching in the form of dramatic dialogues and while the earlier dialogues express the philosophy of Socrates, the later ones use Socrates as a mouthpiece for Plato's own ideas. The most famous of the Platonic dialogues is the *Republic*, in which he put forward his idea of the perfect state, where children would be selected and trained for a specific role in the state. In 367 he attempted to establish an ideal state at Syracuse, but he was unsuccessful.

> ❛ The safest general characterization of the European tradition is that it consists of a series of footnotes to Plato.
> A. N. Whitehead, *Process and Reality* (1929) ❜

Plautus, Titus Maccius (c. 250–184 BC). Roman comic dramatist. He is said to have written 130 plays, of which 21 survive. These are free translations of lost Greek originals, with complicated plots and witty characterization. The plays were still performed long after Plautus's death and influenced many later writers. His *Menaechmi* supplied Shakespeare with the plot of *The Comedy of Errors*.

Pliny, the Elder, full name *Gaius Plinius Secundus* (23–79 AD). Roman author. After service as a cavalry officer, he filled several important administrative posts. Only the *Natural History*, a huge digest of information on astronomy, geography, zoology, and mineralogy, survives from his numerous writings. He was suffocated while directing rescue operations during the eruption of Vesuvius. His nephew **Pliny the Younger,** full name *Gaius Plinius Caecilius Secundus* (61–114 AD), was a writer, lawyer, and administrator. His *Letters* (97–109) deal with various subjects. His correspondence with Emperor Trajan, written while he was a provincial governor, is a valuable historical source.

Plutarch (c. 46–127 AD). Greek essayist and biographer. He travelled widely and held imperial office before finally settling down to an author's life. Although he wrote on many subjects, he is best known for his *Parallel Lives*, a collection of biographies of Greek and Roman soldiers and statesmen. For his Roman plays Shakespeare used Sir Thomas North's translation of Plutarch's *Parallel Lives*; many words and phrases used by North can be detected in the verse of *Julius Caesar* and *Antony and Cleopatra*.

Poe, Edgar Allan (1809–49). US poet and short-story writer. Orphaned at two, he was brought up by a guardian. He left university at his guardian's insistence because of his gambling debts. After publishing two collections of poetry, Poe turned increasingly to writing short stories. His macabre tales, many of which have been made into horror films, include 'The Murders in the Rue Morgue' and 'The Pit and the Pendulum', and can be found in *The Prose Romances* (1843) and *Tales* (1845). His mental health declined as a result of his wife's death and his heavy drinking; he died after a drinking session in Baltimore.

> ❛ There was a reviewer a while back who wrote that my pictures didn't have any beginning or any end. He didn't mean it as a compliment, but it was. It was a fine compliment.
> Jackson Pollock ❜

Pollock, Jackson (1912–56). US painter, the best-known exponent of abstract expressionism. Pollock was born in Wyoming and studied at the Art Students' League in New York. His early paintings, which date from the 1930s, are executed in the realistic style of the US regionalist painters. He held his first exhibition (jointly with William de Kooning) in 1940. After moving through various styles, Pollock adopted his famous technique of 'action painting' in the late 1940s. This involved fixing a large sheet of unstretched canvas to the wall or floor and then dripping, throwing, or spattering paint across it in rhythmic and often violent movements. The resulting work was supposed to express the unconscious feelings of the artist while he was creating it. In his later works Pollock often used such implements as sticks or trowels rather than brushes. His works include *One* and *Echo and Blue Poles*. He was killed in a car accident.

Polo, Marco (1254–1324). Venetian merchant and adventurer, who travelled extensively in Europe and Asia. With his father and uncle he went overland through Baghdad and the Gobi Desert to China (1271–75), where he became ambassador to Kublai Khan, the Mongol emperor. He eventually returned to Venice in 1295. In 1298 he was captured in a sea battle; while imprisoned in Genoa he wrote a detailed account of his travels and adventures.

Pol Pot (1925–   ). Cambodian communist leader, whose rule (1975–79) led to the deaths of over a million people from executions, forced labour, and ill-treatment. Born into a peasant family, he spent part of his youth in a Buddhist monastery. He later became a prominent communist organizer while working as a schoolteacher; from 1963 he devoted himself to a guerrilla struggle against successive Cambodian governments. In 1975 Pol Pot's Khmer Rouge guerrillas took over the government in Phnom Penh and renamed the country Democratic Kampuchea. The new government then attempted to transform the country into a 'pure' peasant state by forcing millions of urban Cambodians to work in labour camps in the countryside, where many perished. Large sections of the middle class were deliberately exterminated. The scale of this brutality was first revealed to the world following the Vietnamese invasion of Cambodia in 1978–79, which forced Pol Pot and his adherents to withdraw to Thailand. Although he officially resigned from the Khmer Rouge leadership in 1985, he appears to remain in control of the movement's political and guerrilla activities. Continuing instability in Cambodia has led to fears that he could even now return to power.

Pompadour, Jeanne Antoinette Poisson, Marquise de (1721–64). Mistress of Louis XV of France. Having married in 1741, she lived at Versailles and was created Marquise in 1745, the year she became the king's mistress. For the next 20 years she exercised control of French public affairs, using large amounts of money to further her ambitions. Her political influence extended to both domestic and foreign policy and may have cost France the Seven Years War (1756–63). A patron of the arts, she founded the Sèvres porcelain factory and the École Militaire.

Pompey, full name *Gnaeus Pompeius Magnus* (106–48 BC). Roman soldier and politician, whose early military successes made him Rome's leading general. After a brilliant campaign to clear the Mediterranean Sea of pirates (67 BC), he defeated Rome's old enemy Mithridates. In 61 BC he formed the first triumvirate, a coalition of three joint rulers, with Ceasar and Crassus. Although he married Caesar's daughter Julia, his support of the aristocratic senate made him Caesar's opponent in the civil war. Defeated at Pharsalus (48 BC), he fled to Egypt, where he was murdered.

Pope, Alexander (1688–1744). British poet, noted mainly for his satires. The son of a Catholic draper, he

---

The Wasp of Twickenham

Such was the nickname of Alexander Pope, who lived in Twickenham for 25 years and became notorious for the ferocity of his satires. Pope's riverside house and gardens at Twickenham were bought with the proceeds of his translation of Homer's *Iliad* (1715–20) and became famous for the embellishments the poet added in the Gothic style, including a grotto lined with rock crystals and an obelisk. The grounds were to have a major effect upon subsequent landscape gardening in Britain. Pope's garden also contained a weeping willow, which — grown from a twig taken from a Turkish basket — was said to be the first such tree to be grown in England. All the weeping willows now growing in Britain and the US are, it has been claimed, descended from this tree.

---

had a tubercular curvature of the spine and grew to only 135 cm. He started writing at an early age and made his name with the *Essay on Criticism* (1711). His subsequent works include the mock epic *The Rape of the Lock* (1714), *The Dunciad* (1728, revised 1743), a biting satire on human pretensions, and *Essay on Man* (1733), a long philosophical poem. He also published successful translations of the *Iliad* and the *Odyssey*.

Porter, Cole (1892–1964). US composer and songwriter. He studied law and music at Harvard, and later went to France, where he took lessons in musical composition. Noted for his witty lyrics and sophistication of style, he wrote words and music for Broadway musicals and revues. His works include the songs 'I Get a

Kick Out of You' (1934) and 'Begin the Beguine' (1936) and the musicals *Kiss Me Kate* (1948) and *Can Can* (1953).

Potter, Beatrix (1866–1943). British writer of children's books. Her stories feature animal characters such as Peter Rabbit, Squirrel Nutkin, Jemima Puddle-Duck, and Mrs Tiggy-Winkle the hedgehog. Her earliest publications, *The Tale of Peter Rabbit* (1900) and *The Tailor of Gloucester* (1902), were written as letters to a sick child and illustrated by Potter with watercolour paintings based on sketches from nature. When she died, she left her extensive farmlands to the National Trust.

Pound, Ezra (1885–1972). US poet and critic. From 1908 he lived in Britain, where he achieved fame with volumes like *Hugh Selwyn Mauberley* (1920). He also encouraged other writers who were then virtually unknown, including D. H. Lawrence and James Joyce, and helped T. S. Eliot to revise *The Waste Land*. During World War II Pound was living in Italy and supported the Fascists by means of a series of radio broadcasts, which led to his arrest in 1945. Declared mentally unfit to stand trial, he spent 12 years in a US hospital, returning to Italy in 1958. His major work is his *Cantos* (published in sections, 1928–70).

Poussin, Nicholas (1594–1665). French painter, regarded as the greatest exponent of neoclassicism in the visual arts. Poussin, who was born in Normandy, struggled to make a living in Paris before moving to Rome in 1624. There he received commissions from the Barberini family and became famous with such biblical and historical paintings as *The Worship of the Golden*

Calf (1635). His scenes were always perfectly balanced and constructed and are noted for the meticulous way in which they are lit. In 1640 he was ordered back to France by Louis XIII, who employed him on a series of mainly unsuitable projects for the next three years. Following his return to Rome in 1643 Poussin concentrated on the painting of idealized landscapes, as in his *Landscape with Diogenes* (1648). The classical perfection of Poussin's work was upheld as an ideal in France until the advent of Romanticism in the late 18th century.

Powell, Michael (1905–90). British film-maker, best known for the movies he wrote and directed with **Emeric Pressburger** (1902–88). Powell directed several films before attracting attention with *The Edge of the World* (1937). His first film with Pressburger, a Hungarian émigré, was the melodrama *The Spy in Black* (1938). The war years saw the production of some of the pair's most remarkable films, notably *The Life and Death of Colonel Blimp* (1943), a gentle satire on the British military establishment that enraged Churchill, and *A Canterbury Tale* (1944). Equally ambitious and imaginative were the metaphysical drama *A Matter of Life and Death* (1946) and *The Red Shoes* (1948), a tragedy set in the world of the ballet. After the break-up of the partnership in 1956, Powell made relatively few films. Press vilification of his *Peeping Tom* (1960), a disturbing movie about a sadistic murderer who films his victims, effectively ended his career in Britain. The film has influenced a number of later directors, notably Martin Scorsese. After several years working in Australia, Powell returned to Britain for a last collaboration with

Pressburger, *The Boy Who Turned Yellow* (1972). He published two highly praised volumes of memoirs, *A Life in Movies* (1986) and *A Million Dollar Movie* (1992).

Praxiteles (fl. 370–330 BC). Greek sculptor, one of the most famous of Greek artists. His works, with the exception of a fine marble Hermes at Olympia, survive only in Roman copies. One of the best known of these is the *Aphrodite of Cnidos*, which displays the sensuousness of form and flowing surfaces that characterized much of Praxiteles's work and influenced Greek, Roman, and Renaissance sculpture.

Presley, Elvis (Aaron) (1935–77). US popular singer. He began by singing country and western songs in Memphis and later combined this style with Black rhythm and blues. His first hit record, 'Heartbreak Hotel' (1956), helped to revolutionize popular music. Though he

> ❛ The hair was a Vaseline cathedral, the mouth a touchingly uncertain sneer of allure...Like a berserk blender the lusty young pelvis whirred and the notorious git-tar slammed forward with a jolt that symbolically deflowered a generation of teenagers... Then out of the half-melted vanilla face a wild black baritone came bawling...
> Brad Darrach on Elvis Presley,
> *Life* Winter 1977 ❜

spent two years doing National Service (1958–60) and much of his subsequent work was inferior, his songs and films enjoyed continuing popularity in the 1960s and 1970s. Known as the 'King of Rock and Roll', he later turned to cabaret work and attracted older audiences. He died of heart failure and was mourned by millions of his fans all over the world. He remains a powerful cult figure.

Priestley, J(ohn) B(oynton) (1894–1984). British dramatist and novelist. Born in Yorkshire, he came to London in 1922 and soon became known as a critic and essayist. *The Good Companions* (1929), which tells of the adventures of a touring concert party, was his first popular novel. Later he wrote mainly dramas, including *When We are Married* (1939) and *An Inspector Calls* (1946), as well as producing and directing plays. He also became well known for his popular broadcasts during World War II.

Prokofiev, Sergei (1891–1953). Russian composer. Prokofiev began composing at an early age and in 1914 won the Rubinstein Prize with his first piano concerto. From 1914 to 1933 he lived mainly in Europe, where he composed such works as the *Classical Symphony* (1916–17) and the opera *The Love of Three Oranges* (1921). In 1933 he returned to Russia. His most famous works include *Peter and the Wolf* (1936), the ballets *Romeo and Juliet* (1935–36) and *Cinderella* (1940–44), and the opera *War and Peace* (1941–52), based on Tolstoy's epic novel.

Prost, Alain (1955–). French motor-racing driver. Born in St Chamond in southern France, he entered his first Formula One event in 1980. With 51 Grand Prix victories, he is the most successful racing driver in history. He won the World Championship four times, in 1985, 1986, 1989, and 1993, the year he retired.

Proust, Marcel (1871–1922). French novelist. The son of a doctor, he suffered from asthma from childhood. Although he took degrees in law and literature, the death of his parents in 1903 and 1905 left him wealthy and he retired to begin work on the nine-volume novel *In Search of Lost Time* (1913–27), which occupied the rest of his life. The first volume, *Swann's Way* (1914), was refused by publishers and had to be produced at his own expense; by the time his second volume was published in 1919 Proust was world-famous. The remaining volumes were published after his death from pneumonia. He is remembered for his eccentricities, such as the cork-lined room in which he worked in total isolation from the outside world.

Ptolemy (fl. 2nd century AD). Egyptian astronomer. He maintained that the earth was at the centre of the universe and that the planets, sun, and stars moved around it, attached to concentric crystalline spheres. This system was accepted by the Christian Church and not challenged until 1543, when Copernicus put forward a system stating that the sun was at the centre of the universe. Ptolemy also wrote treatises on optics, geometry, and music, as well as a famous (if inaccurate) *Guide to Geography*.

Ptolemy dynasty. Macedonian kings of Egypt (323–30 BC). **Ptolemy I,** one of Alexander the Great's generals, seized Egypt after Alexander's death. He went on to conquer Palestine, Cyprus, and part of Asia Minor and made Alexandria his capital. **Ptolemy II**, also known as Ptolemy Philadelphus, was the son of Ptolemy I. Successful in war, he also founded the famous museum and library of Alexandria and was a great patron of learning. Not all of the Ptolemies were equally able or successful, although the women of the dynasty, such as Cleopatra, were often outstanding personalities. The Ptolemies adopted Egyptian customs, including the authorization of marriage between brother and sister, and there were constant intrigues within the dynasty and warfare with neighbouring states. After 80 BC the Ptolemies became subject to Rome. **Ptolemy XIII**, the son of Caesar and Cleopatra and the last of the dynasty, was killed in 30 BC.

Puccini, Giacomo (1858–1924). Italian composer. Puccini was born into a family of musicians stretching back five generations. At the age of 22 he went to the Milan Conservatoire where the composer Ponchielli recognized his talent. His first operatic success, *Manon Lescaut* (1893), was followed in 1896 by *La Bohème*, a picture of Bohemian life in Paris. *Madame Butterfly* (1904) tells the story of the tragic love of a Japanese woman for a US naval officer. Puccini died of cancer of the throat before completing his last opera, *Turandot*.

Purcell, Henry (1659–95). English composer. Purcell became a chorister of the Chapel Royal in 1669, where he studied under Dr John Blow. In 1679 he became organist of Westminster Abbey. His compositions include odes written for such royal occasions as the funeral of Queen Mary, the opera *Dido and Aeneas* (1689), and many songs and instrumental pieces. Although he is usually considered the finest of English composers, little is known about his life and character.

Pushkin, Alexander (1799–1837). Russian poet, dramatist, and prose writer. In 1820 he was exiled as a result of his political writings. Influenced by Byron, he introduced Romanticism to Russia in such works as the verse-novel *Eugene Onegin* (1833). *Boris Godunov* (1831) is a historical tragedy. On his return from exile in 1826 he turned to lyric poetry and prose works such as *The Queen of Spades* (1834). He was killed in a pistol duel. Several of Pushkin's works were made into operas by Russian composers: *Eugene Onegin* and *The Queen of Spades* by Tchaikovsky, *Boris Godunov* by Mussorgsky and *Ruslan and Ludmilla* by Glinka.

> 6 Pythagoras founded a religion, of which the main tenets were the transmigration of souls and the sinfulness of eating beans. His religion was embodied in a religious order which, here and there, acquired control of the state and established a rule of the saints. But the unregenerate still hankered after beans, and sooner or later rebelled.
> Bertrand Russell 9

Pythagoras (c. 580–500 BC). Greek philosopher. He founded a religious society in Croton in southern Italy, already an area of Greek colonization. Although Pythagoras left no writings himself, the doctrines of the Pythagoreans survived his death. These include the theory of the reincarnation of the soul and important studies of mathematics. Pythagoras is best known to the layman for his theorem stating that the square on the hypotenuse of a right-angled triangle is equal to the sum of the squares on the other two sides.

Q

Quintilian (c. 35–96 AD). Roman rhetorician. From 68 he practised law and taught rhetoric in Rome. He retired about 20 years later and was given an honorary consul's title by the emperor Domitian. The text of *The Training of an Orator*, which was published towards the end of his life, was lost for centuries and rediscovered in 1416. He is believed to have died shortly after the assassination of Domitian in 96. His wife and young son died before him.

Quisling, Vidkun (1887–1945). Norwegian officer, who served as minister of defence and in 1933 formed the National Union Party, with a strong allegiance to Hitler's Nazi party. He encouraged the Nazi occupation of Norway in 1940 and was appointed 'minister president' by the Nazis in the occupation government, which ordered 1000 Jews to be sent to their deaths in concentration camps. In 1945 he was arrested, tried for war crimes, and executed. His name has become a synonym for 'traitor'.

R

Rabelais, François (c. 1483–1553). French satirical writer. He became a Franciscan monk in 1521 but after difficulties with the theological authorities moved to a Benedictine community in 1524. After studying medicine at Montpellier, he practised and taught until 1546. His writings were published at irregular intervals over more than 20 years. A vein of coarse humour runs through his comic tales *Pantagruel* (1532), *Gargantua* (1535), and their sequels. His works also contain serious satire of religious abuses and scholastic learning.

Rabin, Yitzhak (1922–95). Israeli statesman and soldier. Born in Jerusalem, Rabin studied agriculture before beginning a military career. He commanded a brigade in Israel's War of Independence (1948–49) and thereafter rose steadily through the ranks. As chief of staff (1964–68) he masterminded Israel's swift victory in the Six Day War (1967). In 1974 he became leader of the Labour Party and Israel's first native-born prime minister. Although he won acclaim for ordering the audacious rescue of Israeli hostages held in Entebbe, Uganda, in 1976, he resigned a year later following a financial scandal. As defence minister (1984–90) he was criticized for his tough handling of the Palestinian uprising known as the *intifada* (from 1987). In 1992 he led the Labour Party back to power and began a second term as prime minister, 18 years after his first. The following year he signed a peace agreement with Yasser Arafat of the PLO, under which Israel allowed the Palestinians autonomy in the West Bank and Gaza Strip. For this he was awarded the 1994 Nobel Peace Prize, jointly with Arafat and Shimon Peres. An accord with Jordan was signed later that year. Rabin was assassinated by a Jewish extremist on 5 November 1995, shortly after speaking at a peace rally in Tel Aviv. His murder caused profound shock and grief throughout Israel.

Rachmaninov, Sergei (1873–1943). Russian composer and pianist. Rachmaninov studied at the Moscow and St Petersburg Conservatoires and soon became famous as a pianist and composer both inside and outside Russia. His second piano concerto (1901) enjoyed great popularity. In 1917 he left Russia and spent the rest of his life in Paris, Switzerland, and the US. His compositions include piano works, symphonies, chamber music, songs, and the choral work *The Bells* (1913). In 1931 Rachmaninov's music was banned in Russia as representing "the decadent attitude of the lower middle classes", but it was later given more appreciative treatment.

Racine, Jean (1639–99). French tragic dramatist. Orphaned in early childhood, he attended the Jansenist school at Port-Royal in Paris before studying theology. His first tragedy, produced by Molière, was a failure, but within a few years he was recognized as France's greatest tragic dramatist with such works as

Andromaque (1667) and *Britannicus* (1669). After the initial failure of *Phèdre* (1677), his masterpiece, Racine gave up the theatre for religion, subsequently writing only two biblical plays for a girls' school.

Raleigh, Sir Walter (1554–1618). English courtier, soldier, explorer, and poet. He became a favourite of Elizabeth I and was knighted in 1584. His expeditions to the Americas (1584–95) led to the introduction of potatoes and tobacco to England and the establishment of a settlement in Virginia. In 1596 he took part in the sack of Cadiz and helped to plan the defeat of the Armada. With the accession of James I he fell out of favour at court and was imprisoned in the Tower of London (1603–16), where he wrote his *History of the World* (1614). He was executed after an unsuccessful expedition in search of El Dorado.

> ❛ I will prove you the notoriousest traitor that ever came to the bar…Nay, I will prove all; thou art a monster: thou has an English face but a Spanish heart. Thou art the most vile and execrable Traitor that ever lived…There never lived a viler viper upon the face of the earth than thou.
>
> Sir Edward Coke to Sir Walter Raleigh, during the latter's trial for treason, 17 November 1603 ❜

Rambert, Dame Marie (1888–1982). British ballet dancer and teacher. Rambert was born in Warsaw and danced with Diaghilev's company (1912–13). In 1920 she started teaching ballet in Britain. As founding director of the Ballet Rambert (now known as the Rambert Dance Company), she played an influential role in the development of British dance from 1935 onwards.

Rameses II (d. c. 1237 BC). King of Egypt from 1304 BC, who restored Egyptian influence after the disastrous reigns of Akhenaton and his successors. His campaigns in the Sudan, Libya, and Palestine protected Egypt's frontiers and enabled him to undertake the building and restoration of her temples. He is thought to be the Pharaoh mentioned in Exodus as the oppressor of the Israelites.

Raphael (1483–1520). Italian painter, born *Raffaello Santi*. Raphael studied with Perugino and was influenced by the works of Michelangelo and Leonardo da Vinci. In 1508 Pope Julius II summoned him to Rome to decorate the papal rooms in the Vatican with frescoes. One of these, *The School of Athens*, a study of famous Greek philosophers, became an influential model of classical order and balance. Another of Raphael's most famous works, the *Sistine Madonna*, reveals his mastery of fine shading and his naturalistic portrayal of the human form. One of the greatest artists of the Italian High Renaissance, Raphael also worked for the pope as an architect on the building of St Peter's.

Rasputin, Grigori Efimovich (c. 1872–1916). Russian monk and political figure. An uneducated peasant, he visited Greece as a young man and on his return to his native village in Siberia claimed to have divine and clairvoyant powers. After settling in St Petersburg (1905) he gained favour with fashionable society and the Imperial court. He had considerable influence over the Tsarina Alexandra, who believed that he could cure her son's haemophilia; while Tsar Nicholas II was pre-occupied with World War I Rasputin used this influence to gain virtual control of domestic affairs. Hated by politicians and the nobility for his power and debauchery, he was assassinated by a group of them in 1916. He survived their attempts to poison and shoot him but was finally drowned.

Ravel, Maurice (1875–1937). French composer of Swiss and Basque parentage. Ravel studied at the Paris Conservatoire under Gabriel Fauré and made his name with the opera *The Spanish Hour* (1911) and the ballet *Daphnis and Chloe* (1912), which was produced by Diaghilev's Ballets Russes. His other works include *Pavane for a Dead Infanta* (1899) and the famous *Boléro* (1928). During World War I Ravel was an ambulance driver. In 1935 he suffered brain damage in a car accident and died after a subsequent operation.

Reagan, Ronald W(ilson) (1911–   ). US film actor and politician; 40th president of the US (1981–89). The son of a shoe salesman, Reagan worked as a sports announcer before going to Hollywood in 1937. Over the next 20 years he appeared in some 50 films, mainly routine B-movies. He was also president of the Screen Actors Guild (1947–52; 1959–60). During the 1960s Reagan became increasingly involved in Republican politics; he was governor of California from 1967 to 1974. In the presidential elections of 1980 he defeated the incumbent, Jimmy Carter, to become (at 69) the oldest-ever president of the US. He survived an assassination attempt in March 1981. As president, Reagan pursued free-market economic policies, cutting income taxes and reducing government spending in nearly all areas except defence. The result was a massive federal budget deficit. In foreign affairs he took a tough line against the Soviet Union and authorized US action in Grenada (1983). The following year he was re-elected by a landslide. His second term saw a major arms-limitation treaty with the Soviet Union (1987), then under Gorbachov. A scandal involving covert arms sales to Iran and the diversion of these funds to right-wing insurgents in Nicaragua failed to dent his popularity. He was succeeded by his vice-president, George Bush. Reagan's folksy laid-back style made him at the same time one of the most popular and one of the most ridiculed

The Best Man?

In 1959 Gore Vidal was having difficulties casting his play *The Best Man*, a satire on the US political system. When an agent suggested Ronald Reagan for the part of a presidential candidate, the offer was dismissed at once, on the grounds that no one would find Reagan believable in such a role. Years later Vidal commented ruefully: "If I had said yes, he would have run two years on Broadway, won all the prizes, and never gone into politics."

figures in US political history. In 1994 he announced that he was suffering from Alzheimer's disease.

Redgrave, Sir Michael (1908–85). British actor. The son of an acting family, he first appeared on stage in 1934. He performed in many Shakespearean roles and acted in and directed modern plays. His numerous films included *The Browning Version* (1951) and *Oh, What a Lovely War!* (1969). His daughter **Vanessa** (1937–   ) is also an actress. Her films include *Camelot* (1967), *Mary Queen of Scots* (1971), *Julia* (1977), and *Howards End* (1992). She is also known for her involvement in left-wing politics, as is her brother **Corin** (1939–   ), a stage actor. Their actress sister **Lynn** (1944–   ) is perhaps best known for her role in the film *Georgy Girl* (1967). Vanessa's daughters Natasha Richardson (1963–   ) and Joely Richardson (1966–   ) have also appeared in films and on television.

Reinhardt, Django, real name *Jean Baptiste Reinhardt* (1910–53). Belgian gypsy jazz guitarist. A French-speaker, Reinhardt spent his youth in gypsy caravans in northern France. He taught himself the guitar and violin at an early age but remained illiterate to the end of his life. Despite incurring severe injuries to his left hand in a fire when he was 18, Reinhardt developed a virtuoso technique. In 1934 he formed the Quintette du Hot Club de Paris with the violinist Stephane Grapelli. The ensemble became internationally famous and made numerous recordings. Reinhardt's own compositions include the popular hit 'Nuages'. After World War II he switched to the electric guitar and played with US jazz greats including Duke Ellington and Dizzy Gillespie.

Reith, John Charles Walsham, Baron (1889–1971). British administrator and businessman, first director-general of the BBC (1927–38). Reith was born in Scotland and brought up as a strict Calvinist. His ideal of public service has had a lasting influence on BBC broadcasting. After leaving the BBC, Reith was chairman of BOAC (British Overseas Airways Corporation) and minister of information and transport during

A Question of Size

Shortly after the British Broadcasting Corporation was created in 1927, the sculptor Eric Gill was commissioned to create a figure of Ariel (the spirit in Shakespeare's *The Tempest*) for the outside of its London headquarters. Trouble should probably have been anticipated; while Gill was notorious for the blatant sexuality of his nudes, Lord Reith, the head of the BBC, was known for his puritanism. Sure enough, when the figure was completed, Reith complained in strong terms about the prominence of its penis. Gill, however, refused to make any alterations. To settle the matter, a panel of distinguished Shakespearean scholars was asked to decide whether Ariel had a male organ and, if so, how large it should be assumed to be. On slender textual evidence, they stated that Ariel was intended to be about 13 years old, prompting a medical expert to rule that the organ was in that case improbably large. Reith had his way and the statue was partially emasculated before being put in place.

World War II. The Reith lectures, broadcast annually, were founded in 1947 and named in his honour.

Rembrandt, full name *Rembrandt Harmensz van Ryn* (1606–69). Dutch painter. He established himself as a portrait painter with a picture of a group of surgeons called *The Anatomy Lesson of Dr Tulp* (1632). Through painting many portraits and other pictures to commission, Rembrandt grew rich, but his lavish life-style led to his bankruptcy in 1656. His many self-portraits and pictures of his wife Saskia are particularly famous for their psychological depth and subtlety of expression. His other works include *Night Watch* (1642) and *The Good Samaritan.*

Renoir, Pierre Auguste (1841–1919). French impressionist painter. A friend of Monet and Alfred Sisley, Renoir contributed pictures to four impressionist exhibitions in the 1870s. He made use of pure bright colours in his pictures, which frequently portrayed women, children, and flowers. Towards the end of his life he adopted a more classical attitude towards the human figure, as in *Women in Hats* (1910). Although increasingly arthritic, he continued to paint and was able to sculpt with the aid of an assistant. He also produced over 150 lithographs. His son **Jean Renoir** (1894–1979) was a film director and screenwriter. He first became interested in the cinema while convalescing from wounds received in World War I and directed his first film in 1924. Most of his early silent films starred his first wife Catherine Hessling. During the 1930s he switched to sound and produced his two masterpieces *La Grande Illusion* (1937), a profound pacifist statement, and *La Règle du jeu* (1939), a satire on French aristocratic society that aroused fierce hostility. During World War II he made a number of films in Hollywood. His last films, directed after his return to France in the 1950s, include *Le Déjeuner sur l'herbe* (1959) and *Le Petit Théâtre de Jean Renoir* (1971).

Reuter, Paul Julius, Baron von (1816–99). German founder of the first telegraphic news organization, born *Israel Beer Josaphat*. During the revolutions of 1848 he sent news articles from Paris to the German papers; and the following year he set up a pigeon post service in Aachen. In 1851 he established his headquarters in London and his telegraphic news service spread throughout the world. He was created a baron in 1871 and his son Herbert took over the news service in 1879. Reuters now transmits over 1.5 million words a day from correspondents in 183 countries.

Reynolds, Sir Joshua (1723–92). British portrait painter. Reynolds studied the works of Raphael and Michelangelo in Rome and developed neoclassical theories of art that proved highly influential. A friend of Dr Johnson and Sheridan, he raised the prestige of artists in Britain. Reynolds became the first president of the newly formed Royal Academy in 1769, a post he held until his sight failed in 1789. He painted over 2000 portraits, including many of the leading figures of his time.

Rhodes, Cecil (1853–1902). British statesman and financier in South Africa. Rhodes first went to South Africa for his health at the age of 16 and worked with his brother on a cotton plantation. He subsequently made his fortune from diamond and gold mines. He was largely responsible for the British annexation of Bechuanaland (1884) and as prime minister of the Cape Colony (1890–96) he extended British territory northwards and gained mineral rights in an area which became known as Southern Rhodesia (1898). In 1896 Rhodes was implicated in the unsuccessful Jameson Raid on the Transvaal and was forced to resign from Parliament. He founded the Rhodes scholarships to Oxford and Cambridge for students from the Commonwealth, the US, and Germany.

Richard I, known as *Richard the Lionheart* (1157–99). King of England from 1189. On his accession to the throne he joined the Third Crusade and while he was absent his brother John attempted to usurp him. Richard tried to return to England in disguise but was captured in Austria and held for ransom by Emperor Henry VI. On the payment of this ransom he returned to England and re-established control. He died while fighting in France. His courage and leadership were celebrated in a number of heroic romances after his death.

Richard III (1452–85). King of England. On the death of his elder brother, Edward IV (1483), the young king Edward V was left in Richard's charge. At Richard's request, Edward V and his brother were declared illegitimate by Parliament and were imprisoned in the Tower. Richard subsequently became king himself. The fate of the two princes was never known but it was widely believed that they were murdered on Richard's

> ❝ Six months were all he devoted
> to his kingdom in ten years'
> reign. He used England as a
> bank on which to draw and
> overdraw to finance his
> ambitious exploits abroad...
> Twice in four years England
> was called upon to furnish
> money on a wholly
> unprecedented scale; first for
> the crusade, and secondly for
> the king's ransom when he fell
> into the hands of the Emperor
> on his return.
>
> A. J. Poole, *From Domesday
> Book to Magna Carta* ❞

orders. He was later killed at the Battle of Bosworth, fighting against Henry Tudor (later Henry VII). Shakespeare's portrayal of Richard as a hunchbacked villain has been shown to be historically inaccurate.

Richardson, Sir Ralph (1902–83). British stage actor, noted particularly for his Shakespearean roles. Having made his debut in 1921, he regularly appeared at the Old Vic from 1930 onwards; many of his famous performances are associated with that theatre. He was knighted in 1947. Although principally a stage actor, he appeared in about 50 films, notably *Anna Karenina* (1948), *The Looking-Glass War* (1968), and *Greystoke* (1984), in which he played Tarzan's grandfather.

Richardson, Samuel (1669–1761). British novelist. He was apprenticed to a printer in 1706 and by 1721 had his own business, later becoming printer to the House of Commons. His novels *Pamela* (1740–44) and *Clarissa* (1747–48) were written in the form of a series of letters between the characters. Although popular in England and Europe and greatly copied, they were also parodied because of their moralistic and sentimental heroines.

Richelieu, Cardinal de (1585–1642). French politician and churchman. He rose to power as an adviser to Marie de' Medici, the mother and regent of Louis XIII of France. In 1624 he became chief of the royal council; later, as Louis XIII's chief minister, he was virtual ruler of France. During the Thirty Years War he aligned France with the Protestant powers to try to reduce the power of the Habsburgs in Europe. He also strengthened royal power at home by ruthlessly crushing the Huguenots and the nobility.

Richthofen, Baron Manfred von (1892–1918). German fighter pilot. Germany's most famous pilot in World War I, he was known as the *Red Baron* because of the colour of his Fokker E2 triplane, which he painted scarlet in defiance of an order to camouflage it. Richthofen shot down 80 enemy aircraft before being killed in action himself. His neice Frieda married the writer D. H. Lawrence.

Rilke, Rainer Maria (1875–1926). Austro-German poet, born in Prague. After an unhappy childhood, he studied in Prague and Munich, where he began to write. He then travelled in Russia and Germany before settling in Paris in 1902. His friendship with the sculptor Rodin at this time was largely responsible for the development of a more objective style in Rilke's poetry, as seen in his *New Poems* (1907–08). In 1911–12 his visits to Duino, on the Dalmatian coast, inspired a major series of poems, the *Duino Elegies*, which he completed in 1922. His reputation rests mainly on these poems and his *Sonnets to Orpheus* (1923). He spent his final years in Switzerland.

> **❝** Works of art are of an infinite solitariness, and nothing is less likely to bring us near to them than criticism. Only love can apprehend and hold them, and can be just towards them.
>
> Rainer Maria Rilke, *Letters to a Young Poet* **❞**

Rimbaud, Arthur (1854–91). French Symbolist poet. In 1871 he sent some of his work to the poet Verlaine, who invited the young Rimbaud to Paris, paying his fare. The two poets began an affair that ended a year later in a quarrel, during which Verlaine shot Rimbaud in the arm. After completing his masterpiece *A Season in Hell* (1873), Rimbaud gave up poetry at the age of 19, the poems in *Illuminations* (1886) having been written earlier. From 1880 he travelled in Europe and Africa, where he worked for a coffee-exporter and became involved in gun-running. He returned to France in 1891 to have a leg amputated, but never recovered.

Rimsky-Korsakov, Nikolai Andreyevich (1844–1908). Russian composer. Born into a naval family, he studied at the Naval College in St Petersburg; as a composer he was largely self-taught. His works include such operas as *The Snow Maiden* (1882) and *Tsar Sultan* (1900), which includes the famous 'Flight of the Bumble Bee'. He also wrote symphonies, piano concertos, and the orchestral suite *Scheherazade* (1888), which was later used for the ballet of the same name (1910).

Robeson, Paul (1898–1976). Black US singer and actor. A leading American football player at university, he abandoned his career as a lawyer to become an actor in 1921. He became famous as a singer, particularly for his interpretation of 'Ol' Man River' in the musical *Showboat*, filmed in 1936. He also appeared in the title role of *Othello* (1928; 1943) and in some of Eugene O'Neill's plays. He was ostracized in the 1950s for his left-wing politics and lived in Britain from 1958 to 1963.

Robespierre, Maximilien de (1758–94). French revolutionary and Jacobin leader, known as 'the Incorruptible'. A lawyer, he became a leader of the radical Jacobin party after the French Revolution. During the Reign of Terror (1793–94) he was the leading figure on the Committee of Public Safety, which condemned those considered to be enemies of the Revolution to the guillotine. These included his rival, Danton. However, following accusations of dictatorial behaviour, Robespierre was himself tried and guillotined.

Rockefeller, John D(avison) (1839–1937). US industrialist and philanthropist. He formed the Standard Oil

> ❝ I believe the power to make money is a gift of God... Having been endowed with the gift I possess, I believe it is my duty to make money and still more money, and to use the money I make for the good of my fellow man according to the dictates of my conscience.
> John D. Rockefeller in Matthew Josephson, *The Robber Barons* ❞

Company and by 1878 had gained control of almost all the oil refineries in the country. He put much of his wealth into the Rockefeller Foundation (1913), an educational and scientific charity. His grandson **Nelson** (1908–79) became governor of New York in 1958 and was vice president of the US (1974–76).

Rodgers, Richard (1902–79). US composer of musical comedies. With the librettist Lorenz Hart (1895–1943) he composed such popular musicals as *Babes in Arms* (1937), which includes the song 'The Lady is a Tramp', and *Pal Joey* (1940). After Hart's death, Rodgers began collaborating with Oscar Hammerstein II (1895–1960). Together they produced the immensely successful musicals *Oklahoma!* (1943), *South Pacific* (1949), *The King and I* (1951), and *The Sound of Music* (1959).

Rodin, August (1840–1917). French sculptor. After failing to get into the School of Fine Arts in Paris, Rodin worked as an ornamental mason. The extreme realism of his first important sculpture, *The Age of Bronze*

(1878) caused a sensation. In 1880 he received a commission for *The Gates of Hell*, a huge sculpture containing over 200 figures; although this was never completed, many of his most famous works, such as *The Thinker* and *The Kiss*, were derived from it. His other works include *The Burghers of Calais* (1886), a copy of which is in the Embankment Gardens at Westminster.

Rodney, Baron George (1718–92). British admiral. Born in London, he entered the navy in 1732. In 1756 and 1760 he destroyed much of the French fleet intended for the invasion of England in the Seven Years' War. While serving in the Leeward Islands, he captured Martinique, St Lucia, and Grenada from the French (1762), and during the American War of Independence he defeated a Spanish fleet off Cape St Vincent (1780). His greatest achievement, on his return to the West Indies, was his victory over the French near Dominica (1782).

Rolling Stones, The. British rock group: the principal members of the original line-up were **Mick Jagger** (1944–), **Keith Richard** (1943–), **Bill Wyman** (1936–), **Charlie Watts** (1941–), and **Brian Jones** (1944–69). The Stones were formed in 1962 and had their first number one hit with the song 'It's All Over Now' in 1964. They subsequently built up a world-wide reputation, based largely on their aggressive style of performance and notorious public behaviour. Their hits of the 1960s included 'Satisfaction', 'Paint It Black', 'Ruby Tuesday', and 'Jumping Jack Flash'. After Jones's death by drowning, he was replaced by guitarist **Mick Taylor** (1948–), who was replaced in turn by **Ron Wood** (1947–   ). Although the late 1960s is still seen as their most creative period, the Stones' success has continued with such albums as *Exile on Main Street* (1972), *Some Girls* (1978), and *Voodoo Lounge* (1994). Now in their fifties, the group show no sign of retiring; in 1995 they undertook their biggest and most profitable tour to date.

Rolls, Charles Stewart (1877–1910). British pioneer motorist and aviator. He became a motor dealer in 1902 and in 1904 met Sir Frederick Henry Royce, who was then producing experimental cars. In 1906 the two men founded a company, Rolls-Royce Limited, to produce luxury cars. Rolls was also the first man to fly across the English Channel and back non-stop (1910); he was killed in a flying accident later that year. Royce designed his first aero-engine, the Eagle, in 1914, and this was widely used in World War I.

Rommel, Erwin (1891–1944). German field marshal. He rose to the rank of captain in World War I, and at the start of World War II became commander of a tank division. He was soon fighting in North Africa, where he earned the nickname 'The Desert Fox'. He made major advances for Germany before his crucial defeat at El Alamein (1942). Soon after the assassination attempt on Hitler (20 July 1944), it was discovered that Rommel had contacts with the conspirators. Although he had no active part in the plot, he was induced to commit suicide rather than stand trial.

Roosevelt, Franklin D(elano) (1882–1945). US statesman; 32nd president of the US (1932–45). A distant cousin of Theodore Roosevelt, he married Eleanor Roosevelt, Theodore's niece, in 1905. Eleanor was herself a social reformer. He was partially crippled by polio in 1921. In 1932 he was elected president and introduced the New Deal, a programme to aid labour, agriculture and the unemployed during the Depression of the 1930s. After being re-elected for a third term as president in 1940 he resisted involving the US in World War II until forced to by the Japanese attack on Pearl Harbor (1941). He died suddenly, after being elected for a record fourth term as president, and was mourned throughout the world.

Roosevelt, Theodore (1858–1919). US statesman; 26th president of the US (1901–09). Although a sickly youth, Roosevelt showed an early love of adventure and physical activity. As a young man he worked as a rancher and campaigned against corruption in public life. He led a volunteer force in Cuba during the Spanish-American War (1898) and on his return was elected Republican governor of New York State. Having been appointed vice-president in 1901, he assumed the presidency on the assassination of McKinley later that year. He was elected president in his own right in 1904. In domestic affairs, Roosevelt is mainly remembered for his championship of the 'Square Deal', a programme of social reform involving improved labour conditions and regulation of monopolies. His approach to foreign affairs is summed up in his dictum "Speak softly and carry a big stick." He built the US navy into a major force and acquired the Panama Canal Zone in 1903. After leaving office in 1909, he helped to split the Republican Party through his bitter feud with president

William Taft. In the presidential elections of 1912 he stood unsuccessfully as candidate for his own Progressive party. Roosevelt was also a keen big-game hunter and explorer.

Rossellini, Roberto (1906–77). Italian film director. Born in Rome, the son of an architect, Rossellini began his career as a director of documentary shorts. His first feature was *The White Ship* (1940), a film about an Italian hospital ship. Rossellini became internationally famous with the release of *Rome, Open City* (1945), a highly realistic story shot on location in the last weeks of World War II. As the first classic of Italian neorealism, the film had a profound impact on film-making in Europe and the US. The director completed his trilogy about the end of the war with *Paisá* (1946) and *Germany Year Zero* (1947). In 1949 Rossellini made the first of five films starring Ingrid Bergman (1915–82), who bore him a son the following year. Although the couple later married, their adulterous relationship caused a huge scandal and damaged both their careers. Their daughter is the actress and model Isabella Rossellini (1952–). In the 1960s and 1970s Rossellini concentrated on making documentaries and biographical films. His later features include *General della Rovere* (1959) and *It Was Night in Rome* (1960).

Rossetti, Dante Gabriel (1828–82). British painter and poet of Italian descent. In 1848, with Holman Hunt and Millais, he formed the Pre-Raphaelite Brotherhood, whose object was to return to the vivid colour and detail of pre-Renaissance art. Rossetti's earlier pictures were inspired by Christianity and the Middle Ages, as well as by his model, Elizabeth Siddal, whom he married in 1860. After her death in 1862 Rossetti placed the manuscripts of his poems in her coffin, but they were retrieved seven years later and published. They include the sonnet sequence *The House of Life*. Many of his later, more sensual, pictures feature Jane Morris, the wife of William Morris. Rossetti's sister **Christina**

Lizzie Siddal

The painter and poet Dante Gabriel Rossetti first met Lizzie Siddal, the beautiful daughter of a milliner's assistant, in 1850. Over the next few years Lizzie acted as a model for several members of the Pre-Raphaelite Brotherhood; on one occasion she became seriously ill after posing in a bath of tepid water for Millais's painting of the drowned Ophelia. Her health was, in fact, always fragile and at the time of her marriage to Rossetti in 1860 she was already in an advanced stage of tuberculosis. Two years later, while suffering from depression brought on by a stillbirth, she died from an overdose of laudanum. On the day of the funeral Rossetti came into the room where her body lay and, wrapping her golden tresses round a small notebook containing all his recent poems, told his dead wife that as she had inspired the verses she must take them with her to the grave. The notebook was buried with her in Highgate Cemetery. However, after seven years of poetic silence, Rossetti — claiming that Lizzie's spirit had visited him in the form of a chaffinch — had the body exhumed, recovered the notebook, and published the verses as *Poems* (1870). One witness at the exhumation, which took place at night by the light of a fire, later claimed that Lizzie Siddal's body was discovered perfectly preserved and that her hair had grown so long it practically filled the coffin.

(1830–94) was also a noted poet. Owing to ill-health and depression, she spent most of her adult life as a recluse. Her poems include *Goblin Market* (1862) and *The Prince's Progress* (1866), as well as many short lyrics. A High Anglican, she devoted her last years to religion.

Rossini, Gioacchino Antonio (1792–1868). Italian composer. Rossini was born into a musical family and studied in Bologna. His first operatic success was *Tancredi* (1813); amongst the many operas that followed the best known are *The Barber of Seville* (1816), *Cinderella* (1817), and *William Tell* (1829). At the age of 37, however, Rossini gave up serious composition. He later wrote some short instrumental pieces collectively called *Sins of My Old Age*. A renowned gourmet, he also became famous for his spectacular recipes, such as Tournedos Rossini.

Rostropovich, Mstislav Leopoldovich (1927–). Russian-born cellist. Rostropovich was taught the cello by his father and studied at the Moscow Conservatoire, where in 1957 he became professor of the cello. He has since performed with acclaim all over the world; Britten and Shostakovich are amongst the composers to have written works especially for him. He also accompanies his wife, the soprano Galina Vishnevskaya, on the piano and is well known as a conductor, particularly of Tchaikovsky. He left Russia in 1975 and now lives in the West.

Rothko, Marc, original name *Marcus Rothkovitch* (1903–70). US abstract painter, born in Russia. Rothko emigrated to the US with his family when he was ten years old. He later studied at Yale (1920–23) but was mainly self-taught as a painter. Although he was a founder of the expressionist group The Ten in 1935 he went on to develop a more surrealist style in the following decade. He developed the style for which he is best known in the late 1940s. His mature paintings tend to juxtapose several rectangular areas of intense colour to create a powerful, almost luminous, effect. These works, which are often very large, were intended to produce a strong emotional reaction, bordering on the religious, in the viewer. His later paintings, which are more sombre in their colouring, seem to reflect the depression that afflicted him at the end of his life. He died by his own hand.

Rothschild, Meyer Amschel (1744–1812). German financier of Jewish origin. He became financial adviser to the ruler of Hesse in 1801 and during the Napoleonic Wars built up a large and influential family banking business. His five sons, who were created barons in 1822, continued the business, which had branches in London, Paris, Vienna and Naples. **Lionel Nathan** (1808–79), a grandson of Meyer, became the first Jewish MP in 1858. **Lionel Walter** (1868–1937) was a naturalist who made important collections of birds and insects. His son **Nathaniel** (1910–90) was a zoologist and administrator, who worked in military intelligence during World War II. The Rothschilds bequeathed to the nation a number of country houses in England, including Waddesdon Manor near Aylesbury, now administered by the National Trust. The origin of the surname Rothschild has been much researched; it probably comes from the red shield that was the sign of the Rothschild house in Frankfurt.

Rousseau, Jean-Jacques (1712–78). Swiss philosopher and novelist. He was apprenticed to an engraver at the age of 13 but ran away in 1728 because of ill-treatment. He then spent some years travelling, his nomadic existence at this time being vividly described in his *Confessions* (1782). In 1744 he settled in Paris and began a relationship with a servant girl, Thérèse le Vasseur, who bore him five children, all of whom he disposed of to a foundlings' hospital. His early works included plays and the essay *Discourse on the Origin and Foundations of Inequality* (1754), which argued that men are naturally innocent and corrupted by society. The novel *Emile* (1762) embodies his educational theories, while *The Social Contract* (1762) is a statement of political principles that influenced the French revolutionaries. In later life Rousseau became subject to attacks of paranoia and finally became insane.

> ❛ Rousseau, sir, is a very bad man. I would sooner sign a sentence for his transportation than that of any felon who has gone from the Old Bailey these many years. Yes, I would like to have him work in the plantations.
>
> Samuel Johnson in
> James Boswell, *The Life of Johnson* (1791) ❜

Royce, Sir Frederick Henry (1863–1933). British engineer. *See* Charles Stewart **Rolls**.

Rubens, Sir Peter Paul (1577–1640). Flemish painter. He travelled widely in Europe before becoming court painter in Antwerp in 1608. His elaborate and colourful paintings, such as *Descent from the Cross* (1611–14), earned him a wide reputation and numerous commissions. After working on a series of paintings for the Luxembourg Palace in Paris he undertook diplomatic missions to Spain and England (1629). He was knighted by Charles I for his designs for the ceiling of the Whitehall banqueting hall. During his years of fame Rubens received more orders than he could cope with at his Antwerp studio; many of his 'middle period' paintings were largely the work of his pupils.

Rubinstein, Artur (1886–1982). US pianist of Polish birth. Famous as an interpreter of Chopin, Rubinstein gave his first public performance at an early age. He made his US debut in 1906 and subsequently gave concerts in Britain, Spain, and South America. During the course of a long career he played in almost every country in the world. Composers to have written works especially for him include Manuel de Falla and Heitor Villa-Lobos. Rubinstein is regarded as one of the greatest pianists of the century.

Rushdie, Salman (1947–   ). British novelist, born in Bombay. Rushdie was educated in Britain, at Rugby School and Cambridge University. After some years working in advertising, he published the novel *Grimus* in 1974. Fame arrived in 1981, when his second novel

Midnight's Children won the Booker Prize and became a bestseller. The book uses a combination of fantasy, satire, and realism to explore the post-independence history of India. *Shame* (1983) takes a similar approach to modern Pakistan. Unhappily, Rushdie is now best known for the international controversy that developed following the publication of *The Satanic Verses* in 1988. Claims that the novel, a complex fantasy about the experience of Muslims in the West, blasphemed against Islam led to violent demonstrations in several countries. In February 1988 the Iranian religious leader Ayatollah Khomeini issued a *fatwa* sentencing Rushdie to death; the author has been obliged to live in hiding under police protection ever since. The Rushdie affair has provoked intense debate about the clash between Islam and Western liberal values. His subsequent publications include *Haroun and the Sea of Stories* (1990) and *The Moor's Last Sigh* (1995). In the mid 1990s Rushdie slowly began to adopt a more public profile.

Ruskin, John (1819–1900). British art critic and essayist. The son of a London wine merchant, he had a very sheltered upbringing. His *Modern Painters* (1843–60) was enormously influential, while his works on architecture and the Pre-Raphaelites confirmed him as the greatest critic of the time. Later, he turned to writing on social and political themes. He married Effie Gray in 1848, but the marriage was annulled after six years on grounds of non-consummation and Effie married the artist Millais (1855). As Slade professor of fine arts at Oxford (1870–84), Ruskin tried to promote community life and craftsmanship. He resigned because of recurring mental illness and retired to the Lake District.

Ruskin's Road

Ruskin, a great champion of handicrafts and traditional industry, believed firmly in the dignity of physical labour. One famous story has him sweeping a London street himself in order to show how it should be kept. Similarly, when he had identified the need for a road to enable villagers to travel between Oxford and North Hinksey, Ruskin enlisted the help of idealistic students at the university to build it (somewhat improbably these included the young Oscar Wilde). Ruskin and his disciples set to with a will to create a road across the muddy fields, under the direction of the writer's gardener. The physical effort involved eventually defeated them and the road was never finished. One bemused local observed: "I don't think the young gentlemen did much harm."

Russell, Bertrand (1872–1970). British philosopher. His earlier works on logic and mathematics include *Principia Mathematica* (1910–13). Russell also wrote widely and controversially on political, moral, and religious topics. During World War I he was dismissed from his lectureship at Cambridge and imprisoned for his pacifist writings. His later works include a popular *History of Western Philosophy* (1945). He inherited the title Earl Russell in 1931 and was awarded the Nobel Prize for literature in 1950; in 1949 he was awarded the OM. In later years Russell was active in peace organizations, including the Campaign for Nuclear Disarmament; in 1961 he was arrested for civil disobedience at the age of 89. His *Autobiography* appeared in two volumes (1967–69).

Russell, Ken (1927–). British film director. He made his reputation at the BBC (1958–66), where he directed a series of biographical films on musicians and artists, including Debussy and Isadora Duncan. His cinema films are highly imaginative and often sensational in their imagery and content. They include *Women in Love* (1969), a version of D. H. Lawrence's novel, *The Devils* (1971), a controversial study of religious hysteria, and the biopics *Mahler* (1973) and *Valentino* (1977). More recent films, such as *Gothic* (1987) and *Whore* (1991), have been somewhat poorly received.

Ruth, Babe, nickname of *George Herman Ruth* (1895–1948). US baseball player, whose outstanding talents and larger than life character did much to popularize the sport in the 1920s. Ruth was brought up in poverty in Baltimore and later went into a boys' home. He began to play for the Baltimore team while still in his teens and was sold to the Boston Red Sox in 1914. Although he achieved record results as a pitcher, his popular fame rested on his aggressive batting. After moving to the New York Yankees in 1919, he took the team to five world series victories. His career total of 714 home runs was not beaten until 1974. He retired in 1936. Away from the pitch Ruth had a reputation for drinking, brawling, and womanizing.

Rutherford, Ernest, Baron (1871–1937). New Zealand physicist, whose work formed a basis for the development of nuclear physics. The son of a farmer, he left New Zealand for Britain in 1895. He was professor of physics at McGill University, Montreal (1898–1907) and then at Manchester (1907). In 1919 he was elected

Cavendish professor of experimental physics at the University of Cambridge. At Cambridge he was also director of the Cavendish Laboratory. His most important work was on the nature of radioactivity. It was Rutherford who distinguished between alpha particles (helium nuclei), beta rays (electrons), and gamma rays (short-wave electromagnetic radiation). In 1906, by bombarding gold foil with alpha particles, he was able to deduce that atoms have a central core, which he called the 'nucleus'. This discovery was of fundamental importance in understanding atomic structure and was the basis of all subsequent nuclear physics. He was awarded the Nobel Prize for chemistry in 1908, the OM in 1925, and a peerage in 1931.

S

Sadat, Anwar el (1918–81). Egyptian statesman. He held important posts under Nasser and succeeded him as president in 1970. In late 1977 he visited Jerusalem on a peace mission to end the Arab-Israeli conflict. His was the first Arab plane to touch down at an Israeli airport since 1948, when the state of Israel was founded. For this peace initiative he and Menachem Begin, the Israeli prime minister, were jointly awarded the 1978 Nobel Peace Prize. Egypt and Israel signed a formal treaty (the Camp David Agreement) in 1979; Israeli troops were withdrawn from the Sinai peninsula a year later. Sadat was assassinated by Islamic extremists.

Sade, Marquis de (1740–1814). French writer and thinker, from whose name the term 'sadism' is derived. From the time of his marriage in 1763, he led an

---

The Marquis in Prison

While in prison the Marquis de Sade used to buy expensive roses, admire them lovingly, and then crush them underfoot. Then he would pick them up tenderly as if to enjoy their scent and throw them into the open drain.

---

ostentatiously licentious life and was imprisoned several times for his perverted treatment of prostitutes. He began his writing career in the Bastille prison, where he indulged his sexual fantasies in his novels. His works, which were still officially banned in France until recently, include *The Adversities of Virtue* (1787) and *Justine* (1791). He died in a lunatic asylum in Charenton after years of confinement. In the 20th century, his nihilistic philosophy has been reappraised as a forerunner of existentialism.

Saint-Saëns, Camille (1835–1921). French composer. A child prodigy, he began to compose at the age of five and at 13 he became an organ scholar at the Paris Conservatoire. In 1857 he became organist of the Madeleine Church in Paris. A brilliant pianist, he composed five piano concertos as well as three symphonies and much chamber music. He is probably best remembered for the humorous *Carnival of the Animals* (1886), in which he parodies the works of various other composers.

Sakharov, Andrei (1921–89). Russian physicist and political figure. A graduate of Moscow University, Sakharov was assigned to military research during World War II. From 1947 he took a leading role in the development of the Soviet hydrogen bomb, which was exploded successfully in 1954. During the 1960s however, he began to campaign against further nuclear testing and to argue for greater freedom of speech in the Soviet Union. The award of the Nobel Peace Prize in 1975 made Sakharov internationally famous; it also provoked a campaign of harassment by the Soviet government, culminating in his exile to Gorky in 1980.

Here he continued to argue outspokenly for disarmament and human rights. Following international protests, Sakharov was finally released in 1986. In 1989 he was elected to the new Chamber of People's Deputies, where he argued for liberal reform until his death a few months later.

Saladin (c. 1138–93). Muslim sultan and commander. By virtue of his military achievements he became sultan of Egypt (1174) and northern Syria (1186). In 1187 he defeated a large Crusader army in northern Palestine and captured Jerusalem. The Third Crusade (1189–92), supported in England by a special tax known as the Saladin Tithe, halted Saladin's advance and he retired to Damascus. Known even among his enemies for his chivalry, he was also a patron of Muslim schools and mosques and contributed his own wealth to the war effort.

Salisbury, Robert Cecil, Marquess of (1830–1903). British statesman; prime minister (1886–92; 1895–1900; 1900–02). A Conservative, he became Disraeli's leading adviser and succeeded him as leader of the opposition (1881). As prime minister he acted as his own foreign secretary, following a policy of 'splendid isolation', as it was later known, in European affairs.

Salk, Jonas Edward (1914–95). US medical scientist. A specialist in public health and epidemic diseases, he produced in 1954 the first vaccine against polio. The vaccine consists of dead polio viruses and is injected into the body, in contrast to Sabin's vaccine, which is usually administered orally on a sugar lump.

> **Patent Truth**
>
> Although Salk made no money from the sale of his vaccine, he worked very hard to publicize the discovery. When someone asked him who owned the patent, he replied "The people – could you patent the sun?"

Sargent, Sir Malcolm (1895–1967). British conductor. Sargent studied at the Royal College of Organists and became Britain's youngest-ever doctor of music. In 1921 he made his conducting debut at a Promenade Concert. Besides teaching at the Royal College of Music, he conducted the Royal Choral Society and the BBC Symphony Orchestra (1950–57). He was conductor-in-chief of the Promenade Concerts, for which he is particularly remembered, and was knighted in 1947.

Sartre, Jean-Paul (1905–80). French philosopher, novelist, and dramatist. He was the leading exponent of existentialism, a philosophical movement that regards man as the product of his own actions and decisions, not governed by heredity or external forces of destiny. He began a lifelong association with Simone de Beauvoir while at the Sorbonne. Among his earlier works were the novel *Nausea* (1938) and his major philosophical text *Being and Nothingness* (1943). He was taken prisoner during World War II, and worked for the Resistance on his return to France. After the war he published the trilogy of novels *Roads to Freedom* (1945–49) and turned increasingly to the theatre, with such plays as *In Camera* (1945). With Beauvoir he established the review *Modern Times* and played a prominent part in left-wing politics. Later in his life he published philosophical works and the autobiography *Words* (1963). He refused the Nobel Prize in 1964.

Savonarola, Girolamo (1452–98). Italian preacher and reformer. Having joined the Dominican order in 1474, he gained considerable influence in Florence with his prophetic sermons and denunciation of corrupt clergy. He ruled Florence as a virtual dictator following the expulsion of the Medici family (1494), introducing a theocratic government. Pope Alexander VI, one of those denounced, summoned him to Rome but he politely refused. He also ignored orders to stop preaching and was finally excommunicated (1497). He was arrested, tortured, found guilty of heresy, and finally hanged and burned.

Scarlatti, Domenico (1685–1757). Italian composer and harpsichordist. The son of the composer Alessandro Scarlatti, he studied with his father and in 1701 became composer and organist to the Naples court. He subsequently worked in Venice and in Rome, where he is said to have taken part in a harpsichord-playing contest with Handel. His works include operas and 600 harpsichord sonatas.

Schiller, Friedrich von (1759–1805). German poet and dramatist. He began writing as a child. His first play, *The Robbers* (1781), caused a furore with its emotional attacks on tyranny. When Schiller, an army officer, was ordered to write no more plays, he fled to Mannheim, where he wrote for the Mannheim National Theatre.

In 1787 he met Goethe at Weimar and the two became close friends. Goethe used his influence to gain Schiller a university post as professor of history and these historical studies inspired the drama *Wallenstein* (1800). He also wrote the hymn 'Ode to Joy', further historical plays including *William Tell* (1804), and important essays on aesthetics.

Schoenberg, Arnold (1874–1951). Austrian composer. Largely self-taught as a musician, the young Schoenberg earned a living by arranging popular operettas. He later taught music in Vienna and Berlin. His works of the 1910s became increasingly dissonant, while those of the 1920s introduced the technique known as serialism, in which all 12 notes of the chromatic scale are used. Having been driven from Germany by the Nazis, he settled in California and became a US citizen in 1941. Besides numerous instrumental works he wrote *Pierrot Lunaire* (1912), for voice and five instruments, and the opera *Moses and Aaron* (1932–51).

> 6 There is still a great deal of music to be written in C major.
> Arnold Schoenberg, attrib. 9

Schopenhauer, Arthur (1788–1860). German philosopher. He began to study medicine, but transferred to philosophy and took a PhD in 1813. Having worked with Goethe on his theory of colours, he made his name with *The World as Will and Idea* (1819), in which he set out his pessimistic antirational philosophy. Overshadowed in his own day by Hegel, Schopenhauer lectured for a time but retired to Frankfurt in 1833 and spent the rest of his life as a recluse.

Schubert, Franz Peter (1797–1828). Austrian composer. Schubert was the son of a schoolmaster and had music lessons from a very early age. He became a teacher himself but hated teaching and in 1816 gave up his job. For the rest of his short life he led a Bohemian existence, rarely leaving Vienna. His outstanding gifts as a melodist are apparent in all his works, which include nine symphonies (one lost and the eighth unfinished), 22 string quartets, the 'Trout' piano quintet, many piano compositions, and over 600 songs. He died of typhoid fever.

Schumann, Robert Alexander (1810–56). German composer. Schumann had piano lessons as a child but was sent to Leipzig University to study law. There he neglected his studies for music and fell in love with the pianist Clara Wieck. Despite her father's opposition, they were married in 1840. Both were fine pianists, but Robert Schumann had to give up his career as a performer after an accident damaged one of his fingers. Schumann was periodically ill with a nervous complaint and in 1852 suffered a mental collapse. After attempting to commit suicide he was confined to an asylum, where he died two years later. His works include four symphonies, a piano concerto, chamber music, and songs.

Schwarzkopf, H. Norman (1935–). US general, who commanded the US-led alliance in the Gulf War against Iraq (1991). The son of a prominent police chief, he quickly made his mark as a young army officer with his remarkable IQ and ebullient personality. The latter is reflected in his nicknames 'Stormin' Norman' and 'The Bear'. During the Vietnam War he was decorated for bravery on five occasions. Following Iraq's invasion of Kuwait in 1990, Schwarzkopf was appointed overall commander of the multinational force assembled in Saudi Arabia, a job requiring considerable diplomatic as well as military skills. His abilities as a strategist were confirmed by his swift liberation of Kuwait with minimal allied casualties (1991). The many honours he received included an honorary knighthood from Queen Elizabeth II.

Schweitzer, Albert (1875–1965). Alsatian theologian, medical missionary, and organist. He is chiefly remembered as a missionary, running both a hospital, which he founded with his wife in 1913, and also a leper colony at Lambaréné in Gabon, West Africa. He used the money raised by his organ recitals for his medical work and received the Nobel Peace Prize in 1952. He wrote a biography of J. S. Bach, as well as a number of religious and philosophical works.

Scorsese, Martin (1942–   ). US film director, the son of Sicilian immigrants, Scorsese grew up in New York. After briefly training for the priesthood, he studied at the New York Film School and began to direct in the late 1960s. He first made his name with *Mean Streets* (1973), the film that began his long collaboration with Robert de Niro. De Niro later appeared in the highly praised *Taxi Driver* (1976), *Raging Bull* (1980), and *Casino* (1995) amongst other Scorsese films. In 1988 the director provoked controversy with *The Last Temptation of Christ* (1988), which portrays Jesus as a troubled man suffering from temptation and doubt. Scorsese's more recent films include the gangster drama *GoodFellas* (1990) and *The Age of Innocence* (1993). He has also made occasional appearances as an actor.

Scott, Robert Falcon (1868–1912). British Antarctic explorer. He became a naval cadet and served in the West Indies (1886) under the explorer Sir Clements Markham. On his first Antarctic expedition (1901–04) Scott carried out surveys of the Ross Sea. In 1910 he sailed for Antarctica again, in the *Terra Nova*, and reached the South Pole in January 1912, a month after Amundsen. Scott died with the rest of his party in severe blizzards on the return journey. His diaries were published as *Scott's Last Expedition* (1913). **Sir Peter Markham Scott** (1909–89) was Scott's son, a famous naturalist, the founder of the Wildfowl Trust at Slimbridge, Gloucestershire, and the author of numerous books on birds.

Scott, Sir Walter (1771–1832). Scottish poet and novelist, who pioneered the historical romance. He was slightly lame, having suffered from infantile paralysis. An Edinburgh lawyer, he made his reputation as a poet with *The Lay of the Last Minstrel* (1805) and *Marmion* (1808). He then turned to writing historical fiction, publishing his novels anonymously until 1827 because he was afraid they might detract from his fame as a poet. The first, *Waverley* (1814), was an immediate success; later works included *The Heart of Midlothian* (1818), *The Bride of Lammermoor* (1819), and

---

Scott and Abbotsford

In 1811 Sir Walter Scott bought a large farmhouse on the banks of the Tweed and renamed it Abbotsford. Over the next 15 years he rebuilt the property at great expense as a gothic mansion, complete with turrets and battlements. Meanwhile the estate grew to 1400 acres. Scott paid for most of this work by issuing bills against his future earnings as a writer, which he could expect to be huge. Unfortunately, both Constable, his publisher, and Ballantyne, a printing firm in which he held a partnership, took to meeting their expenses in the same way. Following the financial crisis of 1825–26, many creditors demanded immediate payment and both concerns were driven into bankruptcy. Scott felt that he had a moral responsibility to shoulder not only his own debts but the liabilities of Constable and Ballantyne as well; a sum amounting to some £200,000. Although his friends offered to help, Scott insisted: "No, this right hand shall work it all off." Within six years he had paid off much of the debt through his own efforts but the strain eventually became too much and in 1832 he became ill. He visited the Mediterranean but died not long after his return to Abbotsford in September that year. Even on his deathbed he continued to dictate, determined to the last to pay off the bills on the house he loved and which had, albeit indirectly, killed him.

Ivanhoe (1820). Heavy spending on Abbotsford, his estate in the Borders, contributed to his bankruptcy in 1826 and for the rest of his life he produced novels at great speed in order to repay his debts.

Segovia, Andrés (1893–1987). Spanish guitarist. Largely self-taught, he gave his first concerts in Spain and in

1924 made his debut in Paris. He subsequently toured all over the world, reviving interest in the guitar as a concert instrument and inspiring many composers to write new works for it. In 1981 he became Marquis of Salobreña.

Sellers, Peter (1925–80). British film actor. He established his reputation as a comic actor on the popular radio programme, *The Goon Show*. His best films have given him scope to display his talent for mimicry and satire. They include *I'm All Right, Jack* (1959), *Dr Strangelove* (1964), *What's New, Pussycat?* (1965), and *Being There* (1979). He also played the accident-prone Inspector Clouseau in Blake Edwards's series of *Pink Panther* films.

Seneca, Lucius Annaeus (4 BC–65 AD). Roman philosopher, author and politician. After the death of Emperor Claudius in 54 AD he became first Nero's tutor and later his chief minister. His writings include moral treatises, tragedies, and philosophical works. Condemned for treason by Nero, he was allowed to select his own means of execution and chose to cut open his veins.

Senna, Ayrton (1960–94). Brazilian motor-racing driver. He started his Formula One career in 1984 and took his first Grand Prix title in Portugal the following year. An aggressive competitor who took many calculated risks on the track, he went on to win the Formula One World Championship in 1988, 1990, and 1991. His records include eight Grand Prix victories in 1988 and four consecutives in 1991. He died of head injuries suffered when he crashed into a wall during the San Marino Grand Prix. His death caused widespread mourning in Brazil, where he was regarded as a national hero.

Shackleton, Sir Ernest Henry (1874–1922). British explorer. He served in the merchant navy and joined Scott's first Antarctic expedition (1901–04). In 1908–09 he commanded an expedition in the *Nimrod*, during which he located the south magnetic pole. In an attempt to cross Antarctica his ship was caught in pack ice and he drifted north on ice floes for months before reaching Elephant Island. He died during a return expedition.

Shaftesbury, Anthony Ashley Cooper, Earl of (1801–85). British politician and social reformer. An MP from 1826 until he succeeded to the peerage in 1851, he was responsible for much social and industrial legislation. The Mines Act (1842) halted the employment of women and children in mines, the Lunacy Act (1845) improved conditions for the mentally handicapped, and the Ten Hours Act (1847) limited working hours in factories. As president of the Ragged Schools Union he secured free education for many poor children.

Shakespeare, William (1564–1616). English dramatist and poet. He spent his early life in Stratford-on-Avon, and at 18 married Anne Hathaway, who bore him three children. By 1584 he was involved in the theatre in London and in 1594 he became a member of the Lord Chamberlain's Company (later the King's Men). Until 1603 he probably acted as well as writing for the company, which performed at the Globe Theatre and on

> ❝ Shakespeare never had six
> lines together without a
> fault.
>> Samuel Johnson in James
>> Boswell, *The Life of Johnson*
>> (1792)

> Was there ever such stuff as
> the greater part of
> Shakespeare? Only one must
> not say so.
>> George III in Fanny Burney, *Diary*
>> (1842–46)

> I have tried lately to read
> Shakespeare, and found it
> so intolerably dull that it
> nauseated me.
>> Charles Darwin, *Autobiography*

> With the single exception of
> Homer, there is no eminent
> writer, not even Sir Walter
> Scott, whom I can despise so
> entirely as I despise
> Shakespeare when I measure
> my mind against his.
>> George Bernard Shaw, review of
>> Irving's *Cymbeline* ❞

tour. His plays were first published posthumously in a folio collection in 1623; consequently it is not possible to assign definite dates to each play. Among the earliest were the three parts of *Henry VI* (1589–92), *Richard III* (1592–93), and *Romeo and Juliet* (1594–95). The comedies date mostly from the middle period and include *A Midsummer Night's Dream* (1595–96), *As You Like It* (1599–1600), and *Twelfth Night* (1601–02). *Hamlet* (1600–01) was the first great tragedy. The other major tragedies, *Othello*, *King Lear*, and *Macbeth*, all date from 1604–06. *The Tempest* (1611–12) is the last major play. Shakespeare died in Stratford on 23 April 1616. In his will he left his wife only his second-best bed.

Shaw, George Bernard (1856–1950). Irish dramatist. He came to London in 1876 to join his mother, who was separated from her husband. Having helped to found the Fabian Society in 1884, he devoted much of his time to political activities, although he was also a successful music and drama critic. His first play was performed in 1892; other early works include *Arms and the Man* (1898), *The Devil's Disciple* (1900), and *Man and Superman* (1903). Not until 1904 were his plays regularly performed, but after that his fame spread rapidly. His most popular plays included *The Doctor's Dilemma* (1906), *Major Barbara* (1907), *Androcles and the Lion* (1912), and *Saint Joan* (1923). *Pygmalion* (1912) has since been adapted as a musical, *My Fair Lady*. Shaw's passion for social reform is apparent in most of his plays, all of which have long prefaces. He also wrote literary and political essays and one of the best popular books on economics ever written, *The Intelligent Woman's Guide to Socialism and Capitalism* (1928). His letters to the actress Ellen Terry were published in 1931. Awarded the Nobel Prize in 1925, he gave away the prize money. A lifelong vegetarian and teetotaller, he died at 94.

Ghost Stories

From May to September 1816 Percy Bysshe Shelley, Mary Godwin (later Shelley's wife), and Claire Clairmont (Mary's stepsister) stayed at the Villa Chapuis on the shores of Lake Geneva. After the arrival of Lord Byron and his personal physician, Dr William Polidori, at the Villa Diodati nearby, the two households became inseparable, enjoying the pleasures of sailing on the lake, walking in the mountains, and talking late into the night. In June, however, the weather broke and rain confined them indoors. Thus restricted, the five friends amused themselves by telling ghost stories. Eventually, at Byron's suggestion, it was agreed that they should write their own tales of horror. Disappointingly, neither Shelley nor Claire wrote anything that is preserved but Byron began a tale about vampires, which was later completed and published by Polidori as *The Vampyre*; it is said that Bram Stoker used this as the basis for his *Dracula* (1897). Mary, preoccupied with her baby son William, found it particularly hard to get started. "Have you thought of a story? I was asked each morning", she recorded in her *Journal*, "and each morning I was forced to reply with a mortifying negative." However, after listening to Byron and Shelley talking about the difference between animate and inanimate matter and the possibility of reanimating corpses, Mary spent a sleepless night, terrifying herself with a "waking dream" about a synthetic man. In the morning she began to write the novel that became *Frankenstein*.

Shelley, Percy Bysshe (1792–1822). British Romantic poet. Shelley was the son of a wealthy landowner who rejected him after his expulsion from Oxford University (1811) for writing an atheist pamphlet. He secretly married Harriet Westbrook in the same year and the couple embarked on a nomadic existence. He came under the influence of the radical philosopher William Godwin and in 1814 eloped abroad with Godwin's daughter **Mary** (1797–1851), later the author of *Frankenstein* (1818). After Shelley's first wife drowned herself in the Serpentine in 1816, he married Mary. They settled in Italy, where Shelley wrote most of his famous poems, including *Prometheus Unbound* (1820), *Epipsychidion* (1821), and *Adonais* (1821). In July 1822 he sailed to Leghorn to visit Byron and was drowned on the return journey.

Sheridan, Richard Brinsley (c. 1751–1816). Irish dramatist and parliamentarian, who lived mostly in Britain. In 1772 he eloped to France with Elizabeth Linley, the daughter of a concert promoter. Their parents forced them to return, and Sheridan fought two duels over the marriage. His first two plays, the social comedies *The Rivals* (1775) and *The Duenna* (1775), brought him fame. His other successful works include *The School for Scandal* (1777) and *The Critic* (1779). He became manager and part-owner of the Drury Lane theatre (from 1776) and was also a Whig MP (1780–1812). When Drury Lane burned down in 1809, Sheridan was ruined. He died in poverty.

Shevardnadze, Eduard (1928–   ). Georgian politician. During the 1960s and 1970s he rose steadily through the Georgian Communist Party to become minister of internal affairs (1965–72) and first secretary (1972–85). In this period he took severe measures against Georgian separatists. As the Soviet minister for foreign affairs (1985–91) under Gorbachov, he negotiated large arms reductions with the US. In 1990 he resigned in protest at Gorbachov's drift away from liberal reform; he was briefly reinstated just before the break-up of the Soviet Union (1991). Following the overthrow of Georgia's president Zviad Ghamsakhurdia in early 1992, Shevardnadze was appointed chairman of the state council. For the next two years he was faced with armed rebellion by Ghamsakhurdia supporters as well as by separatists in the Abkhazia and South Ossetia regions. Although greater stability had been achieved by 1994, this was at the cost of accepting Russia's continuing power in the Black Sea region. Shevardnadze, who narrowly escaped assassination in August 1995, was re-elected by a landslide in November.

Shostakovich, Dmitri (1906–75). Russian composer. He made his name with his first symphony, written when he was 20. Although his operas *The Nose* (1930) and *Lady Macbeth of Mtsenk* (1934) were attacked as decadent and bourgeois, Shostakovich regained official favour with his fifth symphony (1937). His works also include string quartets, the ballet *The Age of Gold* (1938), concertos, and piano music.

Sibelius, Jean (1865–1957). Finnish composer. Although Sibelius studied in Berlin and Vienna, the main influence on his music was the national epic poem of Finland, the *Kalevala*. With financial help from the Finnish government, who gave him a ten-year grant, he wrote music based on episodes from Finnish mythology. His works include seven symphonies, a violin concerto, and a small number of chamber works. Based on Finnish legends, he wrote a number of tone poems, such as *En Saga*, *The Swan of Tuonela*, *Pohjola's Daughter*, and *Tapiola*. Other orchestral works include *Karelia*, *Finlandia*, *Valse Triste*, and *Belshazzar's Feast*. He ceased to compose after 1929.

Simon, Paul (1941–). US folk singer and songwriter. He rose to fame with his former schoolfriend **Art Garfunkel** (1942), with whom he recorded songs blending folk and rock styles, such as those on the album *Bridge over Troubled Waters* (1970). From the 1970s he made a series of successful solo albums, notably *Still Crazy after All These Years* (1975). The highly acclaimed *Graceland* (1986) featured South African musicians, while *The Rhythm of the Saints* (1990) was inspired by Latin American styles.

Simpson, O(renthal) J(ames) (1947–). Black US football player; his sensational trial for murder in 1995 was widely hailed as the 'trial of the century'. Simpson was born in San Francisco and attended the University of Southern California, where he excelled in football and track events. From 1969 he became a running back with the Buffalo Bills. After his retirement as a player in 1979 he made a second career as a television personality and film actor. In June 1994 Simpson's ex-wife Nicole and her friend Ronald Goldman, both white Americans, were found stabbed to death. Simpson was charged with murder and arrested after a televised car chase. His subsequent trial, which lasted nearly a year, was televised in full and transfixed the US public. The case bitterly divided the country, mainly on racial lines. Despite strong circumstantial evidence against Simpson, the prosecution case was fatally weakened when their leading witness, a Los Angeles policeman, was revealed as a racist and a perjurer. Simpson was acquitted.

Sinatra, Frank, full name *Francis Albert Sinatra* (1915–). US singer and film actor. He began his singing career on the radio and with bands such as the Tommy Dorsey Orchestra. His popular recordings include 'My Way' and 'Night and Day'. Sinatra has also starred in a number of films including *From Here to Eternity* (1953), for which he won an Oscar. Though he has given several 'farewell' performances, he has continued to record and give live performances into his late seventies.

Sitting Bull, Indian name *Tatanka Iyotake* (c. 1834–90). Native American warrior, chief of the Dakota Sioux. Born near Grand River in South Dakota, Sitting Bull became a leader of the Sioux resistance to White expansion in the 1870s. In 1876 he led the massacre of General Custer and his men at Little Big Horn. He escaped across the Canadian border but later surrendered (1881) and settled on a reservation. In 1885 he was exhibited in Buffalo Bill's touring Wild West show. He was killed in a further Native American uprising.

> ❛ When I was a boy the Sioux owned the world; the sun rose and set on their land; they sent ten thousand men to battle. Where are the warriors today? Who slew them? Where are our lands?

Who owns them? What white
man can say I ever stole his
land or a penny of his
money? Yet, they say I am a
thief. What white woman,
however lonely, was ever...
insulted by me? Yet they say
I am a bad Indian. What
white man has ever seen me
drunk? Who has ever come to
me hungry and unfed? Who
has ever seen me beat my
wives or abuse my children?
Is it wrong for me to love my
own? Is it wicked for me
because my skin is red?
Because I am a Sioux;
because I was born where
my father lived; because I
would die for my people and
my country?

> Sitting Bull in T. C. McLuhan,
> *Touch the Earth* **,**

Sitwell, Dame Edith (1887–1964). British poet. From 1916 to 1921 she edited *Wheels*, an annual anthology of modern poetry. *Façade*, a sequence of her nonsense poems with music by Sir William Walton, caused an uproar on its first performance in 1923. Her later more serious work includes a number of poems inspired by the Blitz and the atomic bomb. Well known for her eccentric dress and manner, she was made a DBE in 1954. Her brother **Sir Osbert** (1892–1969) wrote satirical verse, short stories, novels, and a notable five-volume autobiography. Their brother **Sacheverell** (1897–88) was a poet, essayist, and art critic.

Smetana, Bedřich (1824–84). Czech composer. Smetana studied music against his father's wishes and worked as a conductor in Sweden from 1856 to 1861. On his return to Bohemia, he composed operas such as *The Bartered Bride* (1866) for the new nationalist opera house in Prague. In 1874 he became totally deaf, but was still able to compose a group of symphonic poems, including *My Country* (1874) and *The Moldau* (1874), inspired by the scenery of Bohemia. The continuous high-pitched whistling that afflicted him in his deafness was represented in one of his string quartets by long high notes on the violin. He died insane.

Smith, Adam (1723–90). Scottish political economist and moral philosopher. He became professor of logic at Glasgow University in 1751 and in 1776 he wrote *The Wealth of Nations*, advocating free trade and private enterprise in place of mercantilism. Smith's doctrines played an important role in establishing economics as a separate science. As well as his work on economics, Smith wrote on the history of astronomy, language, and the arts.

Smith, Ian Douglas (1919–). Rhodesian politician. Following a distinguished career in the RAF in World War II, during which he was shot down twice, he entered Southern Rhodesian politics in 1948. After becoming prime minister in 1964, he made a unilateral declaration of independence for Rhodesia (now Zimbabwe) and set up a constitution with white minority rule. This was considered illegal by Britain. Under US pressure he entered into discussions on black majority rule (1979–80). During this period he was minister without portfolio in the transitional government of Bishop Muzorewa. Following the introduction of majority rule in 1980 he remained an MP until 1988.

Smith, Joseph (1805–44). US founder of the Mormon Church. In 1820 he received his first 'call' to be a prophet. Three years later he was (supposedly) visited by an angel who told him of sacred writings inscribed on gold plates; in 1827 he received the scriptures, published as *The Book of Mormon* (1830). Smith subsequently founded the 'Church of the Latter-day Saints' at Fayette, New York, and sent missionaries to Europe. Despite their numerous converts, the Mormons were persecuted and ridiculed and Smith was often arrested. He was killed by masked raiders during one of his spells of imprisonment.

Smuts, Jan (1870–1950). South African soldier and statesman. A former lawyer, he fought the British during the Boer War (1899–1902) but in the following years sought reconciliation with Britain. Together with Louis Botha he formed the Union of South Africa (1910), later becoming the country's prime minister (1919–24; 1939–48). He was largely responsible for South Africa's involvement in World War II. Smuts also published his philosophical writings.

Sobers, Gary, full name *Sir Garfield Sobers* (1936–   ). West Indian cricketer. He captained the West Indies and Nottinghamshire and also played for Barbados and

South Australia. An all-rounder, he is the only batsman to score 36 runs in one over. In 1958 he made a then-record Test score of 365 not out against Pakistan.

Socrates (469–399 BC). Greek philosopher, the founder of Western moral philosophy. He devoted his life to showing up the absurdity of conventional opinions and spent much of his time discussing the notions of right and wrong with young men, poets, and politicians. When some of his followers conspired against the democratic government, Socrates was tried and condemned to death for atheism and corrupting the young. He died in prison by drinking hemlock. Although he wrote nothing himself, his disciple Plato gives a vivid picture of his courage, integrity, and humour.

> ❝ But already it is time to depart, for you to die, for you to go on living; which of us takes the better course, is not known to anyone except God.
> Socrates in Plato, *Apology* ❞

Solzhenitsyn, Alexander (1918–   ). Russian novelist. A former schoolteacher, he was arrested for criticizing Stalin in 1945 and spent eight years in prison. On his release he began to write. His first published work, *One Day in the Life of Ivan Denisovich* (1962), set in a forced labour camp, was extremely successful. However, the political nature of his novels brought Solzhenitsyn increasingly into official disfavour and from 1964 he published his works abroad. His later novels include *Cancer Ward* (1968) and *The First Circle* (1968). Awarded the Nobel Prize in 1970, he was exiled from the Soviet Union in 1974 following the publication of *The Gulag Archipelago* (1973), which exposes the Russian concentration camp system. After two years in Switzerland he moved to Vermont, USA, where he devoted himself to work on *The Red Wheel*, a multi-volume novel about the Russian Revolution that remains incomplete. In 1991 the Soviet authorities dropped all the charges against him; he returned to his homeland three years later.

Sophocles (c. 496–406 BC). Greek tragic dramatist. Universally popular and successful in his own day, he was treasurer of the Athenian Empire (443–442) and a general of the army. Only seven of his 123 plays survive, the most famous being *Antigone* (442), *Oedipus Rex* (c. 430), and *Oedipus at Colonus* (401).

Soyinka, Wole, full name *Akinwande Oluwole Soyinka* (1934–   ). Nigerian playwright, poet, and novelist. A member of the Yoruba people, he studied at the University of Ibadan and Leeds University, England. In 1960 he returned to Nigeria and formed a national theatre company; later that year his first important play, *The Dance of the Forests*, was staged to mark Nigerian independence. Later plays, such as *The Strong Breed* (1963) and *Death and the King's Horsemen* (1975), combine Western dramatic techniques with traditional African styles and subject matter. His novels include *The Interpreters* (1965) and *Ìsará* (1990). During the Nigerian Civil War he was imprisoned (1967–69) for supposedly aiding the Biafran rebels. This experience inspired his

Poems from Prison (1969) and the prose account *The Man Died* (1972). In 1986 Soyinka became the first Black African to receive the Nobel Prize. Recent work includes the play *A Scourge of Hyacinths* (1992).

Spartacus (d. 71 BC) Thracian gladiator, who led a slave revolt against the Romans. In 73 BC he escaped from gladiatorial school with over 70 other gladiators and, joined by bands of slaves, reached Vesuvius. After resounding victories over Roman legions in southern and northern Italy he was finally defeated by Crassus and executed.

Spencer, Herbert (1820–1903). British philosopher and sociologist. In 1860 he began to compile the major work *Synthetic Philosophy*, which occupied him until 1896. It is a series of volumes including *The Principles of Sociology* (1876–96) and *The Principles of Ethics* (1892–93). Spencer was an adherent of the theory of evolution developed by Charles Darwin and a pioneer of sociology.

Spenser, Edmund (c. 1552–99). English poet. He held various government posts in Ireland and bought an estate near Cork, where he wrote *The Faerie Queene* (1589–1609), an allegorical poem praising the Christian virtues. The poem was published with the aid of Spenser's friend, Sir Walter Raleigh. Spenser planned the work in 12 volumes but only six were published. Later volumes may have been lost in the rebellion that destroyed Spenser's Irish estates and forced him to flee to Cork with his wife and four children. He subsequently returned to London, where he died suddenly in 1599.

> ❛ One unpardonable fault, the
> fault of tediousness,
> pervades the whole of the
> *Faerie Queene*. We become
> sick of cardinal virtues and
> deadly sins, and long for the
> society of plain men and
> women. Of the persons who
> read the first canto one in
> ten reaches the end of the
> first book, and not one in a
> hundred perseveres to the
> end of the poem.
> T. B. Macaulay, *Edinburgh
> Review* December 1831 ❜

Spielberg, Steven (1946–   ). US film director and producer, the most successful in motion-picture history.
Spielberg began to direct for TV and the cinema while
still in his early twenties. He enjoyed his first big success with the shark shocker *Jaws* (1975), which became
the industry's biggest hit to date. Subsequent triumphs
included *Close Encounters of the Third Kind* (1977), the action fantasy *Raiders of the Lost Ark* (1981) and its two sequels, and the science-fiction tearjerker *E.T.: the
Extraterrestrial* (1982), which again broke all box-office
records. Two more serious films, *The Color Purple* (1985)
and *Empire of the Sun* (1987), proved less successful with
the public. In 1993 Spielberg enjoyed a double triumph
with *Schindler's List*, a masterly drama of the Holo-
caust, and *Jurassic Park*, which features convincing
computer-animated dinosaurs. While the former
brought Spielberg Oscars for Best Director and Best

Picture, the latter quickly established itself as the most commercially successful film of all time.

Spinoza, Benedict de (1632–77). Dutch philosopher, of Portuguese Jewish descent. He studied Hebrew and the Jewish scriptures but the unorthodox nature of his thought led to his excommunication by the synagogue authorities in 1656. Subsequently he worked as a tutor and lens-grinder while writing such major works as his *Ethics* (written 1662–75; published 1677). In this book, his masterpiece, Spinoza rejected the idea of a personal God in favour of a pantheist philosophy. In 1673 he refused the offer of the post of professor of philosophy at Heidelberg University in order to preserve his independence. He died of consumption.

Spitz, Mark (1950–). US swimmer. In the 1968 and 1972 Olympic Games he won a record nine gold medals, eight of which were for world-record-breaking performances.

Spock, Dr Benjamin (1903–). US paediatrician. After World War II he became known to millions through his *Book of Baby and Child Care* (1945), which advocated a generally permissive approach. Several generations of parents have considered him an authority on the psychological and physical bringing-up of children. During the Vietnam War he was convicted, but aquitted on appeal, of persuading men to evade conscription. Later publications include *Spock on Spock* (1989).

Springsteen, Bruce (1949–). US rock singer and songwriter. Born in New Jersey, Springsteen played in rock bands from the late 1960s onwards and gained a reputation as an energetic live performer. Although his first album, *Greetings from Asbury Park* (1973), earned him comparisons with Bob Dylan, his real breakthrough came with *Born to Run* (1975), which shows Springsteen at his most exuberant. *Darkness on the Edge of Town* (1978) and *The River* (1981) took a more sombre view of US blue-collar life. He then enjoyed his greatest commercial success with *Born in the USA* (1984), the album that lifted him into the superstar bracket. The 1980s also saw a series of gruelling tours. Subsequent releases, such as *Tunnel of Love* (1988) and *The Ghost of Tom Joad* (1995), have been somewhat bleak and low-key.

Stalin, Joseph, real name *Joseph Vissarionovich Dzhugashvili* (1879–1953). Russian dictator. The son of a poor cobbler, he trained as a priest but was expelled for his revolutionary views. Owing to his political activities, he was arrested seven times between 1902 and 1917. He returned from banishment during the Russian Revolution and in 1922 he became general secretary of the Communist party. Lenin, suspicious of Stalin's aims and methods, tried to have him removed but died before achieving his purpose. Following Lenin's death (1924) Stalin shared the leadership of the party until Trotsky, his chief rival, was ousted. Stalin is believed to have been responsible for Trotsky's assassination in 1940. As dictator of the Soviet Union, Stalin eliminated all opposition through a series of purges in the 1930s during which millions were executed. He also launched a programme of intensive industrialization to be carried out through five-year plans. Agriculture was forcibly collectivized and peasants who did not co-operate were executed or put into concentration camps. During World War II he took command of the armed forces. After the war he maintained Soviet dominance in eastern Europe and regarded the West, particularly the US, as the enemy. Stalin's tyrannical methods were denounced by Khrushchev after his death.

Stanislavsky, Konstantin, stage name of *Konstantin Alexeyev* (1863–1938). Russian actor and theatre producer. In 1898 he founded the Moscow Art Theatre and introduced a new naturalistic style of acting. His productions included classics such a Shakespeare and plays by Chekhov and Gorky. His ideas had a big influence on actors and directors in the West. Modern 'Method' acting, in which actors explore the personality and background of the characters they are playing in order to give a more realistic portrayal, is derived from Stanislavsky's ideas, which are discussed in his book *An Actor Prepares* (1926).

Stanley, Sir Henry Morton (1841–1904). British explorer, born *John Rowlands* in Wales. He sailed as a cabin boy to the US, where he met a cotton merchant called Henry Morton Stanley and took his name. After fighting on both sides in the American Civil War he became a journalist for the *New York Herald* (1867). He was sent to Central Africa to trace the explorer Livingstone, who had been missing for two years. Stanley is reputed to have greeted the explorer with the words "Dr Livingstone, I presume" (1871). The first European to trace the mouth of the Congo, Stanley helped found the Congo Free State (1879). In 1887 he relieved the

> ❛ It was his luck to do
> considerable things exactly
> at the time when exploration
> had become scientific, but
> had not ceased to be
> picturesque. A generation
> before, there was glamour,
> but little good business in
> the conquest of the wild…A
> generation later the glamour
> had largely departed, though
> the business was very good
> business indeed. But in the
> high and palmy days of
> Stanley, the explorer had the
> best of both worlds. He was
> admired as a disinterested
> knight errant, and rewarded
> handsomely for not being
> one.
>
> E. T. Raymond on Sir Henry
> Morton Stanley, in *Portraits
> of the Nineties* ❜

Pasha in Sudan during the Mahdist revolt. He served as an MP (1895–1900) and wrote several books, including *In Darkest Africa* (1890).

Steele, Sir Richard (1672–1729). Anglo-Irish essayist and dramatist. He left Oxford University in 1692 to join the army and was a captain by 1700. His reforming spirit was first shown in his treatise *The Christian Hero* (1701), which was subtitled "An Argument proving that no Principles but those of Religion are Sufficient to make a great Man". In 1709 he and his schoolfriend Joseph Addison founded the periodical *The Tatler*. Steele wrote several hundred essays for *The Tatler* and the other magazines he edited, including *The Spectator*. He also wrote a number of plays, including *The Funeral* (1701). Elected to Parliament in 1713, he was expelled a year later for supporting the Hanoverian succession. He was re-elected and knighted in 1715.

Steinbeck, John (1902–68). US novelist and writer. Born in Salinas, California, Steinbeck studied marine biology at Stanford. He subsequently worked as a journalist and in various menial jobs before publishing his first novel, *Cup of Gold*, in 1929. His work made little impact until *Tortilla Flat* (11935), a tale of poor farm workers in California, became a bestseller. *Of Mice and Men* (1937) and *The Grapes of Wrath* (1939) dealt with similar subject matter but introduced a new note of social criticism. Combining an accessible style with seriousness of purpose, these novels pleased the critics as well as the public; both were successfully filmed. Later novels, such as *Cannery Row* (1945) and *East of Eden* (1952), were less well received. Steinbeck was awarded the Nobel Prize for literature in 1962.

Stendhal, pseudonym of *Marie-Henri Beyle* (1783–1842). French novelist. He served as an officer in the Napoleonic campaigns from 1800 until Napoleon's abdication in 1814, when he retired to Milan to write. Suspected of espionage, he was forced to return to Paris in 1821 and worked as a journalist. From 1830 he was consul-general at Civitavecchia in Italy, where he wrote his two major works, *The Red and the Black* (1830) and *The Charterhouse of Parma* (1839). Standhal died after collapsing in the street in Paris.

Stephenson, George (1781–1848). British engineer. He worked as an engineer in the mines and in 1815 built his first locomotive, the *Blucher*, which could pull 30 tons of coal at 6.4 km per hour (4 mph). He was appointed to build a locomotive for the Stockton–Darlington railway in 1822. This made its historic first journey on 27 September 1825, being the first locomotive to carry passengers and goods. In 1826 Stephenson constructed the 64 km Liverpool–Manchester railway. A competition was held to decide the locomotives to be used on this line and in 1829 Stephenson won the £500 prize with the *Rocket*, a machine designed by his son **Robert** (1803–59). This famous locomotive reached a speed of 57.6 km per hour (36 mph). Robert, who later became a famous civil engineer is also well known for his Britannia railway bridge (1850) over the Menai Strait.

> 6 Every part of the scheme shows that the man has applied himself to a subject of which he has no knowledge and to which he has no science to apply.
> Report of the Parliamentary Commission considering George Stephenson's proposed Liverpool–Manchester railway (1825) 9

Stern, Isaac (1920–   ). US violinist, born in Russia. Stern studied in San Francisco and made his debut there at the age of 11. He has toured all over the world and is widely regarded as one of the greatest living violinists. He was appointed to the Légion d'honneur in 1975.

Sterne, Laurence (1713–68). Anglo-Irish novelist and writer. Sterne was brought up in some poverty in County Tipperary. After studying at Cambridge, he was ordained an Anglican priest and appointed to a living in Yorkshire (1738). His wife suffered a mental breakdown and was committed to an asylum in 1758. The following year saw publication of the first two volumes of his masterpiece, *Tristram Shandy*, an eccentric novel that combines comedy and sentiment. Despite its oddity, the book became highly popular; further volumes appeared between 1761 and 1767. During the 1760s Sterne travelled for his health in France and Italy, an experience that inspired his *A Sentimental Journey* (1768). He died of pleurisy soon after returning to Britain. His other works include volumes of sermons and letters.

Stevens, Wallace (1879–1955). US poet. Born in Reading, Pennsylvania, Stevens attended Harvard (1897–1900) and later trained for the bar. He then worked for many years as a lawyer to an insurance firm, becoming its vice-president in 1934. Although Stevens published a few pieces in magazines and anthologies, poetry remained a private spare-time activity; his first collection, *Harmonium* (1923), did not appear until he was 44. In the 1930s and 1940s a series of landmark collections established Stevens as one of the most gifted and original poets of the century; these include *Ideas of Order* (1936), *The Man with the Blue Guitar* (1937), and *The Auroras of Autumn* (1950). His work, which is extremely difficult to categorize, shows the influence of both European Symbolism and the US romantic tradition of Whitman and Emerson. Its major theme is the interaction between the external world and man as perceiver and creator.

Stevenson, Robert Louis (1850–94). Scottish poet and novelist, best known for his adventure stories, such as *Treasure Island* (1881) and *Kidnapped* (1886). He studied law and engineering before turning to literature in

Tusitala

Having travelled to the South Seas in 1888 for the sake of his health, Robert Louis Stevenson established a warm friendship with the natives of Vailima, Samoa, where he made his home. The writer, who was given the name of Tusitala, or 'storyteller', was made a chief of one of the tribes and received a full ceremonial burial after his death from a brain haemorrhage in 1894. His fellow chiefs subsequently prohibited the use of firearms near the grave, so that he might hear the birds sing there without disturbance. Although the attractions of Samoa, with its climate and friendly people, were obvious, Oscar Wilde doubted that the move was a good one for Stevenson's literary career: "I see that romantic surroundings are the worst surroundings for a romantic writer", he wrote to a friend, "In Gower Street, Stevenson could have written a new *Trois Mousquetaires*. In Samoa he wrote letters to *The Times* about the Germans."

1873. His reputation was made with *Treasure Island* and *Dr Jekyll and Mr Hyde* (1886). He also wrote travel books, literary essays, and poetry. Frequently ill, he travelled throughout Europe and the US, hoping to improve his health. He sailed for the South Seas in 1888 and settled at Vailima in Samoa, where he spent the last five years of his life. During his short time in the Pacific Islands Stevenson became greatly interested in their affairs, and in 1892 wrote *A Footnote to History* about them.

Stockhausen, Karlheinz (1928–   ). German composer, a leading figure of the post-war avant-garde. Stockhausen studied music in Cologne and Paris, where his teachers included Messiaen. In 1953 he co-founded the electronic music studios of the West German state radio, the first of their kind. His works of the 1950s show him experimenting with electronic and synthesized sounds, serial techniques, and unusual spatial arrangements (as in *Gruppen*, 1957, for three orchestras). In the 1960s he dispensed with conventional musical notation and allowed chance to dictate some elements of his works in performance. His ideas about music and its power to unify the human race became increasingly mystical and grandiose during this period. Since 1977 he has been working on a huge opera sequence called *Licht*; when complete this will consist of seven works named after the days of the week. So far *Donnerstag* (1980), *Samstag* (1984), and *Montag* (1988) have been performed.

Stopes, Marie (1880–1958). Scottish advocate of birth control. A botanist and palaeontologist by training, she held university posts in Manchester and London.

Seeing contraception as a way of improving marriages rather than simply a means of decreasing poverty, she founded the first birth-control clinic, at Holloway, London, in 1921. Despite initial opposition from moralists and the medical profession, she influenced the acceptance of contraception by the Church of England.

Stoppard, Tom (1937–). British dramatist, born in Czechoslovakia. His family came to England in 1946. He worked as a journalist for a time and began writing for radio and television in 1960. In 1966 he achieved international fame with his play *Rosencrantz and Guildenstern are Dead*. His subsequent plays, which are noted for their verbal brilliance and ingenious juggling of ideas, include *Jumpers* (1972), *Travesties* (1974), *Night and Day* (1978), *The Real Thing* (1982), *Arcadia* (1993), and *Indian Ink* (1995).

Stradivari, Antonio (1644–1737). Italian violin-maker. Stradivari was born and died in Cremona, where he was a pupil of the violin-maker Niccolò Amati. Stradivari perfected the design and tone of the violin and his formula for varnish has never been discovered. He made violas and cellos as well as violins and all his instruments are now extremely valuable. He signed his instruments with the Latinized 'Stradivarius'.

Strauss, Johann, the Elder (1804–49). Austrian violinist, conductor, and composer, nicknamed 'The Father of the Waltz'. His son **Johann Strauss the Younger** (1825–99) had to study music in secret because his father wanted him to go into business. The debut of his orchestra in 1844 was highly successful, and it soon rivalled his father's orchestra. He composed many dance pieces, including the 'Blue Danube' and 'Emperor' waltzes and the 'Thunder and Lightning' polka. He also wrote such successful operettas as *Die Fledermaus* (1874). Johann's brother **Josef** (1827–70) was also a composer of waltzes.

Strauss, Richard (1864–1949). German composer and conductor. A child prodigy, he began composing at the age of six. Under the influence of Wagner and Liszt he began the composition of a series of symphonic poems that included *Don Juan* (1889) and *Till Eulenspiegel* (1895). In 1905 Strauss had his first operatic success with *Salome*, which he followed with the operas *Elektra* (1909) and *Der Rosenkavalier* (1911). Other well-known works include the *Four Last Songs* (1948). Strauss accepted an important musical post from the Nazis but subsequently resigned when he was criticized for using a libretto by a Jewish writer.

Stravinsky, Igor (1882–1971). Russian composer, who took US citizenship in 1945. Stravinsky studied with Rimsky-Korsakov and had his first major success with the fairy-tale ballet *The Firebird* (1910), written for Diaghilev's Ballets Russes. His third ballet, *The Rite of Spring* (1913), shocked audiences with its dissonant harmonies and unorthodox rhythms. In subsequent works, such as the ballet *Pulcinella* (1920) and the music-theatre piece *Oedipus Rex* (1927), he tried to recall the classicism of 17th- and 18th-century music. Towards the end of his life Stravinsky adopted the twelve-tone technique of composition invented by Arnold Schoenberg.

Streep, Meryl, real name *Mary Louise Streep* (1949–   ). US film actress. Born in New Jersey, she studied drama at Vassar College and Yale before going on Broadway. She first attracted attention with a supporting part in *The Deer Hunter* (1978) and a year later won an Oscar for her performance in the divorce drama *Kramer vs. Kramer* (1979). She went on to play the leads in such distinguished films as *The French Lieutenant's Woman* (1981), *Sophie's Choice* (1982), *Out of Africa* (1985), and *A Cry in the Dark* (1989). After several less successful movies, she made a comeback in the action film *The River Wild* (1994) and *The Bridges of Madison County* (1995), with Clint Eastwood. She is particularly well known for her mastery of foreign accents.

Strindberg, August (1849–1912). Swedish dramatist. His unhappy childhood is described in the autobiographical *The Son of a Servant* (1886). He left university without a degree and became a writer. His earliest dramas were naturalistic 'problem plays' in the style of Ibsen. As a result of his emotional instability and his three unsuccessful marriages, his works became increasingly mysogynistic. *The Father* (1887), *Miss Julie* (1888), and *The Dance of Death* (1901) are the best known. His last plays, such as *The Ghost Sonata*, had an important influence on the symbolist movement.

Suleiman the Magnificent (c. 1494–1566) Sultan of the Ottomon Turks from 1520. He enlarged the Ottoman Empire with campaigns in Europe and North Africa; he also fought against Persia (1534–55). By the end of his reign Belgrade, Budapest, Rhodes, Baghdad, and Algiers had all been added to the Ottoman Empire. He was also a patron of the arts and built several magnificent mosques in Constantinople. His important administrative reforms earned him the title of 'the Lawgiver'.

Sullivan, Sir Arthur (1842–1900). British composer. *See* W. S. **Gilbert**.

Swift, Jonathan (1667–1745). Irish poet, satirist, and prosewriter. He was ordained in 1695 and in 1713 became Dean of St Patrick's, Dublin. His works include *A Tale of a Tub* (written 1696–99) and the political satire *Gulliver's Travels* (1726), now largely read as a children's book. *Journal to Stella* (1710–13) is a series of letters written to Hester Johnson, a lifelong friend. He also wrote a number of pamphlets protesting at Britain's policy in Ireland. After 1739 he was paralysed and unable to speak.

> Swift has sailed into his rest;
> Savage indignation there
> Cannot lacerate his breast.
> Imitate him if you dare,
> World-besotted traveller; he
> Served human liberty.
> W. B. Yeats, 'Swift's Epitaph'

Swinburne, Algernon Charles (1837–1909). British poet. The son of an admiral, he left Oxford University without a degree and became friendly with Dante Gabriel Rossetti and other Pre-Raphaelite artists.

Although *Atlanta in Calydon* (1865) brought him overnight fame, his next work, *Poems and Ballads* (1866), was more controversial and was attacked by critics. Swinburne became an alcoholic, and was saved from possible death in 1879 by a friend who took care of him for the rest of his life and encouraged him to continue writing. Swinburne's later works include plays and criticism.

Synge, John Millington (1871–1909). Irish dramatist. Synge trained as a professional musician and spent several years wandering in Europe. In 1896 the poet W. B. Yeats encouraged him to write, and to visit the Aran Islands to gain material; advice that bore fruit in Synge's *Riders to the Sea* (1904). His portrayal of the Irish peasantry in *The Playboy of the Western World* (1907) caused angry riots among the audience. The play is now considered his masterpiece. *Deirdre of the Sorrows* (1910) was unfinished at his death.

T

Tacitus, Cornelius (c. 56–120 AD). Roman historian. During his distinguished career as a lawyer and in public service he wrote works on oratory, biography, and geography. He then began work on the *Histories* (c. 100) and the *Annals* (c. 115), which are the most reliable sources for the history of Rome between 14 and 70 AD. Tacitus's concise style and his vivid narrative and characterization have earned him a place amongst the world's greatest historians. He enjoyed an eminent reputation in his own time, as is evident from the praise given to him by Pliny in his letters.

Talleyrand-Périgord, Charles Maurice de (1754–1838). French statesman and diplomat. As his club foot prevented him from following the family tradition of entering the army, he went into the Church instead, serving as Bishop of Autun (1788–91). After the fall of the monarchy he was accused of dealings with Louis XVI and banned from France (1794–96). He later became Napoleon's foreign minister (1799–1807) but, worried by Napoleon's ambition, worked secretly for the restoration of the Bourbons. On the accession of Louis XVIII Talleyrand became his foreign minister and secured favourable peace terms for France at the Congress of Vienna (1814–15).

The Survivor

Talleyrand's ability to survive successive changes of regime between 1789 and 1830 attracted both admiration for his political skills and distaste for his somewhat flexible principles. His role in the revolution of 1830, which replaced Charles X with Louis Phillippe, remains particularly obscure. According to one story, Talleyrand was sitting at home in Paris with a friend when the noise of rioting was suddenly broken by a peal of church bells. "Ah!" he remarked mysteriously, "that means we're winning!" "But who's *we*, excellency?" asked the friend. Talleyrand raised a finger to his lips and smiled; "Not a word. I'll tell you who *we* are tomorrow."

Tamerlane (1335–1405). Mongol conqueror, also known as *Timur Leng*. A direct descendant of Genghis Khan, he established himself as a ruler of Turkestan and made Samarkand his capital. His name comes from "Timur-i-leng", meaning "Timur the lame". Infamous for his cruelty, he went on to conquer Persia, southern Russia, and part of India, but died while on his way to attack China. He is the hero of Christopher Marlowe's play *Tamburlaine*.

Tarantino, Quentin (1963–   ). US film director and screenwriter, whose films are known for their violence and quirky black humour. Tarantino was raised in California and developed an early love of film; he wrote his first scripts while working in a video store. In 1993 he supplied the screenplay for *True Romance*, directed by Tony Scott. That same year he made his debut as a director with *Reservoir Dogs*, a brutal but witty crime drama that attracted huge publicity. Tarantino then consolidated his reputation as the most talked-about director of the decade with *Pulp Fiction* (1994), which won seven Oscar nominations and the Palme d'Or at Cannes. He also provided the original script of Oliver Stone's *Natural Born Killers* (1994), but disowned the film in its final form.

Tasman, Abel Janszoon (c. 1603–59). Dutch explorer and navigator. In the service of the Dutch East India Company he led an expedition to explore Australia (1642–43). In the course of this voyage he discovered Van Diemen's Land, which he named after his patron; the island was later renamed Tasmania in his honour. On the same expedition he also discovered New Zealand, Tonga, and Fiji.

Tasso, Torquato (1544–95). Italian Renaissance poet. From the 1560s onwards he wrote epic, lyric, and pastoral poetry mainly under the patronage of the Este family. *Gerusalemme liberata*, his masterpiece, was completed in 1574 but not published until 1581. Tasso later suffered from mental illness (1579–86) but continued to write poetry and prose works during his confinement in an asylum.

Tati, Jacques, original name *Jacques Tatischeff* (1908–82). French film actor and director. A former music-hall star, he later wrote, directed, and acted in several comic films based on visual jokes. His most famous creation is Monsieur Hulot, an eccentric character who has a disastrous way with even the simplest machines or gadgets. His films include *Monsieur Hulot's*

Holiday (1952), *Mon Oncle* (1958), *Traffic* (1970), and *Parade* (1974).

Taylor, Elizabeth (1932–). US film actress, born in Britain. Taylor, who had acted in films since the age of 10 arrived in Hollywood as a child evacuee during World War II. By the age of 16 she had made ten films, the best known of these being *National Velvet* (1944). A famous beauty and screen personality, she has been married eight times, twice to Richard Burton. Her films as an adult include *Cat on a Hot Tin Roof* (1958), *Butterfield 8* (1960), *Who's Afraid of Virginia Woolf?* (1966), *A Little Night Music* (1976), and *The Mirror Crack'd* (1981). She later returned to the stage and campaigned for AIDS charities.

Tchaikovsky, Peter Ilyich (1840–93). Russian composer. He became a professor at the Moscow Conservatoire in 1866. For many years he corresponded with Nadezhda von Meck, a wealthy widow who supplied him with money but whom he never met. In 1877 he made a disastrous marriage, which lasted only a month, to a music student; the breakdown of the marriage was caused by Tchaikovsky's homosexuality. He became universally famous for the ballets *Swan Lake* (1876), *The Sleeping Beauty* (1890), and *The Nutcracker* (1892), the fantasy-overture *Romeo and Juliet* (1880), his six symphonies, and his first piano concerto. His death was officially attributed to cholera contracted from drinking unboiled water; more recent research suggests that he probably committed suicide to avoid a homosexual scandal.

Telford, Thomas (1757–1834). Scottish civil engineer. The son of a shepherd, he learnt the trade of a stone mason and educated himself to be an architect. While working as engineer on the Ellesmere Canal (1796–1801) he made his name with the construction of its two great aqueducts. In Scotland he built the Caledonian Canal and over 1600 km of roads (1801–23), greatly improving communications. While working on the London–Holyhead road he designed and built the Menai suspension bridge (1819–25), his best-known work. Other major constructions include the Göta Canal, Sweden, and St Katherine's Dock, London. He was also responsible for draining part of the East Anglian fens. Telford New Town in Shropshire was named in his honour.

Tennyson, Alfred, Lord (1809–92). British poet. The son of a Lincolnshire rector, he began writing as a child. At Cambridge University he met Arthur Hallam, whose death is commemorated in *In Memoriam* (1850), a long

> ❛ In youth he looked like a gypsy; in age like a dirty old monk; he had the finest ear, perhaps, of any English poet; he was also, undoubtedly, the stupidest; there was little about melancholia that he didn't know; there was little else that he did.
>
> W. H. Auden, introduction to
> *A Selection from the Poems of Alfred Lord Tennyson* ❜

poem sequence that earned Tennyson the position of Poet Laureate. Earlier volumes of poetry contained 'The Lady of Shalott' (1832), 'The Lotus-Eaters' (1832), and *Morte d'Arthur* (1842). From 1853 Tennyson lived on the Isle of Wight; his later works include *Maud* (1855) and the Arthurian poems in *Idylls of the King* (1859). From 1874 he experimented unsuccessfully with poetic drama. He was raised to the peerage in 1884.

Tenzing Norgay (1914–86). Sherpa mountaineer. He worked as a porter on an expedition to Mount Everest in 1935 and became a head porter in 1947. With Sir Edmund Hillary, he made the first complete ascent of Everest (1953). His autobiography, *Tiger of the Snows*, appeared in 1955 and he later became director of the Himalayan Mountaineering Institute in Darjeeling.

Teresa, Mother, original name *Agnes Gonxha Bajahui* (1910–   ). Indian Roman Catholic nun and missionary, born in Albania. Having resolved to become a missionary at the age of 12, she joined the Sisters of Loretto, a community of Irish nuns, in 1928. After a short period in Dublin she travelled to Calcutta, where she worked as a teacher. In 1948, after training as a nurse, she founded her Order of Missionaries of Charity to serve the blind, diseased, and dying among the city's poor. The Shanti Nagar leper colony near Asonol was opened in 1964. Her order now runs schools, clinics, children's homes, and hospices in cities throughout India and in other developing countries. Mother Teresa herself, a tiny woman with evident political skills as well as an unshakable sense of purpose, is now revered throughout the world (although some have criticized her authoritarian style). Her many honours include the Nobel Peace Prize (1979).

Teresa of Avila, St (1515–82). Spanish mystic. In 1533 she entered a Carmelite convent in Avila and in 1555 had an ecstatic vision of Christ. She founded a new convent in 1562, based on an austere rule of meditation and withdrawal from the world. She subsequently founded other convents, and, with St John of the Cross, new Carmelite monasteries. One of the most important figures of the Counter-Reformation, she was canonized in 1622. Her mystical writings include *The Way of Perfection* (1583).

Thackeray, William Makepeace (1811–63). British novelist. After studying law, he began his career as a journalist for *Punch* and other periodicals. In 1840 his wife of four years became insane and he was left to care for their two daughters. *Barry Lyndon* (1844) was his first novel but the satirical *Vanity Fair* (1848) and *Henry Esmond* (1852) proved his greatest successes. He edited the *Cornhill Magazine* from 1860 but resigned in 1862 to concentrate on writing.

Thatcher, Margaret, Baroness (1925–   ). British politician; prime minister (1979–90). The daughter of a grocer, she graduated in chemistry from Oxford. After working as a barrister, she entered Parliament in 1959 as a Conservative. She was a member of the Cabinet (1970–74) and succeeded Edward Heath as leader of the Conservative Party (1975). Following the Conservative victory in the 1979 general election, she became Britain's first woman prime minister. During her first term of office Thatcher adopted a policy of tight monetary control and cuts in government expenditure; this had some success in reducing inflation but caused very high unemployment. In foreign affairs she took a strong anti-Soviet stance, leading to her nickname 'the Iron Lady'. When Argentina invaded the Falkland Islands in 1982, she dispatched a large naval task force; victory in the Falklands War contributed significantly to her re-election by a landslide in 1983. During her second term Thatcher cut income tax and embarked on an ambitious policy of privatizing nationalized industries. She also reduced trade-union powers, defeating a year-long miners' strike in 1984–85. Although unemployment remained high, more prosperous parts of the country enjoyed a short-lived economic boom, leading to a third Conservative victory in 1987. The following year Thatcher became Britain's longest-serving prime minister of the century. During her third term, however, Thatcher's autocratic style made her increasingly unpopular. The imposition of a poll tax to finance local government in 1989–90 led to widespread protests and predictions that the Conservatives could not be re-elected with her as leader. At the same time, her hostile attitude towards the EC split the Cabinet and party, provoking Michael Heseltine to challenge

> ❛ This woman is headstrong, obstinate, and dangerously self-opinionated.
>
> Report by the personnel department at ICI, rejecting the young Margaret Thatcher's application for a job (1948) ❜

her for the leadership in November 1990. When she failed to win an outright victory, she resigned. She entered the House of Lords in 1992.

Themistocles (c. 526–460 BC). Greek statesman and naval commander. He started the building of Piraeus harbour and induced the Athenians to use the revenue from a silver mine to build a sizeable navy. Under his command the Athenian navy, allied with the Spartans and Peloponnesians, defeated Persia under Xerxes I at the Battle of Salamis (480). However, he subsequently lost popularity and was banished from Athens by public vote in 471.

Thomas, Dylan (1914–53). Welsh poet. He began to publish poetry at the age of 20 and later worked for the BBC as a scriptwriter. His exuberant rhetorical poetry began to attract a following during World War II. In 1950 he began a series of popular poetry-reading tours in the US. His *Collected Poems* (1952) was very successful, as was his verse play *Under Milk Wood* (1954), which tells of the colourful inhabitants of a Welsh village. Thomas, an alcoholic, died in New York at 39.

Thomas à Kempis, real name *Thomas Hammerken von Kempen* (c. 1380–1471). German theologian. He spent most of his life in an Augustinian monastery, where he wrote *The Imitation of Christ*. This famous devotional work, which instructs the reader to model his life on that of Christ, has been translated into more languages than any book except the Bible.

Thomson, Sir Joseph John (1856–1940). British physicist. Thomson won a scholarship to Cambridge in 1876 and was associated with the university for the rest of his life; he became Cavendish professor of experimental physics (1884–1918) and later, master of Trinity College (1918). His discovery of the electron (1897) revolutionized the theory of atomic structure. In 1906 he received the Nobel Prize for physics for his researches into the conduction of electricity through gases exposed to X-rays. Thomson was also an outstanding teacher; seven of the men who worked under him were later awarded Nobel Prizes.

Thorpe, Jim, full name *James Francis Thorpe* (1888–1953). US athlete and American football player. Of Native American descent, Thorpe attended the Indian Industrial School in Carlisle, Pennsylvania, where he made his reputation as an outstanding halfback and all-round athlete. At the Stockholm Olympics (1912) he won gold medals in the decathlon and pentathlon. However, a year later he was deprived of his medals when it was revealed that he had played semiprofessional baseball in 1909–10, thereby forfeiting his amateur status. Subsequently Thorpe played baseball for various National League teams (1913–19) and became a professional football star (1919–26). In 1950 a panel of sportswriters voted him the greatest US athlete of the half-century. Despite this, his last years were spent in alcoholism and poverty. In 1982–83, some 30 years after his death, the International Olympic Committee restored his amateur status and returned his medals to his family.

Thucydides (c. 460–400 BC). Greek historian and general. His *History of the Peloponnesian War* (431–404), an account of the war between Athens and Sparta, is the first documented historical record. In 424 the Athenian army was defeated while under his command and Thucydides was exiled from Athens until the end of the war. His *History*, which breaks off at 411, was completed by Xenophon.

Tiberius, full name *Tiberius Claudius Nero Caesar Augustus* (42 BC–37 AD). Roman emperor. As the stepson of Augustus, he soon obtained command in the army and had a brilliant military career. After being passed over several times as Augustus's successor and spending several years in virtual exile on Rhodes (6 BC–2 AD), he finally became emperor in 14 AD. Following the un-

---

Tiberius on Capri

Tiberius's last years on Capri are vividly described by Suetonius in *The Twelve Caesars*. According to Suetonius, the emperor spent his time in a round of orgies and wanton killings; most of his victims seem to have been young boys. He built himself about a dozen ornate villas on the island, each of which was equipped with dungeons, torture chambers, and places of execution. The Villa of Jove, one of these palaces stands at the top of a sheer cliff called 'Tiberius's leap'; those who offended him were hurled over the edge. To add to the horror, Tiberius had begun to suffer from a loathsome skin disease that made him physically repulsive and evil-smelling. He was eventually smothered by a member of his own guard — but not before naming his successor, the still-more depraved Caligula.

---

successful conspiracy of his trusted minister Sejanus (31 AD), he did not leave his home on the island of Capri. In his last years here he gained a reputation for cruelty and depravity.

Tintoretto (1518–94). Venetian painter, born *Jacopo Robusti*. His nickname 'Tintoretto' derived from his father's occupation of dyer (*tintore*). Tintoretto spent most of his life in Venice, where he undertook commissions for religious orders. Working in a style that owed much to Michelangelo and to Titian, he painted religious and mythological subjects as well as many portraits. His most ambitious work was a series of paintings on the life of Christ in the School of Saint Rocco.

Tippett, Sir Michael (1905–   ). British composer. Tippett was imprisoned for three months during World War II for his pacifist convictions. A graduate of the Royal College of Music, he was musical director of Morley College, London, from 1940 to 1951. His many early works remain unpublished, his first mature compositions being the concerto for double string orchestra (1939) and the oratorio *A Child of Our Time* (1941). His later works include the operas *The Midsummer Marriage* (1953), *The Ice Break* (1976), and *New Year* (1989), as well as four symphonies, concertos, piano sonatas, and string quartets.

Titian (c. 1487–1576). Venetian painter, born *Tiziano Vecelli*. Titian was influenced by Bellini, whom he succeeded as Venetian court painter in 1516. In 1533 he became painter to the Emperor Charles V, of whom he painted several famous portraits. After Charles's abdication, Titian produced a number of mythological pictures, including *The Death of Actaeon*, for Charles's son, Philip II of Spain. His other works include *Venus and Adonis* and *The Entombment of Christ*. His subdued and almost impressionistic late style contrasts with the colourful sensuality of his earlier work.

Tito, original name *Joseph Broz* (1892–1980). Yugoslav statesman; president (1953–80). In the 1920s he joined the Communist Party and was imprisoned several times for his activities. During World War II he organized guerrilla resistance against the Nazis. As Yugoslavia's post-war prime minister, he adopted policies that displeased the Soviet Union, leading to his country's expulsion from the Cominform (the Communist Information Bureau) in 1948. After Stalin's death Tito renewed relations with the Soviet Union, while retaining Yugoslavia's independence. In 1974 he was elected president for life.

Tolkien, J(ohn) R(ichard) R(euel) (1892–1973). British scholar and writer. He is best known for the epic trilogy *The Lord of the Rings* (1954–55), which is set in Middle Earth, a world inhabited by hobbits, elves and other fantasy creatures, complete with its own history, culture, and languages. *The Hobbit* (1937) was written as an introduction to the trilogy. His son Christopher edited *The Silmarillion* (1977), a collection of tales and legends of Middle Earth written by Tolkien at various times. As professor of Anglo-Saxon and later of English at Oxford, Tolkien also wrote a number of scholarly works.

Although *The Lord of the Rings* sold millions of copies, Tolkien continued to live quietly at his college.

Tolstoy, Count Leo (1828–1910). Russian novelist. Of noble birth, he left Kazan University before completing his course. In 1852 he joined the army in the Caucasus, where his first stories were written. Ten years later he married the 18-year-old Sofya Bers, known as Sonya, who bore him 13 children. Tolstoy's masterpieces *War and Peace* (1862–69) and *Anna Karenina* (1873–76) are amongst the greatest works of European literature. In 1879 Tolstoy underwent a religious crisis that changed his life; he subsequently gave up smoking and alcohol, became a vegetarian, and renounced literature in favour of ethical teaching. Feeling that his earlier works were worthless and having no desire to gain from them, he divided up his property between his wife and children (1892) and worked as a peasant in

> Tolstoy towered above his age as Dante and Michelangelo and Beethoven had done. His novels are marvels of sustained imagination, but his life was full of inconsistencies. He wanted to be one with the peasants, yet he continued to live like an aristocrat. He preached universal love, yet he quarrelled so painfully with his poor demented wife that at the age of 82 he ran away from her.
> Sir Kenneth Clark, *Civilisation* (1969)

the fields. *What is Art?* (1897) and the novel *Resurrection* (1899) date from this period. In 1910 he left his home and family in a final quest for peace and solitude, but caught a fever on the train journey and died in the station-master's house at Astapovo.

Torquemada, Tomás de (1420–98). Spanish inquisitor. A Dominican friar, he became Spain's first Inquisitor General in 1483. He ruthlessly persecuted heretics, becoming notorious for his use of torture to obtain confessions and for the severity of his punishments. He is said to have condemned 10,000 people to death by burning.

Toscanini, Arturo (1867–1957). Italian conductor. Toscanini made his debut in Rio de Janeiro in 1886 when he was unexpectedly called upon to conduct the opera *Aïda*. After conducting at the La Scala opera house in Milan, he became conductor of the Metropolitan Opera in New York (1908), the New York Philharmonic Orchestra (1928), and the NBC Symphony Orchestra (1937–54). He conducted entirely from memory and was famous for his great energy and perfectionism.

Toulouse-Lautrec, Henri de (1864–1901). French artist. Of noble descent, Lautrec broke both legs as a child, an accident that left him crippled and dwarfed. He achieved recognition with his exhibitions of paintings and posters in the early 1890s. His work is characterized by large areas of colour and the simple but striking portrayal of figures. He usually depicted characters and scenes from cafés, dance-halls, brothels, and the circus. Lautrec's alcoholism seriously affected his health and eventually killed him.

Tracy, Spencer (1900–67). US film actor. Tracy, who originally hoped to enter the priesthood, began his screen career in 1930 and at first played mainly in gangster roles. In his later films he was generally cast as a good character, often playing the leading man opposite Katharine Hepburn, his real-life lover. His films include *Captains Courageous* (1937), *Adam's Rib* (1949), *Bad Day at Black Rock* (1955), *Judgment at Nuremberg* (1961), and *Guess Who's Coming to Dinner* (1967). He is usually considered the leading screen actor of the 1940s and 1950s.

Barsetshire

In his much-loved novels of 'Barsetshire' Trollope created an imaginary county somewhere "in the West of England" as a microcosm of English provincial life. "I had it all in my mind," he later wrote "its roads and railroads, its towns and parishes, its members of Parliament, and the different hunts which rode over it. I knew all the great lords and their castles, the squires and their parks, the rectors and their churches." By the time he reached the fourth novel in the Barsetshire series Trollope had even constructed a map of the county complete with such sites as Courcy Castle, Framley Court, Gatherum Castle, Greshamsbury, Plumstead, and Ullathorne. Trollope finally took leave of his creation in *The Last Chronicle of Barset*: "...to me Barset has been a real county, and its city a real city, and the spires and towers have been before my eyes, and the voices of the people are known to my ears, and the pavements of the city ways are familiar to my footsteps. To them all I now say farewell."

Trollope, Anthony (1815–82). British novelist. Trollope worked for the Post Office in England, Ireland, and abroad until 1867, and is credited with the invention of the pillar box. His first successful novels form a series dealing with middle-class life in the fictional county of Barsetshire; they include *Barchester Towers* (1857) and *The Last Chronicle of Barset* (1867). *Can You Forgive Her?* (1865) introduced the saga of the aristocratic Palliser family, which eventually ran to six volumes. His *Autobiography* (1883) described his disciplined approach to writing; he would be at his table by 5.30 a.m. every day and produce 250 words every quarter of an hour until breakfast. He would then attend to his duties at the GPO.

Trotsky, Leon, original name *Lev Davidovich Bronstein* (1879–1940). Russian revolutionary. He was banished to Siberia in 1898 for his Marxist activities and while there married his fellow conspirator, Aleksandra Sokolovskaya. He escaped in 1902, leaving his wife behind, and married again while in Paris (1903). In 1917 he rejoined the Bolsheviks in Russia and became Lenin's chief partner in organizing the October Revolution. Following their triumph, he took charge of the Red Army in the Civil War (1918–20). After Lenin's death he led the opposition to Stalin but was expelled from the Communist Party in 1927 and later exiled. He continued to oppose Stalin from abroad but was murdered in Mexico by a Spanish communist who is believed to have been one of Stalin's agents. Whilst in exile Trotsky wrote an autobiography and a history of the Russian Revolution. His ideas have provided the foundation for a number of left-wing political groups.

Trudeau, Pierre (Elliot) (1919–). Canadian statesman. A colourful figure with a flair for publicity, he became leader of the Liberal Party and prime minister in 1968. He took a firm stand against Quebec nationalism, one of the major problems of his term of office. His government was defeated in 1979 and he resigned as party leader later that year. He was separated from his young wife Margaret in 1977 when she moved to New York, where her new lifestyle and involvement with the Rolling Stones attracted considerable attention from the press.

Truffaut, François (1932–84). French film director. As a young man Truffaut spent periods in reformatory and prison and deserted from the army. He made a reputation as a film critic in the 1950s. At the end of that decade he emerged as one of an influential group of directors, known as the 'New Wave', who brought a new seriousness and excitement to the cinema. His films include *The 400 Blows* (1959), *Shoot the Pianist* (1960), *Jules and Jim* (1961), *The Story of Adèle H* (1975), and *The Last Metro* (1980).

Truman, Harry S. (1884–1972). US statesman; 33rd president of the US. The names of both his grandfathers began with "S", hence his middle initial, which stood for neither name in particular. He served as Democratic vice-president following Roosevelt's nomination for a fourth term as president and took office on Roosevelt's death just 82 days later. In 1945 he authorized the use of the first atom bomb (1945) against Japan, which ended the Pacific war. After the war he introduced the 'Truman Doctrine' to contain communist expansion. Truman was unexpectedly re-elected in 1948 and his second term of office was occupied chiefly by the Korean War.

Tull, Jethro (1674–1741). English agriculturalist. In 1701 he invented a seed drill that sowed seed mechanically in neat rows; having observed farming techniques abroad, he also used a horse-drawn hoe to loosen soil around the crops. He published *Horse-hoeing Husbandry* in 1733. Although his novel ideas were criticized by other farmers, they were eventually adopted.

Turgenev, Ivan (1818–83). Russian novelist. His first prose work, *A Sportsman's Sketches* (1852), was a major success and was followed by a series of novels including *Fathers and Sons* (1862). His criticisms of Russian country life, including the institution of serfdom, were not well received by the authorities and led to imprisonment and house arrest in 1852–53. From 1856 he lived abroad, mainly in Paris. His plays include the psychological drama *A Month in the Country* (1855). Turgenev's writing reflects his own complex attitude towards Russia, halfway between the reactionary notions of the tsar and the revolutionary ideals of the younger generation. This may explain why his novels were never fully appreciated in Russia.

Turing, Alan Mathison (1912–54). British mathematician who contributed to the development of the computer. After graduating from Cambridge, he taught for several years at Princeton in the US. During World War II he made an important contribution to victory by deciphering the German Enigma codes, thereby giving the Allies advance knowledge of many Axis plans. Turing also carried out important theoretical work in the field of computability, mainly by devising a detailed characterization of an idealized computing machine (known as a Turing Machine), and using this as a criterion to judge whether or not a mathematical problem was decidable. After the war he put theory into practice at the National Physical Laboratory, where he supervised the building of the ACE computer. During his last years he taught at Manchester University, becoming assistant director of the automatic digital machine there. A homosexual, he committed suicide after being charged with alleged public indecency.

Turner, Joseph Mallord William (1775–1851). British landscape painter. Turner had his first exhibition at the age of 16 and became a member of the Royal Academy when he was only 27. Throughout his life he made numerous sketching tours in England and Europe. In his later years he evolved a highly original style of painting featuring luminous atmospheric and scenic effects, which anticipated impressionism and even abstract art. He produced about 300 paintings, including *The Fighting Téméraire* (1839), and over 20,000 drawings and watercolour sketches.

Tussaud, Madame Marie (1760–1850). Swiss wax-modeller, born *Marie Grosholtz*. She learnt the art of wax-modelling from her uncle and during the French Revolution made death masks from the heads of victims of the guillotine. She subsequently married a soldier and escaped to Britain, where she set up a permanent collection of waxworks in Baker Street, London. Madame Tussaud's original wax gallery was a collection of heroes and villains. The present collection, now housed in Marylebone Road, includes many living public figures, film stars, and pop musicians, and is continually being updated. Nevertheless, it still includes some of her original waxworks.

Tutankhamen (c. 1370–1352 BC). King of Egypt. He became king at the age of nine and died suddenly nine years later. Tutankhamen's tomb, the only Egyptian royal grave to escape looting by ancient tomb-robbers, was discovered by Howard Carter in 1922. Its wealth and splendour fascinated the world and brought posthumous fame to the young king. Amongst the treasures unearthed was the gold mask placed over the king's head in his coffin. The mask is an actual portrait of Tutankhamen.

Twain, Mark, pseudonym of *Samuel Langhorne Clemens* (1834–1910). US novelist, creator of Tom Sawyer and

---

Twain and the Comet

Halley's Comet, which passes close to the earth every 76 years, had a peculiar significance in the life of Mark Twain, who was born in 1835, the year in which it made its only 19th-century appearance. Twain himself wrote "It will be the greatest disappointment of my life if I don't go out with Halley's Comet. The Almighty has said, no doubt: 'Now here are two unaccountable freaks; they came in together, they must go out together'." Twain died in April 1910 – just as the comet reappeared.

Huckleberry Finn. Brought up in Missouri, he worked first as a printer's apprentice and from 1857 to 1861 a Mississippi steamboat pilot. 'Mark Twain' was a boatman's phrase, indicating a depth of water of two fathoms. Having become famous for his humorous stories, he made his lasting reputation with *The Adventures of Tom Sawyer* (1876) and *The Adventures of Huckleberry Finn* (1884). In later life Twain suffered from financial problems and became known for his lecture tours.

Tyler, Wat (d. 1381). English rebel leader. In 1381 he led an uprising of peasants protesting against taxes, low wages, and the feudal system. They marched on London via Canterbury and camped on Blackheath, where they put forward their demands to King Richard II. Although Richard was sympathetic to their grievances, Tyler was murdered by the mayor of London and the rebels dispersed.

Tyson, Mike (1966–   ). US heavyweight boxer. A Black, Tyson grew up in poverty in New York City. In 1986 he became the youngest world-heavyweight champion in history when he defeated Trevor Berbick in a World Boxing Championship bout. He went on to establish his supremacy by taking the World Boxing Association title (1986) and that of the International Boxing Federation (1988). A ferociously aggressive fighter, Tyson crushed all challengers until 1990, when a controversial decision gave the IBF title to James Douglas. In 1992 he received a six-year jail sentence for raping a contestant in a beauty contest. Following his release in 1995 he won a comeback fight in 89 seconds, earning $25 million.

U

Uccello, Paolo, real name *Paolo di Dono* (1397–1475). Florentine painter. He experimented with perspective and geometry in his works, some of which have features of abstract design. His best-known paintings are the three-part *Battle of San Romano*, in which he made much use of gold for decorative purposes, and the highly original *Hunt in a Forest at Night*.

Utrillo, Maurice (1883–1955). French painter. The illegitimate son of an artist's model, Utrillo received his name from Miguel Utrillo, a Spanish art critic. After he became an alcoholic and drug addict at an early age, his mother encouraged him to paint as a form of therapy. He developed an original style and usually portrayed streets and buildings, frequently basing his pictures on postcards. Many of his best-known works show scenes from the Montmartre district of Paris.

V

Valentino, Rudolph, original name *Rodolfo d'Antonguolla* (1895–1926). US film actor, born in Italy. Arguably the most famous leading man Hollywood has ever produced, Valentino played exotic romantic heroes and had a devoted female following. Amongst his best-known films are *The Four Horsemen of the Apocalypse* (1921), *The Sheik* (1921), and *Blood and Sand* (1922). Valentino's sudden death at the age of 31 caused a number of his fans to commit suicide; his funeral was a national event.

> ❝ His acting is largely confined to protruding his large, almost occult eyes until the vast areas of white are visible, drawing back the lips of his wide, sensuous mouth to bare his gleaming teeth, and flaring his nostrils.
>
> Adolph Zukor on Rudolph Valentino ❞

Valois, Dame Ninette de, stage name of *Edris Stannus* (1898–   ). British ballerina, choreographer, and ballet director. In 1931 she founded the Sadler's Wells Ballet School and was appointed artistic director of the Vic-Wells Ballet, which later became the Royal Ballet (1956).

Her choreographic works include *The Rake's Progress* and *Don Quixote*. Her autobiography, *Come Dance With Me*, was published in 1957. She was created DBE in 1950.

Vanbrugh, Sir John (1664–1726). English dramatist and architect. His two chief comedies, *The Relapse* (1696) and *The Provok'd Wife* (1697), were highly successful but condemned as licentious by opponents of the theatre. In 1702 Vanbrugh began his career as an architect of the grand and ornate baroque style; in collaboration with Nicholas Hawksmoor he designed Castle Howard in Yorkshire and Blenheim Palace, which was built for the Duke of Marlborough. The grandiose and extravagant nature of his architectural designs is humorously recalled in his epitaph by Abel Evans: "Lie heavy on him, Earth! for he/Laid many heavy loads on thee!"

Van Dyck, Sir Anthony (1599–1641). Flemish portrait painter. He began his career in Rubens's Antwerp workshop and in 1620 became court painter to James I. He soon left England to travel in Italy, where he painted some fine portraits of the Genoese nobility, but returned to England in 1632 to become court painter to Charles I. He painted a number of famous portraits of the king, including an equestrian portrait and a triple portrait, as well as pictures of the royal family.

Van Eyck, Jan (c. 1390–1441). Flemish painter, a pioneer of oil-painting and realism. In 1425 he entered the service of the duke of Burgundy, who employed him on diplomatic missions and as court painter. By 1434 he had married and settled in Bruges. Jan completed the famous altar-piece in Ghent, begun by his brother Hubert, and several other works signed by him survive. These include *Man in a Red Turban* (1433), perhaps a self-portrait, and *The Arnolfini Marriage* (1434), both in the National Gallery, London.

Van Gogh, Vincent (1853–90). Dutch painter. The son of a Lutheran pastor, he gave up his job as an art-dealer to become an evangelist among the Belgian miners, but was dismissed for giving away his possessions. After this his brother Theo financed his painting. Although his early work is sombre, after moving to Paris (1886) he began to use the pure colours of the impressionists. In Arles (1888) he painted many of his best-known works but suffered from fits of depression, in one of which he quarrelled with his friend Gauguin and cut off his own ear. This led to his confinement in the asylum at St Rémy. In May 1890 he moved to Auvers, where he committed suicide. Almost unknown during his lifetime, he is now the most popular of the post-impressionist painters. His works, which now sell for huge sums of money, include *A Cornfield with Cypresses*, *The Yellow Chair*, and *Sunflowers*.

Vaughan Williams, Ralph (1872–1958). British composer. Vaughan Williams was one of the first English composers to collect English folk songs, which he used in such works as the *Norfolk Rhapsody* (1906). His *Fantasia on a Theme by Tallis* (1910) was influenced by music of the Tudor period. His works also include nine symphonies (of which the 'London' and 'Sea' symphonies are the most popular), the ballet *Job* (1931), much choral music, and the opera *The Pilgrim's Progress* (1949).

Vega, Lope de, full name *Lope Félix de Vega Carpio* (1562–1635). Spanish poet and dramatist. As a young man he sailed to the Azores and with the Armada. In the 1590s he began writing plays in Madrid, where he developed a new type of drama called the *comedia*, a mixture of comedy and tragedy. After a series of personal misfortunes, including the deaths of his wife, mistress, and favourite son, he was ordained as a priest in 1614 and began to write religious poetry instead of plays. Over 475 of his reputed 1500 plays have survived, including *Fuenteovejuna* (c. 1613); he also wrote the novel *Dorotea* (1632).

A Death-Bed Confession

When it became clear that he was dying, Lope de Vega asked those who gathered around his bed how much time he had left. Told that his death was imminent, he whispered, "All right, then, I'll say it: Dante makes me sick."

Velasquez, Diego de Silva y (1599–1660). Spanish painter. After training under Francisco de Herrera the Elder, he set up his own studio at the age of 19. In 1623 he became court painter to Philip IV and painted many portraits of the king. A trip to Rome in 1648 produced a portrait of Pope Innocent X and Velasquez's only nude, the *Rokeby Venus*. One of his best-known and most original paintings is *The Maids of Honour* (1656), a study of the infanta with her maids and dwarfs.

Verdi, Giuseppe (1813–1901). Italian composer. He received his earliest musical education from the organist of his village church and in 1831 went to Milan to study music. He married in 1836 but suffered the early loss of his wife and two children (1838–40). His first opera to be staged was *Oberto* (1839) at La Scala. Subsequent successes included *Rigoletto* (1851), *Il Trovatore* (1853), *La Traviata* (1853), and *Aïda* (1871). He continued composing into his eighties and his later works include two Shakespearean operas, the dramatic *Otello* (1887) and the more lighthearted *Falstaff* (1893). Though he became a wealthy man, Verdi continued to live a simple existence and founded a home for retired musicians in Milan.

Verlaine, Paul (1844–96). French poet. His earliest poems date from 1858, when he was 14, and were published five years later. His affair with the 16-year-old poet Rimbaud led to a separation from his wife and ended in 1873, when Verlaine was imprisoned for shooting Rimbaud in the arm. He returned to Catholicism while serving his two-year sentence but soon drifted back into drinking and violence on his release. His major works include the poetry collections *Songs Without Words* (1874) and *Yesteryear and Yesterday* (1884), which contains the poem 'The Art of Poetry'. Verlaine spent his last years in poverty, continuing to frequent the Parisian cafés where he wrote much of his poetry. By the time of his death he was recognized as the leader of the symbolist movement in French literature.

Vermeer, Jan (1632–75). Dutch painter. He struggled to support a large family, receiving little or no income from his paintings, which went unnoticed until the 19th century. Vermeer's mastery of the effect of light on surfaces displayed in most of his pictures, which generally portray one or two figures in a domestic setting, with the light coming from a window on the left of the picture. His paintings, some of the best-known Dutch genre paintings, are also noted for the realism of his interiors.

The Van Meegeren Forgeries

The 20th-century study of Vermeer's works has been gravely hampered by the activities of Hans Van Meegeren (1889–1947), one of art's most notorious forgers. During the 1930s and 1940s, this Dutch painter exploited the art world's ignorance of Vermeer's early life and work by painting a number of fakes that fooled the leading authorities of the day. His deceptions were only exposed in the aftermath of World War II, when a supposed Vermeer was found amongst the numerous works obtained illicitly by Herman Göring. It was soon established that the painting had been sold to Göring by Van Meegeren, who was arrested as a collaborator. In order to escape possible execution, Van Meegeren confessed that he had forged the picture, only to find that no one believed him. To test the claim, Van Meegeren was locked in a studio with a panel of experts and told to produce another 'Vermeer'; so amazing was his technique, that he managed to convince the judges without even completing the picture. He died of a heart attack before beginning a sentence for the lesser crime of forging signatures.

Verne, Jules (1828–1905). French novelist. Verne studied law in Paris before turning to literature. Although he began by writing plays, his scientific interests soon inspired the science-fiction novels for which he is now remembered, notably *Journey to the Centre of the Earth* (1864) and *Twenty Thousand Leagues under the Sea* (1870). A number of the devices invented by Verne for his fiction, such as the submarine and television, have since become fact. On his return to Paris after the Franco-Prussian War, he published the immensely popular *Around the World in Eighty Days* (1872). Verne was made an officer of the Légion d'honneur in 1892.

Veronese, Paolo (c. 1528–88). Italian painter of the Venetian school. Born in Verona, he evolved a rich decorative style, and often included architectural elements in his pictures. His best paintings were of large-scale historical, biblical, and mythological subjects, such as *The Family of Darius before Alexander* (c. 1570) and *Feast in the House of Levi* (1573). However, the naturalism of these pictures brought charges of irreverence from the Inquisition.

Vespucci, Amerigo (1454–1512). Florentine navigator and explorer. Vespucci was originally a provision contractor at Seville, whose services were used by Christopher Columbus on one of his expeditions. He subsequently made several voyages to the New World (1497–1504) on Spanish and Portuguese expeditions. Although Vespucci claimed that he had reached the mainland of America in 1497, there is little other evidence to confirm this. His account of these explorations led to the naming of the new continent after his Christian name.

Victor Emmanuel II (1820–78). King of Sardinia-Piedmont and first king of Italy. He succeeded to the Sardinian throne on the abdication of his father (1849). In 1852 he entrusted the government to his minister Count Cavour (1810–61), who succeeded in creating a new unified Italian kingdom. Victor Emmanuel became king of Italy in 1861 and was successful in maintaining and strengthening the unity of the new state, establishing Rome as its capital in 1870.

Victoria (1819–1901). Queen of Britain and empress of India. She succeeded her uncle, William IV, to the throne in 1837 and in 1840 married her cousin, Prince Albert of Saxe-Coburg-Gotha, who had considerable influence on her policies. She became devoted to him and bore him nine children. Following Albert's early death from typhoid (1861) she withdrew into seclusion for several years in mourning for him. She concerned herself dutifully with affairs of state, her favourite minister being Disraeli, who proclaimed her empress of India (1876). Her long reign (63 years) saw considerable

> ❛ Queen Victoria in her eighties
> was more known, more revered,
> and a more important part of
> the life of the country than she
> had ever been. Retirement, for
> a monarch, is not a good idea.
> Charles, Prince of Wales (1974) ❜

industrial and colonial expansion and restored stability and dignity to the British crown.

Vidal, Gore (1925–). US novelist and writer. The son of a wealthy political family, he served in the army during World War II and then travelled extensively before settling in Italy. His first novel was published when he was 19. Later works include *Myra Breckinridge* (1968), *Burr* (1972), *Empire* (1987), and *Live from Golgotha* (1992). A homosexual, Vidal is known for his witty criticisms of contemporary US society. He has also written essays and screenplays and the autobiography *Palimpsest* (1995).

Villon, François (1431–c. 63). French poet. In 1455 he killed a man, possibly in self-defence, and had to flee from Paris for a while. The following year he returned and robbed a Paris church. Villon's *Poems* includes his famous 'Ballad of the Hanged', probably written in 1463 when he was sentenced to death for brawling. The sentence was commuted to ten years' banishment.

Virgil, full name *Publius Vergilius Maro* (70–19 BC). Roman poet, author of the epic poem the *Aeneid*, the story of the founding of Rome. The son of a farmer, he lived a quiet life as a member of the court of Augustus. The *Eclogues* (42–37 BC), a collection of pastoral poems, were his first major work. He caught a fever on a visit to Greece and died after finishing only 12 books of the *Aeneid*. According to legend, he is buried near Naples.

Visconti, Luchino, full name *Count Don Luchino Visconti di Modrone* (1906–76). Italian film director, who also directed plays and operas. Visconti was born into an aristocratic family and began his career in the performing arts designing sets and costumes. His first film as a director was *Ossessione* (1942), a neorealist work that shows his Marxist sympathies. He later developed a lavish epic style in such films as *Rocco and his Brothers* (1960), *The Leopard* (1963), *Death in Venice* (1971), and *The Innocent* (1976).

Vivaldi, Antonio (1675–1741). Italian composer. Vivaldi studied music with his father and took holy orders in 1693. Because of his red hair he was nicknamed 'The Red Priest'. For many years he was in charge of music at a school for orphaned girls in Venice. His compositions include many concertos, among which are *The Four Seasons* for violin and orchestra, based on poems written by the composer himself. Vivaldi died in poverty in Vienna.

Volta, Alessandro, Count (1745–1827). Italian physicist. His inventions included the electrophorus (1775) to generate static electricity; and he also discovered methane gas (1778). Luigi Galvani had discovered that contact between the muscle of a frog and two different metals produced electricity. In trying to prove that this effect could be obtained without animal tissue Volta produced his 'pile' of layers of metal plates, the first electric battery (1800). In 1801 he demonstrated this to Napoleon, who made him a count and senator of the kingdom of Lombardy. The electrical unit the volt is named after him.

Voltaire, pseudonym of *François Marie Arouet* (1694–1778). French philosophical writer, playwright, poet, and satirist, famous for his attacks on political and religious oppression. His early satirical poems caused him to be banished three times from Paris and imprisoned twice between 1716 and 1726. He began using his pseudonym during one of his periods in the Bastille; it is thought to have been an anagram of *Arouet l(e) j(eune)*. His satirical *Philosophical Letters* (1734) were inspired by a two-year stay in England. In 1750 Voltaire went to Berlin at the invitation of Frederick the Great, but the two men quarrelled and Voltaire left after three years. *Candide* (1759), a parody of Leibniz's optimistic philosophy, was written at Ferney, Voltaire's home from 1758 to 1778. He made a triumphant return to Paris shortly before his death.

A Sceptic to the Last

On his deathbed Voltaire was asked if he renounced the devil. "This is no time to be making new enemies" he replied. Sympathetic priests arranged a hasty interment before the authorities could refuse him a Christian burial.

W

Wagner, Richard (1813–83). German operatic composer. He spent much of his early life travelling in Europe and his first successful opera, *The Flying Dutchman* (1843), was written in Paris. While conductor of the Dresden Opera he composed two works based on German legends, *Tannhäuser* (1845) and *Lohengrin* (1850). After the failure of the revolution of 1848, Wagner fled to Zürich, where he began work on *The Ring of the Nibelung*, an operatic cycle based on German mythology. The *Ring* cycle was first performed complete in 1876 under the patronage of Ludwig II of Bavaria. Wagner's other operas included *Tristan and Isolde* (1865), a tragic love story, the comic *Mastersingers of Nuremberg* (1868), and the 'sacred festival drama' *Parsifal* (1882). For the performance of his later works Wagner built a special theatre at Bayreuth, where a festival of his works is held annually.

> ❛ Damned German stuff. They've been at it for two hours and they're still singing the same bloody tune.
> Sir Thomas Beecham, on an opera by Wagner ❜

Walcott, Derek (1930–   ). St Lucian poet and playwright. The son of a St Lucian mother and a British father, he writes in English with some words and phrases from French and local patois. His work fuses elements of Caribbean folk culture with Western literary traditions. He has published numerous volumes of poetry, including *Sea Grapes* (1976), *Collected Poems 1948–1984* (1986), and the epic *Omeros* (1991), one of several works to show a fascination with Homer. His plays include *Dream on Monkey Mountain* (1970), *A Branch of the Blue Nile* (1986), and an adaptation of *The Odyssey* (1993). Walcott, who is currently professor of English literature at Boston University, was awarded a Nobel Prize in 1992.

Wałesa, Lech (1943–   ). Polish trade-union leader and politician; president (1990–95). Wałesa worked as an electrician in the Gdańsk shipyards from 1966. After being sacked for his defence of workers' rights in 1976, he became involved in various dissident activities. In 1980, as strikes and protests spread throughout Poland, Wałesa emerged at the head of the movement for change and forced a series of concessions from the government. He was appointed chairman of a new independent trade union, Solidarity, later that year. In 1981, however, the government imposed martial law, banned Solidarity, and imprisoned Wałesa. He was released in 1982 and awarded the Nobel Peace Prize a year later. In 1988 a new wave of protests led the government of General Jaruzelski to open talks with Wałesa and other Solidarity leaders. Partially free elections in 1989 resulted in a sweeping victory for Solidarity and Wałesa was elected president of Poland the following year. Although he remained a popular hero to many, his period in office was beset by continuing political and economic instability. In 1995 he was surprisingly defeated in presidential elections by Aleksander Kwasniewski, a former communist.

Wallace, Sir William (c. 1270–1305). Scottish soldier and patriot. After Edward I of England had assumed control of Scotland (1296), Wallace led attacks on the English garrisons and took Stirling Castle (1297). The English were subsequently expelled from Scotland. In 1298 Edward reinvaded Scotland and Wallace's army was crushed at the Battle of Falkirk. He then spent several years waging guerrilla warfare. After his capture in 1304 he was hanged, drawn, and quartered.

Waller, Fats, real name *Thomas Waller* (1904–43). Black US jazz pianist and composer. He played the organ in his father's church before becoming a pianist in cabarets. During the 1930s he helped to pioneer 'stride' style, derived from ragtime. He is remembered for compositions such as 'Honeysuckle Rose' and 'Ain't Misbehavin'', and for his role in the film *Stormy Weather* (1943).

Wallis, Sir Barnes (1887–1979). British aeronautical engineer. His many aeronautical achievements included the R100 airship, the geodetic system used in the Wellington bomber, and the swing-wing aeroplane. However, he is best remembered for his famous bouncing-bombs, developed during World War II, which were used by the historic Dambusters Squadron to breach the allegedly indestructible Ruhr Dams (1943).

Walpole, Sir Robert (1676–1745). British Whig statesman, regarded as Britain's first prime minister. He served as chancellor of the exchequer (1715–17) and took up this office again in the aftermath of the South Sea Bubble crisis (1720), a major financial crash. Having restored economic stability and confidence in Britain following the crisis, Walpole remained the most powerful figure in the land until 1742. During this period he was able to use royal patronage to further his political ends and, by granting positions in the church, army, and royal household, to increase his voting strength in the House of Commons. Accusations of corruption were made against him at various stages of his career, but were dropped through lack of evidence. His unpopular foreign policy culminated in the War of Jenkins's Ear (1738–48) with Spain, which brought about Walpole's resignation (1742). He was created earl of Orford.

Walton, Sir William Turner (1902–83). British composer. A chorister and later an undergraduate at Christ Church, Oxford, Walton was largely self-taught as a composer. He made his name with *Façade* (1923), a set of witty and humorous musical accompaniments to nonsense poems by Edith Sitwell. Walton's other works include the oratorio *Belshazzar's Feast* (1931) and music for Olivier's Shakespeare films *Henry V* (1944) and *Richard III* (1954).

Warbeck, Perkin (c. 1474–99). Pretender to the English throne during the reign of Henry VII. He was persuaded by enemies of the king to impersonate Richard, Duke of York, the younger of the two princes supposedly murdered in 1483 in the Tower of London. After gathering support on the continent, he invaded England and besieged Exeter but was subsequently captured. He was hanged after trying to escape from the Tower.

Warhol, Andy (1926–87). US painter and 'underground' film-maker. The son of Czechoslovak immigrants, Warhol began his career in commercial design. During the late 1950s he emerged as the best-known exponent of Pop Art, with his impersonal paintings of such commonplace objects as soup tins. Many of his later works are portraits of the rich and famous based on newspaper images. His experimental films include the seven-hour-long *Chelsea Girls* (1966), *Trash* (1970), and *Flesh* (1971).

Washington, George (1732–99). American general and first president of the US (1789–97). He began work as a land surveyor at the age of 14 and inherited his brother's large Virginian estate in 1752. His life as a country gentleman was interrupted when he went to fight against the French (1754–58), his first military experience. By his marriage to a rich widow, Martha Custis, he gained a further estate and became one of the wealthiest men in Virginia. He spent the next 15 years managing these estates before commanding the American forces in the American War of Independence (1775). Remarkably, he managed to create, out of a mass of untrained and ill-equipped men, an army capable of defeating experienced British troops. After five years of fighting he captured Yorktown (1781), with French support, and the British surrendered. He was chosen as president of the Constitutional Convention (1787) and in 1789 was elected first president of the republic. He was re-elected in 1793 but refused a third term of office. Queen Elizabeth II is a direct descendant of Washington's great grandfather.

Washington and the Cherry Tree

Generations of schoolchildren have been appalled by the story of young George Washington and the cherry tree, in which the future president emerges as a monster of priggish rectitude. According to the familiar tale, George was given a small hatchet for his sixth birthday. On returning from business, his father was distraught to find that his favourite tree had been killed and gravely asked George if he knew who the culprit might be. "I cannot tell a lie, Pa," came the insufferable response, "you know I can't tell a lie. I did cut it with my hatchet." "Run to my arms, you dearest boy," cried his father in transports, "run to my arms; glad am I, George, that you killed my tree, for you have paid me for it a thousand-fold!" The story is almost certainly the invention of one Pastor Weems, who published his *Life of George Washington: With Curious Anecdotes, Equally Honourable to Himself and Exemplary to His Young Countrymen* in 1806. Among those unimpressed by the tale was Oscar Wilde, who commented "The crude commercialism of America, its materialising spirit are entirely due to the country having adopted for its national hero a man who could not tell a lie."

Watson, James (Dewey) (1928–   ). US biochemist who helped to determine the structure of DNA. A child prodigy, Watson graduated from the University of Chicago at the age of 19. After postgraduate work on viruses, he moved to Cambridge in 1951 and began to work on the structure of DNA (the hereditary material of cells) with Francis Crick. In 1953 they constructed a three-dimensional model of the DNA molecule, which had the form of a spiral ladder (or double helix). This structure fitted in with the physical data for DNA provided by Maurice Wilkins. Watson, Crick, and Wilkins received a Nobel Prize for their work in 1962. Watson's book *The Double Helix* (1968) is a lively and controversial account of their research.

Watt, James (1736–1819). Scottish engineer, a major contributor to the Industrial Revolution. He became a mathematical instrument maker at Glasgow University in 1757 and while repairing a model of Newcomen's steam engine (1764) he saw that improvements could be made. In 1765 he constructed the first steam engine to have a separate condenser. He entered into partnership with Matthew Boulton to produce steam engines and in 1781 invented the 'sun and planet' wheel mechanism, which converts reciprocating (backward and forward) motion into rotary motion. The electrical unit the 'watt' was named in his honour.

Watteau, Jean-Antoine (1684–1721). French rococo painter. He settled in Paris in 1702 and developed a style strongly influenced by Rubens and by Venetian painting. His most characteristic pictures represent courtiers and their ladies in a pastoral landscape. Watteau's most famous picture is the atmospheric and ethereal *Embarkation for the Island of Cythera* (1717). His handling of colour has led critics to describe him as a forerunner of the impressionists.

Waugh, Evelyn (1903–66). British novelist and satirist. After graduating from Oxford, he worked as a teacher; his first published work was a biography of the poet Rossetti and his first novel the farcical *Decline and Fall* (1928). In 1930 he joined the Catholic Church. Most of his early novels, including *Vile Bodies* (1930), are satirical. Those written after World War II, such as *Brideshead Revisited* (1945) and the trilogy *Men of Arms* (1952), *Officers and Gentlemen* (1955), and *Unconditional Surrender* (1961), are more serious in content and style.

Wayne, John, stage name of *Marion Michael Morrison* (1907–79). US film actor. Nicknamed 'The Duke', he was the slow-speaking tough hero of scores of action films and Westerns. During his 40-year career he appeared in over 150 films, including *Stagecoach* (1939), *The High and the Mighty* (1954), *The Searchers* (1956), and *True Grit* (1969), for which he received an Oscar. His last film was *The*

> ❛ John Wayne has been the success he has been over the years because he does what he does better than anybody else can. A lot of people have said he doesn't really act. Just let them try to act like he does and they'll find they can't do it.
> Clint Eastwood ❜

Shootist (1976). Wayne was also known for his right-wing patriotic views.

Webb, Sidney, Baron Passfield (1859–1947) and his wife **Beatrice** (1858–1943). British social reformers and historians. Sidney Webb was a founder member of the socialist Fabian Society, while Beatrice studied social problems. In 1894 they collaborated on the classic *History of Trade Unionism*. Their other books included *English Local Government* (1906–29) and *Soviet Communism* (1935). They were involved in the establishment of the London School of Economics (1895), and they founded the *New Statesman* magazine (1913).

Wedgwood, Josiah (1730–95). British pottery designer and manufacturer. He set up his own business in his native town of Burslem, Staffordshire, in 1759. The characteristic Wedgwood stonewares, decorated in white relief on an unglazed background of blue, green, or black, were strongly influenced in design by ancient Greek vases. Wedgwood's porcelain rivalled that of Sèvres and Meissen. He was made a Fellow of the Royal Society for his invention of the pyrometer, an instrument for measuring high temperatures, and he was also the first industrialist to install steam-powered engines in his factory.

Weill, Kurt (1900–50). German composer, best known for the satirical operas he wrote in collaboration with Bertolt Brecht. Weill worked as a conductor and studied under the composer Busoni before turning to composition in the mid 1920s. He made his name with his first Brecht collaboration, *The Rise and Fall of the City* *of Mahagonny* (1927). Brecht also provided the libretto for the classic *The Threepenny Opera* (1928), which includes the hit 'Mack the Knife', and *The Seven Deadly Sins* (1933). In these works Brecht and Weill pioneered a new kind of political opera that incorporated elements of jazz and other popular styles. After fleeing Germany (1933) to escape the Nazi persecution of the Jews, Weill settled in New York and produced a series of similar works for the Broadway stage. A number of these, including *Knickerbocker Holiday* (1938) and *Lost in the Stars* (1949), had libretti by the playwright Maxwell Anderson. He also wrote various nondramatic works, including two symphonies. Weill was married to the singer Lotte Lenya (1900–81), who appeared in many of his works.

Weissmuller, Johnny (1904–84). US swimmer and film actor. The son of Austrian immigrants, he won five gold medals for freestyle races in the 1924 and 1928 Olympic Games. Between 1932 and 1948 he played the character of Tarzan in 12 MGM films made from the stories by Edgar Rice Burroughs.

Weizmann, Chaim (1874–1952). Jewish statesman and chemist, born in Russia. Through his research work for the British War Office during World War I he discovered a process to produce acetone, used in explosives. An active Zionist, he negotiated with the British to establish a Jewish homeland in Palestine and was head of the World Zionist Organization (1920–30; 1935–46). He later became the first president of the state of Israel (1949–52).

Welles, Orson (1915–85). US film director, writer, and actor. He became famous for his radio adaptation of H. G. Wells's *The War of the Worlds* (1938), which was so realistic that it caused many panic-stricken listeners to flee from what they thought was a Martian invasion. In 1940 Welles went to Hollywood, where he co-wrote, directed, and starred in his masterpiece, *Citizen Kane* (1941). His later films as a director include *The Magnificent Ambersons* (1942), *Touch of Evil* (1958), and *Chimes at Midnight* (1966), one of several Shakespeare adaptations. He also starred as Harry Lime in *The Third Man* (1949).

Wellington, Duke of (1769–1852). British field marshal and statesman, known as 'The Iron Duke'. He was born *Arthur Wesley* in Dublin, the family name being changed to *Wellesley* in the 1790s. From 1796 to 1805 he commanded troops in India, resisting French influence there. In the Peninsular War (1808–14) he ousted Napoleon's forces from Portugal and Spain. With the Prussian general Blücher he finally defeated Napoleon at the Battle of Waterloo (1815). He subsequently concentrated on politics, becoming a Tory cabinet minister in 1818. As prime minister (1828–30) he accepted Catholic Emancipation but opposed parliamentary reform. He was later foreign secretary (1834–35) under Sir Robert Peel.

Wells, H(erbert) G(eorge) (1866–1946). British novelist. The son of a failed tradesman and professional cricketer, he was apprenticed to a draper for several unhappy years but later won a scholarship to study science in London. He wrote over 60 novels, including the science-fiction stories *The Time Machine* (1895) and *The Invisible Man* (1897), and such social comedies as *Kipps* (1905), *Tono-Bungay* (1909), and *The History of Mr Polly* (1910). His numerous historical, political, and scientific works were also widely popular and made him one of the most influential thinkers of the age.

The Draper's Assistant's Revenge

As a young man, H. G. Wells was obliged by his family's poverty to spend two years working as a draper's assistant. He later described this period at Hyde's Drapery Establishment in Southsea as "the most unhappy, hopeless period" of his life. Nevertheless, it provided him with experiences he could draw upon in several of his novels of frustrated lower-middle-class life. The hero of *The History of Mr Polly* (1910), for example, is obliged to work in the Port Burdock Drapery Bazaar, "one of those large, rather low-class establishments which sell everything from pianos and furniture to books and millinery... He spent most of the time inattentive to business, in a sort of uncomfortable happiness, increasing his indigestion." When Mr Polly later burns down his own shop Wells seems to be enjoying a vicarious revenge; some of the details of Polly's subsequent wanderings were probably based upon events in the life of Wells's brother Frank, who actually *did* run away from his job at a draper's. Wells also milked his memories of Hyde's Drapery Establishment in the novel *Kipps* (1905), in which Artie Kipps escapes the drapery trade to great wealth. When the book was first published Wells suggested that sales of the book might be promoted by having posters displayed in the Southsea area, proclaiming 'Kipps worked here'.

Wesley, John (1703–91). British founder of Methodism. After studying at Oxford, Wesley became a missionary in Georgia, where he met members of the Protestant Moravian brethren. He underwent a decisive religious experience during a church service in 1738, after which he turned away from High Anglican doctrines and began travelling and preaching all over Britain. The numerous religious societies he organized were united as the Methodist Church in 1784. His brother **Charles** (1707–88) was a member of the first 'methodists', a group of students at Oxford who attracted this name because of their methodical observance of religious practices. He also wrote many well-known hymns, such as 'Jesu, Lover of My Soul'.

West, Mae (1892–1980). US stage and screen actress, noted for her buxom figure and bawdy wisecracking style. West was born in Brooklyn, the daughter of a boxer. Having appeared in burlesque and revue from an early age, she staged her first play, *Sex*, in 1926; the production led to her arrest on charges of obscenity. After further stage work, including the Broadway triumph *Diamond Lil* (1928), she made her film debut in 1932, when she was 40. Her best-known movies include *She Done Him Wrong* (1933), with Cary Grant, and *My Little Chickadee* (1940), with W. C. Fields. After World War II she returned to Broadway, later making a camp comeback (at the age of 78) in *Myra Breckenridge* (1970). Most of West's famous double entendres ("Why don't you come up sometime and see me" "I was Snow White, but I drifted") were scripted by the actress herself.

Whistler, James Abbott McNeill (1834–1903). US painter. He abandoned his career as a soldier to study art and from 1855 lived in Paris and London, where he developed a style of painting influenced by realism, impressionism, and oriental art. In 1877 Ruskin described Whistler's painting *Nocturne in Black and Gold* as "flinging a pot of paint in the public's face" and Whistler sued for libel. At the trial he was awarded a farthing in damages; he retaliated with the book *The Gentle Art of Making Enemies* (1890). Whistler supported the idea of 'art for art's sake' and was also well known as a wit.

White, Patrick (1912–90). Australian novelist and writer. White was brought up on his father's sheep farm in Australia but educated mainly in England. After graduating from Cambridge he settled in London and began to write, finding success with his first published novel, *Happy Valley* (1939). During World War II he served with RAF intelligence in the Mediterranean and Middle East. He returned to live in Australia in 1948. The novels that established White as his country's leading imaginative writer appeared in the later 1950s and early 1960s. *The Tree of Man* (1955) was followed by *Voss* (1957), an epic tale of a German immigrant in 19th-century Australia, and *Riders in the Chariot* (1961). White also had a number of plays produced in the 1960s. His later novels include *A Fringe of Leaves* (1976) and *The Twyborn Affair* (1980). In his old age White became an outspoken advocate of complete Australian independence from Britain. In 1988 he led protests against bicentennial celebrations of European settlement in Australia.

Whitman, Walt(er) (1819–92). US poet and essayist. He left school at 11 and had a number of jobs, including printing and teaching. The poetry collection *Leaves of Grass* (1855), which he continued to revise and expand throughout his life, made him controversially famous and was judged obscene by some critics. During the Civil War, he spent much time visiting the wounded soldiers of both sides in Washington hospitals. A pioneer of free verse, he is considered America's greatest poet.

> ❛ In Whitman's works the elemental parts of a man's mind and the fragments of imperfect education may be seen merging together, floating and sinking in a sea of insensate egotism and rhapsody, repellent, divine, disgusting, extraordinary.
> John Jay Chapman, 'Walt Whitman'
>
> Do I contradict myself?
> Very well then I contradict myself,
> (I am large, I contain multitudes).
> Walt Whitman, *Song of Myself* ❜

Whittle, Sir Frank (1907–   ). British aeronautical engineer and RAF officer. He invented the first British jet propulsion unit, which was fitted to the specially constructed Gloster E28/39 and made its maiden flight on 15 May 1941. In 1948 he received a government award of £100,000 for his work. His autobiography *Jet: The Story of a Pioneer* was published in 1953.

Wilberforce, William (1759–1833). British politician and reformer. He was a close friend of William Pitt the Younger, a fellow student at Cambridge, and they both entered Parliament in 1780. Wilberforce's major concern was for the abolition of slavery. His first success was a bill banning the slave trade, passed in 1807. He died just one month before the passing of the act that effectively abolished slavery altogether in the British Empire.

Wilde, Oscar (1854–1900). Irish dramatist, essayist, and poet. After a brilliant academic career in Dublin and Oxford, a lecture tour of the US confirmed his reputation as a wit before he had published anything of note. His novel *The Picture of Dorian Gray* (1891) was attacked as immoral, but his plays, including *Lady Windermere's Fan* (1892) and *The Importance of Being Earnest* (1895), were runaway successes. Although married with two sons, in 1891 he began the homosexual relationship with Lord Alfred Douglas that was to ruin him; in 1895 he was sentenced to two years' hard labour for homosexual offences. *The Ballad of Reading Gaol* (1895) was written during his imprisonment. Released bankrupt in 1897, he went to France and lived in poverty. He was converted to Catholicism on his deathbed.

The Trials of Oscar Wilde

Oscar Wilde's tragic downfall was precipitated by the scheming of the Marquess of Queensberry, father of Wilde's lover Lord Alfred Douglas. Determined to remove his son from Wilde's influence, Queensberry left a calling card at the writer's club inscribed "Oscar Wilde...Posing as Somdomite" (*sic*); Wilde responded by suing the marquess for libel. The decision was foolhardy in the extreme; Wilde had set himself against the Establishment, which now grasped the opportunity for revenge. Wilde himself quite failed to see the danger, reassuring a friend: "Don't distress yourself. All is well. The working classes are with me...to a boy." Under cross-examination Wilde was forced to admit to homosexual affairs and lost his case; he was then arrested and tried for homosexual offences under the Criminal Law Amendment Act of 1895. The trial created a sensation; Wilde's conviction was inevitable, despite the only direct evidence being a woman's testimony that she saw Wilde "drive away in a hansom cab" from Park Lane, where the offences were alleged to have taken place. Wilde was sentenced to two years hard labour in Reading gaol, from which – broken in health, bankrupt, and bitter at his treatment by Lord Alfred and other friends – he never recovered. His wife, Constance, wrote of him: "I think his fate is rather like Humpty Dumpty's, quite as tragic and quite as impossible to put right."

Wilhelm II (1859–1941). German kaiser (emperor) and king of Prussia. He was one of Queen Victoria's grandchildren and had a deep conviction that he ruled by divine right. Crowned emperor in 1888, he forced the resignation of Bismarck, his father's chief minister, two years later. Although he strengthened Germany's power in Europe by colonial expansion, his involvement in foreign policy generally did more harm than good. He has often been accused of being the prime instigator of World War I through his initial support for Austria-Hungary's stand against Serbia. However, as the war progressed its control passed to the hands of his generals and his influence declined. He was forced to abdicate in 1918 and fled to the Netherlands, where he led the life of a country gentleman until his death.

William I, known as *William the Conqueror* (c. 1028–87). King of England. The illegitimate son of Robert I, duke of Normandy, he effectively ruled Normandy from about 1042. On a visit to Edward the Confessor in 1051 he was reputedly promised the throne of England, but on Edward's death in 1066 Harold succeeded to the throne. William invaded England, killed Harold at the Battle of Hastings, and took the crown. He then followed a policy of consolidation, by building castles and introducing the feudal system. He also organized the countrywide survey known as the Domesday Book.

William III, known as *William of Orange* (1650–1702). King of England, Scotland, and Ireland from 1689 and prince of Orange. He was governor of the Netherlands from 1672 and in 1677 he married his cousin Mary, daughter of James II. On the invitation of James's opponents, he invaded England in 1688, landing a small force at Torbay, and was crowned joint sovereign with Mary (1689). He defeated James in Ireland at the Battle of the Boyne (1690). During the 1690s William spent much time on the continent involved in the Dutch struggle against Louis XIV of France. Despite his excellent qualities as a diplomat and military leader,

William III never really won the sympathy of the mass of the English people. He died from a fall when his horse stumbled on a molehill.

William the Silent (1533–84). Dutch soldier and statesman, the founder of the Dutch Republic. He became prince of Orange in 1544 and in 1559 he was appointed governor of Holland, Zeeland, and Utrecht by Philip II of Spain. Later, however, he led a movement against Spanish rule and Philip's persecution of Protestants (1568–76). Under his leadership the seven northern Dutch provinces declared their independence from Spain (1581). William was assassinated by a Catholic fanatic.

Williams, Tennessee (1914–83). US dramatist, born *Thomas Lanier Williams*. His plays were often controversial, being criticized for their sensational treatment of sex and violence. The son of a salesman, he grew up in some poverty in the American Deep South. His first major success was *The Glass Menagerie* (1945), a play based largely on his own troubled family life. *A Streetcar Named Desire* (1947) and *Cat on a Hot Tin Roof* (1955) both won Pulitzer Prizes. Williams's work suffered during the 1960s, when his addiction to alcohol and sleeping pills caused a complete physical and mental breakdown.

Williams, William Carlos (1883–1963). US poet and writer. Williams was born in Rutherford, New Jersey, the son of a British father and a Puerto Rican mother. Although educated mainly in Europe, he later studied medicine and settled in his home town to work as a GP for some 40 years. He published his first book, *Poems*, in 1909. By bringing him into contact with all sections of US society, Williams's work as a doctor had a profound influence on his poetry. In his mature work, which began to appear in the early 1920s, he attempted to forge a new poetic idiom based on colloquial American speech. He summarized his 'objectivist' approach to writing in the phrase "No ideas but in things". His major work is the five-volume *Paterson* (1946–58), a free-verse evocation of the modern industrial city. Other volumes include *Spring and Fall* (1923), *Collected Later Poems* (1950), and *Pictures from Brueghel* (1963).

Wilson, Harold, Lord (1916–95). British statesman; prime minister (1964–70; 1974–76). An economics lecturer at Oxford, he acted as a government adviser during World War II and entered Parliament as a Labour member in 1945. He was elected leader of the Labour party in 1963 and became prime minister a year later, when Labour was returned after 13 years in opposition. Although he was re-elected in 1966, his government's economic plans were knocked off course by a balance of payments crisis. Defeated in 1970, he was re-elected at the head of minority Labour governments in the two elections of 1974. He resigned unexpectedly in 1976.

Wilson, Woodrow (1856–1924). US statesman; 28th president of the US (1913–21). A lawyer and academic, he became Democratic governor of New Jersey in 1911 and a year later was elected president. Re-elected in 1916, he kept the US out of World War I until the German U-boat campaign forced him to enter it in 1917.

He argued for "peace without victory" and put forward a list of 'Fourteen Points', upholding democracy and self-determination, which were intended to form the basis for the peace treaty at Paris. He was also mainly responsible for the establishment of the League of Nations. His presidency ended in tragic failure when the Versailles treaty was rejected by the US Senate. Wilson suffered a stroke and retired soon afterwards.

Wittgenstein, Ludwig (1889–1951). Austrian philosopher. His interest in mathematics developed from his early researches in aeronautics. From 1911 he studied logic under Bertrand Russell at Cambridge. He fought in the Austrian army during World War I and the manuscript of his *Tractatus Logico-Philosophicus* (1921) was sent to Russell from an Italian prison camp. This complex and influential treatise explores the relationship between language and things. On his release in 1919, Wittgenstein gave up philosophy to work as a teacher until 1929, when he returned to Cambridge as a lecturer and, later, professor. *Philosophical Investigations* (1953) was published after his death from cancer.

Wodehouse, P(elham) G(renville) (1881–1975). British novelist. Although his first works were school stories and romances, in 1913 he began writing the humorous novels and short stories for which he is famous. His stories usually feature members of the English gentry involved in farcical situations. Two of his most popular characters are Bertie Wooster and his manservant Jeeves, who first appeared in *The Man with Two Left Feet* (1917) and made their last appearance in *Much Obliged, Jeeves* (1971). Wodehouse lived mostly abroad from 1909 and became a US citizen in 1955. He was knighted shortly before his death.

The Berlin Broadcasts

In 1940 P. G. Wodehouse was staying with his wife in Le Touquet, France, when the Germans invaded. After a brief period of internment, he was released on condition that he did not leave Germany. Very naively, and much to the detriment of his reputation, Wodehouse also agreed to broadcast five short nonpolitical talks from Berlin. These were intended by Wodehouse to reassure friends in the US of his safety and included fairly innocuous accounts of his experiences as an internee: "Young men, starting out in life, have often asked me 'How can I become an Internee?' Well, there are several methods. My own was to buy a villa...on the coast of France and stay there until the Germans came along. This is probably the best and simplest system. You buy the villa and the Germans do the rest." Nonetheless, these Berlin Broadcasts created a furore and caused Wodehouse to be branded a traitor in his native country. After the war the stigma remained and it was not until the very end of his life that the award of a knighthood signified that Wodehouse had been forgiven by the Establishment. His rehabilitation was largely the result of the efforts of fellow-writers, notably Evelyn Waugh and George Orwell, who wrote in his *In Defence of P G Wodehouse*: "...it is nonsense to talk of 'Fascist tendencies' in his books. There are no post-1918 tendencies at all."

Wolfe, James (1727–59). British general. Having helped to put down the 1745 rebellion in Scotland, he was sent to command British forces fighting the French for control of North America during the Seven Years'

War (1756–63). In 1758 he took Louisbourg in Nova Scotia, and a year later he successfully besieged Quebec. There he surprised the defenders by sending troops up a steep unguarded path from the St Lawrence River on to the Plains of Abraham beside the city. Although he was killed during this battle, his victory led eventually to British supremacy in Canada.

Wolsey, Thomas (c. 1473–1530). English churchman and statesman. The son of a butcher, he was educated at Oxford and progressed rapidly in the church, becoming archbishop of York in 1514 and a cardinal in 1515. As Lord Chancellor to Henry VIII, Wolsey controlled both church and state. He made various alliances in Europe designed to further his ambition to become pope, which effectively brought about a decline in English power. Wolsey's failure to obtain an annulment of Henry VIII's marriage to Catherine of Aragon led to his downfall. In 1530 he was arrested for high treason but died on his way to London.

> ❛ I see the matter against me, how it is framed. But if I had served God as diligently as I have done the King, he would not have given me over in my grey hairs.
> Cardinal Wolsey to the Constable of the Tower of London, on his arrest for treason, 3 November 1530 ❜

Wood, Sir Henry (1869–1944). British conductor. He began his musical career as a composer but soon turned to conducting. In 1895 he inaugurated the Promenade Concerts in the Queen's Hall, London. Wood was particularly interested in Russian music and introduced many new works to British audiences. He was knighted in 1911.

Woolf, Virginia (1882–1941). British novelist, born *Adeline Virginia Stephen*. Her father, the critic and biographer Sir Leslie Stephen, educated her at home. After his death she became a leading figure in the 'Bloomsbury group' of artists and writers. In 1912 she married Leonard Woolf, and together they established the Hogarth Press in 1917. Her reputation was made with *Mrs Dalloway* (1925) and *To the Lighthouse* (1927); later novels include the historical fantasy *Orlando* (1928) and *The Waves* (1931). She used a number of experimental techniques in her works, including the 'stream of consciousness' technique developed by James Joyce. Her essays, reviews, and diaries are also well known. She had several periods of mental breakdown and in 1941 drowned herself in a river near her Sussex home.

Wordsworth, William (1770–1850). British poet. His early life is described in the long autobiographical poem *The Prelude* (1850). He visited France in 1791–92 and became a supporter of the French Revolution; while there he met Annette Vallon, who bore him a daughter. His first volume of poetry was published in 1793. In 1795 he settled in Dorset with his devoted sister Dorothy. In the same year he met Coleridge, with whom he collaborated on *Lyrical Ballads* (1798).

Wordsworth's contributions included *Tintern Abbey* and *The Idiot Boy*, as well as a critical preface. During a trip to Germany in 1798 he wrote the 'Lucy' poems and began *The Prelude*, which he continued to revise until his death. In 1802 he married Mary Hutchinson, who joined him and Dorothy in their Lake District home. *Poems in Two Volumes* (1807) included the *Ode: Intimations of Immortality*. Wordsworth was Poet Laureate from 1843 until his death.

Wren, Sir Christopher (1632–1723). English architect and scientist. He became professor of astronomy at Gresham College in London and subsequently at Oxford (when he was only 28). However, he gradually abandoned science for architecture. After the Great Fire of London (1666) he rebuilt 51 London churches, as well as St Paul's Cathedral, one of his greatest achievements. His style was largely neoclassical and he often decorated his churches with elaborate steeples; he also showed considerable ingenuity in fitting his buildings into irregular sites. He also built the library of Trinity College, Cambridge (1676) and Greenwich Hospital (1696). Wren was also elected an MP (1685–87; 1701–02). He was buried in St Paul's Cathedral; his epitaph reads '*Si monumentum requiris, circumspice*' (If you seek a monument, look around you).

Wright, Frank Lloyd (1869–1959). US architect, one of the leading architectural innovators of the 20th century. Born in Wisconsin, he studied architecture under Louis H. Sullivan in Chicago. During his early career he built a number of private houses in a functional style, using modern materials and incorporating open-plan areas. He also designed some of the first skyscrapers and the unique spiral form of the Guggenheim Museum in New York (1956). His standing as an architect was not fully recognized until after World War II.

> ❛ The physician can bury his mistakes, but the architect can only advise his clients to plant vines.
> Frank Lloyd Wright,
> *Autobiography* (1945) ❜

Wright, Orville (1871–1948) and his brother **Wilbur** (1867–1912). US pioneers of aviation. The Wright brothers designed and built bicycles before turning to glider design. They constructed a biplane in 1899 and made the first sustained powered flight on 17 December 1903 near Kitty Hawk in North Carolina. There is a replica of their plane in the Science Museum in South Kensington, London. Although their early flights did not succeed in making news or in interesting the US government, the brothers continued to improve their flying machines. In 1908 they had their plane sent by sea to France, where they were received enthusiastically. The Wright brothers gained a US army contract for the first military plane in 1909.

Wycliffe, John (c. 1329–84). English religious reformer. He studied at Oxford and was briefly master of Balliol College. A forerunner of the Reformation and Protestantism in England, Wycliffe made many attacks on the Church, condemning the doctrine of transubstantiation (the belief that the bread and wine of the Eucharist changes into the body and blood of Christ on consecration), the payment of papal taxes, and the sale of indulgences. This led to his enforced retirement from Oxford and his condemnation as a heretic. His followers, known as Lollards, travelled the country to preach his doctrines. Wycliffe was denounced by the pope and eventually had his works banned by the Church. His greatest achievement was the first complete translation of the Bible into English.

X

Xenophon (c. 432–350 BC). Greek soldier and author. In 400 BC he led 10,000 Greek mercenaries, the survivors of an unsuccessful expedition against Persia, through hostile territory to safety by the Black Sea. This adventure is recorded in his *Anabasis*. Having been exiled from Athens for fighting against the Athenians for Sparta, he served as a mercenary officer until about 394, when he settled at his country estate near Olympia. Here he wrote a history of Greece, to continue the work of Thucydides, and *Memoirs of Socrates*.

Xerxes (c. 529–465 BC). King of Persia. He succeeded his father Darius in 486 BC and in 480 invaded Greece with enormous forces. After meeting unexpected resistance at Thermopylae, he was defeated by sea at Salamis (480) and by land at Plataea (479). Xerxes continued his father's massive building project at Persepolis. A harsh ruler, he was assassinated in a palace intrigue.

Y

Yeats, William Butler (1865–1939). Irish poet and dramatist. The son of a painter, he studied art until 1889, when he published his first volume of poems, *The Wanderings of Oisin* (1889). Like much of his early poetry, this was based on Irish folklore. During the 1890s he involved himself in nationalist politics, partly out of love for the activist Maud Gonne. With a friend and patron, Lady Gregory, he established the Abbey theatre in Dublin (1904) and continued to manage it until the end of his life. Key works of Yeats's middle period include the volumes *Responsibilities* (1914) and *The Wild Swans at Coole* (1917) and the poem 'Easter 1916' (1921). Having been rejected by Maud, he married Georgie Hyde-Lees in 1917. Her psychic talents encour-

> ❛ Yeats stood for enchantment...He was the real original rationalist who said that the fairies stand to reason. He staggered the materialists by attacking their abstract materialism with a completely concrete mysticism.
> G. K. Chesterton, *Autobiography* (1936) ❜

aged Yeats's use of mystic symbolism in his later work. He was a member of the Irish Senate (1922–28) and won the Nobel Prize in 1923. Much of his greatest poetry, including *The Tower* (1927) and *The Winding Stair* (1933), was written in old age.

Yeltsin, Boris (1931–) Russian politician; president (1991–). Born in Sverdlovsk, he worked in the construction industry before becoming a full-time Communist Party worker in the 1960s. He went on to achieve national prominence as first secretary of the Moscow Communist Party (1985–87). A dynamic character, he clashed frequently with Gorbachov, whom he accused of being over-cautious in his reforms. Although Gorbachov eventually sacked him, Yeltsin was subsequently elected president of the Russian Republic (1990) and renounced his party membership. When communist hardliners staged a coup the following year, Yeltsin led popular resistance to the new rulers, who soon stood down. Although Gorbachov was reinstated, his authority was now weaker than that of Yeltsin. On the break-up of the Soviet Union in December 1991, Yeltsin became president of independent Russia. During the next two years he introduced a series of free-market reforms designed to rescue the Soviet economy. An attempted coup by communists in October 1993 was suppressed by the army. Yeltsin also used the military to crush separatists in Chechenia (1994–95). Both his handling of this crisis and his sometimes erratic public behaviour led to mounting international criticism in the mid 1990s. In 1995 Yeltsin suffered a heart attack. His authority took a further

blow when elections resulted in the communists becoming the largest party in parliament.

Yevtushenko, Yevgeny (1933–   ). Russian poet and
writer. He was already publishing poems in journals at
the age of 17, but made his name in the 'thaw' years
that followed Stalin's death. His works mark a return
to personal rather than political poetry in the Soviet
Union. The long poems *Babiy Yar* (1961), concerned with
the massacre of Ukrainian Jews by the Nazis, and
Bratsk Station (1966) were international successes. With
their strong rhythms and narrative drive, Yevtushenko's poems are ideally suited to the author's
flamboyant style of public performance. He has been
an outspoken commentator on topical issues for some
40 years (although, with hindsight, his attitude to the
communist regime has been criticized as over-timid).

Z

Zátopek, Emil (1922–   ). Czech athlete. The greatest runner of his time, he won his first Olympic gold medal in the 10,000 metres in 1948. Four years later, at the Helsinki Olympics, he won gold medals for the 5000 and 10,000 metres and the marathon. In the 10,000 metres he set five new world records during his career.

Zeffirelli, Franco (1923–   ). Italian opera, stage, and film director. Born illegitimate and orphaned as a young child, he began his career as an actor and theatrical designer. After working as an assistant to Luchino Visconti, he established his reputation for splendid opera productions at La Scala in Milan and the Metropolitan Opera in New York. His films include the Shakespeare adaptations *Romeo and Juliet* (1968) and *Hamlet* (1990), the biopic *Brother Sun, Sister Moon* (1973), about St Francis of Assisi, and several films of operas. His television series *Jesus of Nazareth* enjoyed great popularity in the late 1970s. Since 1993 Zeffirelli has been a member of the Italian Senate.

Zola, Émile (1840–1902). French novelist, who founded the naturalist movement in writing. He began work as a journalist and made his name in the literary world with *Thérèse Raquin* (1867). In 1871 he embarked on *The Rougon Macquarts* (1871–93), a series of 20 novels about the members of a single family. The novels cover all aspects of French society during the Second Empire, and include *Nana* (1880), the story of a prostitute, and *Germinal* (1885), set in a mining community. In 1898 Zola published an open letter in support of Dreyfus, a Jewish army officer falsely imprisoned for treason, and was obliged to flee to England for a time. His works were influenced by contemporary ideas of heredity and scientific fatalism.